MW00723804

PROGRAMMING WITH UNIX SYSTEM CALLS AND LIBRARIES

UNIX SVR4.2 MP

UNIX
PRESS

Copyright © 1993, 1992, 1991 Novell, Inc.
Copyright © 1990, 1989, 1988, 1987, 1986, 1985, 1984 AT&T
All Rights Reserved
Printed in USA

Published by Prentice-Hall, Inc.
A Simon & Schuster Company
Englewood Cliffs, New Jersey 07632

No part of this publication may be reproduced or transmitted in any form or by any means - graphic,
electronic, electrical, mechanical, or chemical, including photocopying, recording in any medium, taping,
by any computer or information storage and retrieval systems, etc., without prior permissions in writing
from Novell, Inc. (Novell).

IMPORTANT NOTE TO USERS

While every effort has been made to ensure the accuracy and completeness of all information in this
document, Novell assumes no liability to any party for any loss or damage caused by errors or omissions
or by statements of any kind in this document, its updates, supplements, or special editions, whether such
errors, omissions, or statements result from negligence, accident, or any other cause. Novell further
assumes no liability arising out of the application or use of any product or system described herein; nor any
liability for incidental or consequential damages arising from the use of this document. **Novell DISCLAIMS
ALL WARRANTIES REGARDING THE INFORMATION CONTAINED HEREIN, WHETHER EXPRESSED,
IMPLIED OR STATUTORY, INCLUDING IMPLIED WARRANTIES OF MERCHANTABILITY OR FITNESS
FOR A PARTICULAR PURPOSE.** Novell makes no representation that the interconnection of products in the
manner described herein will not infringe on existing or future patent rights, nor do the descriptions contained
herein imply the granting of any license to make, use or sell equipment constructed in accordance with this
description.

Novell reserves the right to make changes to any products herein without further notice.

TRADEMARKS

Intel386 is a registered trademark of Intel Corporation.
OPEN LOOK is a registered trademark of Novell, Inc.
UNIX is a registered trademark in the United States and other countries
   licensed exclusively through X/Open Company Ltd.
X Window System is a trademark of the Massachusetts Institute of Technology.

10 9 8 7 6 5 4 3 2 1

ISBN 0-13-157942-8

UNIX
PRESS
A Prentice Hall Title

Contents

Figures and Tables

1 Introduction

Introduction

This book, *Programming with UNIX System Calls and Libraries*, concentrates on how to use the system services provided by the UNIX operating system kernel. It is designed to give you information about application programming in a UNIX system environment. It does not attempt to teach you how to write programs. Rather, it is intended to supplement texts on programming by concentrating on the other elements that are part of getting application programs into operation.

Audience and Prerequisite Knowledge

Programming with UNIX System Calls and Libraries is intended for the Independent Software Vendor (ISV) who develops UNIX System software applications.

As the title suggests, we are addressing software developers. No special level of programming involvement is assumed. We hope the book will be useful to people who work on or manage large application development projects.

Programmers in the expert class, or those engaged in developing system software, may find that *Programming with UNIX System Calls and Libraries* lacks the depth of information they need. For them we recommend the *Operating System API Reference*.

Knowledge of terminal use, of a UNIX system editor, and of the UNIX system directory/file structure is assumed. If you feel shaky about your mastery of these basic tools, you might want to look over the *User's Guide* before tackling this one.

Related Books and Documentation

Throughout this book, you will find pointers and references to other guides and manuals where information is described in more detail. In particular, you will find references to other programming guides (this document being a part of the programming guide series) and reference manuals. Both of these document sets are described below.

UNIX System V Programming Books

The components of UNIX System V include the Graphical User Interface (GUI), the shell command line interface (CLI), the Application Program Interface (API), and the Device Driver Interface/Driver Kernel Interface (DDI/DKI). This document is part of a series of UNIX System V programming guides that includes the following:

- *Programming in Standard C* — Describes the C programming environment, libraries, compiler, link editor and file formats as well as tools for analyzing and debugging C programs.

- *UNIX Software Development Tools* — Describes the tools provided in the UNIX System environment for building, maintaining and packaging programs.

- *Character User Interface Programming* — Provides guidelines on how to develop a menu and form-based interface that operates on ASCII character terminals running on UNIX System V Release 4.2 (SVR4.2).

- *Graphical User Interface Programming* — Describes how to develop application software using the MoOLIT toolkit, 3D visuals, and mouseless operation.

- *Network Programming Interfaces* — Describes networking services such as the Transport Library Interface (TLI), the Remote Procedure Call (RPC) and the Network Selection facility.

Reference Manual Set

The reference manual set contains manual pages that formally and comprehensively describe features of the UNIX operating system. References to this documentation can be found throughout this book. Therefore, the reference manual set is recommended as a companion set to the UNIX System V programming guides. It is composed of the following:

- *Command Reference* — Describes all user and administrator commands in the UNIX system.

- *Operating System API Reference* — Describes UNIX system calls and C language library functions.

- *System Files and Devices Reference* — Describes file formats, special files (devices), and miscellaneous system facilities.

■ *Device Driver Reference* — Describes functions used by device driver software.

The C Connection

The UNIX system supports many programming languages, and C compilers are available on many different operating systems. Nevertheless, the relationship between the UNIX operating system and C has always been and remains very close. Most of the code in the UNIX operating system is written in the C language, and over the years many organizations using the UNIX system have come to use C for an increasing portion of their application code. Thus, while *Programming with UNIX System Calls and Libraries* is intended to be useful to you no matter what language(s) you are using, you will find that, unless there is a specific language-dependent point to be made, the examples assume you are programming in C. *Programming in Standard C* gives you detailed information about C language programming in the UNIX environment.

Hardware/Software Dependencies

Nearly all the text in this book is accurate for any computer running UNIX System V Release 4 or later, with the exception of hardware-specific information such as addresses.

If you find commands that work a little differently in your UNIX system environment, it may be because you are running under a different release of the software. If some commands just don't seem to exist at all, they may be members of packages not installed on your system. If you do find yourself trying to execute a nonexistent command, talk to the administrators of your system to find out what you have available.

Information in the Examples

While every effort has been made to present displays of information just as they appear on your terminal, it is possible that your system may produce slightly different output. Some displays depend on a particular machine configuration that may differ from yours. Changes between releases of the UNIX system software may cause small differences in what appears on your terminal.

Where complete code samples are shown, we have tried to make sure they compile and work as represented. Where code fragments are shown, while we can't say that they have been compiled, we have attempted to maintain the same standards of coding accuracy for them.

Notation Conventions

Whenever the text includes examples of output from the computer and/or commands entered by you, we follow the standard notation scheme that is common throughout UNIX System V documentation:

- All computer input and output is shown in a **constant-width** font. Commands that you type in from your terminal are shown in constant-width type. Text that is printed on your terminal by the computer is shown in constant-width type.

- Comments added to a display to show that part of the display has been omitted are shown in *italic* type and are indented to separate them from the text that represents computer output or input. Comments that explain the input or output are shown in the same type font as the rest of the display. An italic font is used to show substitutable text elements, such as the word *"filename"* for example.

- Because you are expected to press the [**RETURN**] key after entering a command or menu choice, the [**RETURN**] key is not explicitly shown in these cases. If, however, during an interactive session, you are expected to press [**RETURN**] without having typed any text, the notation is shown.

- Control characters are shown by the string "CTRL-" followed by the appropriate character, such as " d " (this is known as "CTRL-d"). To enter a control character, hold down the key marked " [**CTRL**] " (or " [**CONTROL**] ") and press the [**d**] key.

- The standard default prompt signs for an ordinary user and **root** are the dollar sign (**$**) and the pound sign (**#**).

- When the **#** prompt is used in an example, the command illustrated may be executed only by **root**.

Manual Page References

Manual pages are referred to with the function name showing first in constant width font, followed by the section number appearing in parenthesis in normal font. For example, the Executable and Linking Format Library (ELF) manual page appears as `elf`(3E). Reference manuals are not referred to individually; however, individual sections are referred to as "Section 3E in the Reference Manuals."

Section (1)   *Command Reference*

Sections (2), (3)   *Operating System API Reference*

Sections (4), (5), (7), (8)   *System Files and Devices Reference*

Note that the *Command Reference* describes commands appropriate for general users and system administrators as well as for programmers.

Application Programming in the UNIX System Environment

This section introduces application programming in a UNIX system environment. It briefly describes what application programming is and then moves on to a discussion on UNIX system tools and where you can read about them, and to languages supported in the UNIX system environment and where you can read about them.

Programmers working on application programs develop software for the benefit of other, nonprogramming users. Most large commercial computer applications involve a team of applications development programmers. They may be employees of the end-user organization or they may work for a software development firm. Some of the people working in this environment may be more in the project management area than working programmers.

Application programming has some of the following characteristics:

- Applications are often large and are developed by a team of people who write requirements, designs, tests, and end-user documents. This implies use of a project management methodology, including version control (described in the *UNIX Software Development Tools*). change requests, tracking, and so on.

- Applications must be developed more robustly.

    - They must be easy to use, implying character or graphical user interfaces.

    - They must check all incoming data for validity (for example, using the Data Validation Tools described in *UNIX Software Development Tools*).

    - They should be able to handle large amounts of data.

- Applications must be easy to install and administer

    (see "Application Software Packaging" and "Modifying the **sysadm** Interface" in *UNIX Software Development Tools*).

UNIX System Tools and Languages

Let's clarify the term "UNIX system tools." In simple terms, it means an existing piece of software used as a component in a new task. In a broader context, the term is used often to refer to elements of the UNIX system that might also be called features, utilities, programs, filters, commands, languages, functions, and so on. It gets confusing because any of the things that might be called by one or more of these names can be, and often are, used simply as components of the solution to a programming problem. The chapter's aim is to give you some sense of the situations in which you use these tools, and how the tools fit together. It refers you to other chapters in this book or to other documents for more details.

Facilities Covered and Not Covered in This Guide

Programming with UNIX System Calls and Libraries is about facilities used by application programs in a UNIX system environment, so let's take a minute to talk about which tools we mean, which ones are not going to be covered in this book, and where you might find information about those not covered here. Actually, the subject of things not covered in *Programming with UNIX System Calls and Libraries* might be even more important to you than the things that are. We couldn't possibly cover everything you ever need to know about UNIX system tools in this one volume.

Tools not covered in this text:

- the **login** procedure
- UNIX system editors and how to use them
- how the file system is organized and how you move around in it
- shell programming

Information about these subjects can be found in the *User's Guide* and a number of commercially available texts.

Tools that are covered in this text apply to application software development. This text also covers tools for packaging application and device driver software and for customizing the administrative interface.

Programming Tools and Languages in the UNIX System Environment

In this section we describe a variety of programming tools supported in the UNIX system environment. By "programming tools" we mean those offered for use on a computer running a current release of UNIX System V. Since these are separately purchasable items, not all of them will necessarily be installed on your machine. On the other hand, you may have programming tools and languages available on your machine that came from another source and are not mentioned in this discussion.

The C Language

C is intimately associated with the UNIX system since it was originally developed for use in recoding the UNIX system kernel. If you need to use a lot of UNIX system function calls for low-level I/O, memory or device management, or interprocess communication, C is a logical first choice. Most programs, however, don't require such direct interfaces with the operating system, so the decision to choose C might better be based on one or more of the following characteristics:

- a variety of data types: characters, integers of various sizes, and floating point numbers

- low-level constructs (most of the UNIX system kernel is written in C)

- derived data types such as arrays, functions, pointers, structures, and unions

- multidimensional arrays

- scaled pointers and the ability to do pointer arithmetic

- bitwise operators

- a variety of flow-of-control statements: `if`, `if-else`, `switch`, `while`, `do-while`, and `for`

- a high degree of portability

Refer to the *Programming in Standard C* for complete details on C.

It takes fairly concentrated use of the C language over a period of several months to reach your full potential as a C programmer. If you are a casual programmer, you might make it easier for yourself if you choose a less demanding programming facility such as those described below.

Shell

You can use the shell to create programs (new commands). Such programs are also called shell procedures. Refer to the *UNIX Software Development Tools* for information on how to create and execute shell programs using commands, variables, positional parameters, return codes, and basic programming control structures.

awk

The **awk** program (its name is an acronym constructed from the initials of its developers) scans an input file for lines that match pattern(s) described in a specification file. When **awk** finds a line that matches a pattern, it performs actions also described in the specification. It is not uncommon that an **awk** program can be written in a couple of lines to do functions that would take a couple of pages to describe in a programming language like FORTRAN or C. For example, consider a case where you have a set of records that consist of a key field and a second field that represents a quantity, and the task is to output the sum of the quantities for each key. The pseudocode for such a program might look like this:

```
SORT RECORDS
Read the first record into a hold area;
Read additional records until EOF;
{
If the key matches the key of the record in the hold area,
   add the quantity to the quantity field of the held record;
If the key does not match the key of the held record,
   write the held record,
   move the new record to the hold area;
}
At EOF, write out the last record from the hold area.
```

An **awk** program to accomplish this task would look like this:

```
        { qty[$1] += $2 }
END     { for (key in qty) print key, qty[key] }
```

This illustrates only one characteristic of **awk**; its ability to work with associative arrays. With **awk**, the input file does not have to be sorted, which is a requirement of the pseudoprogram.

For detailed information on **awk**, see the "**awk** Tutorial" chapter in the *UNIX Software Development Tools* and **awk**(1) in the *Command Reference*.

lex

lex is a lexical analyzer that can be added to C or FORTRAN programs. A lexical analyzer is interested in the vocabulary of a language rather than its grammar, which is a system of rules defining the structure of a language. **lex** can produce C language subroutines that recognize regular expressions specified by the user, take some action when a regular expression is recognized, and pass the output stream on to the next program.

For detailed information on **lex**, see the "**lex**" chapter in the *UNIX Software Development Tools* and **lex**(1) in the *Command Reference*.

yacc

yacc (Yet Another Compiler Compiler) is a tool for describing an input language to a computer program. **yacc** produces a C language subroutine that parses an input stream according to rules laid down in a specification file. The **yacc** specification file establishes a set of grammatical rules together with actions to be taken when tokens in the input match the rules. **lex** may be used with **yacc** to control the input process and pass tokens to the parser that applies the grammatical rules.

For detailed information on **yacc**, see the "**yacc**" chapter in *UNIX Software Development Tools* and **yacc**(1) in the *Command Reference*.

m4

m4 is a macro processor that can be used as a preprocessor for assembly language and C programs. For details, see the "**m4**" chapter of *Programming in Standard C* and **m4**(1) in the *Command Reference*.

bc and dc

bc enables you to use a computer terminal as you would a programmable calculator. You can edit a file of mathematical computations and call **bc** to execute them. The **bc** program uses **dc**. You can use **dc** directly, if you want, but it takes a little getting used to since it works with reverse Polish notation. **bc** and **dc** are described in Section 1 of the *Command Reference*.

Character User Interfaces

curses

Actually a library of C functions, **curses** is included in this list because the set of functions comprise a sublanguage for dealing with terminal screens. If you are writing programs that include interactive user screens, you will want to become familiar with this group of functions.

For detailed information on **curses**, see the *Character User Interface Programming*.

FMLI

The Form and Menu Language Interpreter (FMLI) is a high-level programming tool having two main parts:

- The Form and Menu Language, a programming language for writing scripts that define how an application will be presented to users. The syntax of the Form and Menu Language is very similar to that of the UNIX system shell programming language, including variable setting and evaluation, built-in commands and functions, use of and escape from special characters, redirection of input and output, conditional statements, interrupt signal handling, and the ability to set various terminal attributes. The Form and Menu Language also includes sets of "descriptors," which are used to define or customize attributes of frames and other objects in your application.

- The Form and Menu Language Interpreter, **fmli**, which is a command interpreter that sets up and controls the video display screen on a terminal, using instructions from your scripts to supplement FMLI's predefined screen control mechanisms. FMLI scripts can also invoke UNIX system commands and C executables, either in the background or in full screen mode. The Form and Menu Language Interpreter operates similarly to the UNIX command interpreter **sh**. At run time it parses the scripts you have written, thus giving you the advantages of quick prototyping and easy maintenance.

FMLI provides a framework for developers to write applications and application interfaces that use menus and forms. It controls many aspects of screen management for you. This means that you do not have to be concerned with the low-level details of creating or placing frames, providing users with a means of navigating between or within frames, or processing the use of forms and menus. Nor do you need to worry about on which kind of terminal your application will be run. FMLI takes care of all that for you.

For details see the FMLI chapter in the *Character User Interface Programming*.

ETI

The Extended Terminal Interface (ETI) is a set of C library routines that promote the development of application programs displaying and manipulating windows, panels, menus, and forms and that run under the UNIX system. ETI consists of

- the low-level (**curses**) library
- the **panel** library
- the **menu** library
- the **form** library
- the TAM Transition library

The routines are C functions and macros; many of them resemble routines in the standard C library. For example, there's a routine **printw** that behaves much like **printf** and another routine **getch** that behaves like **getc**. The automatic teller program at your bank might use **printw** to print its menus and **getch** to accept your requests for withdrawals (or, better yet, deposits). A visual screen editor like the UNIX system screen editor **vi** might also use these and other ETI routines.

A major feature of ETI is cursor optimization. Cursor optimization minimizes the amount a cursor has to move around a screen to update it. For example, if you designed a screen editor program with ETI routines and edited the sentence

> `ETI is a great package for creating forms and menus.`

to read

> `ETI is the best package for creating forms and menus.`

the program would change only "`the best`" in place of "`a great`". The other characters would be preserved. Because the amount of data transmitted—the output—is minimized, cursor optimization is also referred to as output optimization.

Cursor optimization takes care of updating the screen in a manner appropriate for the terminal on which an ETI program is run. This means that ETI can do whatever is required to update many different terminal types. It searches the **terminfo** database to find the correct description for a terminal.

How does cursor optimization help you and those who use your programs? First, it saves you time in describing in a program how you want to update screens. Second, it saves a user's time when the screen is updated. Third, it reduces the load on your UNIX system's communication lines when the updating takes place. Fourth, you don't have to worry about the myriad of terminals on which your program might be run.

Here's a simple ETI program. It uses some of the basic ETI routines to move a cursor to the middle of a terminal screen and print the character string **BullsEye**. For now, just look at their names and you will get an idea of what each of them does:

Figure 1-1: A Simple ETI Program

```
#include <curses.h>

main()
{
    initscr();

    move( LINES/2 - 1, COLS/2 - 4 );
    addstr("Bulls");
    refresh();
    addstr("Eye");
    refresh();
    endwin();
}
```

For complete information on ETI, refer to the ETI chapter in the *Character User Interface Programming*.

Graphical User Interfaces

XWIN Graphical Windowing System

The XWIN Graphical Windowing System is a network-transparent window system. X display servers run on computers with either monochrome or color bitmap display hardware. The server distributes user input to and accepts output requests from various application programs (referred to as "clients"). Each client is located on either the same machine or on another machine in the network.

The clients use **Xlib**, a C library routine, to interface with the window system by means of a stream connection.

"Widgets" are a set of code and data that provide the look and feel of a user interface. The C library routines used for creating and managing widgets are called the X Intrinsics. They are built on top of the X Window System, monitor events related to user interactions, and dispatch the correct widget code to handle the display. Widgets can then call application-registered routines (called callbacks) to handle the specific application semantics of an interaction. The X Intrinsics also monitor application-registered, nongraphical events and dispatch application routines to handle them. These features allow programmers to use this implementation of an OPEN LOOK toolkit in data base management, network management, process control, and other applications requiring response to external events.

Clients sometimes use a higher level library of the X Intrinsics and a set of widgets in addition to **xlib**. Refer to the "XWIN Graphical Windowing System" chapter of the *Graphical User Interface Programming* guide for general information about the design of X.

OPEN LOOK Graphical User Interface

The OPEN LOOK Graphical User Interface is a software application that creates a user-friendly graphical environment for the UNIX system. It replaces the traditional UNIX system commands with graphics that include windows, menus, icons, and other symbols. Using a hand-held pointing device (a "mouse"), you manipulate windows by moving them, changing their size and running them in the background. You can have multiple applications running at the same time by creating more than one window on your screen.

For more information, refer to the *Graphical User Interface Programming*.

UNIX System Calls and Libraries

This section describes the UNIX system services supplied by UNIX system calls and libraries for the C programming language. It introduces such topics as the process scheduler, virtual memory, interprocess communication, file and record locking, and symbolic links. The system calls and libraries that programs use to access these UNIX system services are described in detail later in this book.

File and Device Input/Output

UNIX system applications can do all I/O by reading or writing files, because all I/O devices, even a user's terminal, are files in the file system. Each peripheral device has an entry in the file system hierarchy, so that device names have the same structure as filenames, and the same protection mechanisms apply to devices as to files. Using the same I/O calls on a terminal as on any file makes it easy to redirect the input and output of commands from the terminal to another file. Besides the traditionally available devices, names exist for disk devices regarded as physical units outside the file system, and for absolutely addressed memory.

STREAMS Input/Output

STREAMS is a general, flexible facility and a set of tools for development of UNIX system communication services. It supports the implementation of services ranging from complete networking protocol suites to individual device drivers. STREAMS defines standard interfaces for character input/output within the kernel, and between the kernel and the rest of the UNIX system. The associated mechanism is simple and open-ended. It consists of a set of system calls, kernel resources, and kernel routines.

The standard interface and mechanism enable modular, portable development and easy integration of high-performance network services and their components. STREAMS does not impose any specific network architecture. The STREAMS user interface is upwardly compatible with the character I/O user level functions such as **open**, **close**, **read**, **write**, and **ioctl**. Benefits of STREAMS are discussed in more detail later in this chapter.

A "Stream" is a full-duplex processing and data transfer path between a STREAMS driver in kernel space and a process in user space.

Figure 1-2: Simple Streams

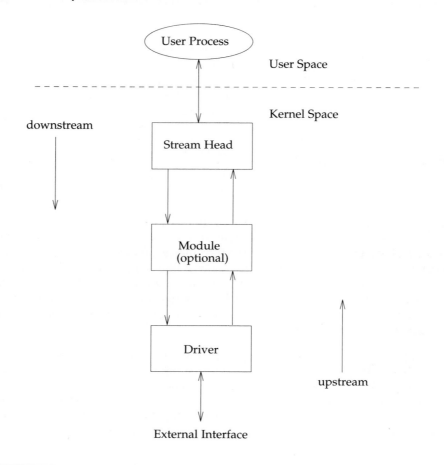

In the kernel, a Stream is constructed by linking a Stream head, a driver, and zero or more modules between the Stream head and driver. The "Stream head" is the end of the Stream nearest to the user process. All system calls made by a user level process on a Stream are processed by the Stream head.

Pipes are also STREAMS-based. A STREAMS-based pipe is a full-duplex (bidirectional) data transfer path in the kernel. It implements a connection between the kernel and one or more user processes and also shares properties of STREAMS-based devices.

Figure 1-3: STREAMS-based Pipe

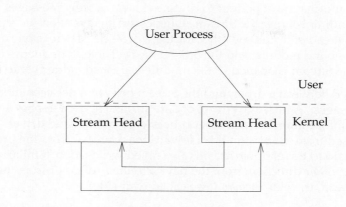

A STREAMS driver may be a device driver that provides the services of an external I/O device, or a software driver, commonly referred to as a pseudo-device driver. The driver typically handles data transfer between the kernel and the device and does little or no processing of data other than conversion between data structures used by the STREAMS mechanism and data structures that the device understands.

A STREAMS module represents processing functions to be performed on data flowing on the Stream. The module is a defined set of kernel-level routines and data structures used to process data, status, and control information. Data processing may involve changing the way the data is represented, adding/deleting header and trailer information to data, and/or packetizing/depacketizing data. Status and control information includes signals and input/output control information.

Each module is self-contained and functionally isolated from any other component in the Stream except its two neighboring components. The module communicates with its neighbors by passing messages. The module is not a required component in STREAMS, whereas the driver is, except in a STREAMS-based pipe where only the Stream head is required.

One or more modules may be inserted into a Stream between the Stream head and driver to perform intermediate processing of messages as they pass between the Stream head and driver. STREAMS modules are dynamically interconnected in a Stream by a user process. No kernel programming, assembly, or link editing is required to create the interconnection.

STREAMS uses queue structures to keep information about given instances of a pushed module or opened STREAMS device. A queue is a data structure that contains status information, a pointer to routines for processing messages, and pointers for administering the Stream. Queues are always allocated in pairs; one queue for the read-side and the other for the write-side. There is one queue pair for each driver and module, and the Stream head. The pair of queues is allocated whenever the Stream is opened or the module is pushed (added) onto the Stream.

Data is passed between a driver and the Stream head and between modules in the form of messages. A message is a set of data structures used to pass data, status, and control information between user processes, modules, and drivers. Messages that are passed from the Stream head toward the driver or from the process to the device, are said to travel downstream (also called write-side). Similarly, messages passed in the other direction, from the device to the process or from the driver to the Stream head, travel upstream (also called read-side).

A STREAMS message is made up of one or more message blocks. Each block consists of a header, a data block, and a data buffer. The Stream head transfers data between the data space of a user process and STREAMS kernel data space. Data to be sent to a driver from a user process is packaged into STREAMS messages and passed downstream. When a message containing data arrives at the Stream head from downstream, the message is processed by the Stream head, which copies the data into user buffers.

Within a Stream, messages are distinguished by a type indicator. Certain message types sent upstream may cause the Stream head to perform specific actions, such as sending a signal to a user process. Other message types are intended to carry information within a Stream and are not directly seen by a user process.

File and Record Locking

The provision for locking files, or portions of files, is primarily used to prevent the sort of error that can occur when two or more users of a file try to update information at the same time. The classic example is the airlines reservation system where two ticket agents each assign a passenger to Seat A, Row 5 on the 5 o'clock flight to Detroit. A locking mechanism is designed to prevent such mishaps by blocking Agent B from even seeing the seat assignment file until Agent A's transaction is complete.

File locking and record locking are really the same thing, except that file locking implies the whole file is affected; record locking means that only a specified portion of the file is locked. (Remember, in the UNIX system, file structure is undefined; a record is a concept of the programs that use the file.)

Two types of locks are available: read locks and write locks. If a process places a read lock on a file, other processes can also read the file but all are prevented from writing to it, that is, changing any of the data. If a process places a write lock on a file, no other processes can read or write in the file until the lock is removed. Write locks are also known as exclusive locks. The term shared lock is sometimes applied to read locks.

Another distinction needs to be made between mandatory and advisory locking. Mandatory locking means that the discipline is enforced automatically for the system calls that read, write, or create files. This is done through a permission flag established by the file's owner (or the superuser). Advisory locking means that the processes that use the file take the responsibility for setting and removing locks as needed. Thus, mandatory may sound like a simpler and better deal, but it isn't so. The mandatory locking capability is included in the system to comply with an agreement with **/usr/group**, an organization that represents the interests of UNIX system users. The principal weakness in the mandatory method is that the lock is in place only while the single system call is being made. It is extremely common for a single transaction to require a series of reads and writes before it can be considered complete. In cases like this, the term atomic is used to describe a transaction that must be viewed as an indivisible unit. The preferred way to manage locking in such a circumstance is to make certain the lock is in place before any I/O starts, and that it is not removed until the transaction is done. That calls for locking of the advisory variety.

Where to Find More Information

The "File and Device Input/Output" chapter in this book discusses file and device I/O including file and record locking in detail with a number of examples. There is an example of file and record locking in the sample application in the "UNIX System Calls and Libraries" chapter. The manual pages that specifically address file and record locking are **fcntl**(2), **lockf**(3) and **chmod**(2) in the *Operating System API Reference* and **fcntl**(5) in the *System Files and Devices Reference*. **fcntl**(2) describes the system call for file and record locking (although it isn't limited to that only) **fcntl**(5) tells you the file control options. The subroutine **lockf**(3) can also be used to lock sections of a file or an entire file. Setting **chmod** so that all portions of a file are locked will ensure that parts of files are not corrupted.

Memory Management

The UNIX system includes a complete set of memory-mapping mechanisms. Process address spaces are composed of a vector of memory pages, each of which can be independently mapped and manipulated. The memory-management facilities

- unify the system's operations on memory
- provide a set of kernel mechanisms powerful and general enough to support the implementation of fundamental system services without special-purpose kernel support
- maintain consistency with the existing environment, in particular using the UNIX file system as the name space for named virtual-memory objects

The system's virtual memory consists of all available physical memory resources including local and remote file systems, processor primary memory, swap space, and other random-access devices. Named objects in the virtual memory are referenced though the UNIX file system. However, not all file system objects are in the virtual memory; devices that the UNIX system cannot treat as storage, such as terminal and network device files, are not in the virtual memory. Some virtual memory objects, such as private process memory and shared memory segments, do not have names.

The Memory Mapping Interface

The applications programmer gains access to the facilities of the virtual memory system through several sets of system calls.

- **mmap** establishes a mapping between a process's address space and a virtual memory object.
- **mprotect** assigns access protection to a block of virtual memory.
- **munmap** removes a memory mapping.
- **getpagesize** returns the system-dependent size of a memory page.
- **mincore** tells whether mapped memory pages are in primary memory.

Where to Find More Information

The "Process Management" chapter in this book gives a detailed description of the virtual memory system. Refer to **mmap**(2), **mprotect**(2), **munmap**(2), **getpagesize**(2) and **mincore**(2) in the *Operating System API Reference* for these manual pages.

Process Management and Scheduling

Beginning with System V Release 4.2 MP (SVR4.2 MP), the schedulable entity is always a lightweight process (LWP). Scheduling priorities and classes are attributes of LWPs and not processes. When scheduling system calls accept a process on which to operate, the operation is applied to each LWP in the process. The UNIX system scheduler determines when LWPs run. It maintains priorities based on configuration parameters, process behavior, and user requests; it uses these priorities to assign LWPs to the CPU.

UNIX System V gives users absolute control over the sequence in which certain LWPs run, and the amount of time each LWP may use the CPU before another LWP gets a chance.

By default, the scheduler uses a time-sharing policy similar to the policy used in previous releases. A time-sharing policy adjusts priorities dynamically in an attempt to provide good response time to interactive LWPs and good throughput to CPU-intensive LWPs.

A fixed class scheduling policy is available, also. It is similar to the time-sharing policy except that the time slices given to fixed class processes or LWPs do not degrade over time.

The scheduler offers a fixed priority scheduling policy as well as a time-sharing policy. Fixed priority scheduling allows users to set fixed priorities on a per-process or LWP basis. The highest-priority fixed priority LWP always gets the CPU as soon as it is runnable, even if system processes are runnable. An application can therefore specify the exact order in which LWPs run. An application may also be written so that its fixed priority LWPs have a guaranteed response time from the system.

For most UNIX environments, the default scheduler configuration works well and no fixed priority LWPs are needed: administrators should not change configuration parameters and users should not change scheduler properties of their applications. However, for some applications with strict timing constraints, fixed priority LWPs are the only way to guarantee that the application's requirements are met.

Where to Find More Information

The "Process Management" chapter in this book gives detailed information on the process scheduler, along with relevant code examples. See also **priocntl**(1) in the *Command Reference*, **priocntl**(2) in the *Operating System API Reference*, and **dispadmin**(1M) in the *Command Reference*.

Interprocess Communications

Pipes, named pipes, and signals are all forms of interprocess communication. Business applications running on a UNIX system computer, however, often need more sophisticated methods of communication. In applications, for example, where fast response is critical, a number of processes may be brought up at the start of a business day to be constantly available to handle transactions on demand. This cuts out initialization time that can add seconds to the time required to deal with the transaction. To go back to the ticket reservation example again for a moment, if a customer calls to reserve a seat on the 5 o'clock flight to Detroit, you don't want to have to say, "Yes, sir; just hang on a minute while I start up the reservations program." In transaction-driven systems, the normal mode of processing is to have all the components of the application standing by waiting for some sort of an indication that there is work to do.

To meet requirements of this type, the UNIX system offers a set of nine system calls and their accompanying header files, all under the umbrella name of inter-process communications (IPC).

The IPC system calls come in sets of three; one set each for messages, semaphores, and shared memory. These three terms define three different styles of communication between processes:

messages   Communication is in the form of data stored in a buffer. The buffer can be either sent or received.

semaphores   Communication is in the form of positive integers with a value between 0 and 32,767. Semaphores may be contained in an array the size of which is determined by the system administrator. The default maximum size for the array is 25.

shared memory   Communication takes place through a common area of main memory. One or more processes can attach a segment of memory and as a consequence can share whatever data is placed there.

The sets of IPC system calls are:

```
msgget    semget    shmget
msgctl    semctl    shmctl
msgop     semop     shmop
```

The "get" calls each return to the calling program an identifier for the type of IPC facility that is being requested.

The "ctl" calls provide a variety of control operations that include obtaining (IPC_STAT), setting (IPC_SET) and removing (IPC_RMID), the values in data structures associated with the identifiers picked up by the "get" calls.

The "op" manual pages describe calls that are used to perform the particular operations characteristic of the type of IPC facility being used. msgop has calls that send or receive messages. semop (the only one of the three that is actually the name of a system call) is used to increment or decrement the value of a semaphore, among other functions. shmop has calls that attach or detach shared memory segments.

Where to Find More Information

The "Interprocess Communications" chapter in this book gives a detailed description of IPC, with many code examples that use the IPC system calls. An example of the use of some IPC features is included in the liber application in "Interprocess Communications". The system calls are described in Section 2 of the *Operating System API Reference*.

Symbolic Links

A symbolic link is a special type of file that represents another file. The data in a symbolic link consists of the path name of a file or directory to which the symbolic link file refers. The link that is formed is called symbolic to distinguish it from a regular (also called a hard) link. A symbolic link differs functionally from a regular link in three major ways.

- Files from different file systems may be linked.

- Directories, as well as regular files, may be symbolically linked by any user.

- A symbolic link can be created even if the file it represents does not exist.

When a user creates a regular link to a file, a new directory entry is created containing a new filename and the inode number of an existing file. The link count of the file is incremented.

In contrast, when a user creates a symbolic link (using the ln(1) command with the -s option), both a new directory entry and a new inode are created. A data block is allocated to contain the path name of the file to which the symbolic link refers. The link count of the referenced file is not incremented.

Symbolic links can be used to solve a variety of common problems. For example, it frequently happens that a disk partition (such as **root**) runs out of disk space. With symbolic links, an administrator can create a link from a directory on that file system to a directory on another file system. Such a link provides extra disk space and is, in most cases, transparent to both users and programs.

Symbolic links can also help deal with the built-in path names that appear in the code of many commands. Changing the path names would require changing the programs and recompiling them. With symbolic links, the path names can effectively be changed by making the original files symbolic links that point to new files.

In a shared resource environment like NFS, symbolic links can be very useful. For example, if it is important to have a single copy of certain administrative files, symbolic links can be used to help share them. Symbolic links can also be used to share resources selectively. Suppose a system administrator wants to do a remote mount of a directory that contains sharable devices. These devices must be in **/dev** on the client system, but this system has devices of its own so the administrator does not want to mount the directory onto **/dev**. Rather than do this, the administrator can mount the directory at a location other than **/dev** and then use symbolic links in the **/dev** directory to refer to these remote devices. (This is similar to the problem of built-in path names since it is normally assumed that devices reside in the **/dev** directory.)

Finally, symbolic links can be valuable within the context of the virtual file system (VFS) architecture. With VFS, new services, such as higher performance files and network IPC, may be provided on a file system basis. Symbolic links can be used to link these services to home directories or to places that make more sense to the application or user. Thus, you might create a data base index file in a RAM-based file system type and symbolically link it to the place where the data base server expects it and manages it.

Where to Find More Information

The "Directory and File Management" chapter in this book discusses symbolic links in detail. Refer to **symlink**(2) in the *Operating System API Reference* for information on creating symbolic links. See also **stat**(2), **rename**(2), **link**(2), **readlink**(2) and **unlink**(2) in the same manual, and **ln**(1) in the *Command Reference*.

2 UNIX System Calls and Libraries

Table of Contents

Introduction

This chapter introduces the system calls and other system services you can use to develop application programs. Each application performs a different function, but goes through the same basic steps: input, processing, and output. For the input and output steps, most applications interact with an end user at a terminal. During the processing step, sometimes an application needs access to special services provided by the operating system (for example, to interact with the file system, control processes, manage memory, and more). Some of these services are provided through system calls and some through libraries of functions.

Libraries and Header Files

The standard libraries supplied by the C compilation system contain functions that you can use in your program to perform input/output, string handling, and other high-level operations that are not explicitly provided by the C language. Header files contain definitions and declarations that your program will need if it calls a library function. They also contain function-like macros that you can use in your program as you would a function.

In this part, we'll talk a bit more about header files and show you how to use library functions in your program. We'll also describe the contents of some of the more important standard libraries, and tell you where to find them in the *Operating System API Reference*. We'll close with a brief discussion of standard I/O.

Header Files

Header files serve as the interface between your program and the libraries supplied by the C compilation system. Because the functions that perform standard I/O, for example, very often use the same definitions and declarations, the system supplies a common interface to the functions in the header file **<stdio.h>**. By the same token, if you have definitions or declarations that you want to make available to several source files, you can create a header file with any editor, store it in a convenient directory, and include it in your program as described in the first part of this chapter.

Header files traditionally are designated by the suffix **.h**, and are brought into a program at compile time. The preprocessor component of the compiler does this because it interprets the **#include** statement in your program as a directive. The two most commonly used directives are **#include** and **#define**. As we have seen, the **#include** directive is used to call in and process the contents of the named file. The **#define** directive is used to define the replacement token string for an identifier. For example,

```
#define NULL    0
```

defines the macro **NULL** to have the replacement token sequence **0**. See the section on "C Language", in the *Programming in Standard C* guide for the complete list of preprocessing directives.

Many different **.h** files are named in the *Operating System API Reference*. Here we are going to list a number of them, to illustrate the range of tasks you can perform with header files and library functions. When you use a library function in your program, the manual page will tell you which header file, if any, needs to be included. If a header file is mentioned, it should be included before you use any of the associated functions or declarations in your program. It's generally best to put the `#include` right at the top of a source file.

`assert.h`	assertion checking
`ctype.h`	character handling
`errno.h`	error conditions
`float.h`	floating point limits
`limits.h`	other data type limits
`locale.h`	program's locale
`math.h`	mathematics
`setjmp.h`	nonlocal jumps
`signal.h`	signal handling
`stdarg.h`	variable arguments
`stddef.h`	common definitions
`stdio.h`	standard input/output
`stdlib.h`	general utilities
`string.h`	string handling
`time.h`	date and time
`unistd.h`	system calls

How to Use Library Functions

The manual page for each function describes how you should use the function in your program. Manual pages follow a common format; although, some manual pages may omit some sections:

- The "NAME" section names the component(s) and briefly states its purpose.

- The "SYNOPSIS" section specifies the C language programming interface(s).

- The "DESCRIPTION" section details the behavior of the component(s).

- The "EXAMPLE" section gives examples, caveats and guidance on usage.

- The "FILES" section gives the file names that are built into the program.

- The "SEE ALSO" section lists related component interface descriptions.

- The "DIAGNOSTICS" section outlines return values and error conditions.

The "NAME" section lists the names of components described in that manual page with a brief, one-line statement of the nature and purpose of those components.

The "SYNOPSIS" section summarizes the component interface by compactly representing the order of any arguments for the component, the type of each argument (if any) and the type of value the component returns.

The "DESCRIPTION" section specifies the functionality of components without stipulating the implementation; it excludes the details of how UNIX System V implements these components and concentrates on defining the external features of a standard computing environment instead of the internals of the operating system, such as the scheduler or memory manager. Portable software should avoid using any features or side-effects not explicitly defined.

The "SEE ALSO" section refers the reader to other related manual pages in the UNIX System V reference manual set as well as other documents. The "SEE ALSO" section identifies manual pages by the title which appears in the upper corners of each page of a manual page.

Some manual pages cover several commands, functions or other UNIX System V components; thus, components defined along with other related components share the same manual page title. For example, references to the function `calloc` cite `malloc`(3) because the function `calloc` is described with the function `malloc` in the manual page entitled `malloc`(3). As an example manual page, we'll look at the `strcmp` function, which compares character strings. The routine is described on the `string` manual page in Section 3, Subsection 3C, of the *Operating System API Reference*. Related functions are described there as well, but only the sections relevant to `strcmp` are shown in the following figure.

Figure 2-1: Excerpt from `string`(3C) Manual Page

NAME

     `string: strcat, strdup, strncat, strcmp, strncmp, strcpy, strncpy, strlen,`
     `strchr, strrchr, strpbrk, strspn, strcspn, strok` – string operations

SYNOPSIS

     `#include <string.h>`   . . .
     `int strcmp(const char *`*sptr1*`, const char *`*sptr2*`);`   . . .

DESCRIPTION

     . . . `strcmp` compares its arguments and returns an integer less than, equal to, or
     greater than 0, according as the first argument is lexicographically less than, equal
     to, or greater than the second . . .

As shown, the "DESCRIPTION" section tells you what the function or macro does. It's the "SYNOPSIS" section, though, that contains the critical information about how you use the function or macro in your program. Note that the first line in the "SYNOPSIS" is

     `#include <string.h>`

That means that you should include the header file **<string.h>** in your program because it contains useful definitions or declarations relating to **strcmp**.

In fact, **<string.h>** contains the **strcmp** "function prototype" as follows:

     `extern int strcmp(const char *, const char *);`

A function prototype describes the kinds of arguments expected and returned by a C language function. Function prototypes afford a greater degree of argument type checking than old-style function declarations, and reduce the chance of using the function incorrectly. Including **<string.h>**, assures that the C compiler checks calls to **strcmp** against the official interface. You can, of course, examine **<string.h>** in the standard place for header files on your system, usually the **/usr/include** directory.

The "SYNOPSIS" for a C library function closely resembles the C language declaration of the function and its arguments. The "SYNOPSIS" tells the reader:

- the type of value returned by the function;
- the arguments the function expects to receive when called, if any;
- the argument types.

For example, the "SYNOPSIS" for the macro **feof** is:

```
#include <stdio.h>
int feof( FILE *sfp )
```

The "SYNOPSIS" section for **feof** shows that:

- The macro **feof** requires the header file **<stdio.h>**
- The macro **feof** returns a value of type **int**
- The argument *sfp* is a pointer to an object of type **FILE**

To use **feof** in a program, you need only write the macro call, preceded at some point by the **#include** control line, as in the following:

```
#include <stdio.h>    /* include definitions */
main() {
    FILE *infile;      /* define a file pointer */
    while (!feof(infile)) {   /* until end-of-file */
        /* operations on the file */
    }

}
```

By way of further illustration, let's look at how you might use **strcmp** in your own code. The following figure shows a program fragment that will find the bird of your choice in an array of birds.

Figure 2-2: How `strcmp` Is Used in a Program

```c
#include <string.h>

/* birds must be in alphabetical order */
char *birds[] = { "albatross",  "canary", "cardinal", "ostrich", "penguin" };

/* Return the index of the bird in the array. */
/* If the bird is not in the array, return -1 */

int is_bird(const char *string)
{
    int low, high, midpoint;
    int cmp_value;

    /* use a binary search to find the bird */
    low = 0;
    high = sizeof(birds)/sizeof(char *) - 1;
    while(low <= high)
    {
        midpoint = (low + high)/2;
        cmp_value = strcmp(string, birds[midpoint]);
        if (cmp_value < 0)
            high = midpoint - 1;
        else if (cmp_value > 0)
            low = midpoint + 1;
        else /* found a match */
            return midpoint;
    }
    return -1;
}
```

The format of a "SYNOPSIS" section only resembles, but does not duplicate, the format of C language declarations. To show that some components take varying numbers of arguments, the "SYNOPSIS" section uses additional conventions not found in actual C function declarations:

- Text in **courier** represents source-code typed just as it appears.

- Text in *italic* usually represents substitutable argument prototypes.

- Square brackets [ ] around arguments indicate optional arguments.

- Ellipses . . . indicate that the previous arguments may repeat.

- If the type of an argument may vary, the "SYNOPSIS" omits the type.

For example, the "SYNOPSIS" for the function **printf** is:

```
#include <stdio.h>

int printf( char *fmt [ , arg . . . ] )
```

The "SYNOPSIS" section for **printf** shows that the argument *arg* is optional, may be repeated and is not always of the same data type. The "DESCRIPTION" section of the manual page provides any remaining information about the function **printf** and the arguments to it.

The "DIAGNOSTICS" section specifies return values and possible error conditions. The text in the "DIAGNOSTICS" takes a conventional form which describes the return value in case of successful completion followed by the consequences of an unsuccessful completion, as in the following example:

Figure 2-3: Sample DIAGNOSTICS Section

On success, **lseek** returns the value of the resulting file-offset, as measured in bytes from the beginning of the file.

On failure, **lseek** returns **-1**, it does not change the file-offset, and **errno** equals:

    EBADF if **fildes** is not a valid open file-descriptor.

    EINVAL if **whence** is not **SEEK_SET**, **SEEK_CUR** or **SEEK_END**.

    ESPIPE if **fildes** denotes a pipe or FIFO.

The **<errno.h>** header file defines symbolic names for error conditions which are described in **intro**(2) of the *Operating System API Reference*. For more information on error conditions, see the section entitled "UNIX System Call Error Handling" in this chapter.

C Library (libc)

In this section, we describe some of the more important routines in the standard C library. As we indicated in the first part of this chapter, **libc** contains the system calls described in Section 2 of the *Operating System API Reference*, and the C language functions described in Section 3, Subsections 3C and 3S. We'll explain what each of these subsections contains below. We'll look at system calls at the end of the section.

Subsection 3C Routines

Subsection 3C of the *Operating System API Reference* contains functions and macros that perform a variety of tasks:

- string manipulation
- character classification
- character conversion

Figure 2-4 lists string-handling functions that appear on the **string** page in Subsection 3C of the *Operating System API Reference*. Programs that use these functions should include the header file **<string.h>**.

Figure 2-4: String Operations

strcat	Append a copy of one string to the end of another.
strncat	Append no more than a given number of characters from one string to the end of another.
strcmp	Compare two strings. Returns an integer less than, greater than, or equal to 0 to show that one is lexicographically less than, greater than, or equal to the other.
strncmp	Compare no more than a given number of characters from the two strings. Results are otherwise identical to **strcmp**.
strcpy	Copy a string.
strncpy	Copy a given number of characters from one string to another. The destination string will be truncated if it is longer than the given number of characters, or padded with null characters if it is shorter.

Figure 2-4: String Operations (continued)

`strdup`	Return a pointer to a newly allocated string that is a duplicate of a string pointed to.
`strchr`	Return a pointer to the first occurrence of a character in a string, or a null pointer if the character is not in the string.
`strrchr`	Return a pointer to the last occurrence of a character in a string, or a null pointer if the character is not in the string.
`strlen`	Return the number of characters in a string.
`strpbrk`	Return a pointer to the first occurrence in one string of any character from the second, or a null pointer if no character from the second occurs in the first.
`strspn`	Return the length of the initial segment of one string that consists entirely of characters from the second string.
`strcspn`	Return the length of the initial segment of one string that consists entirely of characters not from the second string.
`strstr`	Return a pointer to the first occurrence of the second string in the first string, or a null pointer if the second string is not found.
`strtok`	Break up the first string into a sequence of tokens, each of which is delimited by one or more characters from the second string. Return a pointer to the token, or a null pointer if no token is found.

Figure 2-5 lists functions and macros that classify 8-bit character-coded integer values. These routines appear on the **conv**(3C) and **ctype**(3C) pages in Subsection 3C of the *Operating System API Reference*. Programs that use these routines should include the header file **<ctype.h>**.

Figure 2-5: Classifying 8-Bit Character-Coded Integer Values

`isalpha`	Is *c* a letter?
`isupper`	Is *c* an uppercase letter?
`islower`	Is *c* a lowercase letter?
`isdigit`	Is *c* a digit [0-9]?
`isxdigit`	Is *c* a hexadecimal digit [0-9], [A-F], or [a-f]?
`isalnum`	Is *c* alphanumeric (a letter or digit)?
`isspace`	Is *c* a space, horizontal tab, vertical tab, new-line, form-feed, or carriage return?
`ispunct`	Is *c* a punctuation character (neither control nor alphanumeric)?
`isprint`	Is *c* a printing character?
`isgraph`	Same as `isprint` except false for a space.
`iscntrl`	Is *c* a control character or a delete character?
`isascii`	Is *c* an ASCII character?
`toupper`	Change lower case to upper case.
`_toupper`	Macro version of `toupper`.
`tolower`	Change upper case to lower case.
`_tolower`	Macro version of `tolower`.
`toascii`	Turn off all bits that are not part of a standard ASCII character; intended for compatibility with other systems.

Figure 2-6 lists functions and macros in Subsection 3C of the *Operating System API Reference* that are used to convert characters, integers, or strings from one representation to another. The left-hand column contains the name that appears at the top of the manual page; the other names in the same row are related functions or macros described on the same manual page. Programs that use these routines should include the header file **<stdlib.h>**.

Figure 2-6: Converting Characters, Integers, or Strings

`a64l`	`l64a`		Convert between long integer and base-64 ASCII string.
`ecvt`	`fcvt`	`gcvt`	Convert floating point number to string.
`l3tol`	`ltol3`		Convert between 3-byte packed integer and long integer.
`strtod`	`atof`		Convert string to double-precision number.
`strtol`	`atol`	`atoi`	Convert string to integer.
`strtoul`			Convert string to unsigned long.

Subsection 3S Routines

Subsection 3S of the *Operating System API Reference* contains the so-called standard I/O library for C programs. Frequently, one manual page describes several related functions or macros. In Figure 2-7, the left-hand column contains the name that appears at the top of the manual page; the other names in the same row are related functions or macros described on the same manual page. Programs that use these routines should include the header file **<stdio.h>**. We'll talk a bit more about standard I/O in the last subsection of this chapter.

Figure 2-7: Standard I/O Functions and Macros

`fclose`	`fflush`			Close or flush a stream.
`ferror`	`feof`	`clearerr`	`fileno`	Stream status inquiries.
`fopen`	`freopen`	`fdopen`		Open a stream.
`fread`	`fwrite`			Input/output.
`fseek`	`rewind`	`ftell`		Reposition a file pointer in a stream.
`getc`	`getchar`	`fgetc`	`getw`	Get a character or word from a stream.
`gets`	`fgets`			Get a string from a stream.
`popen`	`pclose`			Begin or end a pipe to/from a process.
`printf`	`fprintf`	`sprintf`		Print formatted output.
`putc`	`putchar`	`fputc`	`putw`	Put a character or word on a stream.
`puts`	`fputs`			Put a string on a stream.
`scanf`	`fscanf`	`sscanf`		Convert formatted input.
`setbuf`	`setvbuf`			Assign buffering to a stream.
`system`				Issue a command through the shell.
`tmpfile`				Create a temporary file.
`tmpnam`	`tempnam`			Create a name for a temporary file.
`ungetc`				Push character back into input stream.
`vprintf`	`vfprintf`	`vsprintf`		Print formatted output of a **varargs** argument list.

Math Library (libm)

The math library, `libm`, contains the mathematics functions supplied by the C compilation system. These appear in Subsection 3M of the *Operating System API Reference*. Here we describe some of the major functions, organized by the manual page on which they appear. Note that functions whose names end with the letter `f` are single-precision versions, which means that their argument and return types are `float`. Programs that use math functions should include the header file `<math.h>`.

Figure 2-8: Math Functions

erf(3M)		
erf		Compute the error function of x, defined as $$\frac{2}{\sqrt{\pi}} \int_0^x e^{-t^2}\, dt.$$
erfc		Compute 1.0 - `erf(x)`, which is used because of the extreme loss of relative accuracy if `erf` is called for large x and the result subtracted from 1.0 (e.g., for $x = 5$, 12 places are lost).
exp(3M)		
exp	expf	Compute e^x.
cbrt		Compute the cube root of x.
log	logf	Compute the natural logarithm of x. The value of x must be positive.
log10	log10f	Compute the base-ten logarithm of x. The value of x must be positive.
pow	powf	Compute x^y. If x is zero, y must be positive. If x is negative, y must be an integer.
sqrt	sqrtf	Compute the non-negative square root of x. The value of x must be non-negative.
floor(3M)		
floor	floorf	Compute the largest integer not greater than x.
ceil	ceilf	Compute the smallest integer not less than x.

UNIX System Calls and Libraries

Figure 2-8: Math Functions (continued)

copysign		Compute x but with the sign of y.
fmod	fmodf	Compute the floating point remainder of the division of x by y: x if y is zero, otherwise the number f with same sign as x, such that $x = iy + f$ for some integer i, and $|f| < |y|$.
fabs	fabsf	Compute $|x|$, the absolute value of x.
rint		Compute as a double-precision floating point number the integer value nearest the double-precision floating point argument x, and rounds the return value according to the currently set machine rounding mode.
remainder		Compute the floating point remainder of the division of x by y: **NaN** if y is zero, otherwise the value $r = x - yn$, where n is the integer value nearest the exact value of x/y, and n is even whenever $|n - x/y| = 1/2$.
gamma(3M)		
gamma	lgamma	Compute $\ln(|\Gamma(x)|)$, where $\Gamma(x)$ is defined as $\int_0^x e^{-t}t^{x-1}\,dt$.
hypot(3M)		
hypot		Compute **sqrt**$(x * x + y * y)$, taking precautions against overflows.
matherr(3M)		
matherr		Error handling.
trig(3M)		
sin	sinf	Compute the sine of x, measured in radians.
cos	cosf	Compute the cosine of x, measured in radians.
tan	tanf	Compute the tangent of x, measured in radians.
asin	asinf	Compute the arcsine of x, in the range $[-\pi/2, +\pi/2]$.
acos	acosf	Compute the arccosine of x, in the range $[0, +\pi]$.

Figure 2-8: Math Functions (continued)

atan	atanf	Compute the arctangent of x, in the range $(-\pi/2, +\pi/2)$.
atan2	atan2f	Compute the arctangent of y/x, in the range $(-\pi, +\pi]$, using the signs of both arguments to determine the quadrant of the return value.

sinh(3M)		
sinh	sinhf	Compute the hyperbolic sine of x.
cosh	coshf	Compute the hyperbolic cosine of x.
tanh	tanhf	Compute the hyperbolic tangent of x.
asinh		Compute the inverse hyperbolic sine of x.
acosh		Compute the inverse hyperbolic cosine of x.
atanh		Compute the inverse hyperbolic tangent of x.

General Purpose Library (libgen)

libgen contains general purpose functions, and functions designed to facilitate internationalization. These appear in Subsection 3G of the *Operating System API Reference*. Figure 2-9 describes functions in libgen. The header files <libgen.h> and, occasionally, <regexp.h> should be included in programs that use these functions.

Figure 2-9: libgen Functions

advance	step	Execute a regular expression on a string.
basename		Return a pointer to the last element of a path name.
bgets		Read a specified number of characters into a buffer from a stream until a specified character is reached.
bufsplit		Split the buffer into fields delimited by tabs and new-lines.

Figure 2-9: `libgen` **Functions** (continued)

`compile`		Return a pointer to a compiled regular expression that uses the same syntax as **ed**.
`copylist`		Copy a file into a block of memory, replacing new-lines with null characters. It returns a pointer to the copy.
`dirname`		Return a pointer to the parent directory name of the file path name.
`eaccess`		Determine if the effective user ID has the appropriate permissions on a file.
`gmatch`		Check if name matches shell file name pattern.
`isencrypt`		Use heuristics to determine if contents of a character buffer are encrypted.
`mkdirp`		Create a directory and its parents.
`p2open`	`p2close`	**p2open** is similar to **popen** [see **popen**(3S)]. It establishes a two-way connection between the parent and the child. **p2close** closes the pipe.
`pathfind`		Search the directories in a given path for a named file with given mode characteristics. If the file is found, a pointer is returned to a string that corresponds to the path name of the file. A null pointer is returned if no file is found.
`regcmp`		Compile a regular expression and return a pointer to the compiled form.
`regex`		Compare a compiled regular expression against a subject string.
`rmdirp`		Remove the directories in the specified path.
`strccpy`	`strcadd`	**strccpy** copies the input string to the output string, compressing any C-like escape sequences to the real character. **strcadd** is a similar function that returns the address of the null byte at the end of the output string.
`strecpy`		Copy the input string to the output string, expanding any non-graphic characters with the C escape sequence. Characters in a third argument are not expanded.

Figure 2-9: `libgen` **Functions** (continued)

`strfind`	Return the offset of the first occurrence of the second string in the first string. `-1` is returned if the second string does not occur in the first.
`strrspn`	Trim trailing characters from a string. It returns a pointer to the last character in the string not in a list of trailing characters.
`strtrns`	Return a pointer to the string that results from replacing any character found in two strings with a character from a third string. This function is similar to the `tr` command.

Standard I/O Library

The functions in Subsection 3S of the *Operating System API Reference* constitute the standard I/O library for C programs. In this section, we want to discuss standard I/O in a bit more detail. First, let's briefly define what I/O involves. It has to do with

- reading information from a file or device to your program;

- writing information from your program to a file or device;

- opening and closing files that your program reads from or writes to.

Three Files You Always Have

Programs automatically start off with three open files: standard input, standard output, and standard error. These files with their associated buffering are called streams, and are designated **stdin**, **stdout**, and **stderr**, respectively. The shell associates all three files with your terminal by default.

This means that you can use functions and macros that deal with **stdin**, **stdout**, or **stderr** without having to open or close files. **gets**, for example, reads a string from **stdin**; **puts** writes a string to **stdout**. Other functions and macros read from or write to files in different ways: character at a time, **getc** and **putc**; formatted, **scanf** and **printf**; and so on. You can specify that output be directed to **stderr** by using a function such as **fprintf**. **fprintf** works the same way as **printf** except that it delivers its formatted output to a named stream, such as **stderr**.

Named Files

Any file other than standard input, standard output, and standard error must be explicitly opened by you before your program can read from or write to the file. You open a file with the standard library function **fopen**. **fopen** takes a path name, asks the system to keep track of the connection between your program and the file, and returns a pointer that you can then use in functions that perform other I/O operations.

The pointer is to a structure called **FILE**, defined in **<stdio.h>**, that contains information about the file: the location of its buffer, the current character position in the buffer, and so on. In your program, then, you need to have a declaration such as

```
FILE *fin;
```

which says that **fin** is a pointer to a **FILE**. The statement

```
fin = fopen("filename", "r");
```

associates a **FILE** structure with **filename**, the path name of the file to open, and returns a pointer to it. The **"r"** means that the file is to be opened for reading. This argument is known as the mode. There are modes for reading, writing, and both reading and writing.

In practice, the file open function is often included in an **if** statement:

```
if ((fin = fopen("filename", "r")) == NULL)
    (void)fprintf(stderr,"Cannot open input file %s\n",
        "filename");
```

which takes advantage of the fact that **fopen** returns a **NULL** pointer if it cannot open the file. To avoid falling into the immediately following code on failure, you can call **exit**, which causes your program to quit:

```
if ((fin = fopen("filename", "r")) == NULL) {
    (void)fprintf(stderr,"Cannot open input file %s\n",
        "filename");
    exit(1);
}
```

Once you have opened the file, you use the pointer **fin** in functions or macros to refer to the stream associated with the opened file:

```
int c;
c = getc(fin);
```

brings in one character from the stream into an integer variable called **c**. The variable **c** is declared as an integer even though we are reading characters because **getc** returns an integer. Getting a character is often incorporated in some flow-of-control mechanism such as

```
while ((c = getc(fin)) != EOF)
       .
       .
       .
```

that reads through the file until **EOF** is returned. **EOF**, **NULL**, and the macro **getc** are all defined in **<stdio.h>**. **getc** and other macros in the standard I/O package keep advancing a pointer through the buffer associated with the stream; the UNIX system and the standard I/O functions are responsible for seeing that the buffer is refilled if you are reading the file, or written to the output file if you are producing output, when the pointer reaches the end of the buffer.

Your program may have multiple files open simultaneously, 20 or more depending on system configuration. If, subsequently, your program needs to open more files than it is permitted to have open simultaneously, you can use the standard library function **fclose** to break the connection between the **FILE** structure in **<stdio.h>** and the path names of the files your program has opened. Pointers to **FILE** may then be associated with other files by subsequent calls to **fopen**. For output files, an **fclose** call makes sure that all output has been sent from the output buffer before disconnecting the file. **exit** closes all open files for you, but it also gets you completely out of your process, so you should use it only when you are sure you are finished.

BSD System Libraries and Header Files

If you are migrating to UNIX System V from a BSD System environment, or want to run BSD system applications, you may need to install and access the BSD libraries and header files included in the BSD Compatibility Package.

The BSD Compatibility Package is a separately installed, optional package that contains the following, which are either different from UNIX System V or don't exist in UNIX System V:

- BSD commands

- Library routines
  For example, **printf** returns different values under BSD and UNIX System V; the BSD routine **re_comp** doesn't exist in UNIX System V.

- Header files
  For example, **sysexits.h** doesn't exist in UNIX System V; and the BSD **sys/file.h** has additional **#define**s not in UNIX System V.

- System Calls and Signals
  Routines to emulate BSD system calls. For example, the BSD system call, **killpg**, has been implemented as a library routine with the same name.

By using the BSD Compatibility Package, you can take advantage of a comprehensive BSD environment compatibility.

The subsections below discuss BSD header files, libraries, and how to access them. BSD commands included in the BSD Compatibility Package are listed in "Appendix B" of the *User's Guide*. Manual pages for BSD commands and functions appear in the *Command Reference* and *Operating System API Reference*.

To install the BSD Compatibility Package, see the *Installation Guide*.

Accessing BSD Libraries and Header Files

Once the BSD Compatibility Package is installed, compatibility package header files and libraries called by the C compiler (**cc**) and linker (**ld**) are located in **/usr/ucbinclude** and **/usr/ucblib**. To access these header files and libraries, set your **PATH** variable so that **/usr/ucb** comes before the default UNIX System V path directories **/sbin**, **/usr/sbin**, **/usr/bin**, and **/usr/ccs/bin**.

To find out what your path is currently, use the **echo** command as shown in the following example.

```
$ echo $PATH
PATH=.:/home/medici/bin:/usr/bin:/usr/ucb:/etc
$
```

To make the BSD Compatibility Package commands the default, change the order of the directories in your path, as shown in the example below:

```
$ PATH=.:/home/medici/bin:/usr/ucb:/usr/bin:/etc
$
```

To make this change permanent, put a line like the above **PATH** command in your
.profile file (or your **.cshrc** file, if you're using the C shell).

By setting your path as shown above, you'll use **/usr/ucb/cc** when you compile
C programs. **/usr/ucb/cc** sets its default paths to pick up, in this order:

1. user-specified include directories and libraries

2. the compatibility include files and directories

3. the default UNIX System V headers and libraries, if unresolved symbols
    remain

BSD Library Routines

The BSD Compatibility Package libraries contain the routines listed in the following table. These routines are either not in UNIX System V or have a different
interface and a different system call "wrapper" than their UNIX System V counterparts; these latter routines are marked with an asterisk (*).

Not all entries in this table appear on their own manual pages. See the permuted
index in the *Operating System API Reference* for the name of the manual page that
explains a particular routine.

BSD Library Routines

_longjmp	getwd	setreuid
_setjmp	ieee_functions	setstate
alloca	ieee_handler	settimeofday*
alphasort	index	setusershell
bcmp	initstate	setvbuf*
bcopy	itom	sfconvert
closelog	killpg	sgconvert
copysign	longjmp*	sigblock
dbm_clearerr	madd	sigfpe
dbm_delete	mcmp	siginterrupt
dbm_error	mctl	siglongjmp*
dbm_fetch	mdiv	sigmask

dbm_firstkey	mfree	signal*
dbm_nextkey	min	sigpause
dbm_open	mkstemp	sigsetjmp*
dbm_store	mout	sigsetmask
dbmclose	msqrt	sigstack
dbminit	msub	sigvec
decimal_to_double	mtox	single_to_decimal
decimal_to_extended	mult	sleep*
decimal_to_single	nextkey	sprintf*
delete	nice*	srand*
double_to_decimal	nlist*	srandom
econvert	pow	stejmp*
endusershell	printf*	store
extended_to_decimal	psignal*	strcasecmp
fconvert	rand*	strncasecmp
fetch	random	sys_siglist
firstkey	re_comp	syscall
floatingpoint	re_exec	syslog
fopen*	reboot	times*
fp_class	reboot	ualarm
fprintf*	regex*	usleep
freopen*	rindex	utimes
ftime	rpow dbm_close	vfprintf*
gcd	scalbn	vprintf*
gconvert	scandir	vsprintf*
getdtablesize	sdiv	wait3
gethostid	seconvert	wait*
gethostname	setbuf*	wiFEXITED
getpagesize	setbuffer	wiFSIGNALED
getpriority	sethostname	wiFSTOPPED
getrusage	setlinebuf	xtom
gettimeofday*	setpriority	
getusershell	setregid	

BSD Header Files

The BSD Compatibility Package includes a set of header files that provide a high degree of source compatibility for applications that were originally written to work on BSD.

Some BSD header files do not exist in UNIX System V. Others differ in ways that cannot be reconciled in a single file and are listed in the following table with an asterisk (*).

assert.h*	strings.h	sys/reboot.h
dbm.h	struct.h	sys/resource.h*
fp.h	sunfp.h	sys/signal.h*
mp.h	sys/dirent.h*	sys/types.h*
ndbm.h	sys/fcntl.h*	sys/vfs.h*
regexp.h*	sys/file.h*	sys/wait.h*
setjmp.h*	sys/ieeefp.h	sysexits.h
signal.h*	sys/mtio.h	ufs/quota.h
stdio.h*	sys/param.h*	unistd.h*

How C Programs Communicate with the Shell

Information or control data can be passed to a C program as an argument on the command line, which is to say, by the shell. When you execute a C program, command line arguments are made available to the function **main** in two parameters, an argument count, conventionally called **argc**, and an argument vector, conventionally called **argv**. (Every C program is required to have an entry point named **main**.) **argc** is the number of arguments with which the program was invoked. **argv** is an array of pointers to character strings that contain the arguments, one per string. Since the command name itself is considered to be the first argument, or **argv[0]**, the count is always at least one. Here is the declaration for **main**:

```
int
main(int argc, char *argv[])
```

For two examples of how you might use run-time parameters in your program, see the last subsection of this chapter.

The shell, which makes arguments available to your program, considers an argument to be any sequence of non-blank characters. Characters enclosed in single quotes (**'abc def'**) or double quotes (**"abc def"**) are passed to the program as one argument even if blanks or tabs are among the characters. You are responsible for error checking and otherwise making sure that the argument received is what your program expects it to be.

In addition to **argc** and **argv**, you can use a third argument: **envp** is an array of pointers to environment variables. You can find more information on **envp** in the *Operating System API Reference* under **exec** in Section 2 and in the *System Files and Devices Reference* under **environ** in Section 5.

C programs exit voluntarily, returning control to the operating system, by returning from **main** or by calling the **exit** function. That is, a **return(***n***)** from **main** is equivalent to the call **exit(***n***)**. (Remember that **main** has type "function returning **int**.") Your program should return a value to say whether it completed successfully or not. The value gets passed to the shell, where it becomes the value of the **$?** shell variable if you executed your program in the foreground. By convention, a return value of zero denotes success, a non-zero return value means some sort of error occurred. You can use the macros **EXIT_SUCCESS** and **EXIT_FAILURE**, defined in the header file **<stdlib.h>**, as return values from **main** or argument values for **exit**.

Passing Command Line Arguments

As described above, information or control data can be passed to a C program as an argument on the command line. When you execute the program, command line arguments are made available to the function **main** in two parameters, an argument count, conventionally called **argc**, and an argument vector, conventionally called **argv**. **argc** is the number of arguments with which the program was invoked. **argv** is an array of pointers to characters strings that contain the arguments, one per string. Since the command name itself is considered to be the first argument, or **argv[0]**, the count is always at least one.

If you plan to accept run-time parameters in your program, you need to include code to deal with the information. Figure 2-10 and Figure 2-11 show program fragments that illustrate two common uses of run-time parameters:

- Figure 2-10 shows how you provide a variable file name to a program, such that a command of the form

    ```
    $ prog filename
    ```

    will cause **prog** to attempt to open the specified file.

- Figure 2-11 shows how you set internal flags that control the operation of a program, such that a command of the form

    ```
    $ prog -opr
    ```

    will cause **prog** to set the corresponding variables for each of the options specified. The **getopt** function used in the example is the most common way to process arguments in UNIX system programs. **getopt** is described in Subsection 3C of the *Operating System API Reference*.

Figure 2-10: Using `argv[1]` **to Pass a File Name**

```c
#include <stdio.h>

int
main(int argc, char *argv[])
{
    FILE *fin;
    int ch;

    switch (argc)
    {
    case 2:
        if ((fin = fopen(argv[1], "r")) == NULL)
        {
            /* First string (%s) is program name (argv[0]).  */
            /* Second string (%s) is name of file that could */
            /* not be opened (argv[1]). */

            (void)fprintf(stderr, "%s: Cannot open input file %s\n",
                argv[0], argv[1]);
            return(2);
        }
        break;
    case 1:
        fin = stdin;
        break;

    default:
        (void)fprintf(stderr, "Usage: %s [file]\n", argv[0]);
        return(2);
    }

    while ((ch = getc(fin)) != EOF)
        (void)putchar(ch);

    return (0);

}
```

Figure 2-11: Using Command Line Arguments to Set Flags

```c
#include <stdio.h>
#include <stdlib.h>

int
main(int argc, char *argv[])
{
        int oflag = 0;
        int pflag = 0;          /* Function flags */
        int rflag = 0;
        int ch;

        while ((ch = getopt(argc, argv, "opr")) != -1)
        {
                /* For options present, set flag to 1.         */
                /* If unknown options present, print error message. */

                switch (ch)
                {
                case 'o':
                        oflag = 1;
                        break;
                case 'p':
                        pflag = 1;
                        break;
                case 'r':
                        rflag = 1;
                        break;
                default:
                        (void)fprintf(stderr, "Usage: %s [-opr]\n", argv[0]);
                        return(2);
                }
        }
        /* Do other processing controlled by oflag, pflag, rflag. */
        return(0);
}
```

System Calls

UNIX system calls are the interface between the kernel and the user programs that run on top of it. The UNIX system kernel is the software on which everything else in the UNIX operating system depends. The kernel manages system resources, maintains file systems and supports system calls. **read, write** and the other system calls in Section 2 of the *Operating System API Reference* define what the UNIX system is. Everything else is built on their foundation. Strictly speaking, they are the only way to access such facilities as the file system, interprocess communication primitives, and multitasking mechanisms.

Of course, most programs do not need to invoke system calls directly to gain access to these facilities. If you are writing a C program, for example, you can use the library functions described in Section 3 of the *Operating System API Reference*. When you use these functions, the details of their implementation on the UNIX system are transparent to the program, for example, that the system call **read** underlies the **fread** implementation in the standard C library. In other words, the program will generally be portable to any system, UNIX or not, with a conforming C implementation. (See the *Programming in Standard C* guide for a discussion of the standard C library.)

In contrast, programs that invoke system calls directly are portable only to other UNIX or UNIX-like systems; for that reason, you would not use **read** in a program that performed a simple input/output operation. Other operations, however, including most multitasking mechanisms, do require direct interaction with the UNIX system kernel. These operations are the subject of the first part of this book. This chapter lists the system calls in functional groups, and includes brief discussions of error handling. For details on individual system calls, see Section 2 of the *Operating System API Reference*.

A C program is automatically linked with the system calls you have invoked when you compile the program. The procedure may be different for programs written in other languages. Check the *Programming in Standard C* guide for details on the language you are using.

Input/Output and File System Calls

File and Device I/O

These system calls perform basic input/output operations on UNIX system files.

Figure 2-12: File and Device I/O Functions

open		open a file for reading or writing
creat		create a new file or rewrite an existing one
close		close a file descriptor
read	write	transfer data from/onto a file or device
getmsg	putmsg	get/put message from/onto a stream
lseek		move file I/O pointer
fcntl		file I/O control
ioctl		device I/O control

Terminal Device Control

These system calls deal with a general terminal interface for the control of asynchronous communications ports.

Figure 2-13: Terminal Device Control Functions

tcgetattr	tcsetattr	get and set terminal attributes
tcdrain	tcflush	line control functions
tcflow	tcsendbreak	line control functions
cfgetispeed	cfgetospeed	get baud rate functions
cfsetispeed	cfsetospeed	set baud rate functions
tcgetsid		get terminal session ID
tcgetpgrp		get terminal foreground process group ID
tcsetpgrp		set terminal foreground process group ID

Directory and File System Control

These system calls allow creation of new directories (and other types of files), linking to existing files, obtaining or modifying file status information, and allow you to control various aspects of the file system.

Figure 2-14: Directory and File System Control Functions

link			link to a file
access			determine accessibility of a file
mknod			make a directory, special, or regular file
chmod	fchmod		change mode of file
chown	fchown	lchown	change owner and group of a file
utime			set file access and modification times
stat	fstat	lstat	get file status
pathconf	fpathconf		get configurable path name variables
getdents			read directory entries and put in file system-independent format
mkdir			make a directory
readlink			read the value of a symbolic link
rename			change the name of a file
rmdir			remove a directory
symlink			make a symbolic link to a file
unlink			remove directory entry
ustat			get file system statistics
sync			update super block
mount	umount		mount/unmount a file system
statfs	fstatfs		get file system information
sysfs			get file system type information

Process and Memory System Calls

Processes

These system calls control user processes.

Figure 2-15: Process Management Functions

fork			create a new process
execl	execle	execlp	execute a file with a list of arguments
execv	execve	execvp	execute a file with a variable list
exit	_exit		terminate process
wait	waitpid	waitid	wait for child process to change state
setuid	setgid		set user and group IDs
getpgrp	setpgrp		get and set process group ID
chdir	fchdir		change working directory
chroot			change root directory
nice			change priority of a process
getcontext	setcontext		get and set current user context
getgroups	setgroups		get or set supplementary group IDs
getpid	getppid	getpgid	get process and parent process IDs
getuid	geteuid		get real user and effective user
getgid	getegid		get real group and effective group
pause			suspend process until signal
priocntl			process scheduler control
setpgid			set process group ID
setsid			set session ID
kill			send a signal to a process or group of processes

Signals

Signals are messages passed by the UNIX system to running processes.

Figure 2-16: Signal Management Functions

`sigaction`		detailed signal management
`sigaltstack`		set/get signal alternate stack context
`sigignore`	`sigpause`	simplified signal management
`sighold`	`sigrelse`	simplified signal management
`sigset`	`signal`	simplified signal management
`sigpending`		examine blocked and pending signals
`sigprocmask`		change or examine signal mask
`sigsuspend`		install a signal mask and suspend process
`sigsend`	`sigsendset`	send a signal to a process or group of processes

Basic Interprocess Communication

These system calls connect processes so they can communicate. `pipe` is the system call for creating an interprocess channel. `dup` is the call for duplicating an open file descriptor. (These IPC mechanisms are not applicable for processes on separate hosts.)

Figure 2-17: Basic Interprocess Communication Functions

`pipe`	open file-descriptors for a pipe
`dup`	duplicate an open file-descriptor

Advanced Interprocess Communication

These system calls support interprocess messages, semaphores, and shared memory and are effective in data base management. (These IPC mechanisms are also not applicable for processes on separate hosts.)

Figure 2-18: Advanced Interprocess Communication Functions

msgget	get message queue
msgctl	message control operations
msgop	message operations
semget	get set of semaphores
semctl	semaphore control operations
semop	semaphore operations
shmget	get shared memory segment identifier
shmctl	shared memory control operations
shmop	shared memory operations

Memory Management

These system calls give you access to virtual memory facilities.

Figure 2-19: Memory Management Functions

getpagesize		get system page size
memcntl		memory management control
mmap		map pages of memory
mprotect		set protection of memory mapping
munmap		unmap pages of memory
plock		lock process, text, or data in memory
brk	sbrk	dynamically allocate memory space

Miscellaneous System Calls

These are system calls for such things as administration, timing, and other miscellaneous purposes.

Figure 2-20: Miscellaneous System Functions

acct		enable or disable process accounting
alarm		set a process alarm clock
getrlimit	setrlimit	control maximum system resource consumption
modload		loads dynamically loadable kernel module
moduload		unloads kernel module
modpath		change path from which modules are loaded
modadm		module administration
profil		execution time profile
sysconf		method for application's determination of value for system configuration
sysi86		machine-specific functions (available only on Intel processors)
time	stime	get/set time
uadmin		administrative control
ulimit		get and set user limits
uname		get/set name of current UNIX system

XENIX System Calls

The system calls listed in this section are provided in the Application Compatibility Package installed by default as part of the Foundation Set. They are intended to be used by XENIX applications installed on UNIX System V. See the associated Section 2 manual pages for these system calls for more information.

File Management

chsize
Changes the size of the file to a specified length by either truncating the file or padding it with an appropriate number of bytes.

locking
Allows a specified number of bytes in a file to be controlled by the locking process, to lock or unlock a file region for reading or writing.

`mknod`	Creates a new file name by the pathname pointed to by *path*.
`rdchk`	Checks to see if a process will block if it attempts to read the data in a file.
`stat`	Obtains information about the named file pointed to by *path*.

Process Management

`lock`	Locks a process in primary memory.
`nap`	Suspends the execution of a current process for a short interval.
`ftime`	Gets the time and date and returns the time in a structure pointed to by its argument.

Inter-Process Communications

`creatsem`	Defines a binary semaphore and returns a unique semaphore number used by the **waitsem** and **sigsem** system calls to set parameters. **creatsem** also manages mutually exclusive access to a resource, shared variable or critical section of a program.
`nbwaitsem`	Will fail if a semaphore is busy instead of waiting [see **waitsem**(2)].
`opensem`	Opens a named semaphore and returns the unique semaphore identification number used by **waitsem** and **sigsem**.
`stat`	Puts data returned by **stat** system call in a special format.
`sdenter`	Synchronizes access to a shared data segment by indicating that the current process is about to access the contents of the same.
`sdfree`	Detaches the current process from the shared data segment that is attached at the specified address [see **sdget**(2)].
`sdget`	Attaches a shared data segment to the data space of the current process.
`sdgetv`	Synchronizes cooperating processes that are using shared data segments.
`sdleave`	Used in conjunction with **sdenter** to synchronize processes using shared data segments [see **sdenter**(2)].

sdwaitv	Used in conjunction with **sdgetv** to synchronize processes using shared data segments [see **sdgetv**(2)].
sigsem	Signals a process that is waiting on the semaphore that it may proceed and use the resource governed by the semaphore.
waitsem	Awaits and checks access to a resource governed by a semaphore. It is used in conjunction with **sigsem**.

BSD System Calls

The optional BSD Compatibility Package includes system calls and library routines that provide BSD system call functionality not present in or different from UNIX System V's system call functionality. See the section "BSD System Libraries and Header Files", in this chapter, for details.

UNIX System Call Error Handling

UNIX system calls that fail to complete successfully almost always return a value of **-1** to your program. (If you look through the system calls in Section 2, you will see that there are a few calls for which no return value is defined, but they are the exceptions.) In addition to the **-1** returned to the program, the unsuccessful system call places an integer in an externally declared variable, **errno**. In a C program, you can determine the value in **errno** if your program contains the following statement:

```
#include <errno.h>
```

The C language function **perror**(3C) can be used to print an error message (on **stderr**) based on the value of **errno**. The value in **errno** is not cleared on successful calls, so your program should check it only if the system call returned a **-1** indicating an error. The following list identifies the error numbers and symbolic names defined in the **<errno.h>** header file, and described in **intro**(2) of the *Operating System API Reference*.

Error Number	Symbolic Name	Description
1	EPERM	Not privileged. Typically this error indicates an attempt to modify a file in some way forbidden except to its owner or a process with the appropriate privilege. It is also returned for attempts by ordinary users to do things allowed only to the super-user.
2	ENOENT	No such file or directory. A file name is specified and the file should exist but fails to, or one of the directories in a path name fails to exist.
3	ESRCH	No such process. No process can be found corresponding to the that specified by PID in the **kill** or **ptrace** routine.
4	EINTR	Interrupted system call. An asynchronous signal (such as interrupt or quit), which the user has elected to catch, occurred during a system service routine. If execution is resumed after processing the signal, it will appear as if the interrupted routine call returned this error condition.
5	EIO	I/O error. Some physical I/O error has occurred. This error may in some cases occur on a call following the one to which it actually applies.
6	ENXIO	No such device or address. I/O on a special file refers to a subdevice which does not exist, or exists beyond the limit of the device. It may also occur when, for example, a tape drive is not on-line or no disk pack is loaded on a drive.
7	E2BIG	Arg list too long. An argument list longer than **ARG_MAX** bytes is presented to a member of the **exec** family of routines. The argument list limit is sum of the size of the argument list plus the size of the environment's exported shell variables.
8	ENOEXEC	Exec format error. A request is made to execute a file which, although it has the appropriate permissions, does not start with a valid format [see **a.out**(4)].
9	EBADF	Bad file number. Either a file descriptor refers to no open file, or a **read** [respectively, **write**] request is made to a file that is open only for writing (respectively, reading).

Error Number	Symbolic Name	Description
10	ECHILD	No child processes. A **wait** routine was executed by a process that had no existing or unwaited-for child processes.
11	EAGAIN	Resource is temporarily unavailable. For example, the **fork** routine failed because the system's process table is full or the user is not allowed to create any more processes. Or a system call failed because of insufficient memory or swap space.
12	ENOMEM	Not enough space. During execution of an **exec, brk,** or **sbrk** routine, a program asks for more space than the system is able to supply. This is not a temporary condition; the maximum size is a system parameter. The error may also occur if the arrangement of text, data, and stack segments requires too many segmentation registers, or if there is not enough swap space during the **fork** routine. If this error occurs on a resource associated with Remote File Sharing (RFS), it indicates a memory depletion which may be temporary, dependent on system activity at the time the call was invoked. (The RFS feature is no longer supported.)
13	EACCES	Permission denied. An attempt was made to access a file in a way forbidden by the protection system.
14	EFAULT	Bad address. The system encountered a hardware fault in attempting to use an argument of a routine. For example, **errno** potentially may be set to **EFAULT** any time a routine that takes a pointer argument is passed an invalid address, if the system can detect the condition. Because systems will differ in their ability to reliably detect a bad address, on some implementations passing a bad address to a routine will result in undefined behavior.

Error Number	Symbolic Name	Description
15	ENOTBLK	Block device required. A non-block file was mentioned where a block device was required (e.g., in a call to the **mount** routine).
16	EBUSY	Device busy. An attempt was made to mount a device that was already mounted or an attempt was made to dismount a device on which there is an active file (open file, current directory, mounted-on file, active text segment). It will also occur if an attempt is made to enable accounting when it is already enabled. The device or resource is currently unavailable.
17	EEXIST	File exists. An existing file was mentioned in an inappropriate context (e.g., call to the **link** routine).
18	EXDEV	Cross-device link. A link to a file on another device was attempted.
19	ENODEV	No such device. An attempt was made to apply an inappropriate operation to a device (e.g., read a write-only device).
20	ENOTDIR	Not a directory. A non-directory was specified where a directory is required (e.g., in a path prefix or as an argument to the **chdir** routine).
21	EISDIR	Is a directory. An attempt was made to write on a directory.
22	EINVAL	Invalid argument. An invalid argument was specified (e.g., unmounting a non-mounted device, mentioning an undefined signal in a call to the **signal** or **kill** routine. Also set by the functions described in the math package (3M).
23	ENFILE	File table overflow. The system file table is full (i.e., **SYS_OPEN** files are open, and temporarily no more files can be opened).

Error Number	Symbolic Name	Description
24	**EMFILE**	Too many open files. No process may have more than **OPEN_MAX** file descriptors open at a time.
25	**ENOTTY**	Not a typewriter. A call was made to the **ioctl** routine specifying a file that is not a special character device.
26	**ETXTBSY**	Text file busy. An attempt was made to execute a pure-procedure program that is currently open for writing. Also an attempt to open for writing or to remove a pure-procedure program that is being executed.
27	**EFBIG**	File too large. The size of a file exceeded the maximum file size, **FCHR_MAX** [see **getrlimit**(2)].
28	**ENOSPC**	No space left on device. While writing an ordinary file or creating a directory entry, there is no free space left on the device. In the **fcntl** routine, the setting or removing of record locks on a file cannot be accomplished because there are no more record entries left on the system.
29	**ESPIPE**	Illegal seek. A call to the **lseek** routine was issued to a pipe.
30	**EROFS**	Read-only file system. An attempt to modify a file or directory was made on a device mounted read-only.
31	**EMLINK**	Too many links. An attempt to make more than the maximum number of links, **LINK_MAX**, to a file.
32	**EPIPE**	Broken pipe. A write on a pipe for which there is no process to read the data. This condition normally generates a signal; the error is returned if the signal is ignored.

Error Number	Symbolic Name	Description
33	EDOM	Math argument out of domain of func. The argument of a function in the math package (3M) is out of the domain of the function.
34	ERANGE	Math result not representable. The value of a function in the math package (3M) is not representable within machine precision.
35	ENOMSG	No message of desired type. An attempt was made to receive a message of a type not existing on the specified message queue [see **msgop**(2)].
36	EIDRM	Identifier removed. This error is returned to processes that resume execution due to the removal of an identifier from the file system's name space [see **msgctl**(2), **semctl**(2), and **shmctl**(2)].
37	ECHRNG	Channel number out of range.
38	EL2NSYNC	Level 2 not synchronized.
39	EL3HLT	Level 3 halted.
40	EL3RST	Level 3 reset.
41	ELNRNG	Link number out of range.
42	EUNATCH	Protocol driver not attached.
43	ENOCSI	No CSI structure available.
44	EL2HLT	Level 2 halted.
45	EDEADLK	Deadlock condition. A deadlock situation was detected and avoided. This error pertains to file and record locking.
46	ENOLCK	No record locks available. There are no more locks available. The system lock table is full [see **fcntl**(2)].

Error Number	Symbolic Name	Description
60	ENOSTR	Device not a stream. A **putmsg** or **getmsg** system call was attempted on a file descriptor that is not a STREAMS device.
61	ENODATA	No data available.
62	ETIME	Timer expired. The timer set for a STREAMS **ioctl** call has expired. The cause of this error is device specific and could indicate either a hardware or software failure, or perhaps a timeout value that is too short for the specific operation. The status of the **ioctl** operation is indeterminate.
63	ENOSR	Out of stream resources. During a STREAMS **open**, either no STREAMS queues or no STREAMS head data structures were available. This is a temporary condition; one may recover from it if other processes release resources.
64	ENONET	Machine is not on the network. This error is Remote File Sharing (RFS) specific. (The RFS feature is no longer supported.) This error occurs when users try to advertise, unadvertise, mount, or unmount remote resources while the machine has not done the proper startup to connect to the network.
65	ENOPKG	Package not installed. This error occurs when users attempt to use a system call from a package which has not been installed.
66	EREMOTE	Object is remote. This error is RFS specific. (The RFS feature is no longer supported.) This error occurs when users try to advertise a resource which is not on the local machine, or try to mount/unmount a device (or pathname) that is on a remote machine.
67	ENOLINK	Link has been severed. This error is RFS specific. (The RFS feature is no longer supported.) This error occurs when the link (virtual circuit) connecting to a remote machine is gone.

Error Number	Symbolic Name	Description
68	EADV	Advertise error. This error is RFS specific. (The RFS feature is no longer supported.) This error occurs when users try to advertise a resource which has been advertised already, or try to stop the RFS while there are resources still advertised, or try to force unmount a resource when it is still advertised.
69	ESRMNT	Srmount error. This error is RFS specific. (The RFS feature is no longer supported.) This error occurs when an attempt is made to stop RFS while resources are still mounted by remote machines, or when a resource is readvertised with a client list that does not include a remote machine that currently has the resource mounted.
70	ECOMM	Communication error on send. This error is RFS specific. (The RFS feature is no longer supported.) This error occurs when the current process is waiting for a message from a remote machine, and the virtual circuit fails.
71	EPROTO	Protocol error. Some protocol error occurred. This error is device specific, but is generally not related to a hardware failure.
74	EMULTIHOP	Multihop attempted. This error is RFS specific. (The RFS feature is no longer supported.) This error occurs when users try to access remote resources which are not directly accessible.
76	EDOTDOT	Error 76. This error is RFS specific. (The RFS feature is no longer supported.) A way for the server to tell the client that a process has transferred back from mount point.
77	EBADMSG	Not a data message. During a **read**, **getmsg**, or **ioctl I_RECVFD** system call to a STREAMS device, something has come to the head of the queue that can't be processed. That something depends on the system call: **read**: control information or a passed file descriptor. **getmsg**: passed file descriptor. **ioctl**: control or data information.

Error Number	Symbolic Name	Description
78	ENAMETOOLONG	File name too long. The length of the path argument exceeds **PATH_MAX**, or the length of a path component exceeds **NAME_MAX** while **_POSIX_NO_TRUNC** is in effect; [see **limits**(4)].
79	EOVERFLOW	Error 79. Value too large to be stored in data type.
80	ENOTUNIQ	Name not unique on network. Given log name not unique.
81	EBADFD	File descriptor in bad state. Either a file descriptor refers to no open file or a read request was made to a file that is open only for writing.
82	EREMCHG	Remote address changed.
83	ELIBACC	Cannot access a needed shared library. Trying to **exec** an **a.out** that requires a shared library and the shared library doesn't exist or the user doesn't have permission to use it.
84	ELIBBAD	Accessing a corrupted shared library. Trying to **exec** an **a.out** that requires a shared library (to be linked in) and **exec** could not load the shared library. The shared library is probably corrupted.
85	ELIBSCN	**.lib** section in **a.out** corrupted Trying to **exec** an **a.out** that requires a shared library (to be linked in) and there was erroneous data in the **.lib** section of the **a.out**. The **.lib** section tells **exec** what shared libraries are needed. The **a.out** is probably corrupted.
86	ELIBMAX	Attempting to link in more shared libraries than system limit. Trying to **exec** an **a.out** that requires more static shared libraries than is allowed on the current configuration of the system. See the *Advanced System Administration System Performance Administration* guide.

Error Number	Symbolic Name	Description
87	ELIBEXEC	Cannot **exec** a shared library directly Attempting to **exec** a shared library directly.
88	EILSEQ	Error 88. Illegal byte sequence. Handle multiple characters as a single character.
89	ENOSYS	Operation not applicable.
90	ELOOP	Number of symbolic links encountered during path name traversal exceeds **MAXSYMLINKS**
91	ERESTART	Error 91. Interrupted system call should be restarted.
92	ESTRPIPE	Error 92. Streams pipe error (not externally visible).
93	ENOTEMPTY	Directory not empty.
94	EUSERS	Too many users. Too many users.
95	ENOTSOCK	Socket operation on non-socket. Self-explanatory.
96	EDESTADDRREQ	Destination address required. A required address was omitted from an operation on a transport endpoint. Destination address required.
97	EMSGSIZE	Message too long. A message sent on a transport provider was larger than the internal message buffer or some other network limit.
98	EPROTOTYPE	Protocol wrong type for socket. A protocol was specified that does not support the semantics of the socket type requested.
99	ENOPROTOOPT	Protocol not available. A bad option or level was specified when getting or setting options for a protocol.

Error Number	Symbolic Name	Description
120	EPROTONOSUPPORT	Protocol not supported. The protocol has not been configured into the system or no implementation for it exists.
121	ESOCKTNOSUPPORT	Socket type not supported. The support for the socket type has not been configured into the system or no implementation for it exists.
122	EOPNOTSUPP	Operation not supported on transport endpoint. For example, trying to accept a connection on a datagram transport endpoint.
123	EPFNOSUPPORT	Protocol family not supported. The protocol family has not been configured into the system or no implementation for it exists. Used for the Internet protocols.
124	EAFNOSUPPORT	Address family not supported by protocol family. An address incompatible with the requested protocol was used.
125	EADDRINUSE	Address already in use. User attempted to use an address already in use, and the protocol does not allow this.
126	EADDRNOTAVAIL	Cannot assign requested address. Results from an attempt to create a transport endpoint with an address not on the current machine.
127	ENETDOWN	Network is down. Operation encountered a dead network.
128	ENETUNREACH	Network is unreachable. Operation was attempted to an unreachable network.
129	ENETRESET	Network dropped connection because of reset. The host you were connected to crashed and rebooted.
130	ECONNABORTED	Software caused connection abort. A connection abort was caused internal to your host machine.

Error Number	Symbolic Name	Description
131	ECONNRESET	Connection reset by peer. A connection was forcibly closed by a peer. This normally results from a loss of the connection on the remote host due to a timeout or a reboot.
132	ENOBUFS	No buffer space available. An operation on a transport endpoint or pipe was not performed because the system lacked sufficient buffer space or because a queue was full.
133	EISCONN	Transport endpoint is already connected. A connect request was made on an already connected transport endpoint; or, a **sendto** or **sendmsg** request on a connected transport endpoint specified a destination when already connected.
134	ENOTCONN	Transport endpoint is not connected. A request to send or receive data was disallowed because the transport endpoint is not connected and (when sending a datagram) no address was supplied.
143	ESHUTDOWN	Cannot send after transport endpoint shutdown. A request to send data was disallowed because the transport endpoint had already been shut down.
144	ETOOMANYREFS	Too many references: cannot splice.
145	ETIMEDOUT	Connection timed out. A connect or send request failed because the connected party did not properly respond after a period of time. (The timeout period is dependent on the communication protocol.)
146	ECONNREFUSED	Connection refused. No connection could be made because the target machine actively refused it. This usually results from trying to connect to a service that is inactive on the remote host.
147	EHOSTDOWN	Host is down. A transport provider operation failed because the destination host was down.

Error Number	Symbolic Name	Description
148	**EHOSTUNREACH**	No route to host. A transport provider operation was attempted to an unreachable host.
149	**EALREADY**	Operation already in progress. An operation was attempted on a non-blocking object that already had an operation in progress.
150	**EINPROGRESS**	Operation now in progress. An operation that takes a long time to complete (such as a **connect**) was attempted on a non-blocking object.
151	**ESTALE**	Stale NFS file handle.
152	**ENOLOAD**	Cannot load required module. An attempt made to load a module failed.
153	**ERELOC**	Relocation error in loading module. Symbolic referencing error.
154	**ENOMATCH**	No symbol is found matching the given spec.
156	**EBADVER**	Version number mis-matched. The version number associated with a module is not supported by the kernel.
157	**ECONFIG**	Configured kernel resource exhausted.

3 File and Device Input/Output

Introduction

This chapter discusses the UNIX System file and record locking facility. Mandatory and advisory file and record locking are both available on current releases of the UNIX System. The intent of this capability is to provide a synchronization mechanism for programs accessing the same stores of data simultaneously. Such processing is characteristic of many multiuser applications, and the need for a standard method of dealing with the problem has been recognized by standards advocates like **/usr/group**, an organization of UNIX System users from businesses and campuses across the country.

Advisory file and record locking can be used to coordinate self-synchronizing processes. In mandatory locking, the standard I/O subroutines and I/O system calls enforce the locking protocol. In this way, at the cost of a little efficiency, mandatory locking double checks the programs against accessing the data out of sequence.

Also included in this chapter is a description of how file and record locking capabilities can be used. Examples are given for the correct use of record locking. Misconceptions about the amount of protection that record locking affords are dispelled. Record locking should be viewed as a synchronization mechanism, not a security mechanism.

The remainder of this chapter describes the STREAMS mechanism as it relates to input/output operations.

Input/Output System Calls

The lowest level of I/O in UNIX System V provides no buffering or other such services, but it offers the most control over what happens. System calls that represent direct entries into the UNIX System V kernel control all user I/O. UNIX System V keeps the system calls that do I/O simple, uniform and regular to eliminate differences between files, devices and styles of access. The same read and write system calls apply to ordinary disk files and I/O devices such as terminals, tape-drives and line-printers. They do not distinguish between "random" and "sequential" I/O, nor do they impose any logical record size on files. Thus, a single, uniform interface handles all communication between programs and peripheral devices, and programmers can defer specifying devices from program-development until program-execution time.

All I/O is done by reading or writing files, because all peripheral I/O devices, even a user's terminal, are files in the file system. Each supported device has an entry in the file system hierarchy, so that device names have the same structure as filenames, and the same protection mechanisms work on both devices and files.

A file is an ordered set of bytes of data on a I/O-device. The size of the file on input is determined by an end-of-file condition dependent on device-specific characteristics. The size of a regular file is determined by the position and number of bytes written on it, no predetermination of the size of a file is necessary or possible.

Besides the traditionally available devices, names exist for disk devices regarded as physical units outside the file system, and for absolutely addressed memory. The most important device in practice is the user's terminal. Treating a communication-device in the same way as any file by using the same I/O calls make it easy to redirect the input and output of commands from the terminal to another file; although, some differences are inevitable. For example, UNIX System V ordinarily treats terminal input in units of lines because character-erase and line-delete processing cannot be completed until a full line is typed. Programs trying to read some large number of bytes from a terminal must wait until a full line is typed, and then may be notified that some smaller number of bytes were actually read. All programs must prepare for this eventuality in any case, because a read from any disk file returns fewer bytes than requested when it reaches the end of the file. Ordinarily, reads from a terminal are fully compatible with reads from a disk file.

File Descriptors

UNIX System V File and Device I/O functions denote a file by a small positive integer called a "file-descriptor" and declared as follows:

> `int` *fildes*

where *fildes* represents the file-descriptor, and the file-descriptor denotes an open file from which data is read or onto which data is written. UNIX System V maintains all information about an open file; the user program refers to the file only by the file-descriptor. Any I/O on the file uses the file-descriptor instead of the filename to denote the file.

Multiple file-descriptors may denote the same file, and each file-descriptor has associated with it information used to do I/O on the file:

- a file-offset that shows which byte in the file to read or write next;

- file-status and access-modes (e.g., *read, write, read/write*) [see **open**(2)];

- the 'close-on-exec' flag [see **fcntl**(2)].

Doing I/O on the user's terminal occurs commonly enough that special arrangements make this convenient. When the command interpreter (the "shell") runs a program, it opens three files, called the *standard input*, the *standard output* and the *standard error output*, with file-descriptors `0`, `1` and `2`. All of these are normally connected to the terminal; thus, a program reading file-descriptor `0` and writing file-descriptors `1` and `2`, can do terminal I/O without opening the files. If I/O is redirected to and from files with `<` and `>`, as in:

> `prog <infile >outfile`

the shell changes the default assignments for file-descriptors `0` and `1` from the terminal to the named files. Similar conventions hold for I/O on a pipe. Normally file-descriptor `2` remains attached to the terminal, so error messages can go there. In all cases, the shell changes the file assignments, the program does not. The program can ignore where its output goes, as long as it uses file-descriptor `0` for input and `1` and `2` for output.

Reading and Writing Files

The functions **read** and **write** do I/O on files. For both, the first argument is a file-descriptor, the second argument is a buffer in the user program where the data comes from or goes to and the third argument is the number of bytes of data to transfer. Each call returns a count of the number of bytes actually transferred. These calls look like:

$$n = \textbf{read}(\textit{fildes, buffer, count});$$

$$n = \textbf{write}(\textit{fildes, buffer, count});$$

Up to *count* bytes are transferred between the file denoted by *fildes* and the byte array pointed to by *buffer*. The returned value *n* is the number of bytes actually transferred.

For writing, the returned value is the number of bytes actually written; it is generally an error if this fails to equal the number of bytes requested. In the **write** case, *n* is the same as *count* except under exceptional conditions, such as I/O errors or end of physical medium on special files; in a **read**, however, *n* may without error be less than *count*.

For reading, the number of bytes returned may be less than the number requested, because fewer than *count* bytes remained to be read. If the file-offset is so near the end of the file that reading *count* characters would cause reading beyond the end, only sufficient bytes are transferred to reach the end of the file, also, typewriter-like terminals never return more than one line of input. (When the file is a terminal, **read** normally reads only up to the next new-line, which is generally less than what was requested.)

When a **read** call returns with *n* equal to zero, the end of the file has been reached. For disk files this occurs when the file-offset equals the current size of the file. It is possible to generate an end-of-file from a terminal by use of an escape sequence that depends on the device used. The function **read** returns 0 to signify end-of-file, and returns −1 to signify an error.

The number of bytes to be read or written is quite arbitrary. The two most common values are 1, which means one character at a time ("unbuffered"), and 512, which corresponds to a physical block size on many peripheral devices. This latter size is most efficient, but even character at a time I/O is not overly expensive. Bytes written affect only those parts of a file implied by the position of the file-offset and the count; no other part of the file is changed. If the last byte lies beyond the end of the file, the file grows as needed.

A simple program using the **read** and **write** functions to copy its input to its output can copy anything, since the input and output can be redirected to any file or device.

```
#define  BUFSIZE  512

main()    /* copy input to output */
{
    char buf[BUFSIZE];
    int  n;

    while ((n = read(0, buf, BUFSIZE)) > 0)
        write( 1, buf, n);
    exit(0);
}
```

If the file size is not a multiple of **BUFSIZE**, some **read** will return a smaller number of bytes to be written by **write**: the next call to **read** after that will return zero indicating end-of-file.

To see how **read** and **write** can be used to construct higher level functions like **getchar** and **putchar**, here is an example of **getchar** which does unbuffered input:

```
#define  CMASK   0377  /* for making char's > 0 */

getchar() /* unbuffered single character input */
{
    char c;

    return((read(0, &c, 1) > 0) ? c & CMASK : EOF);
}
```

The variable **c** must be declared **char**, because **read** accepts a character pointer. The character returned must be masked with **0377** to ensure that it is positive; otherwise, sign extension may make it negative.

The second version of **getchar** does input in big chunks, and hands out the characters one at a time.

```
#define  CMASK    0377  /* for making char's > 0 */
#define  BUFSIZE  512

getchar()  /* buffered version */
{
    static char    buf[BUFSIZE];
    static char    *bufp = buf;
    static int     n = 0;

    if (n == 0) {    /* buffer is empty */
        n = read(0, buf, BUFSIZE);
        bufp = buf;
    }
    return((--n >= 0) ? *bufp++ & CMASK : EOF);
}
```

Opening, Creating and Closing Files

Other than the default standard input, output and error files, you must explicitly open files in order to read or write them. The two functions that do this are: **open** and **creat** [see **open**(2) and **creat**(2) in the *Operating System API Reference*]. To read or write a file assumed to exist already, it must be opened by the following call:

fildes = **open**(*name*, *oflag*);

The argument *name* is a character string that represents a UNIX System V file system pathname. The *oflag* argument indicates whether the file is to be read, written, or "updated", that is, read and written simultaneously. The returned value *fildes* is a file-descriptor used to denote the file in subsequent calls that read, write or otherwise manipulate the file.

The function **open** resembles the function **fopen** in the Standard I/O Library, except that instead of returning a pointer to **FILE**, **open** returns a file-descriptor which is just an **int** [see **fopen**(3S) and **stdio**(3S) in the *Operating System API Reference*]. Moreover, the values for the access mode argument *oflag* are different (the flags are found in **/usr/include/fcntl.h**):

- **O_RDONLY** for read access.
- **O_WRONLY** for write access.
- **O_RDWR** for read and write access.

The function **open** returns **-1** if any error occurs; otherwise it returns a valid open file-descriptor.

Trying to **open** a file that does not exist causes an error; hence, **creat** is used to create new files, or to re-write old ones. The **creat** system call creates the given file if it does not exist, or truncates it to zero length if it does exist; **creat** also opens the new file for writing and, like **open**, returns a file-descriptor. Calling **creat** as follows:

> *fildes* = **creat**(*name, pmode*);

returns a file-descriptor if it created the file identified by the string **name**, and **-1** if it did not. Trying to **creat** a file that already exists does not cause an error, but if the file already exists, **creat** truncates it to zero length.

If the file is brand new, **creat** creates it with the protection mode specified by the **pmode** argument. The UNIX System V file system associates nine bits of protection information with a file, controlling *read, write* and *execute* permission for the *owner* of the file, for the owner's *group*, and for any *other* users. Thus, a three-digit octal number specifies the permissions most conveniently. For example, **0755** specifies *read, write* and *execute* permission for the *owner*, and *read* and *execute* permission for the *group* and all *other* users.

A simplified version of the UNIX System V utility **cp** (a program which copies one file to another) illustrates this:

Figure 3-1: simplified version of cp

```
#define  NULL 0
#define  BUFSIZE 512
#define  PMODE 0644 /* RW owner, R group & others */

main(argc, argv)     /* cp: copy fd1 to fd2 */
    int argc;
    char *argv[ ];
{
    int  fd1, fd2, n;
    char buf[BUFSIZE];

    if (argc != 3)
        error("Usage: cp from to", NULL);
    if ((fd1 = open(argv[1], 0)) == -1)
        error("cp: can't open %s", argv[1]);
    if ((fd2 = creat(argv[2], PMODE)) == -1)
        error("cp: can't create %s", argv[2]);

    while ((n = read(fd1, buf, BUFSIZE)) > 0)
        if (write(fd2, buf, n) != n)
            error("cp: write error", NULL);

    exit(0);
}
error(s1, s2)   /* print error message and die */
    char *s1, *s2;
{
    printf(s1, s2);
    printf("\n");

    exit(1);
}
```

The main simplification is that this version copies only one file, and does not permit the second argument to be a directory.

As stated earlier, there is a limit, **OPEN_MAX**, on the number of files which a process may have open simultaneously. Accordingly, any program which intends to process many files must be prepared to re-use file-descriptors. The function **close** breaks the connection between a file-descriptor and an open file, and frees the file-descriptor for use with some other file. Termination of a program via **exit** or return from the main program closes all open files.

Random Access — lseek

Normally, file I/O is sequential: each **read** or **write** proceeds from the point in the file right after the previous one. This means that if a particular byte in the file was the last byte written (or read), the next I/O call implicitly refers to the immediately following byte. For each open file, UNIX System V maintains a file-offset that indicates the next byte to be read or written. If n bytes are read or written, the file-offset advances by n bytes. When necessary, however, a file can be read or written in any arbitrary order using **lseek** to move around in a file without actually reading or writing.

To do random (direct-access) I/O it is only necessary to move the file-offset to the appropriate location in the file with a call to **lseek**. Calling **lseek** as follows:

        lseek(*fildes*, *offset*, *whence*);

or as follows:

        location = **lseek**(*fildes*, *offset*, *whence*);

forces the current position in the file denoted by file-descriptor *fildes* to move to position *offset* as specified by *whence*. Subsequent reading or writing begins at the new position. The file-offset associated with *fildes* is moved to a position *offset* bytes from the beginning of the file, from the current position of the file-offset or from the end of the file, depending on *whence*; *offset* may be negative. For some devices (e.g., paper tape and terminals) **lseek** calls are ignored. The value of **location** equals the actual offset from the beginning of the file to which the file-offset was moved. The argument *offset* is of type **off_t** defined by the header file **<types.h>** as a **long**; *fildes* and *whence* are **int**'s.

The argument *whence* can be **SEEK_SET**, **SEEK_CUR** or **SEEK_END** to specify that *offset* is to be measured from the beginning, from the current position, or from the end of the file respectively. For example, to append a file, seek to the end before writing:

lseek(*fildes*, **0L, SEEK_END**);

To get back to the beginning ("rewind"),

lseek(*fildes*, **0L, SEEK_SET**);

Notice the **0L** argument; it could also be written as **(long)** **0**.

With **lseek**, you can treat files more or less like large arrays, at the price of slower access. For example, the following simple function reads any number of bytes from any arbitrary point in a file:

```
get(fd, p, buf, n) /* read n bytes from position p */
    int fd, n;
    long p;
    char *buf;
{
    lseek(fd, p, SEEK_SET);  /* move to p */
    return(read(fd, buf, n));
}
```

File and Record Locking

Mandatory and advisory file and record locking both are available on current releases of the UNIX system. The intent of this capability to is provide a synchronization mechanism for programs accessing the same stores of data simultaneously. Such processing is characteristic of many multiuser applications, and the need for a standard method of dealing with the problem has been recognized by standards advocates like **/usr/group**, an organization of UNIX system users from businesses and campuses across the country.

Advisory file and record locking can be used to coordinate self-synchronizing processes. In mandatory locking, the standard I/O subroutines and I/O system calls enforce the locking protocol. In this way, at the cost of a little efficiency, mandatory locking double checks the programs against accessing the data out of sequence.

The remainder of this chapter describes how file and record locking capabilities can be used. Examples are given for the correct use of record locking. Misconceptions about the amount of protection that record locking affords are dispelled. Record locking should be viewed as a synchronization mechanism, not a security mechanism.

The manual pages for the **fcntl** system call, the **lockf** library function, and **fcntl** data structures and commands are referred to throughout this section [see fcntl(5)]. You should read them before continuing.

Terminology

Before discussing how to use record locking, let us first define a few terms.

Record

> A contiguous set of bytes in a file. The UNIX operating system does not impose any record structure on files. This may be done by the programs that use the files.

Cooperating Processes

> Processes that work together in some well-defined fashion to accomplish the tasks at hand. Processes that share files must request permission to access the files before using them. File access permissions must be carefully set to restrict noncooperating processes from accessing those files. The term process will be used interchangeably with cooperating process to refer to a task obeying such protocols.

Read (Share) Locks

These are used to gain limited access to sections of files. When a read lock is put on a record, other processes may also read lock that record, in whole or in part. No other process, however, may have or obtain a write lock on an overlapping section of the file. If a process holds a read lock it may assume that no other process will be writing or updating that record at the same time. This access method also lets many processes read the given record. This might be necessary when searching a file, without the contention involved if a write or exclusive lock were used.

Write (Exclusive) Locks

These are used to gain complete control over sections of files. When a write lock is put on a record, no other process may read or write lock that record, in whole or in part. If a process holds a write lock it may assume that no other process will be reading or writing that record at the same time.

Advisory Locking

A form of record locking that does not interact with the I/O subsystem. Advisory locking is not enforced, for example, by **creat**, **open**, **read**, or **write**. The control over records is accomplished by requiring an appropriate record lock request before I/O operations. If appropriate requests are always made by all processes accessing the file, then the accessibility of the file will be controlled by the interaction of these requests. Advisory locking depends on the individual processes to enforce the record locking protocol; it does not require an accessibility check at the time of each I/O request.

Mandatory Locking

A form of record locking that does interact with the I/O subsystem. Access to locked records is enforced by the **creat**, **open**, **read** and **write** system calls. If a record is locked, then access of that record by any other process is restricted according to the type of lock on the record. The control over records should still be performed explicitly by requesting an appropriate record lock before I/O operations, but an additional check is made by the system before each I/O operation to ensure the record locking protocol is being honored. Mandatory locking offers an extra synchronization check, but at the cost of some additional system overhead.

File Protection

There are access permissions for UNIX system files to control who may read, write, or execute such a file. These access permissions may only be set by the owner of the file or by a process with the appropriate privilege. The permissions of the directory in which the file resides can also affect the ultimate disposition of a file. Note that if the directory permissions allow anyone to write in it, then files within the directory may be removed, even if those files do not have read, write or execute permission for that user. Any information that is worth protecting, is worth protecting properly. If your application warrants the use of record locking, make sure that the permissions on your files and directories are set properly. A record lock, even a mandatory record lock, will only protect the portions of the files that are locked. Other parts of these files might be corrupted if proper precautions are not taken.

Only a known set of programs and/or administrators should be able to read or write a data base. This can be done easily by setting the set-group-ID bit of the data base accessing programs [see **chmod**(1)]. The files can then be accessed by a known set of programs that obey the record locking protocol. An example of such file protection, although record locking is not used, is the **mail** command. In that command only the particular user and the **mail** command can read and write in the unread mail files.

Opening a File for Record Locking

The first requirement for locking a file or segment of a file is having a valid open file descriptor. If read locks are to be done, then the file must be opened with at least read accessibility, and with write accessibility for write locks.

NOTE | Mapped files cannot be locked: if a file has been mapped, any attempt to use file or record locking on the file fails. See **mmap**(2).

For our example we will open our file for both read and write access:

```
#include <stdio.h>
#include <errno.h>
#include <fcntl.h>

int fd;                 /* file descriptor */
char *filename;


main(argc, argv)
int argc;
char *argv[];
{
        extern void exit(), perror();

        /* get data base file name from command line and open the
         * file for read and write access.
         */
        if (argc < 2) {
             (void) fprintf(stderr, "usage: %s filename\n", argv[0]);
             exit(2);
             }
        filename = argv[1];
        fd = open(filename, O_RDWR);
        if (fd < 0) {
             perror(filename);
             exit(2);
             }
        .
        .
        .
```

The file is now open for us to perform both locking and I/O functions. We then proceed with the task of setting a lock.

Setting a File Lock

There are several ways for us to set a lock on a file. In part, these methods depend on how the lock interacts with the rest of the program. There are also questions of performance as well as portability. Two methods will be given here, one using the **fcntl** system call, the other using the **/usr/group** standards compatible **lockf** library function call.

Locking an entire file is just a special case of record locking. For both these methods the concept and the effect of the lock are the same. The file is locked starting at a byte offset of zero (0) until the end of the maximum file size. This point extends beyond any real end of the file so that no lock can be placed on this file beyond this point. To do this the value of the size of the lock is set to zero. The code using the **fcntl** system call is as follows:

File and Device Input/Output

```
#include <fcntl.h>
#define MAX_TRY    10
int try;
struct flock lck;

try = 0;

/* set up the record locking structure, the address of which
 * is passed to the fcntl system call.
 */
lck.l_type = F_WRLCK;    /* setting a write lock */
lck.l_whence = 0;        /* offset l_start from beginning of file */
lck.l_start = 0L;
lck.l_len = 0L;          /* until the end of the file address space */

/* Attempt locking MAX_TRY times before giving up.
 */
while (fcntl(fd, F_SETLK, &lck) < 0) {
        if (errno == EAGAIN || errno == EACCES) {
                /* there might be other errors cases in which
                 * you might try again.
                 */
                if (++try < MAX_TRY) {
                        (void) sleep(2);
                        continue;
                }
                (void) fprintf(stderr,"File busy try again later!\n");
                return;
        }
        perror("fcntl");
        exit(2);
}
        .
        .
        .
```

This portion of code tries to lock a file. This is attempted several times until one of the following things happens:

- the file is locked

- an error occurs

- it gives up trying because **MAX_TRY** has been exceeded

To perform the same task using the **lockf** function, the code is as follows:

```
#include <unistd.h>
#define MAX_TRY    10
int try;
try = 0;

/* make sure the file pointer
 * is at the beginning of the file.
 */
lseek(fd, 0L, 0);

/* Attempt locking MAX_TRY times before giving up.
 */
while (lockf(fd, F_TLOCK, 0L) < 0) {
        if (errno == EAGAIN || errno == EACCES) {
                /* there might be other errors cases in which
                 * you might try again.
                 */
                if (++try < MAX_TRY) {
                        sleep(2);
                        continue;
                }
                (void) fprintf(stderr,"File busy try again later!\n");
                return;
        }
        perror("lockf");
        exit(2);
}
        .
        .
        .
```

It should be noted that the **lockf** example appears to be simpler, but the **fcntl** example exhibits additional flexibility. Using the **fcntl** method, it is possible to set the type and start of the lock request simply by setting a few structure variables. **lockf** merely sets write (exclusive) locks; an additional system call, **lseek**, is required to specify the start of the lock.

Setting and Removing Record Locks

Locking a record is done the same way as locking a file except for the differing starting point and length of the lock. We will now try to solve an interesting and real problem. There are two records (these records may be in the same or different file) that must be updated simultaneously so that other processes get a consistent view of this information. (This type of problem comes up, for example, when updating the interrecord pointers in a doubly linked list.) To do this you must decide the following questions:

- What do you want to lock?

- For multiple locks, in what order do you want to lock and unlock the records?

- What do you do if you succeed in getting all the required locks?

- What do you do if you fail to get all the locks?

In managing record locks, you must plan a failure strategy if you cannot obtain all the required locks. It is because of contention for these records that we have decided to use record locking in the first place. Different programs might:

- wait a certain amount of time, and try again

- abort the procedure and warn the user

- let the process sleep until signaled that the lock has been freed

- some combination of the above

Let us now look at our example of inserting an entry into a doubly linked list. For the example, we will assume that the record after which the new record is to be inserted has a read lock on it already. The lock on this record must be changed or promoted to a write lock so that the record may be edited.

Promoting a lock (generally from read lock to write lock) is permitted if no other process is holding a read lock in the same section of the file. If there are processes with pending write locks that are sleeping on the same section of the file, the lock promotion succeeds and the other (sleeping) locks wait. Promoting (or demoting) a write lock to a read lock carries no restrictions. In either case, the lock is merely reset with the new lock type. Because the **/usr/group lockf** function does not have read locks, lock promotion is not applicable to that call. An example of record locking with lock promotion follows:

```
struct record {
        .
        .               /* data portion of record */
        .
        long prev;      /* index to previous record in the list */
        long next;      /* index to next record in the list */
};

/* Lock promotion using fcntl(2)
 * When this routine is entered it is assumed that there are read
 * locks on "here" and "next".
 * If write locks on "here" and "next" are obtained:
 *      Set a write lock on "this".
 *      Return index to "this" record.
 * If any write lock is not obtained:
 *      Restore read locks on "here" and "next".
 *      Remove all other locks.
 *      Return a -1.
 */
long
set3lock (this, here, next)
long this, here, next;
{
        struct flock lck;

        lck.l_type = F_WRLCK;    /* setting a write lock */
        lck.l_whence = 0;        /* offset l_start from beginning of file */
        lck.l_start = here;
        lck.l_len = sizeof(struct record);

        /* promote lock on "here" to write lock */
        if (fcntl(fd, F_SETLKW, &lck) < 0) {
                return (-1);
        }
        /* lock "this" with write lock */
        lck.l_start = this;
        if (fcntl(fd, F_SETLKW, &lck) < 0) {
                /* Lock on "this" failed;
                 * demote lock on "here" to read lock.
                 */
                lck.l_type = F_RDLCK;
                lck.l_start = here;
                (void) fcntl(fd, F_SETLKW, &lck);
                return (-1);
        }
        /* promote lock on "next" to write lock */
        lck.l_start = next;
        if (fcntl(fd, F_SETLKW, &lck) < 0) {
                /* Lock on "next" failed;
                 * demote lock on "here" to read lock,
                 */
```

(continued on next page)

```
                lck.l_type = F_RDLCK;
                 lck.l_start = here;
                (void) fcntl(fd, F_SETLK, &lck);
                /* and remove lock on "this".
                 */
                lck.l_type = F_UNLCK;
                lck.l_start = this;
                (void) fcntl(fd, F_SETLK, &lck);
                return (-1);/* cannot set lock, try again or quit */
        }

        return (this);
}
```

The locks on these three records were all set to wait (sleep) if another process was blocking them from being set. This was done with the **F_SETLKW** command. If the **F_SETLK** command was used instead, the **fcntl** system calls would fail if blocked. The program would then have to be changed to handle the blocked condition in each of the error return sections.

Let us now look at a similar example using the **lockf** function. Since there are no read locks, all (write) locks will be referenced generically as locks.

```
/* Lock promotion using lockf(3)
 * When this routine is entered it is assumed that there are
 * no locks on "here" and "next".
 * If locks are obtained:
 *     Set a lock on "this".
 *     Return index to "this" record.
 * If any lock is not obtained:
 *     Remove all other locks.
 *     Return a -1.
 */

#include <unistd.h>

long
set3lock (this, here, next)
long this, here, next;

{

        /* lock "here" */
        (void) lseek(fd, here, 0);
```

(continued on next page)

File and Record Locking

```
        if (lockf(fd, F_LOCK, sizeof(struct record)) < 0) {
                return (-1);
        }
        /* lock "this" */
        (void) lseek(fd, this, 0);
        if (lockf(fd, F_LOCK, sizeof(struct record)) < 0) {
                /* Lock on "this" failed.
                 * Clear lock on "here".
                 */
                (void) lseek(fd, here, 0);
                (void) lockf(fd, F_ULOCK, sizeof(struct record));
                return (-1);

        }

        /* lock "next" */
        (void) lseek(fd, next, 0);
        if (lockf(fd, F_LOCK, sizeof(struct record)) < 0) {

                /* Lock on "next" failed.
                 * Clear lock on "here",
                 */
                (void) lseek(fd, here, 0);
                (void) lockf(fd, F_ULOCK, sizeof(struct record));

                /* and remove lock on "this".
                 */
                (void) lseek(fd, this, 0);
                (void) lockf(fd, F_ULOCK, sizeof(struct record));
                return (-1);/* cannot set lock, try again or quit */

        }
        return (this);
}
```

Locks are removed in the same manner as they are set, only the lock type is different (**F_UNLCK** or **F_ULOCK**). An unlock cannot be blocked by another process and will only affect locks that were placed by this process. The unlock only affects the section of the file defined in the previous example by **lck**. It is possible to unlock or change the type of lock on a subsection of a previously set lock. This may cause an additional lock (two locks for one system call) to be used by the operating system. This occurs if the subsection is from the middle of the previously set lock.

Getting Lock Information

You can determine which processes, if any, are blocking a lock from being set. This can be used as a simple test or as a means to find locks on a file. A lock is set up as in the previous examples and the **F_GETLK** command is used in the **fcntl** call. If the lock passed to **fcntl** would be blocked, the first blocking lock is returned to the process through the structure passed to **fcntl**. That is, the lock data passed to **fcntl** is overwritten by blocking lock information. This information includes two pieces of data that have not been discussed yet, **l_pid** and **l_sysid**, that are only used by **F_GETLK**. (For systems that do not support a distributed architecture the value in **l_sysid** should be ignored.) These fields uniquely identify the process holding the lock.

If a lock passed to **fcntl** using the **F_GETLK** command would not be blocked by another process's lock, then the **l_type** field is changed to **F_UNLCK** and the remaining fields in the structure are unaffected. Let us use this capability to print all the segments locked by other processes. Note that if there are several read locks over the same segment only one of these will be found.

```
struct flock lck;

/* Find and print "write lock" blocked segments of this file. */
        (void) printf("sysid    pid type     start    length\n");
        lck.l_whence = 0;
        lck.l_start = 0L;
        lck.l_len = 0L;
        do {
                lck.l_type = F_WRLCK;
                (void) fcntl(fd, F_GETLK, &lck);
                if (lck.l_type != F_UNLCK) {
                        (void) printf("%5d %5d    %c  %8d %8d\n",
                                        lck.l_sysid,
                                        lck.l_pid,
                                        (lck.l_type == F_WRLCK) ? 'W' : 'R',
                                        lck.l_start,
                                        lck.l_len);
                        /* if this lock goes to the end of the address
                         * space, no need to look further, so break out.
                         */
                        if (lck.l_len == 0)
                                break;
                        /* otherwise, look for new lock after the one
                         * just found.
                         */
                        lck.l_start += lck.l_len;
                }
        } while (lck.l_type != F_UNLCK);
```

fcntl with the **F_GETLK** command will always return correctly (that is, it will not sleep or fail) if the values passed to it as arguments are valid.

The **lockf** function with the **F_TEST** command can also be used to test if there is a process blocking a lock. This function does not, however, return the information about where the lock actually is and which process owns the lock. A routine using **lockf** to test for a lock on a file follows:

```
/* find a blocked record. */
/* seek to beginning of file */
(void) lseek(fd, 0, 0L);
/* set the size of the test region to zero (0)
 * to test until the end of the file address space.
 */
if (lockf(fd, F_TEST, 0L) < 0) {
        switch (errno) {
                case EACCES:
                case EAGAIN:
                (void) printf("file is locked by another process\n");
                break;
                case EBADF:
                /* bad argument passed to lockf */
                perror("lockf");
                break;
                default:
                (void) printf("lockf: unknown error <%d>\n", errno);
                break;
                }
        }
```

When a process forks, the child receives a copy of the file descriptors that the parent has opened. The parent and child also share a common file pointer for each file. If the parent were to seek to a point in the file, the child's file pointer would also be at that location. This feature has important implications when using record locking. The current value of the file pointer is used as the reference for the offset of the beginning of the lock, as described by **l_start**, when using a **l_whence** value of 1. If both the parent and child process set locks on the same file, there is a possibility that a lock will be set using a file pointer that was reset by the other process. This problem appears in the **lockf** function call as well and is a result of the **/usr/group** requirements for record locking. If forking is used in a record locking program, the child process should close and reopen the file if either locking method is used. This will result in the creation of a new and separate file pointer that can be manipulated without this problem occurring. Another solution is to use the **fcntl** system call with a **l_whence** value of 0 or 2. This makes the locking function atomic, so that even processes sharing file pointers can be locked without difficulty.

File and Device Input/Output

Deadlock Handling

There is a certain level of deadlock detection/avoidance built into the record locking facility. This deadlock handling provides the same level of protection granted by the **/usr/group** standard **lockf** call. This deadlock detection is only valid for processes that are locking files or records on a single system. Deadlocks can only potentially occur when the system is about to put a record locking system call to sleep. A search is made for constraint loops of processes that would cause the system call to sleep indefinitely. If such a situation is found, the locking system call will fail and set **errno** to the deadlock error number. If a process wishes to avoid the use of the systems deadlock detection it should set its locks using **F_GETLK** instead of **F_GETLKW**.

Selecting Advisory or Mandatory Locking

The use of mandatory locking is not recommended for reasons that will be made clear in a subsequent section. Whether or not locks are enforced by the I/O system calls is determined at the time the calls are made by the permissions on the file [see **chmod**(2)]. For locks to be under mandatory enforcement, the file must be a regular file with the set-group-ID bit on and the group execute permission off. If either condition fails, all record locks are advisory. Mandatory enforcement can be assured by the following code:

```
#include <sys/types.h>
#include <sys/stat.h>

int mode;
struct stat buf;
                    .
                    .
                    .
        if (stat(filename, &buf) < 0) {
                perror("program");
                exit (2);
        }
        /* get currently set mode */
        mode = buf.st_mode;
        /* remove group execute permission from mode */
        mode &= ~(S_IEXEC>>3);
        /* set 'set group id bit' in mode */
        mode |= S_ISGID;
        if (chmod(filename, mode) < 0) {
                perror("program");
                exit(2);
        }
                    .
                    .
                    .
```

Files that are to be record locked should never have any type of execute permission set on them. This is because the operating system does not obey the record locking protocol when executing a file.

The **chmod**(1) command can also be easily used to set a file to have mandatory locking. This can be done with the command:

> **chmod +l** *file*

The **ls**(1) command shows this setting when you ask for the long listing format:

> **ls -l** *file*

causes the following to be printed:

> **-rw---l---**   1   *user*   *group*   *size*   *mod_time*   *file*

Caveat Emptor—Mandatory Locking

- Mandatory locking only protects those portions of a file that are locked. Other portions of the file that are not locked may be accessed according to normal UNIX system file permissions.

- If multiple reads or writes are necessary for an atomic transaction, the process should explicitly lock all such pieces before any I/O begins. Thus advisory enforcement is sufficient for all programs that perform in this way.

- As stated earlier, arbitrary programs should not have unrestricted access permission to files that are important enough to record lock.

- Advisory locking is more efficient because a record lock check does not have to be performed for every I/O request.

Record Locking and Future Releases of the UNIX System

Provisions have been made for file and record locking in a UNIX system environment. In such an environment the system on which the locking process resides may be remote from the system on which the file and record locks reside. In this way multiple processes on different systems may put locks upon a single file that resides on one of these or yet another system. The record locks for a file reside on the system that maintains the file. It is also important to note that deadlock detection/avoidance is only determined by the record locks being held by and for a single system. Therefore, it is necessary that a process only hold record locks on a single system at any given time for the deadlock mechanism to be effective. If a process needs to maintain locks over several systems, it is suggested that the process avoid the sleep-when-blocked features of **fcntl** or **lockf** and that the process maintain its own deadlock detection. If the process uses the sleep-when-blocked feature, then a timeout mechanism should be provided by the process so that it does not hang waiting for a lock to be cleared.

Basic STREAMS Operations

This section describes the basic set of operations for manipulating STREAMS entities.

A STREAMS driver is similar to a traditional character I/O driver in that it has one or more nodes associated with it in the file system, and it is accessed using the **open** system call. Typically, each file system node corresponds to a separate minor device for that driver. Opening different minor devices of a driver causes separate Streams to be connected between a user process and the driver. The file descriptor returned by the **open** call is used for further access to the Stream. If the same minor device is opened more than once, only one Stream is created; the first **open** call creates the Stream, and subsequent **open** calls return a file descriptor that references that Stream. Each process that opens the same minor device shares the same Stream to the device driver.

Once a device is opened, a user process can send data to the device using the **write** system call and receive data from the device using the **read** system call. Access to STREAMS drivers using **read** and **write** is compatible with the traditional character I/O mechanism.

The **close** system call closes a device and dismantles the associated Stream when the last open reference to the Stream is given up.

The following example shows how a simple Stream is used. In the example, the user program interacts with a communications device that provides point-to-point data transfer between two computers. Data written to the device transmitted over the communications line, and data arriving on the line can be retrieved by reading from the device.

```
#include <fcntl.h>

main( )
{
    char buf[1024];
    int fd, count;

    if ((fd = open("/dev/comm/01", O_RDWR)) < 0) {
        perror("open failed");
        exit(1);
    }
    while ((count = read(fd, buf, 1024)) > 0) {
        if (write(fd, buf, count) != count) {
            perror("write failed");
            break;
        }
    }
    exit(0);
}
```

In the example, **/dev/comm/**01 identifies a minor device of the communications device driver. When this file is opened, the system recognizes the device as a STREAMS device and connects a Stream to the driver. Figure 3-2 shows the state of the Stream following the call to **open**.

Figure 3-2: Stream to Communication Driver

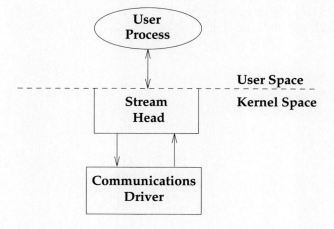

This example illustrates a user reading data from the communications device and then writing the input back out to the same device. In short, this program echoes all input back over the communications line. The example assumes that a user sends data from the other side of the communications line. The program reads up to 1024 bytes at a time, and then writes the number of bytes just read.

The **read** call returns the available data, which may contain fewer than 1024 bytes. If no data is currently available at the Stream head, the **read** call blocks until data arrive.

Similarly, the **write** call attempts to send *count* bytes to **/dev/comm/01**. However, STREAMS implements a flow control mechanism that prevents a user from exhausting system resources by flooding a device driver with data.

Flow control controls the rate of message transfer among the modules, drivers, Stream head, and processes. Flow control is local to each Stream and advisory (voluntary). It limits the number of characters that can be queued for processing at any queue in a Stream, and limits buffers and related processing at any queue and in any one Stream, but does not consider buffer pool levels or buffer usage in other Streams. Flow control is not applied to high-priority messages.

If the Stream exerts flow control on the user, the **write** call blocks until flow control is relieved. The call does not return until it has sent *count* bytes to the device. **exit**, which is called to terminate the user process, also closes all open files, and thereby dismantling the Stream in this example.

Benefits of STREAMS

STREAMS provides the following benefits:

- A flexible, portable, and reusable set of tools for development of UNIX system communication services.

- Easy creation of modules that offer standard data communications services and the ability to manipulate those modules on a Stream.

- From user level, modules can be dynamically selected and interconnected; kernel programming, assembly, and link editing are not required to create the interconnection.

STREAMS also greatly simplifies the user interface for languages that have complex input and output requirements.

Standardized Service Interfaces

STREAMS simplifies the creation of modules that present a service interface to any neighboring application program, module, or device driver. A service interface is defined at the boundary between two neighbors. In STREAMS, a service interface is a specified set of messages and the rules that allow passage of these messages across the boundary. A module that implements a service interface receives a message from a neighbor and responds with an appropriate action (for example, sends back a request to retransmit) based on the specific message received and the preceding sequence of messages.

In general, any two modules can be connected anywhere in a Stream. However, rational sequences are generally constructed by connecting modules with compatible protocol service interfaces. For example, a module that implements an X.25 protocol layer, as shown in Figure 3-2, presents a protocol service interface at its input and output sides. In this case, other modules should only be connected to the input and output side if they have the compatible X.25 service interface.

Manipulating Modules

STREAMS provides the capabilities to manipulate modules from the user level, to interchange modules with common service interfaces, and to change the service interface to a STREAMS user process. These capabilities yield further benefits when implementing networking services and protocols, including:

- User level programs can be independent of underlying protocols and physical communication media.

- Network architectures and higher level protocols can be independent of underlying protocols, drivers, and physical communication media.

- Higher level services can be created by selecting and connecting lower level services and protocols.

The following examples show the benefits of STREAMS capabilities for creating service interfaces and manipulating modules. These examples are only illustrations and do not necessarily reflect real situations.

Protocol Portability

Figure 3-3 shows how the same X.25 protocol module can be used with different drivers on different machines by implementing compatible service interfaces. The X.25 protocol module interfaces are Connection Oriented Network Service (CONS) and Link Access Protocol - Balanced (LAPB).

Figure 3-3: X.25 Multiplexing Stream

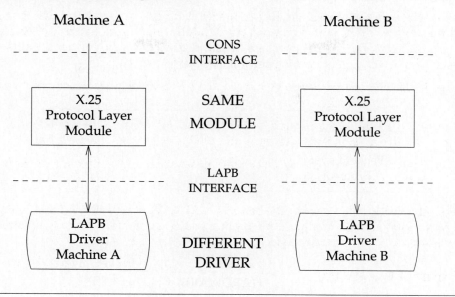

Protocol Substitution

Alternate protocol modules (and device drivers) can be interchanged on the same machine if they are implemented to an equivalent service interface.

Protocol Migration

Figure 3-4 illustrates how STREAMS can move functions between kernel software and front-end firmware. A common downstream service interface allows the transport protocol module to be independent of the number or type of modules below. The same transport module connects without change to either an X.25 module or X.25 driver that has the same service interface.

By shifting functions between software and firmware, developers can produce cost effective, functionally equivalent systems over a wide range of configurations. They can rapidly incorporate technological advances. The same transport protocol module can be used on a lower capacity machine, where economics may preclude the use of front-end hardware, and also on a larger scale system where a front-end is economically justified.

Figure 3-4: Protocol Migration

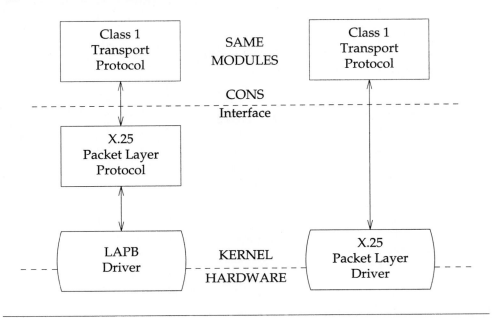

Module Reusability

Figure 3-5 shows the same canonical module (for example, one that provides delete and kill processing on character strings) reused in two different Streams. This module is typically implemented as a filter, with no downstream service interface. In both cases, a tty interface is presented to the Stream's user process because the module is nearest to the Stream head.

Figure 3-5: Module Reusability

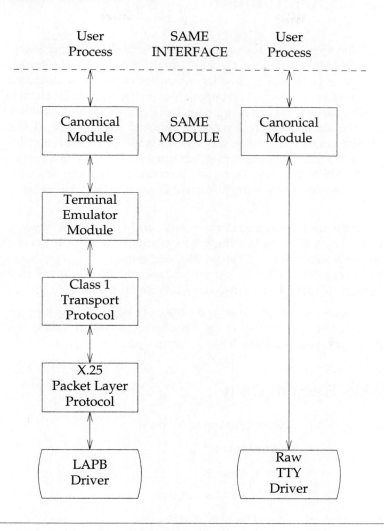

STREAMS Mechanism

This chapter shows how to construct, use, and dismantle a Stream using STREAMS-related systems calls. General and STREAMS-specific system calls provide the user level facilities required to implement application programs. This system call interface is upwardly compatible with the traditional character I/O facilities. The **open** system call recognizes a STREAMS file and creates a Stream to the specified driver. A user process can receive and send data on STREAMS files using **read** and **write** in the same way as with traditional character files. The **ioctl** system call enables users to perform functions specific to a particular device. STREAMS **ioctl** commands [see **streamio**(7)] support a variety of functions for accessing and controlling Streams. The last **close** in a Stream dismantles a Stream.

In addition to the traditional **ioctl** commands and system calls, there are other system calls used by STREAMS. The **poll** system call enables a user to poll multiple Streams for various events. The **putmsg** and **getmsg** system calls enable users to send and receive STREAMS messages, and are suitable for interacting with STREAMS modules and drivers through a service interface.

STREAMS provides kernel facilities and utilities to support development of modules and drivers. The Stream head handles most system calls so that the related processing does not have to be incorporated in a module or driver.

STREAMS System Calls

The STREAMS-related system calls are as follows:

open	Open a Stream
close	Close a Stream
read	Read data from a Stream
write	Write data to a Stream
ioctl	Control a Stream
getmsg	Receive a message at the Stream head
putmsg	Send a message downstream

`poll`	Notify the application program when selected events occur on a Stream
`pipe`	Create a channel that provides a communication path between multiple processes

A STREAMS device responds to the standard character I/O system calls, such as `read` and `write`, by turning the request into a message. This feature ensures that STREAMS devices may be accessed from the user level in the same manner as non-STREAMS character devices. However, additional system calls provide other capabilities.

getmsg and putmsg

The `putmsg` and `getmsg` system calls enable a user process to send and receive STREAMS messages, in the same form the messages have in kernel modules and drivers. `read` and `write` are not designed to include the message boundaries necessary to encode messages.

The advantage of this capability is that a user process, as well as a STREAMS module or driver, can implement a service interface.

poll

The `poll` system call allows a user process to monitor a number of streams to detect expected I/O events. Such events might be the availability of a device for writing, input data arriving from a device, a hangup occurring, an error being detected, or the arrival of a priority message. See `poll`(2) in the *Operating System API Reference* for more information.

Opening a STREAMS Device File

One way to construct a Stream is to open [see `open`(2)] a STREAMS-based driver file.

If the **open** call is the initial file open, a Stream is created. (There is one Stream per major/minor device pair.)

If this is the initial open of this Stream, the driver open routine is called. If modules have been specified to be autopushed, they are pushed immediately after the driver open. When a Stream is already open, further opens of the same Stream result in calls to the open procedures of all pushable modules and the driver open. Note that this is done in the reverse order from the initial Stream open. In other words, the initial open processes from the Stream end to the Stream head, while later opens process from the Stream head to the Stream end.

Creating a STREAMS-based Pipe

In addition to opening a STREAMS-based driver, a Stream can be created by creating a pipe [see **pipe**(2)]. Because pipes are not character devices, STREAMS creates and initializes a **streamtab** structure for each end of the pipe.

When the **pipe** system call is executed, two Streams are created. STREAMS follows the procedures similar to those of opening a driver; however, duplicate data structures are created. That is, two entries are allocated in the user's file table and two **vnode**s are created to represent each end of the pipe. The file table entries are initialized to point to the allocated **vnode**s and each **vnode** is initialized to specify a file of type **FIFO**.

Each Stream header represents one end of the pipe, and it points to the downstream half of each Stream head queue pair. Unlike STREAMS-based devices, however, the downstream portion of the Stream terminates at the upstream portion of the other Stream.

Adding and Removing Modules

As part of constructing a Stream, a module can be added (pushed) with an **ioctl** **I_PUSH** [see **streamio**(7)] system call. The push inserts a module beneath the Stream head. Because of the similarity of STREAMS components, the push operation is similar to the driver open. First, the address of the **qinit** structure for the module is obtained.

Next, STREAMS allocates a pair of **queue** structures and initializes their contents as in the driver open.

Then, **q_next** values are set and modified so that the module is interposed between the Stream head and its neighbor immediately downstream. Finally, the module open procedure (located using **qinit**) is called.

Each push of a module is independent, even in the same Stream. If the same module is pushed more than once on a Stream, there will be multiple occurrences of that module in the Stream. The total number of pushable modules that may be contained on any one Stream is limited by the kernel parameter **NSTRPUSH**.

An **ioctl** **I_POP** [see **streamio**(7)] system call removes (pops) the module immediately below the Stream head. The pop calls the module close procedure. On return from the module close, any messages left on the module's message queues are freed (deallocated). Then, STREAMS connects the Stream head to the component previously below the popped module and deallocates the module's **queue** pair. **I_PUSH** and **I_POP** enable a user process to alter dynamically the configuration of a Stream by pushing and popping modules as required. For example, a module may be removed and a new one inserted below the Stream head. Then the original module can be pushed back after the new module has been pushed.

Closing the Stream

The last **close** to a STREAMS file dismantles the Stream. Dismantling consists of popping any modules on the Stream and closing the driver. Before a module is popped, the **close** may delay to allow any messages on the write message queue of the module to be drained by module processing. Similarly, before the driver is closed, the **close** may delay to allow any messages on the write message queue of the driver to be drained by driver processing. If O_NDELAY (or O_NONBLOCK) is clear, **close** waits up to 15 seconds for each module to drain and up to 15 seconds for the driver to drain [see **open**(2)]. If O_NDELAY (or O_NONBLOCK) is set, the pop is performed immediately and the driver is closed without delay. Messages can remain queued, for example, if flow control is inhibiting execution of the write queue **service** procedure. When all modules are popped and any wait for the driver to drain is completed, the driver close routine is called. On return from the driver close, any messages left on the driver's queues are freed, and the **queue** and **stdata** structures are deallocated.

 NOTE STREAMS frees only the messages contained on a message queue. Any message or data structures used internally by the driver or module must be freed by the driver or module close procedure.

Finally, the user's file table entry and the **vnode** are deallocated and the file is closed.

Stream Construction Example

The following example extends the previous communications device echoing example (see the section "Basic STREAMS Operations" in this chapter) by inserting a module in the Stream. The (hypothetical) module in this example can convert (change case, delete, and/or duplicate) selected alphabetic characters.

Inserting Modules

An advantage of STREAMS over the traditional character I/O mechanism stems from the ability to insert various modules into a Stream to process and manipulate data that pass between a user process and the driver. In the example, the character conversion module is passed a command and a corresponding string of characters by the user. All data passing through the module are inspected for instances of characters in this string; the operation identified by the command is performed on all matching characters. The necessary declarations for this program are shown below:

```
#include <string.h>
#include <fcntl.h>
#include <stropts.h>

#define    BUFLEN       1024

/*
 * These defines would typically be
 * found in a header file for the module
 */
#define    XCASE      1   /* change alphabetic case of char */
#define    DELETE     2   /* delete char */
#define    DUPLICATE  3   /* duplicate char */

main()
{
    char buf[BUFLEN];
    int fd, count;
    struct strioctl strioctl;
```

The first step is to establish a Stream to the communications driver and insert the character conversion module. The following sequence of system calls accomplishes the following display:

```
    if ((fd = open("/dev/comm/01", O_RDWR)) < 0) {
        perror("open failed");
        exit(1);
    }
    if (ioctl(fd, I_PUSH, "chconv") < 0) {
        perror("ioctl I_PUSH failed");
        exit(2);
    }
```

The **I_PUSH ioctl** call directs the Stream head to insert the character conversion module between the driver and the Stream head, creating the Stream shown in Figure 3-6. As with drivers, this module resides in the kernel and must have been configured into the system before it was booted, unless the system has an autoload capability.

Figure 3-6: Case Converter Module

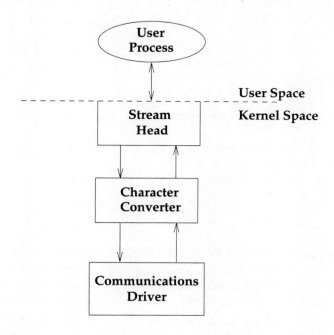

An important difference between STREAMS drivers and modules is illustrated here. Drivers are accessed through a node or nodes in the file system and may be opened just like any other device. Modules, on the other hand, do not occupy a file system node. Instead, they are identified through a separate naming convention, and are inserted into a Stream using **I_PUSH**. The name of a module is defined by the module developer.

Modules are pushed onto a Stream and removed from a Stream in Last-In-First-Out (LIFO) order. Therefore, if a second module was pushed onto this Stream, it would be inserted between the Stream head and the character conversion module.

Module and Driver Control

The next step in this example is to pass the commands and corresponding strings to the character conversion module. This can be done by issuing **ioctl** calls to the character conversion module as follows:

```
/* change all uppercase vowels to lowercase */
strioctl.ic_cmd = XCASE;
strioctl.ic_timout = 0;          /* default timeout (15 sec) */
strioctl.ic_dp = "AEIOU";
strioctl.ic_len = strlen(strioctl.ic_dp);

if (ioctl(fd, I_STR, &strioctl) < 0) {
    perror("ioctl I_STR failed");
    exit(3);
}
/* delete all instances of the chars 'x' and 'X' */
strioctl.ic_cmd = DELETE;
strioctl.ic_dp = "xX";
strioctl.ic_len = strlen(strioctl.ic_dp);

if (ioctl(fd, I_STR, &strioctl) < 0) {
    perror("ioctl I_STR failed");
    exit(4);
}
```

ioctl requests are issued to STREAMS drivers and modules indirectly, using the **I_STR ioctl** call [see **streamio**(7)]. The argument to **I_STR** must be a pointer to a **strioctl** structure, which specifies the request to be made to a module or driver. This structure is defined in **<stropts.h>** and has the following format:

```
struct strioctl {
    int   ic_cmd;    /* ioctl request */
    int   ic_timout; /* ACK/NAK timeout */
    int   ic_len;    /* length of data argument */
    char *ic_dp;     /* ptr to data argument */
};
```

where **ic_cmd** identifies the command intended for a module or driver, **ic_timout** specifies the number of seconds an **I_STR** request should wait for an acknowledgement before timing out, **ic_len** is the number of bytes of data to accompany the request, and **ic_dp** points to that data.

In the example, two separate commands are sent to the character conversion module. The first sets `ic_cmd` to the command **XCASE** and sends as data the string "AEIOU"; it converts all uppercase vowels in data passing through the module to lowercase. The second sets `ic_cmd` to the command **DELETE** and sends as data the string "xX"; it deletes all occurrences of the characters 'x' and 'X' from data passing through the module. For each command, the value of `ic_timout` is set to zero, which specifies the system default timeout value of 15 seconds. The `ic_dp` field points to the beginning of the data for each command; `ic_len` is set to the length of the data.

`I_STR` is intercepted by the Stream head, which packages it into a message, using information contained in the **strioctl** structure, and sends the message downstream. Any module that does not understand the command in `ic_cmd` passes the message further downstream. The request will be processed by the module or driver closest to the Stream head that understands the command specified by `ic_cmd`. The `ioctl` call will block up to `ic_timout` seconds, waiting for the target module or driver to respond with either a positive or negative acknowledgement message. If an acknowledgement is not received in `ic_timout` seconds, the `ioctl` call will fail.

> **NOTE** Only one `I_STR` request can be active on a Stream at one time. Further requests will block until the active `I_STR` request is acknowledged and the system call completes.

The **strioctl** structure is also used to retrieve the results, if any, of an `I_STR` request. If data is returned by the target module or driver, `ic_dp` must point to a buffer large enough to hold that data, and `ic_len` will be set on return to show the amount of data returned:

```
while ((count = read(fd, buf, BUFLEN)) > 0) {
    if (write(fd, buf, count) != count) {
        perror("write failed");
        break;
    }
}
exit(0);
}
```

Note that the character conversion processing was realized with no change to the communications driver.

The **exit** system call dismantles the Stream before terminating the process. The character conversion module is removed from the Stream automatically when it is closed. Alternatively, modules may be removed from a Stream using the **I_POP** **ioctl** call described in **streamio**(7). This call removes the topmost module on the Stream, and enables a user process to alter the configuration of a Stream dynamically, by popping modules as needed.

A few of the important **ioctl** requests supported by STREAMS have been discussed. Several other requests are available to support operations such as determining if a given module exists on the Stream, or flushing the data on a Stream. These requests are described fully in **streamio**(7).

4   Process Management

Introduction

A process is the execution of a program; most UNIX System V commands execute as separate processes. Each process is a distinct entity, able to execute and terminate independently of all other processes. Each user can have many processes in the system simultaneously. In fact, it is not always necessary for the user to be logged into the system while those processes are executing.

Beginning with UNIX System V Release 4.2 MP (SVR4.2 MP), the operating system supports a schedulable entity called a *lightweight process* (LWP). Each process contains one or more LWPs. LWPs allow multiple threads of control within a single process. The Threads Library provides interfaces with which applications may be multithreaded. See the chapter entitled, "Programming with the Threads Library," for information about threads and LWPs. When a process does not explicitly create any new LWPs, it contains one LWP and has the same semantics that a process had in previous releases.

Whenever you execute a command in the UNIX system you are initiating a process that is numbered and tracked by the operating system. A flexible feature of the UNIX system is that processes can be generated by other processes. This happens more than you might ever be aware of. For example, when you log in to your system you are running a process, very probably the shell. If you then use an editor such as **vi**, take the option of invoking the shell from **vi**, and execute the **ps** command, you will see a display something like the one in the following figure (which shows the results of a **ps -f** command):

Figure 4-1: Process Status

UID	PID	PPID	C	STIME	TTY	TIME	COMD
abc	24210	1	0	06:13:14	tty29	0:05	-sh
abc	24631	24210	0	06:59:07	tty29	0:13	vi c2.uli
abc	28441	28358	80	09:17:22	tty29	0:01	ps -f
abc	28358	24631	2	09:15:14	tty29	0:01	sh -i

As you can see, user **abc** (who went through the steps described above) now has four processes active. It is an interesting exercise to trace the chain that is shown in the Process ID (PID) and Parent Process ID (PPID) columns. The shell that was started when user abc logged on is process 24210; its parent is the initialization process (process ID 1). Process 24210 is the parent of process 24631, and so on.

The four processes in the example above are all UNIX system shell-level commands, but you can spawn new processes from your own program. You might think, "Well, it's one thing to switch from one program to another when I'm at my terminal working interactively with the computer; but why would a program want to run other programs, and if one does, why wouldn't I just put everything together into one big executable module?"

Overlooking the case where your program is itself an interactive application with diverse choices for the user, your program may need to run one or more other programs based on conditions it encounters in its own processing. (If it's the end of the month, go do a trial balance, for example.) The usual reasons why it might not be practical to create one large executable are:

- The load module may get too big to fit in the maximum process size for your system.

- You may not have control over the object code of all the other modules you want to include.

Suffice it to say, there are legitimate reasons why this creation of new processes might need to be done. There are two ways to do it:

- **exec**(2)—stop this process and start another

- **fork**(2)—start an additional copy of this process

Program Execution & Process Creation

Program Execution – exec

Overlays, performed by the family of **exec** system calls, can change the executing program, but can not create new processes. Processes are created (or spawned) by the system call **fork**, which is discussed later.

exec is the name of a family of functions that includes **execl**, **execv**, **execle**, **execve**, **execlp**, and **execvp**. They all have the function of transforming the calling process into a new process. The reason for the variety is to provide different ways of pulling together and presenting the arguments of the function. An example of one version (**execl**) might be:

```
execl("/usr/bin/prog2", "prog", progarg1, progarg2, (char *)0);
```

For **execl** the argument list is

/usr/bin/prog2	path name of the new process file
prog	the name the new process gets in its argv[0]
progarg1, progarg2	arguments to prog2 as char *'s
(char *)0	a null char pointer to mark the end of the arguments

Check the **exec**(2) manual page in the *Operating System API Reference* for the rest of the details. The key point of the **exec** family is that there is no return from a successful execution: the new process overlays the process that makes the **exec** system call. The new process also takes over the process ID and other attributes of the old process. If the call to **exec** is unsuccessful, control is returned to your program with a return value of **-1**. You can check **errno** to learn why it failed.

The system call **execl** executes another program, *without returning*; thus, to print the date as the last action of a running program, use:

```
execl("/bin/date", "date", NULL);
```

The first argument to **execl** is the *filename* of the command; you have to know where it is found in the file system. The second argument is conventionally the program name (that is, the last component of the filename), but this is seldom used except as a placeholder. If the command takes arguments, they are strung out after this; the end of the list is marked by a **NULL** argument.

The **execl** call overlays the existing program with the new one, runs that, then exits, without returning to the original program.

 NOTE When a multithreaded process calls **exec**, the new process will be created with a single thread (and LWP), effectively terminating all other threads (and LWPs) in the process. If **exec** fails, no threads (or LWPs) are terminated.

The one exception to the rule that the original program never gets control back occurs when there is an error, for example if the file can't be found or is not executable. If you don't know where **date** is located, say:

```
execl("/bin/date", "date", NULL);
execl("/usr/bin/date", "date", NULL);
printf(stderr, "Someone stole 'date'\n");
```

A variant of **execl** called **execv** is useful when you don't know in advance how many arguments there are going to be. The call is:

```
execv(filename, argp);
```

Where *argp* is an array of pointers to the arguments; the last pointer in the array must be **NULL** so **execv** can tell where the list ends. As with **execl**, *filename* is the file in which the program is found, and *argp[0]* is the name of the program. (This arrangement is identical to the *argv* array for C program arguments.)

Neither of these functions provides the niceties of normal command execution. There is no automatic search of multiple directories – you have to know precisely where the command is located. Nor do you get the expansion of metacharacters like "<", ">", "*", "?" and "[]" in the argument list. If you want these, use **execl** to invoke the shell **sh**, which then does all the work. Construct a string **cmdline** that contains the complete command as it would have been typed at the terminal, then say:

```
execl("/bin/sh", "sh", "-c", cmdline, NULL);
```

The shell is assumed to be at a fixed place, **/bin/sh**. Its argument **-c** says to treat the next argument as a whole command line, so it does just what you want. The only problem is in constructing the right information in **cmdline**.

To summarize:

- Any process may **exec** (cause execution of) a file.

- Doing an **exec** does not change the process ID; the process that did the **exec** persists, but after the **exec** it is executing a different program.

■ Files that were open before the **exec** remain open afterwards.

Many programs want to regain control after **exec**ing another program; these should use a combination of **fork** and **exec** (see the next section). However, a program with two or more phases that communicate only through temporary files might use an **exec** function without a **fork**. Here it is natural to make the second pass simply an **execl** call from the first. For example, the first pass of a compiler might overlay itself with the second pass of the compiler. This is analogous to a "goto" in programming.

Process Creation – fork

If a process wishes to regain control after **exec**ing a second program, it should **fork** a child process, have the child **exec** the second program, and the parent **wait** for the child. This is analogous to a "call" except that the **fork** system call creates a new process that is an exact copy of the calling process. The following figure depicts what is involved in executing a program with a typical **fork** as the first step:

Figure 4-2: Process Primitives

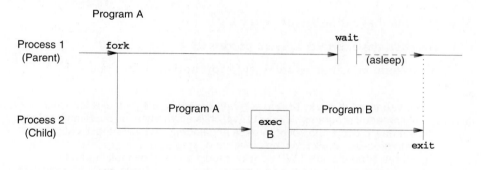

Because the **exec** functions simply overlay the new program on the old one, to save the old one requires that it first be split into two copies; one of these can be overlaid, while the other waits for the new overlaying program to finish.

The system call **fork** does the splitting as in the following call:

```
proc_id = fork();
```

The newly created process, known as the *child process*, is a copy of the image of the original process, called the *parent process*. The system call **fork** splits the program into two copies, both of which continue to run, and which differ only in the value returned in **proc_id**. In the child process, **proc_id** equals zero; in the parent process, **proc_id** equals a non-zero value that is the process number of the child process. Thus, the basic way to call, and return from, another program is:

```
if (fork() == 0)    /* in child */
    execl("/bin/sh", "sh", "-c", cmd, NULL);
```

And in fact, except for handling errors, this is sufficient. The **fork** is zero, so it calls **execl** which does the *cmd* and then dies. In the parent, **fork** returns non-zero so it skips the **execl**. (If there is any error, **fork** returns **-1**).

A child inherits its parent's permissions, working-directory, root-directory, open files, etc. This mechanism permits processes to share common input streams in various ways. Files that were open before the **fork** are shared after the **fork**. The processes are informed through the return value of **fork** as to which is the parent and which is the child. In any case the child and parent differ in three important ways:

- The child has a different process ID.

- The child has a different parent process ID.

- All accounting variables are reset to appropriate values in the child.

> **NOTE** Two variations of **fork**, **forkall(2)** and **fork1(2)**, are intended for use in multithreaded programs. **forkall** (which is a synonym for **fork**) duplicates in the new process the set of threads and underlying LWPs that exist in the calling process. **fork1**, on the other hand, creates a new process with a single thread and a single LWP. **fork1** should be used by multithreaded processes that will have the new process call **exec**. Since **exec** will terminate all but one thread (and LWP), there is no need to duplicate all threads with **forkall**.

The **fork** system call creates a child process with code and data copied from the parent process that created the child process. Once the copying is completed, the new (child) process is placed on the runnable queue to be scheduled. Each child process executes independently of its parent process, although the parent may explicitly wait for the termination of that child or any of its children. Usually the parent waits for the death of its child at some point, since this **wait** call is used to free the process-table entry used by the child. See the discussion under "Process Termination" for more detail.

Process Management

Calling **fork** creates a new process that is an exact copy of the calling process. The one major difference between the two processes is that the child gets its own unique process ID. When the **fork** process has completed successfully, it returns a **0** to the child process and the child's process ID to the parent. If the idea of having two identical processes seems a little funny, consider this:

■ Because the return value is different between the child process and the parent, the program can contain the logic to determine different paths.

■ The child process could say, "Okay, I'm the child; I'm supposed to issue an **exec** for an entirely different program."

■ The parent process could say, "My child is going to **exec** a new process; I'll issue a **wait** until I get word that the new process is finished."

Your code might include statements like the following:

Figure 4-3: Example of fork

```
#include <errno.h>
pid_t ch_pid;
int ch_stat, status;
char *p_arg1, *p_arg2;
void exit();
    if ((ch_pid = fork()) < 0) {
        /* Could not fork... check errno */
    }
    else if (ch_pid == 0) {              /* child */
        (void)execl("/usr/bin/prog2", "prog", p_arg1, p_arg2, (char *)NULL);
        exit(2);   /* execl() failed */
    }
    else {                    /* parent */
        while ((status = wait(&ch_stat)) != ch_pid) {
            if (status < 0 && errno == ECHILD)
                break;
            errno = 0;
        }
    }
```

Because the new **exec**'d process takes over the child process ID, the parent knows the ID. What this boils down to is a way of leaving one program to run another, returning to the point in the first program where processing left off.

Keep in mind that the fragment of code above includes minimal checking for error conditions, and has potential for confusion about open files and which program is writing to a file. Leaving out the possibility of named files, the new process created by the **fork** or **exec** has the three standard files that are automatically opened: **stdin**, **stdout**, and **stderr**. If the parent has buffered output that should appear before output from the child, the buffers must be flushed before the fork. Also, if the parent and the child processes both read input from a stream, whatever is read by one process will be lost to the other. That is, once something has been delivered from the input buffer to a process the pointer has moved on.

Process creation is essential to the basic operation of UNIX System V because each command run by the Shell executes in its own process. In fact, execution of a Shell command or Shell procedure involves both a **fork** and an overlay. This scheme makes a number services easy to provide. I/O redirection, for example, is basically a simple operation; it is performed entirely in the child process that executes the command, and thus no memory in the Shell parent process is required to rescind the change in standard input and output. Background processes likewise require no new mechanism; the Shell merely refrains from waiting for commands executing in the background to complete. Finally, recursive use of the Shell to interpret a sequence of commands stored in a file is in no way a special operation.

Control of Processes – fork and wait

A parent process can suspend its execution to wait for termination of a child process with **wait** or **waitpid**. More often, the parent wants to wait for the child to terminate before continuing itself as follows:

```
int status;

if (fork() == 0)
    execl( ... );
wait(&status);
```

The previous code fragment avoids handling any abnormal conditions, such as a failure of the **execl** or **fork**, or the possibility that there might be more than one child running simultaneously. (The function **wait** returns the process-id of the terminated child, which can be checked against the value returned by **fork**.) In addition, this fragment avoids dealing with any funny behavior on the part of the child (which is reported in **status**).

The low-order eight bits of the value returned by **wait** encodes the termination status of the child process; 0 signifies normal termination and non-zero to signify various kinds of abnormalities. The next higher eight bits are taken from the argument of the call to **exit** which caused a normal termination of the child process. It is good coding practice for all programs to return meaningful status.

When a program is called by the shell, the three file-descriptors are available for use. When this program calls another one, correct etiquette suggest making sure the same conditions hold. Neither **fork** nor the **exec** calls affects open files in any way. If the parent is buffering output that must come out before output from the child, the parent must flush its buffers before the **execl**. Conversely, if a caller buffers an input stream, the called program loses any information that has been read by the caller.

Process Termination

Processes terminate in one of two ways:

- Normal Termination occurs by a return from **main** or when requested by an explicit call to **exit** or **_exit**.

- Abnormal Termination occurs as the default action of a signal or when requested by **abort**.

On receiving a signal, a process looks for a signal-handling function. Failure to find a signal-handling function forces the process to call **exit**, and therefore to terminate. The functions **_exit**, **exit** and **abort** terminate a process with the same effects except that **abort** makes available to **wait** or **waitpid** the status of a process terminated by the signal **SIGABRT** [see **exit**(2) and **abort**(2)].

As a process terminates, it can set an eight-bit exit status code available to its parent. Usually, this code indicates success (zero) or failure (non-zero), but it can be used in any manner the user wishes. If a signal terminated the process, the system first tries to dump an image of core, then modifies the exit code to indicate which signal terminated the process and whether core was dumped. This is provided that the signal is one that produces a core dump [see **signal**(5)]. Next, all signals are set to be ignored, and resources owned by the process are released, including open files and the working directory. The terminating process is now a "zombie" process, with only its process-table entry remaining; and that is unavailable for use until the process has finally terminated. Next, the process-table is searched for any child or zombie processes belonging to the terminating process. Those children are then adopted by **init** by changing their parent process ID to 1). This is necessary since there must be a parent to record the death of the child. The last actions of **exit** are to record the accounting information and exit code for the terminated process in the zombie process-table entry and to send the parent the death-of-child signal, **SIGCHLD** [see "Signals, Job Control and Pipes"].

If the parent wants to wait until a child terminates before continuing execution, the parent can call **wait**, which causes the parent to sleep until a child zombie is found (meaning the child terminated). When the child terminates, the death-of-child signal is sent to the parent although the parent ignores this signal. (Ignore is the default disposition. Applications that fork children and need to know the return status should set this signal to other than ignore.) The search for child zombies continues until the terminated child is found; at which time, the child's exit status and accounting information is reported to the parent (remember the call to **exit** in the child put this information in the child's process-table entry) and the zombie process-table entry is freed. Now the parent can wake up and continue executing.

Timer Operations

A process can suspend itself for a specific period of time with the function **sleep** or suspend itself indefinitely with the function **pause** until a signal arrives to reactivate the process. The function **alarm** schedules a signal to arrive at a specific time, so a **pause** suspension need not be indefinite.

```
#include <stdio.h>
#include <signal.h>

struct sigaction new_act, old_act;
int alarm_count = 5;     /* initialize number of alarms */

main () {
   void alarm_action();
/*
 * pass signal and function to sigaction
 */
   new_act.sa_handler = alarm_action;
   sigaction(SIGALRM, &new_act, &old_act);

   alarm(5);            /* set alarm clock for 5 seconds */

   pause(); /* suspend process until receipt of signal */
}

void alarm_action() {
/*
 * print the number of alarms remaining
 */
   printf("\t<%d\007>", alarm_count);
/*
 * pass signal and function to sigaction
 */
   new_act.sa_handler = alarm_action;
   sigaction(SIGALRM, &new_act, &old_act);

   alarm(5);               /* set alarm clock for 5 seconds */
   if (--alarm_count)      /* decrement alarm count */
      pause();             /* suspend process */
}
```

The preceding example shows how you can use the **signal**, **alarm** and **pause** system calls to alternately suspend and resume a program.

Process Scheduling

In UNIX System V Release 4.2 MP (SVR4.2 MP), the schedulable entity is always a lightweight process (LWP). Scheduling priorities and classes are attributes of LWPs and not processes. When scheduling system calls accept a process on which to operate, the operation is applied to each LWP in the process. The UNIX system scheduler determines when LWPs run. It maintains priorities based on configuration parameters, process behavior, and user requests; it uses these priorities to assign LWPs to the CPU.

UNIX System V gives users absolute control over the sequence in which certain LWPs run, and the amount of time each LWP may use the CPU before another LWP gets a chance.

By default, the scheduler uses a time-sharing policy similar to the policy used in previous releases. A time-sharing policy adjusts priorities dynamically in an attempt to provide good response time to interactive LWPs and good throughput to CPU-intensive LWPs.

The scheduler offers a fixed priority scheduling policy as well as a time-sharing policy. Fixed priority scheduling allows users to set fixed priorities on a per-process or LWP basis. The highest-priority fixed priority LWP always gets the CPU as soon as it is runnable, even if system processes are runnable. An application can therefore specify the exact order in which LWPs run. An application may also be written so that its fixed priority LWPs have a guaranteed response time from the system.

For most UNIX environments, the default scheduler configuration works well and no fixed priority LWPs are needed: administrators should not change configuration parameters and users should not change scheduler properties of their applications. However, for some applications with strict timing constraints, fixed priority LWPs are the only way to guarantee that the application's requirements are met.

| NOTE | Fixed priority LWPs used carelessly can have a dramatic negative effect on the performance of time-sharing LWPs. |

You can manage the relationship between processes and processors. Processors can be taken offline or brought online. Processes can be bound to a specific processor and processors can be bound exclusively by a process. Note that exclusive binding applies only to user level processes and not to kernel drivers. That is, the exclusive binding of a user level process excludes other user level processes, but not a kernel driver.

This chapter is addressed to programmers who need more control over order of process and LWP execution than they get using default scheduler parameters.

Because changes in scheduler administration can affect scheduler behavior, programmers may also need to know about scheduler administration. For administrative information on the scheduler, see the *System Administration* guide. There are also a few reference manual entries with information on scheduler administration:

- **dispadmin**(1M) tells how to change scheduler configuration in a running system.

- **ts_dptbl**(4), **fc_dptbl**(4), and **fp_dptbl**(4) describe the time-sharing, fixed class, and fixed priority parameter tables that are used to configure the scheduler.

The rest of this chapter is organized as follows:

- "How the Process Scheduler Works" tells what the scheduler does and how it does it. It also introduces scheduler classes.

- The "Commands and Function Calls" section describes and gives examples of the **priocntl**(1) command and the **priocntl**(2), **priocntllist**(2), and **priocntlset**(2) system calls, the user interface to scheduler services. The **priocntl** functions allow you to retrieve scheduler configuration information and to get or set scheduler parameters for a process or LWP, or a set of processes or LWPs.

- The "Interaction with Other Functions" section describes the interactions between the scheduler and related functions.

- The "Performance" section discusses scheduler latencies of which some applications must be aware, and mentions some considerations other than the scheduler that application designers must take into account to ensure that their requirements are met.

- The "Managing Processors and Processes" section describes how you can manage the relationship between processors and processes. It tells how you can take processors offline or bring them online.

How the Process Scheduler Works

The following figure shows how the UNIX System V Release 4 process and LWP scheduler works. Fixed Class Priorities overlap the default Time-Sharing Priorities.

Figure 4-4: The UNIX System V Release 4 Process Scheduler

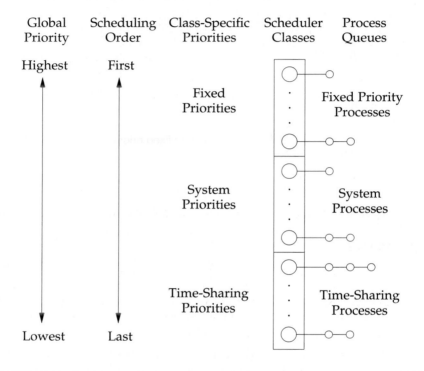

When a process or LWP is created, it inherits its scheduler parameters, including scheduler class and a priority within that class. A process or LWP changes class only as a result of a user request. The system manages the priority of an LWP based on user requests and a policy associated with the scheduler class of the LWP.

In the default configuration, the initialization process belongs to the time-sharing class. Because processes inherit their scheduler parameters, all user login shells begin as time-sharing processes in the default configuration.

The scheduler converts class-specific priorities into global priorities. The global priority of an LWP determines when it runs—the scheduler always runs the runnable LWP with highest global priority. Numerically higher priorities run first. Once the scheduler assigns an LWP to the CPU, the LWP runs until it uses up its time slice, sleeps, or is preempted by a higher-priority LWP. LWPs with the same priority run round-robin.

Administrators specify default time slices in the configuration tables, but users may assign time slices to fixed priority LWPs.

You can display the global priority of a process or LWP with the **-cl** options of the **ps**(1) command. You can display configuration information about class-specific priorities with the **priocntl**(1) command and the **dispadmin**(1M) command.

By default, all fixed priority processes or LWPs have higher priorities than any kernel process, and all kernel processes have higher priorities than any time-sharing process.

 NOTE As long as there is a runnable fixed priority fixed priority process or LWP, no kernel process and no time-sharing process runs.

The following sections describe the scheduling policies of the default classes.

Time-Sharing Class and Fixed Class

The goal of the time-sharing policy is to provide good response time to interactive processes and LWPs and good throughput to CPU-bound processes and LWPs. The scheduler switches CPU allocation frequently enough to provide good response time, but not so frequently that it spends too much time doing the switching. Time slices are typically a few hundred milliseconds.

The time-sharing policy changes priorities dynamically and assigns time slices of different lengths. The scheduler raises the priority of an LWP that sleeps after only a little CPU use (an LWP sleeps, for example, when it starts an I/O operation such as a terminal read or a disk read); frequent sleeps are characteristic of interactive tasks such as editing and running simple shell commands. On the other hand, the time-sharing policy lowers the priority of an LWP that uses the CPU for long periods without sleeping.

The default time-sharing policy gives larger time slices to LWPs with lower priorities. An LWP with a low priority is likely to be CPU-bound. Other LWPs get the CPU first, but when a low-priority LWP finally gets the CPU, it gets a bigger chunk of time. If a higher-priority LWP becomes runnable during a time slice, however, it preempts the running process or LWP.

The scheduler manages time-sharing processes and LWPs using configurable parameters in the time-sharing parameter table `ts_dptbl`. This table contains information specific to the time-sharing class.

The default fixed class policy is similar to the default time-sharing policy except that the priorities and time slices given to fixed class processes or LWPs do not degrade over time. The `fc_dptbl` parameter table contains information specific to the fixed class.

System Class

The system class uses a fixed-priority policy to run kernel processes such as servers and housekeeping processes like the paging demon. The system class is reserved for use by the kernel; users may neither add nor remove a process from the system class. Priorities for system class processes are set up in the kernel code for those processes; once established, the priorities of system processes do not change. (User processes and LWPs running in kernel mode are not in the system class.)

Fixed Priority Class

The fixed priority class uses a fixed-priority scheduling policy so that critical processes and LWPs can run in predetermined sequence. Real-time Fixed priorities never change except when a user requests a change. Contrast this fixed-priority policy with the time-sharing policy, for which the system changes priorities to provide good interactive response time.

Privileged users can use the `priocntl` command or the `priocntl` system call to assign fixed priorities.

The scheduler manages fixed priority processes and LWPs using configurable parameters in the fixed priority parameter table `fp_dptbl`. This table contains information specific to the fixed priority class.

Scheduler Commands and Function Calls

Below is a programmer's view of default LWP priorities. Fixed Class Priorities overlap the default Time-Sharing Priorities.

Figure 4-5: Process Priorities (Programmer View)

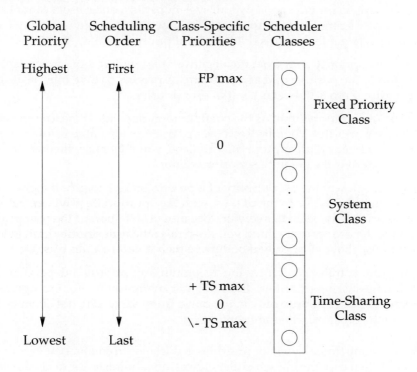

From a user or programmer's point of view, a process or LWP priority has meaning only in the context of a scheduler class. You specify an LWP priority by specifying a class and a class-specific priority value. The class and class-specific value are mapped by the system into a global priority that the system uses to schedule LWPs.

- Fixed priorities run from zero to a configuration-dependent maximum. The system maps them directly into global priorities. They never change except when a user changes them.

- System priorities are controlled entirely in the kernel. Users cannot affect them.

- Time-sharing priorities have a user-controlled component (the "user priority") and a component controlled by the system. The system does not change the user priority except as the result of a user request. The system changes the system-controlled component dynamically on a per-process or LWP basis to provide good overall system performance; users cannot affect the system-controlled component. The scheduler combines these two components to get the process or LWP global priority.

  The user priority runs from the negative of a configuration-dependent maximum to the positive of that maximum. A process or LWP inherits its user priority. Zero is the default initial user priority.

  The "user priority limit" is the configuration-dependent maximum value of the user priority. You may set a user priority to any value below the user priority limit. With appropriate privilege, you may raise the user priority limit. Zero is the default user priority limit.

  You may lower the user priority of a process or LWP to give the process or LWP reduced access to the CPU or, with the appropriate privilege, raise the user priority to get better service. Because you cannot set the user priority above the user priority limit, you must raise the user priority limit before you raise the user priority if both have their default values of zero.

  An administrator configures the maximum user priority independent of global time-sharing priorities. In the default configuration, for example, a user may set a user priority only in the range from −20 to +20, but 60 time-sharing global priorities are configured.

A system administrator's view of priorities is different from that of a user or programmer. When configuring scheduler classes, an administrator deals directly with global priorities. The system maps priorities supplied by users into these global priorities. See the *System Administration* guide.

The `ps -cel` command reports global priorities for all active processes and LWPs. The `priocntl` command reports the class-specific priorities that users and programmers use.

NOTE	Global priorities and user-supplied priorities are in ascending order: numerically higher priorities run first.

The **priocntl**(1) command and the **priocntl**(2), **priocntllist**(2), and **priocntlset**(2) system calls set or retrieve scheduler parameters for processes and LWPs. Setting priorities is similar for all these functions:

- Specify the target processes and LWPs.

- Specify the scheduler parameters you want for those processes and LWPs.

- Do the command or system call to set the parameters for the processes and LWPs.

You specify the target processes and LWPs using an ID type and an ID. The ID type tells how to interpret the ID. [This concept of a set of processes and LWPs applies to signals as well as to the scheduler; see **sigsend**(2)]. The following table lists the valid ID types that you may specify.

priocntl ID types

LWP ID
process ID
parent process ID
process group ID
session ID
class ID
effective user ID
effective group ID
all processes

These IDs are basic properties of UNIX processes and LWPs. [See **intro**(2)]. The class ID refers to the scheduler class of the process or LWP. **priocntl** works only for the time-sharing, fixed class, and the fixed priority classes, not for the system class. Processes in the system class have fixed priorities assigned when they are started by the kernel.

The priocntl Command

The **priocntl** command comes in four forms:

- **priocntl -l** displays configuration information.

- **priocntl -d** displays the scheduler parameters of processes and LWPs.

- **priocntl -s** sets the scheduler parameters of processes and LWPs.

- **priocntl -e** executes a command with the specified scheduler parameters.

1. Here is the output of the **-l** option for the default configuration.

```
$ priocntl -l
CONFIGURED CLASSES
==================

SYS (System Class)

FC (Time sharing)
        Configured FC User Priority Range: -30 through 30

TS (Time Sharing)
        Configured TS User Priority Range: -20 through 20

FP (Fixed Priority)
        Maximum Configured FP Priority: 59
```

2. The **-d** option displays the scheduler parameters of a process or LWP or a set of processes or LWPs. The syntax for this option is

        priocntl -d -i *idtype*   *idlist*

idtype tells what kind of IDs are in *idlist*. *idlist* is a list of IDs separated by white space. Here are the valid values for *idtype* and their corresponding ID types in *idlist*:

idtype	*idlist*
lwpid	LWP IDs
pid	process IDs
ppid	parent process IDs
pgid	process group IDs
sid	session IDs
class	class names (**TS** or **FP**)
uid	effective user IDs
gid	effective group IDs
all	

Here are some examples of the **-d** option of **priocntl**:

```
$ # display info on all processes and LWPs
$ priocntl -d -i all
            .
            .
            .
$ # display info on all time-sharing processes and LWPs:
$ priocntl -d -i class TS
            .
            .
            .
$ # display info on all processes and LWPs with user ID 103 or 6626
$ priocntl -d -i uid 103 6626
            .
            .
            .
```

3. The **-s** option sets scheduler parameters for a process or LWP or a set of processes or LWPs. The syntax for this option is

> **priocntl -s -c** *class   class_options* **-i** *idtype   islist*

idtype and *idlist* are the same as for the **-d** option described above.

class is **TS** for time-sharing or **FP** for fixed priority. You must have appropriate privilege to create a fixed priority process or LWP, to raise a time-sharing user priority above a per-process or LWP limit, or to raise the per-process or LWP limit above zero. Class options are class-specific:

Class-specific options for **priocntl**

class	-c *class*	options	meaning
fixed priority	FP	-p *pri*	priority
		-t *tslc*	time slice
		-r *res*	resolution
time-sharing	TS	-p *upri*	user priority
		-m *uprilim*	user priority limit
fixed class	FC	-p *upri*	user priority
		-m *uprilim*	user priority limit

For a fixed priority process or LWP you may assign a priority and a time slice.

- The priority is a number from 0 to the fixed priority maximum as reported by **priocntl -l**; the default maximum is 59.

- You specify the time slice as a number of clock intervals and the resolution of the interval. Resolution is specified in intervals per second. The time slice, therefore, is *tslc/res* seconds. To specify a time slice of one-tenth of a second, for example, you could specify a *tslc* of 1 and a *res* of 10. If you specify a time slice without specifying a resolution, millisecond resolution (a *res* of 1000) is assumed.

If you change a time-sharing process or LWP into a fixed priority process or LWP, it gets a default priority and time slice if you don't specify one. If you want to change only the priority of a fixed priority process or LWP and leave its time slice unchanged, omit the **-t** option. If you want to change only the time slice of a fixed priority process or LWP and leave its priority unchanged, omit the **-p** option.

For a time-sharing process or LWP you may assign a user priority and a user priority limit.

- The user priority is the user-controlled component of a time-sharing priority. The scheduler calculates the global priority of a time-sharing process or LWP by combining this user priority with a system-controlled component that depends on process or LWP behavior. The user priority has the same effect as a value set by **nice** (except that **nice** uses higher numbers for lower priority).

- The user priority limit is the maximum user priority a process or LWP may set for itself without being a privileged user. By default, the user priority limit is 0. You must have appropriate privilege to set a user priority limit above 0.

Both the user priority and the user priority limit must be within the user priority range reported by the **priocntl -l** command. The default range is –20 to +20.

There is no limit for the number of times a process or LWP may lower and raise its user priority, as long as the value is below its user priority limit. As a courtesy to other users, lower your user priority for big chunks of low-priority work. However, remember that if you lower your user priority limit, you must have appropriate privilege to raise it. A typical use of the user priority limit is to reduce permanently the priority of child processes or LWPs, or another set of low-priority processes or LWPs.

The user priority can never be greater than the user priority limit. If you set the user priority limit below the user priority, the user priority is lowered to the new user priority limit. If you attempt to set the user priority above the user priority limit, the user priority is set to the user priority limit.

Here are some examples of the **-s** option of **priocntl**:

```
# # make process with ID 24668 a fixed priority process with default parameters:
# priocntl -s -c FP -i pid 24668

# # make 3608 FP with priority 55 and a one-fifth second time slice:
# priocntl -s -c FP -p 55 -t 1 -r 5 -i pid 3608

# # change all processes or LWPs into time-sharing processes or LWPs:
# priocntl -s -c TS -i all

# # for uid 1122, reduce TS user priority and user priority limit to -10:
# priocntl -s -c TS -p -10 -m -10 -i uid 1122
```

4. The **-e** option sets scheduler parameters for a specified command and executes the command. The syntax for this option is

      priocntl -e -c *class class_options command [command arguments]*

The class and class options are the same as for the **-s** option described above.

```
# # start a fixed priority shell with default fixed priority:
# priocntl -e -c FP /bin/sh

$ # run make with a time-sharing  user priority of -10:
$ priocntl -e -c TS -p -10 make bigprog
```

The **priocntl** command subsumes the function of **nice**, which continues to work as in previous releases. **nice** works only on time-sharing processes and LWPs and uses higher numbers to assign lower priorities. The final example above is equivalent to using **nice** to set an "increment" of 10:

      nice -10 make bigprog

The priocntl System Call

```
#include      <sys/types.h>
#include      <sys/procset.h>
#include      <sys/priocntl.h>
#include      <sys/fppriocntl.h>
#include      <sys/tspriocntl.h>

long priocntl(idtype_t idtype, id_t id, int cmd, void *arg);
```

The **priocntl** system call gets or sets scheduler parameters of a set of processes or LWPs. The input arguments:

- *idtype* is the type of ID you are specifying.

- *id* is the ID.

- *cmd* specifies which **priocntl** function to perform. The functions are listed in the table below.

- *arg* is a pointer to a structure that depends on *cmd*.

Here are the valid values for *idtype* that are defined in **<priocntl.h>**, and their corresponding ID types in *id*. In this table, "process" also means LWP.

idtype	Interpretation of id
P_PID	process ID (of a single process)
P_PPID	parent process ID
P_PGID	process group ID
P_LWPID	LWP ID
P_SID	session ID
P_CID	class ID
P_UID	effective user ID
P_GID	effective group ID
P_ALL	all processes and LWPs

Here are the valid values for *cmd*, their meanings, and the type of *arg*:

priocntl Commands

cmd	*arg* Type	Function
PC_GETCID	pcinfo_t	get class ID and attributes
PC_GETCLINFO	pcinfo_t	get class name and attributes
PC_SETPARMS	pcparms_t	set class and scheduling parameters
PC_GETPARMS	pcparms_t	get class and scheduling parameters

Here are the values **priocntl** returns on success:

- The GETCID and GETCLINFO commands return the number of configured scheduler classes.

- **PC_SETPARMS** returns 0.

- **PC_GETPARMS** returns the process ID of the process or LWP whose scheduler properties it is returning.

On failure, **priocntl** returns **-1** and sets **errno** to indicate the reason for the failure. See **priocntl**(2) for the complete list of error conditions.

PC_GETCID, PC_GETCLINFO

The **PC_GETCID** and **PC_GETCLINFO** commands retrieve scheduler parameters for a class based on the class ID or class name. Both commands use the **pcinfo** structure to send arguments and receive return values:

```
typedef struct pcinfo {
    id_t  pc_cid;                    /* class id */
    char  pc_clname[PC_CLNMSZ];      /* class name */
    long  pc_clinfo[PC_CLINFOSZ];    /* class information */
} pcinfo_t;
```

The **PC_GETCID** command gets scheduler class ID and parameters given the class name. The class ID is used in some of the other **priocntl** commands to specify a scheduler class. The valid class names are **TS** for time-sharing, **FC** for fixed class, and **FP** for fixed priority.

For the fixed priority class, `pc_clinfo` contains an **fpinfo** structure, which holds **fp_maxpri**, the maximum valid fixed priority; in the default configuration, this is the highest priority any process or LWP can have. The minimum valid fixed priority is zero. **fp_maxpri** is a configurable value; the *System Administration* guide tells how to configure process and LWP priorities.

```
typedef struct fpinfo {
    short  fp_maxpri;  /* maximum fixed priority */
} fpinfo_t;
```

For the time-sharing class, `pc_clinfo` contains a **tsinfo** structure, which holds **ts_maxupri,** the maximum time-sharing user priority. The minimum time-sharing user priority is **-ts_maxupri**. **ts_maxupri** is also a configurable value.

```
typedef struct tsinfo {
    short  ts_maxupri;  /* limits of user priority range */
} tsinfo_t;
```

For the fixed class, `pc_clinfo` contains a **fcinfo** structure, which holds **fc_maxupri,** the maximum fixed class user priority. The minimum fixed class user priority is **-fc_maxupri**. **fc_maxupri** is also a configurable value.

```
typedef struct fcinfo {
    short  fc_maxupri;  /* limits of user priority range */
} fcinfo_t;
```

The following program is a cheap substitute for **priocntl -l**; it gets and prints the range of valid priorities for the time-sharing and fixed priority scheduler classes.

```
/*
 * Get scheduler class IDs and priority ranges.
 */

#include <sys/types.h>
#include <sys/priocntl.h>
#include <sys/fppriocntl.h>
#include <sys/tspriocntl.h>
#include <stdio.h>
#include <string.h>
#include <stdlib.h>
#include <errno.h>

main ()
{
        pcinfo_t        pcinfo;
        tsinfo_t        *tsinfop;
        fpinfo_t        *fpinfop;
        short           maxtsupri, maxfppri;

    /* time sharing */
        (void) strcpy (pcinfo.pc_clname, "TS");
        if (priocntl (0L, 0L, PC_GETCID, &pcinfo) == -1L) {
                perror ("PC_GETCID failed for time-sharing class");
                exit (1);
        }
        tsinfop = (struct tsinfo *) pcinfo.pc_clinfo;
        maxtsupri = tsinfop->ts_maxupri;
        (void) printf("Time sharing: ID %ld, priority range -%d through %d\n",
                pcinfo.pc_cid, maxtsupri, maxtsupri);

    /* fixed priority */
        (void) strcpy(pcinfo.pc_clname, "FP");
        if (priocntl (0L, 0L, PC_GETCID, &pcinfo) == -1L) {
                perror ("PC_GETCID failed for fixed priority class");
                exit (2);
        }
        fpinfop = (struct fpinfo *) pcinfo.pc_clinfo;
        maxfppri = fpinfop->fp_maxpri;
        (void) printf("Fixed priority:    ID %ld, priority range 0 through %d\n",
                pcinfo.pc_cid, maxfppri);
        return (0);
}
```

The following screen shows the output of this program, called **getcid** in this
example.

```
$ getcid
Time sharing: ID 1, priority range -20 through 20
Fixed priority:   ID 2, priority range 0 through 59
```

The following function is useful in the examples below. Given a class name, it uses **PC_GETCID** to return the class ID and maximum priority in the class.

> **NOTE** All the following examples omit the lines that include header files. The examples compile with the same header files as in the first example above.

```c
/*
 *  Return class ID and maximum priority.
 *  Input argument name is class name.
 *  Maximum priority is returned in *maxpri.
 */

id_t
schedinfo (name, maxpri)
        char *name;
        short *maxpri;
{
        pcinfo_t        info;
        tsinfo_t        *tsinfop;
        fpinfo_t        *fpinfop;

        (void) strcpy(info.pc_clname, name);
        if (priocntl (0L, 0L, PC_GETCID, &info) == -1L) {
                return (-1);
        }
        if (strcmp(name, "TS") == 0) {
                tsinfop = (struct tsinfo *) info.pc_clinfo;
                *maxpri = tsinfop->ts_maxupri;
        } else if (strcmp(name, "FP") == 0) {
                fpinfop = (struct fpinfo *) info.pc_clinfo;
                *maxpri = fpinfop->fp_maxpri;
        } else {
                return (-1);
        }
        return (info.pc_cid);
}
```

The **PC_GETCLINFO** command gets a scheduler class name and parameters given the class ID. This command makes it easy to write applications that make no assumptions about what classes are configured.

The following program uses **PC_GETCLINFO** to get the class name of a process or LWP based on the process ID. This program assumes the existence of a function **getclassID**, that retrieves the class ID of a process or LWP given the process ID; this function is given in the following section.

```
/*  Get scheduler class name given process ID. */

main (argc, argv)
        int argc;
        char *argv[];
{
        pcinfo_t        pcinfo;
        id_t            pid, classID;
        id_t            getclassID();

        if ((pid = atoi(argv[1])) <= 0) {
                perror ("bad pid");
                exit (1);
        }
        if ((classID = getclassID(pid)) == -1) {
                perror ("unknown class ID");
                exit (2);
        }
        pcinfo.pc_cid = classID;
        if (priocntl (0L, 0L, PC_GETCLINFO, &pcinfo) == -1L) {
                perror ("PC_GETCLINFO failed");
                exit (3);
        }
        (void) printf("process ID %d, class %s\n", pid, pcinfo.pc_clname);
}
```

PC_GETPARMS, PC_SETPARMS

The **PC_GETPARMS** command gets and the **PC_SETPARMS** command sets scheduler parameters for processes and LWPs. Both commands use the **pcparms** structure to send arguments or receive return values:

```
typedef struct pcparms {
    id_t  pc_cid;                        /* process or LWP class */
    long  pc_clparms[PC_CLPARMSZ];       /* class specific */
} pcparms_t;
```

Ignoring class-specific information for the moment, we can write a simple function for returning the scheduler class ID of a process or LWP, as promised in the previous section.

```
/*
 *  Return scheduler class ID of process or LWP with ID pid.
 */

getclassID (pid)
        id_t pid;
{
        pcparms_t        pcparms;

        pcparms.pc_cid = PC_CLNULL;
        if (priocntl(P_PID, pid, PC_GETPARMS, &pcparms) == -1) {
                return (-1);
        }
        return (pcparms.pc_cid);
}
```

For the real-time class, For the fixed priority class, **pc_clparms** contains an **fpparms** structure. **fpparms** holds scheduler parameters specific to the

```
typedef struct fpparms {
    short  fp_pri;        /* fixed priority */
    ulong  fp_tqsecs;     /* seconds in time quantum */
    long   fp_tqnsecs;    /* additional nsecs in quantum */
} fpparms_t;
```

fp_pri is the fixed priority; **fp_tqsecs** is the number of seconds and **fp_tqnsecs** is the number of additional nanoseconds in a time slice. That is, **fp_tqsecs** seconds plus **fp_tqnsecs** nanoseconds is the interval an LWP may use the CPU without sleeping before the scheduler gives another LWP a chance at the CPU.

For the time-sharing class, **pc_clparms** contains a **tsparms** structure. **tsparms** holds the scheduler parameter specific to the time-sharing class:

```
typedef struct tsparms {
    short  ts_uprilim;  /* user priority limit */
    short  ts_upri;     /* user priority */
} tsparms_t;
```

ts_upri is the user priority, the user-controlled component of a time-sharing priority. ts_uprilim is the user priority limit, the maximum user priority a process or LWP may set for itself without being a privileged user. These values are described above in the discussion of the -s option of the priocntl command. Both the user priority and the user priority limit must be within the range reported by the priocntl -1 command; this range is also reported by the PC_GETCID and PC_GETCLINFO commands to the priocntl system call.

The PC_GETPARMS command gets the scheduler class and parameters of a single process or LWP. The return value of the priocntl is the process ID of the process or LWP whose parameters are returned in the pcparms structure. The process or LWP chosen depends on the idtype and id arguments to priocntl and on the value of pcparms.pc_cid, which contains PC_CLNULL or a class ID returned by PC_GETCID:

Table 4-1: What Gets Returned by PC_GETPARMS

Number of Processes Selected by idtype and id	pc_cid		
	FP class ID	TS class ID	PC_CLNULL
1	FP parameters of process or LWP selected	TS parameters of process or LWP selected	class and parameters of process or LWP selected
More than 1	FP parameters of highest-priority FP process or LWP	TS parameters of process or LWP with highest user priority	(error)

If idtype and id select a single process or LWP and pc_cid does not conflict with the class of that process or LWP, priocntl returns the scheduler parameters of the process or LWP. If they select more than one process or LWP of a single scheduler class, priocntl returns parameters using class-specific criteria as shown in the table. priocntl returns an error in the following cases:

■ idtype and id select one or more processes or LWPs and none is in the class specified by pc_cid.

■ idtype and id select more than one process or LWP and pc_cid is PC_CLNULL.

■ **idtype** and **id** select no processes or LWPs.

The following program takes a process ID as its input and prints the scheduler class and class-specific parameters of that process or LWP:

```
/*
 *  Get scheduler class and parameters of
 *  process or LWP whose pid is input argument.
 */

main (argc, argv)
        int argc;
        char *argv[];
{
        pcparms_t       pcparms;
        fpparms_t       *fpparmsp;
        tsparms_t       *tsparmsp;
        id_t            pid, fpID, tsID;
        id_t            schedinfo();
        short           priority, tsmaxpri, fpmaxpri;
        ulong           secs;
        long            nsecs;

        pcparms.pc_cid = PC_CLNULL;
        fpparmsp = (fpparms_t *) pcparms.pc_clparms;
        tsparmsp = (tsparms_t *) pcparms.pc_clparms;
        if ((pid = atoi(argv[1])) <= 0) {
                perror ("bad pid");
                exit (1);
        }

    /* get scheduler properties for this pid */
        if (priocntl(P_PID, pid, PC_GETPARMS, &pcparms) == -1) {
                perror ("GETPARMS failed");
                exit (2);
        }

    /* get class IDs and maximum priorities for TS and FP */
        if ((tsID = schedinfo ("TS", &tsmaxpri)) == -1) {
                perror ("schedinfo failed for TS");
                exit (3);
        }
        if ((fpID = schedinfo ("FP", &fpmaxpri)) == -1) {
                perror ("schedinfo failed for FP");
                exit (4);
        }

    /* print results */
        if (pcparms.pc_cid == fpID) {
                priority = fpparmsp->fp_pri;
                secs = fpparmsp->fp_tqsecs;
```

(continued on next page)

Process Management

```
                nsecs =  fpparmsp->fp_tqnsecs;
                (void) printf ("process %d: FP priority %d\n",
                        pid, priority);
                (void) printf ("  time slice %ld secs, %ld nsecs\n",
                        secs, nsecs);
        } else if (pcparms.pc_cid == tsID) {
                priority = tsparmsp->ts_upri;
                (void) printf ("process %d: TS priority %d\n",
                        pid, priority);
        } else {
                printf ("Unknown scheduler class %d\n",
                        pcparms.pc_cid);
                exit (5);
        }
        return (0);
}
```

The **PC_SETPARMS** command sets the scheduler class and parameters of a set of processes or LWPs. The **idtype** and **id** input arguments specify the processes or LWPs to be changed. The **pcparms** structure contains the new parameters: **pc_cid** contains the ID of the scheduler class to which the processes or LWPs are to be assigned, as returned by **PC_GETCID**; **pc_clparms** contains the class-specific parameters:

- If **pc_cid** is the fixed priority class ID, **pc_clparms** contains an **fpparms** structure in which **fp_pri** contains the fixed priority and **fp_tqsecs** plus **fp_tqnsecs** contains the time slice to be assigned to the processes or LWPs.

- If **pc_cid** is the time-sharing class ID, **pc_clparms** contains a **tsparms** structure in which **ts_uprilim** contains the user priority limit and **ts_upri** contains the user priority to be assigned to the processes or LWPs.

The following program takes a process ID as input, makes the process or LWP a fixed priority process or LWP with the highest valid priority minus 1, and gives it the default time slice for that priority. The program calls the **schedinfo** function listed above to get the real-time fixed priority class ID and maximum priority.

```
/*
 *  Input arg is proc ID.  Make process or LWP a fixed priority
 *  process or LWP with highest priority minus 1.
 */

main (argc, argv)
        int argc;
        char *argv[];
{
        pcparms_t       pcparms;
        fpparms_t       *fpparmsp;
        id_t            pid, fpID;
        id_t            schedinfo();
        short           maxrtpri;
        short           maxfppri;

        if ((pid = atoi(argv[1])) <= 0) {
                perror ("bad pid");
                exit (1);
        }

   /* Get highest valid FP priority. */
        if ((fpID = schedinfo ("FP", &maxfppri)) == -1) {
                perror ("schedinfo failed for FP");
                exit (2);
        }

   /*  Change proc to FP, highest prio - 1, default time slice */
        pcparms.pc_cid = fpID;
        fpparmsp = (struct fpparms *) pcparms.pc_clparms;
        fpparmsp->fp_pri = maxfppri - 1;
        fpparmsp->fp_tqnsecs = FP_TQDEF;

        if (priocntl(P_PID, pid, PC_SETPARMS, &pcparms) == -1) {
                perror ("PC_SETPARMS failed");
                exit (3);
        }
}
```

The following table lists the special values **fp_tqnsecs** can take when
PC_SETPARMS is used on fixed priority processes and LWPs. When any of these is
used, **fp_tqsecs** is ignored. These values are defined in the header file
fppriocntl.h:

fp_tqnsecs	Time Slice
FP_TQINF	infinite
FP_TQDEF	default
FP_NOCHANGE	unchanged

FP_TQINF specifies an infinite time slice. FP_TQDEF specifies the default time slice configured for the fixed priority being set with the SETPARMS call. FP_NOCHANGE specifies no change from the current time slice; this value is useful, for example, when you change process or LWP priority but do not want to change the time slice. (You can also use FP_NOCHANGE in the fp_pri field to change a time slice without changing the priority.)

The priocntllist System Call

```
#include        <sys/types.h>
#include        <sys/procset.h>
#include        <sys/priocntl.h>
#include        <sys/fppriocntl.h>
#include        <sys/tspriocntl.h>

long priocntllist(lwpid_t *lwpidp, int idcnt, int cmd, void *arg);
```

The priocntllist system call provides the programming interface to scheduling policies and policy specific parameters for an arbitrary list of LWPs within the calling process. priocntllist has the same functions as priocntl system call, but a more general way of specifying the set of LWPs whose scheduling properties are to be changed. The input argument *lwpidp* points to an array in user memory of LWP IDs that identify the LWPs to which the system call applies, and *idcnt* is the number of elements in the array. *cmd* specifies the function to be performed and *arg* is a pointer to a structure whose type depends on *cmd*.

The priocntlset System Call

```
#include        <sys/types.h>
#include        <sys/signal.h>
#include        <sys/procset.h>
#include        <sys/priocntl.h>
#include        <sys/fppriocntl.h>
#include        <sys/tspriocntl.h>

long priocntlset(procset_t *psp, int cmd, void *arg);
```

The **priocntlset** system call changes scheduler parameters of a set of processes or LWPs, just like **priocntl**. **priocntlset** has the same command set as **priocntl**; the *cmd* and *arg* input arguments are the same. But while **priocntl** applies to a set of processes or LWPs specified by a single **idtype/id** pair, **priocntlset** applies to a set of processes or LWPs that results from a logical combination of two **idtype/id** pairs. The input argument *psp* points to a **procset** structure that specifies the two **idtype/id** pairs and the logical operation to perform. This structure is defined in **procset.h**:

```
typedef struct procset {
        idop_t     p_op;              /* operator connecting */
                                      /* left and right sets */
    /* left set:  */
        idtype_t   p_lidtype;         /* left ID type */
        id_t       p_lid;             /* left ID */

    /* right set:  */
        idtype_t   p_ridtype;         /* right ID type */
        id_t       p_rid;             /* right ID */
} procset_t;
```

p_lidtype and **p_lid** specify the ID type and ID of one ("left") set of processes or LWPs; **p_ridtype** and **p_rid** specify the ID type and ID of a second ("right") set of processes or LWPs. **p_op** specifies the operation to perform on the two sets of processes or LWPs to get the set of processes or LWPs to operate on. The valid values for **p_op** and the processes or LWPs they specify are:

- **POP_DIFF**: set difference—processes or LWPs in left set and not in right set

- **POP_AND**: set intersection—processes or LWPs in both left and right sets

- **POP_OR**: set union—processes or LWPs in either left or right sets or both

- **POP_XOR**: set exclusive-or—processes or LWPs in left or right set but not in both

The following macro, also defined in **procset.h**, offers a convenient way to initialize a **procset** structure :

```
#define setprocset(psp, op, ltype, lid, rtype, rid) \
            (psp)->p_op        = (op); \
            (psp)->p_lidtype   = (ltype); \
            (psp)->p_lid       = (lid); \
            (psp)->p_ridtype   = (rtype); \
            (psp)->p_rid       = (rid);
```

Here is a situation where **priocntlset** can be useful: an application has both real-time fixed priority and time-sharing processes that run under a single user ID. If the application wants to change the priority of only its fixed priority processes without changing the time-sharing processes to fixed priority processes, it can do so as follows. (This example uses the function **schedinfo**, which is defined above in the section on **PC_GETCID**.)

```
/*
 * Change fixed priorities of this uid
 * to highest fixed priority minus 1.
 */
main (argc, argv)
        int argc;
        char *argv[];
{
        procset_t          procset;
        pcparms_t          pcparms;
        struct fpparms    *fpparmsp;
        id_t               fpclassID;
        id_t               schedinfo();
        short              maxfppri;
    /* left set: select processes with same uid as this process */
        procset.p_lidtype = P_UID;
        procset.p_lid = getuid();
    /* get info on fixed priority class */
        if ((fpclassID = schedinfo ("FP", &maxfppri)) == -1) {
                perror ("schedinfo failed");
                exit (1);
        }
    /* right set: select fixed priority processes */
        procset.p_ridtype = P_CID;
        procset.p_rid = fpclassID;
    /* select only my FP processes */
        procset.p_op = POP_AND;
    /* specify new scheduler parameters */
        pcparms.pc_cid = fpclassID;
        fpparmsp = (struct fpparms *) pcparms.pc_clparms;
        fpparmsp->fp_pri = maxfppri - 1;
        fpparmsp->fp_tqnsecs = FP_NOCHANGE;
        if (priocntlset (&procset, PC_SETPARMS, &pcparms) == -1) {
                perror ("priocntlset failed");
                exit (2);
        }
}
```

`priocntl` offers a simple scheduler interface that is adequate for many applications; applications that need a more powerful way to specify sets of processes or LWPs can use `priocntlset`.

Scheduler Interaction with Other Functions

Kernel Processes

The kernel assigns its demon and housekeeping processes to the system scheduler class. Users may neither add processes or LWPs to nor remove processes or LWPs from this class, nor may they change the priorities of these processes or LWPs. The command `ps -cel` lists the scheduler class of all processes or LWPs. Processes in the system class are identified by a `SYS` entry in the `CLS` column.

If the workload on a machine contains fixed priority processes or LWPs that use too much CPU, they can lock out system processes, which can lead to all sorts of trouble. Fixed priority applications must ensure that they leave some CPU time for system and other processes and LWPs.

fork, exec

Scheduler class, priority, and other scheduler parameters are inherited across the `fork`(2) and `exec`(2) system calls.

nice

The `nice`(1) command and the `nice`(2) system call work as in previous versions of the UNIX system. They allow you to change the priority of only a time-sharing process or LWP. You still use lower numeric values to assign higher time-sharing priorities with these functions.

To change the scheduler class of a process or LWP or to specify a fixed priority, you must use one of the `priocntl` functions. Use higher numeric values to assign higher priorities with the `priocntl` functions.

init

The `init` process (process ID 1) may be assigned to any class configured on the system. Because most processes and LWPs normally inherit the scheduler properties of `init`, `init` must be the only process specified by `idtype` and `id` or by the `procset` structure. However, `init` should be assigned to the time-sharing class unless there are compelling reasons to do otherwise.

Scheduler Performance

Because the scheduler determines when and for how long LWPs run, it has an overriding importance in the performance and perceived performance of a system.

By default, all processes and LWPs are time-sharing processes or LWPs. A process or LWP changes class only as a result of one of the **priocntl** functions.

In the default configuration, all real-time fixed priority process priorities are above any time-sharing process priority. This implies that as long as any fixed priority process or LWP is runnable, no time-sharing process or LWP or system process ever runs. So if a fixed priority application is not written carefully, it can completely lock out users and essential kernel housekeeping.

Besides controlling process and LWP class and priorities, a fixed priority application must also control several other factors that influence its performance. The most important factors in performance are CPU power, amount of primary memory, and I/O throughput. These factors interact in complex ways. For more information, see the chapter on performance management in the *System Administration* guide. In particular, the **sar**(1) command has options for reporting on all the factors discussed in this section.

LWP State Transition

Applications that have strict fixed priority constraints may need to prevent processes and LWPs from being swapped or paged out to secondary memory. Here's a simplified overview of UNIX system LWP states and the transitions between states:

Figure 4-6: LWP State Transition Diagram

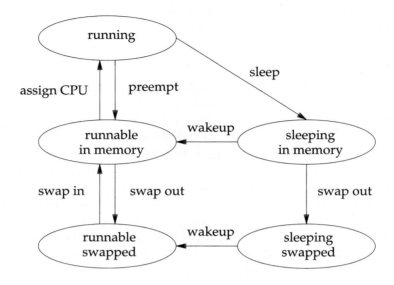

An active LWP is normally in one of the five states in the diagram. The arrows show how it changes states.

- An LWP is running if it is assigned to a CPU. An LWP is preempted—that is, removed from the running state—by the scheduler if an LWP with a higher priority becomes runnable. An LWP is also preempted if it consumes its entire time slice and An LWP of equal priority is runnable.

- An LWP is runnable in memory if it is in primary memory and ready to run, but is not assigned to a CPU.

- An LWP is sleeping in memory if it is in primary memory but is waiting for a specific event before it can continue execution. For example, an LWP is sleeping if it is waiting for an I/O operation to complete, for a locked resource to be unlocked, or for a timer to expire. When the event occurs, the process is sent a wakeup; if the reason for its sleep is gone, the LWP becomes runnable.

- An LWP is runnable and swapped if it is not waiting for a specific event but has had its whole address space written to secondary memory to make room in primary memory for other LWPs.

- An LWP is sleeping and swapped if it is both waiting for a specific event and has had its whole address space written to secondary memory to make room in primary memory for other processes or LWPs.

If a machine does not have enough primary memory to hold all its active processes and LWPs, it must page or swap some address space to secondary memory:

- When the system is short of primary memory, it writes individual pages of some processes and LWPs to secondary memory but leaves those processes and LWPs runnable. When an LWP runs, if it accesses those pages, it must sleep while the pages are read back into primary memory.

- When the system gets into a more serious shortage of primary memory, it writes all the pages of some processes and LWPs to secondary memory and marks those processes and LWPs as swapped. Such processes and LWPs get back into a schedulable state only by being chosen by the system scheduler demon process, then read back into memory.

Both paging and swapping, and especially swapping, introduce delay when a process or LWP is ready to run again. For processes and LWPs that have strict timing requirements, this delay can be unacceptable. To avoid swapping delays, fixed priority processes and LWPs are never swapped, though parts of them may be paged. An application can prevent paging and swapping by locking its text and data into primary memory. For more information see **memcntl**(2) in the *Operating System API Reference*. Of course, how much can be locked is limited by how much memory is configured. Also, locking too much can cause intolerable delays to processes and LWPs that do not have their text and data locked into memory. Tradeoffs between performance of fixed priority processes and LWPs and performance of other processes and LWPs depend on local needs. On some systems, process locking may be required to guarantee the necessary fixed priority response.

Software Latencies

Designers of some fixed priority applications must have information on software latencies to analyze the performance characteristics of their applications and to predict whether performance constraints can be met. These latencies depend on kernel implementation and on system hardware, so it is not practical to list the latencies. It is useful, however, to describe some of the most important latencies. Consider the following time-line:

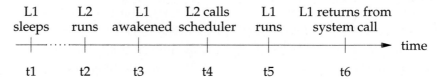

L1 and L2 represent LWPs; t1 through t6 represent points in time. Suppose that L1 has a higher priority than all other active LWPs, including L2. L1 runs and does a system call that causes it to sleep at time t1, waiting for I/O. L2 runs. The I/O device interrupts, resulting in a wakeup at time t3 that makes L1 runnable. If L2 is running in user mode at time t3, it is preempted immediately and the interval (t4 – t3) is, for practical purposes, zero. If L2 is running in kernel mode at time t3, it is preempted as soon as it gets to a safe place for preemption, a point in kernel code where no spin locks are held and where the state of the current LWP (L2 in this example) may be saved and a different LWP run. Therefore, if L2 is running in kernel mode at time t3, the interval (t4 – t3) depends on how long the kernel code needs to run before getting to such a safe point. It is useful to know both a typical time to preemption and a maximum time to preemption; these times depend on kernel implementation and on hardware. Eventually, the scheduler runs (at time t4), finds that a higher-priority LWP L1 is runnable, and runs it. We refer to the interval (t5 – t4) as the software switch latency of the system. This latency is, for practical purposes, a constant; again, it is an implementation-dependent value. At time t6, L1 returns to the user program from the system call that put it to sleep at time t1. For simplicity, suppose that the program is getting only a few bytes of data from the I/O device. In this simple case, the interval (t6 – t5) consists primarily of the overhead of getting out of the system call. We refer to the interval (t6 – t3) as the software wakeup latency of the system; this is the interval from the I/O device interrupt until the user LWP returns to application level to deal with the interrupt (if it is the highest priority LWP). So the software wakeup latency is composed of a preemption latency, context-switch time, and a part of system call overhead. Of course, the latency increases as the system call asks for more data.

This discussion of latencies assumes that the text and data of the processes and LWPs are in primary memory. An application may have to use process locking to guarantee that its processes and LWPs do not get swapped or paged out of primary memory. See the discussion in the previous section.

Managing Processors and Processes

Processor Administration Information

Processors are identified with a processor ID number that gives them a unique tag within the system. The state of the processors in your system can be examined by using the **psrinfo**(1M) command or the **processor_info**(2) system call. They report whether the processor is online or offline.

Taking Processors Online and Offline

When a processor is online, it can dispatch processes and perform normal operating system functions. You can bring a processor online with the **psradm**(1M) command or the **p_online**(2) system call. Taking a processor offline removes the processor from operational status. The processor retains its place in the system but does not perform any useful operations while it is idle.

Only processors with no bound processes can be taken offline. Some hardware platforms may require some processors to be online at all times. A processor can be taken offline with the **psradm**(1M) command or the **p_online**(2) system call. Once a processor has been taken offline, it remains idle until it is brought back online using the **psradm**(1M) command or the **p_online**(2) system call.

Binding Processes to Processors

By default, an LWP can execute on any processor in the system. You can use the **pbind**(1M) command or the **processor_bind**(2) system call to bind a process (all of the associated LWPs) or LWP to a processor. This restricts the LWPs to execute only on the specified processor. Once bound, all child processes created by this process or timeout routines requested by this process are bound by default to the same processor. The **-P** option of the **ps**(1) command can be used to display the processor binding status of all processes in the system. The **pbind**(1M) command can also be used to unbind a process (all the associated LWPs) or LWP from a processor. Once unbound, the process or LWP can execute on any processor in the system.

Placing Processors in an Exclusive Binding Mode

You can use the **pexbind**(1M) command or the **processor_exbind**(2) system call to place a processor in an exclusive binding mode, or to unbind it. When a processor has been placed in an exclusive binding mode, it will execute only LWPs bound to that processor. It will not execute any other LWPs in the system even when the processor is idle. If a kernel driver requires a resource that is available only in the exclusively bound processor, the processor is still available for the kernel driver even though it is not available for user level LWPs that are not exclusively bound to it.

For example, if a driver is exclusively bound to the processor, and a process requires the service of this device driver, the operating system will temporarily bind the process to the processor and execute the process on the processor for the duration of the driver routine. Once the driver operation is complete, the operating system will unbind the outside process from the processor and restrict itself again only to processes that are bound to the processor. Also, processes that are exclusively bound to a processor are restricted to run only on that processor.

Memory Management Facilities

The UNIX system provides a complete set of memory management mechanisms, providing applications complete control over the construction of their address space and permitting a wide variety of operations on both process address spaces and the variety of memory objects in the system. Process address spaces are composed of a vector of memory pages, each of which can be independently mapped and manipulated. Typically, the system presents the user with mappings that simulate the traditional UNIX process memory environment, but other views of memory are useful as well.

The UNIX memory-management facilities:

- Unify the system's operations on memory.

- Provide a set of kernel mechanisms powerful and general enough to support the implementation of fundamental system services without special-purpose kernel support.

- Maintain consistency with the existing environment, in particular using the UNIX file system as the name space for named virtual-memory objects.

Virtual Memory, Address Spaces and Mapping

The system's virtual memory (VM) consists of all available physical memory resources. Examples include local and remote file systems, processor primary memory, swap space, and other random-access devices. Named objects in the virtual memory are referenced though the UNIX file system. However, not all file system objects are in the virtual memory; devices that cannot be treated as storage, such as terminal and network device files, are not in the virtual memory. Some virtual memory objects, such as private process memory and shared memory segments, do not have names.

A process's address space is defined by mappings onto objects in the system's virtual memory (usually files). Each mapping is constrained to be sized and aligned with the page boundaries of the system on which the process is executing. Each page may be mapped (or not) independently. Only process addresses which are mapped to some system object are valid, for there is no memory associated with processes themselves—all memory is represented by objects in the system's virtual memory.

Each object in the virtual memory has an object address space defined by some physical storage. A reference to an object address accesses the physical storage that implements the address within the object. The virtual memory's associated physical storage is thus accessed by transforming process addresses to object addresses, and then to the physical store.

A given process page may map to only one object, although a given object address may be the subject of many process mappings. An important characteristic of a mapping is that the object to which the mapping is made is not affected by the mere existence of the mapping. Thus, it cannot, in general, be expected that an object has an "awareness" of having been mapped, or of which portions of its address space are accessed by mappings; in particular, the notion of a "page" is not a property of the object. Establishing a mapping to an object simply provides the potential for a process to access or change the object's contents.

The establishment of mappings provides an access method that renders an object directly addressable by a process. Applications may find it advantageous to access the storage resources they use directly rather than indirectly through **read** and **write**. Potential advantages include efficiency (elimination of unnecessary data copying) and reduced complexity (single-step updates rather than the **read**, modify buffer, **write** cycle). The ability to access an object and have it retain its identity over the course of the access is unique to this access method, and facilitates the sharing of common code and data.

Networking, Heterogeneity and Integrity

VM is designed to fit well with the larger UNIX heterogeneous environment. This environment makes extensive use of networking to access file systems—file systems that are now part of the system's virtual memory. Networks are not constrained to consist of similar hardware or to be based upon a common operating system; in fact, the opposite is encouraged, for such constraints create serious barriers to accommodating heterogeneity. While a given set of processes may apply a set of mechanisms to establish and maintain the properties of various system objects—properties such as page sizes and the ability of objects to synchronize their own use—a given operating system should not impose such mechanisms on the rest of the network.

As it stands, the access method view of a virtual memory maintains the potential for a given object (say a text file) to be mapped by systems running the UNIX memory management system and also to be accessed by systems for which virtual memory and storage management techniques such as paging are totally foreign, such as PC-DOS. Such systems can continue to share access to the object, each using and providing its programs with the access method appropriate to that system. The unacceptable alternative would be to prohibit access to the object by less capable systems.

Another consideration arises when applications use an object as a communications channel, or otherwise try to access it simultaneously. In both cases, the object is shared; thus, applications must use some synchronization mechanism to maintain the integrity of their actions on it. The scope and nature of the synchronization mechanism is best left to the application. For example, file access on systems which do not support virtual memory access methods must be indirect, by way of `read` and `write`. Applications sharing files on such systems must coordinate their access using semaphores, file locking, or some application-specific protocols. What is required in an environment where mapping replaces `read` and `write` as the access method is an operation, such as `fsync`, that supports atomic update operations.

The nature and scope of synchronization over shared objects is application-defined from the outset. If the system tried to impose automatic semantics for sharing, it might prohibit other useful forms of mapped access that have nothing to do with communication or sharing. By providing the mechanism to support integrity, and leaving it to cooperating applications to apply the mechanism, the needs of applications are met without eliminating diversity. Note that this design does not prohibit the creation of libraries that provide abstractions for common application needs. Not all abstractions on which an application builds need be supplied by the "operating system."

Memory Management Interfaces

The applications programmer gains access to VM facilities through several sets of system calls. The next sections summarize these calls, and provide examples of their use. For details, see the *Operating System API Reference*.

Creating and Using Mappings

```
caddr_t
mmap(caddr_t addr, size_t len, int prot, int flags, int fd, off_t off);
```

`mmap` establishes a mapping between a process's address space and an object in the system's virtual memory. All other system functions that contribute to the definition of an address space are built from `mmap`, the system's most fundamental function for defining the contents of an address space. The format of an `mmap` call is:

```
paddr = mmap(addr, len, prot, flags, fd, off);
```

mmap establishes a mapping from the process's address space at an address *paddr* for *len* bytes to the object specified by *fd* at offset *off* for *len* bytes. A successful call to **mmap** returns *paddr* as its result, which is an implementation-dependent function of the parameter *addr* and the setting of the **MAP_FIXED** bit of *flags*, as described below. The address range *[paddr, paddr + len)* must be valid for the address space of the process and the range *[off, off + len)* must be valid for the virtual memory object. (The notation *[start, end)* denotes the interval from *start* to *end*, including *start* but excluding *end*.)

> **NOTE** The mapping established by **mmap** replaces any previous mappings for the process's pages in the range *[paddr, paddr + len)*.

The parameter *prot* determines whether read, execute, write or some combination of accesses are permitted to the pages being mapped. To deny all access, set *prot* to **PROT_NONE**. Otherwise, specify permissions by an OR of **PROT_READ**, **PROT_EXECUTE**, and **PROT_WRITE**.

A write access must fail if **PROT_WRITE** has not been set, though the behavior of the write can be influenced by setting **MAP_PRIVATE** in the *flags* parameter, which provides other information about the handling of mapped pages, as described below:

- **MAP_SHARED** and **MAP_PRIVATE** specify the mapping type, and one of them must be specified. The mapping type describes the disposition of store operations made by this process into the address range defined by the mapping operation. If **MAP_SHARED** is specified, write references will modify the mapped object. No further operations on the object are necessary to effect a change — the act of storing into a **MAP_SHARED** mapping is equivalent to doing a **write** system call.

> **NOTE** The private copy is not created until the first write; until then, other users who have the object mapped **MAP_SHARED** can change the object. That is, if one user has an object mapped **MAP_PRIVATE** and another user has the same object mapped **MAP_SHARED**, and the **MAP_SHARED** user changes the object before the **MAP_PRIVATE** user does the first write, then the changes appear in the **MAP_PRIVATE** user's copy that the system makes on the first write. If an application needs isolation from changes made by other processes, it should use **read** to make a copy of the data it wishes to keep isolated.

On the other hand, if **MAP_PRIVATE** is specified, an initial write reference to a page in the mapped area will create a copy of that page and redirect the initial and successive write references to that copy. This operation is sometimes referred to as copy-on-write and occurs invisibly to the process causing the store. Only pages actually modified have copies made in this manner. **MAP_PRIVATE** mappings are used by system functions such as **exec**(2) when mapping files containing programs for execution. This permits operations by programs such as debuggers to modify the "text" (code) of the program without affecting the file from which the program is obtained.

The mapping type is retained across a **fork**.

- **MAP_FIXED** informs the system that the value returned by **mmap** must be *addr*, exactly. The use of **MAP_FIXED** is discouraged, as it may prevent an implementation from making the most effective use of system resources. When **MAP_FIXED** is not set, the system uses *addr* as a hint to arrive at *paddr*. The *paddr* so chosen is an area of the address space that the system deems suitable for a mapping of *len* bytes to the specified object. An *addr* value of zero grants the system complete freedom in selecting *paddr*, subject to constraints described below. A non-zero value of *addr* is taken as a suggestion of a process address near which the mapping should be placed. When the system selects a value for *paddr*, it never places a mapping at address 0, nor replaces any extant mapping, nor maps into areas considered part of the potential data or stack "segments." The system strives to choose alignments for mappings that maximize the performance of the its hardware resources.

The file descriptor used in a **mmap** call need not be kept open after the mapping is established. If it is closed, the mapping will remain until such time as it is replaced by another call to **mmap** that explicitly specifies the addresses occupied by this mapping; or until the mapping is removed either by process termination or a call to **munmap**. Although the mapping endures independent of the existence of a file descriptor, changes to the file can influence accesses to the mapped area, even if they do not affect the mapping itself. For instance, should a file be shortened by a call to **truncate**, such that the mapping now "overhangs" the end of the file, then accesses to that area of the file which "does not exist" will result in **SIGBUS** signals. It is possible to create the mapping in the first place such that it "overhangs" the end of the file — the only requirement when creating a mapping is that the addresses, lengths, and offsets specified in the operation be possible (that is, within the range permitted for the object in question), not that they exist at the time the mapping is created (or subsequently.)

Similarly, if a program accesses an address in a manner inconsistently with how it has been mapped (for instance, by attempting a store operation into a mapping that was established with only **PROT_READ** access), then a **SIGSEGV** signal will result. **SIGSEGV** signals will also result on any attempt to reference an address not defined by any mapping.

In general, if a program makes a reference to an address that is inconsistent with the mapping (or lack of a mapping) established at that address, the system will respond with a **SIGSEGV** violation. However, if a program makes a reference to an address consistent with how the address is mapped, but that address does not evaluate at the time of the access to allocated storage in the object being mapped, then the system will respond with a **SIGBUS** violation. In this manner a program (or user) can distinguish between whether it is the mapping or the object that is inconsistent with the access, and take appropriate remedial action.

Using **mmap** to access system memory objects can simplify programs in a variety of ways. Keeping in mind that **mmap** can really be viewed as just a means to access memory objects, it is possible to program using **mmap** in many cases where you might program with **read** or **write**. However, it is important to realize that **mmap** can only be used to gain access to memory objects — those objects that can be thought of as randomly accessible storage. Thus, terminals and network connections cannot be accessed with **mmap** because they are not "memory." Magnetic tapes, even though they are memory devices, can not be accessed with **mmap** because storage locations on the tape can only be addressed sequentially. Some examples of situations which can be thought of as candidates for use of **mmap** over more traditional methods of file access include:

- Random access operations — either map the entire file into memory or, if the address space can not accommodate the file or if the file size is variable, create "windows" of mappings to the object.

- Efficiency — even in situations where access is sequential, if the object being accessed can be accessed via **mmap**, an efficiency gain may be obtained by avoiding the copying operations inherent in accesses via **read** or **write**.

- Structured storage — if the storage being accessed is collected as tables or data structures, algorithms can be more conveniently written if access to the file is treated just as though the tables were in memory. Previously, programs could not simply make storage or table alterations in memory and save them for access in subsequent runs; however, when the addresses of a table are defined by mappings to a file, then changes to that storage are changes to the file, and are thus automatically recorded in it.

- Scattered storage — if a program requires scattered regions of storage, such as multiple heaps or stack areas, such areas can be defined by mapping operations during program operation.

The remainder of this section will illustrate some other concepts surrounding mapping creation and use.

Mapping **/dev/zero** gives the calling program a block of zero-filled virtual memory of the size specified in the call to **mmap**. **/dev/zero** is a special device, that responds to **read** as an infinite source of bytes with the value 0, but when mapped creates an unnamed object to back the mapped region of memory. The following code fragment demonstrates a use of this to create a block of scratch storage in a program, at an address of the system's choosing.

```
/*
 * Function to allocate a block of zeroed storage.  Parameter
 * is the number of bytes desired.  The storage is mapped as
 * MAP_SHARED, so that if a fork occurs, the child process
 * will be able to access and modify the storage.  If we wished
 * to cause the child's modifications (as well as those by the
 * parent) to be invisible to the ancestry of processes, we
 * would use MAP_PRIVATE.
 */
caddr_t
get_zero_storage(int len);
{
      int fd;
      caddr_t result;

      if ((fd = open("/dev/zero", O_RDWR)) == -1)
            return ((caddr_t)-1);
      result = mmap(0, len, PROT_READ|PROT_WRITE, MAP_SHARED, fd, 0);
      (void) close(fd);
      return (result);
}
```

As written, this function permits a hierarchy of processes to use the area of allocated storage as a region of communication (for implicit interprocess communication purposes). Later in this chapter we will describe a set of system facilities that provide a similar function packaged for accomplishing the same purpose without requiring that the processes be in a parent-child hierarchy.

In some cases, devices or files are only useful if accessed via mapping. An example of this is frame buffer devices used to support bit-mapped displays, where display management algorithms function best if they can operate randomly on the addresses of the display directly.

Finally, it is important to remember that mappings can be operated upon at the granularity of a single page. Even though a mapping operation may define multiple pages of an address space, there is no restriction that subsequent operations on those addresses must operate on the same number of pages. For instance, an **mmap** operation defining ten pages of an address space may be followed by subsequent **munmap** (see below) operations that remove every other page from the address space, leaving five mapped pages each followed by an unmapped page. Those

unmapped pages may subsequently be mapped to different locations in the same
or different objects, or the whole range of pages (or any partition, superset, or subset of the pages) used in other **mmap** or other memory management operations.
Further, it must be noted that any mapping operation that operates on more than
a single page can "partially succeed" in that some parts of the address range can
be affected even though the call returns a failure. Thus, an **mmap** operation that
replaces another mapping, if it fails, may have deleted the previous mapping and
failed to replace it. Similarly, other operations (unless specifically stated otherwise) may process some pages in the range successfully before operating on a
page where the operation fails.

Not all device drivers support memory mapping. **mmap** fails if you try to map a
device that does not support mapping.

Removing Mappings

```
int
munmap(caddr_t addr, size_t len);
```

munmap removes all mappings for pages in the range [addr, addr + len) from the
address space of the calling process. It is not an error to remove mappings from
addresses that do not have them, and any mapping, no matter how it was established, can be removed with **munmap**. **munmap** does not in any way affect the
objects that were mapped at those addresses.

Cache Control

The UNIX memory management system can be thought of as a form of "cache
management", in which a processor's primary memory is used as a cache for
pages from objects from the system's virtual memory. Thus, there are a number of
operations which control or interrogate the status of this "cache", as described in
this section.

Memory Cache Control

```
int
memcntl(caddr_t addr, size_t len, int cmd, caddr_t arg, int attr, int mask);
```

`memcntl` provides several control operations over mappings in the range *[addr, addr + len)*, including locking pages into physical memory, unlocking them, and writing pages to secondary storage. The functions described in the rest of this section offer simplified interfaces to the `memcntl` operations.

Memory Page Locking

```
int
mlock(caddr_t addr, size_t len);

int
munlock(caddr_t addr, size_t len);
```

`mlock` causes the pages referenced by the mapping in the range *[addr, addr + len)* to be locked in physical memory. References to those pages (through other mappings in this or other processes) will not result in page faults that require an I/O operation to obtain the data needed to satisfy the reference. Because this operation ties up physical system resources, and has the potential to disrupt normal system operation, use of this facility is restricted to the superuser. The system prohibits more than a configuration-dependent limit of pages to be locked in memory simultaneously, the call to `mlock` will fail if this limit is exceeded.

`munlock` releases the locks on physical pages. If multiple `mlock` calls are made through the same mapping, only a single `munlock` call will be required to release the locks (in other words, locks on a given mapping do not nest.) However, if different mappings to the same pages are processed with `mlock`, then the pages will stay locked until the locks on all the mappings are released.

Locks are also released when a mapping is removed, either through being replaced with an `mmap` operation or removed explicitly with `munmap`. A lock will be transferred between pages on the "copy-on-write" event associated with a **MAP_PRIVATE** mapping, thus locks on an address range that includes **MAP_PRIVATE** mappings will be retained transparently along with the copy-on-write redirection (see `mmap` above for a discussion of this redirection).

Address Space Locking

```
int
mlockall(int flags);

int
munlockall(void);
```

mlockall and **munlockall** are similar in purpose and restriction to **mlock** and **munlock**, except that they operate on entire address spaces. **mlockall** accepts a *flags* argument built as a bit-field of values from the set:

> **MCL_CURRENT**   Current mappings
> **MCL_FUTURE**   Future mappings

If *flags* is **MCL_CURRENT**, the lock is to affect everything currently in the address space. If *flags* is **MCL_FUTURE**, the lock is to affect everything added in the future. If *flags* is **(MCL_CURRENT | MCL_FUTURE)**, the lock is to affect both current and future mappings.

munlockall removes all locks on all pages in the address space, whether established by **mlock** or **mlockall**.

Memory Cache Synchronization

```
int
msync(caddr_t addr, size_t len, int flags);
```

msync supports applications which require assertions about the integrity of data in the storage backing their mapping, either for correctness or for coherent communications in a distributed environment. **msync** causes all modified copies of pages over the range *[addr, addr + len)* to be flushed to the objects mapped by those addresses. In the cache analogy discussed previously, **msync** is the cache "write-back," or flush, operation. It is similar in purpose to the **fsync** operation for files.

msync optionally invalidates such cache entries so that further references to the pages cause the system to obtain them from their permanent storage locations.

The *flags* argument provides a bit-field of values that influences the behavior of **msync**. The bit names and their interpretations are:

MS_SYNC	synchronized write
MS_ASYNC	return immediately
MS_INVALIDATE	invalidate caches

MS_SYNC causes **msync** to return only after all I/O operations are complete. MS_ASYNC causes **msync** to return immediately once all I/O operations are scheduled. MS_INVALIDATE causes all cached copies of data from mapped objects to be invalidated, requiring them to be reobtained from the object's storage upon the next reference.

Memory Page Residency

```
int
mincore(caddr_t addr, size_t len, char *vec);
```

mincore determines the residency of the memory pages in the address space covered by mappings in the range *[addr, addr + len)*. Using the "cache concept" described earlier, this function can be viewed as an operation that interrogates the status of the cache, and returns an indication of what is currently resident in the cache. The status is returned as a char-per-page in the character array referenced by **vec* (which the system assumes to be large enough to encompass all the pages in the address range). Each character contains either a "1" (indicating that the page is resident in the system's primary storage), or a "0" (indicating that the page is not resident in primary storage.) Other bits in the character are reserved for possible future expansion — therefore, programs testing residency should test only the least significant bit of each character.

mincore returns residency information that is accurate at an instant in time. Because the system may frequently adjust the set of pages in memory, this information may quickly be outdated. Only locked pages are guaranteed to remain in memory.

Other Mapping Functions

```
long
sysconf(PAGESIZE);
```

sysconf returns the system-dependent size of a memory page. For portability, applications should not embed any constants specifying the size of a page, and instead should make use of **sysconf** to obtain that information. Note that it is not unusual for page sizes to vary even among implementations of the same instruction set, increasing the importance of using this function for portability.

```
int
mprotect(caddr_t addr, size_t len, int prot);
```

mprotect has the effect of assigning protection *prot* to all pages in the range *[addr, addr + len)*. The protection assigned can not exceed the permissions allowed on the underlying object. For instance, a read-only mapping to a file that was opened for read-only access can not be set to be writable with **mprotect** (unless the mapping is of the **MAP_PRIVATE** type, in which case the write access is permitted since the writes will modify copies of pages from the object, and not the object itself).

Address Space Layout

Traditionally, the address space of a UNIX process has consisted of exactly three segments: one each for write-protected program code (text), a heap of dynamically allocated storage (data), and the process's stack. Text is read-only and shared, while the data and stack segments are private to the process.

System V Release 4 still uses text, data, and stack segments, though these should be thought of as constructs provided by the programming environment rather than by the operating system. As such, it is possible to construct processes that have multiple segments of each "type," or of types of arbitrary semantic value — no longer are programs restricted to being built only from objects the system was capable of representing directly. For instance, a process's address space may contain multiple text and data segments, some belonging to specific programs and some shared among multiple programs. Text segments from shared libraries, for example, typically appear in the address spaces of many processes. A process's address space is simply a vector of pages, and there is no necessary division between different address-space segments. Process text and data spaces are simply groups of pages mapped in ways appropriate to the function they provide the program.

While the system may have multiple areas that can be considered "data" segments, for programming convenience the system maintains operations to operate on an area of storage associated with a process's initial "heap storage area." A process can manipulate this area by calling **brk** and **sbrk**:

```
caddr_t
brk(caddr_t addr);

caddr_t
sbrk(int incr);
```

brk sets the system's idea of the lowest data segment location not used by the caller to *addr* (rounded up to the next multiple of the system's page size).

sbrk, the alternate function, adds *incr* bytes to the caller's data space and returns a pointer to the start of the new data area.

A process's address space is usually sparsely populated, with data and text pages intermingled. The precise mechanics of the management of stack space is machine-dependent. By convention, page 0 is not used. Process address spaces are often constructed through dynamic linking when a program is **exec**'ed. Operations such as **exec** and dynamic linking build upon the mapping operations described previously. Dynamic linking is described further in the *Programming in Standard C* guide.

5 Terminal Device Control

Introduction

This chapter discusses the general terminal interface to control asynchronous communication ports. The functions on the **termio**(7) manual page are used to access and configure the hardware interface to a terminal.

Also included in this chapter is a discussion of the mechanisms involved with opening and closing a terminal device file, as well as input/output processing.

The remainder of this chapter addresses the STREAMS mechanism as it relates to terminal device control. The STREAMS-based terminal subsystem provides a uniform interface for implementing character I/O devices and networking protocols in the kernel. Also discussed here is the notion of the STREAMS-based pseudo-terminal subsystem which provides the user with an identical interface to the STREAMS-based terminal subsystem.

Terminal Device Control Functions

General Terminal Interface

Terminal Device Control functions offer a general terminal interface for controlling asynchronous communication-ports in a device-independent manner using parameters stored in the **termios** structure which is defined by the **<termios.h>** header file [see **termios**(7)]. UNIX System V also uses **termios** to control the operation of network-connections.

Table 5-1: Terminal Device Control Functions

Feature/Function Description	Interface
General Terminal Characteristics	
– get output baud-rate	cfgetospeed
– set output baud-rate	cfsetospeed
– get input baud-rate	cfgetispeed
– set input baud-rate	cfsetispeed
General Terminal Control Functions	
– get state of terminal	tcgetattr
– set state of terminal	tcsetattr
– line control function	tcsendbreak
– line control function	tcdrain
– line control function	tcflush
– line control function	tcflow
– get foreground process-group-id	tcgetpgrp
– set foreground process-group-id	tcsetpgrp

The **termios** structure stores the values of settable terminal I/O parameters used by functions to control terminal I/O characteristics and the operation of a terminal-device-file. The **<termios.h>** header file defines the **termios** structure to contain at least the following members [see **termios**(7)]:

```
tcflag_t  c_iflag;       /* input modes */
tcflag_t  c_oflag;       /* output modes */
tcflag_t  c_cflag;       /* control modes */
tcflag_t  c_lflag;       /* local modes */
cc_t      c_cc[NCCS];    /* control chars */
```

The <termios.h> header file defines the type tcflag_t as long, the type cc_t as char. The <termios.h> header file also defines the symbolic-constant NCCS as the size of the control-character array.

Baud Rates

The structure termios stores the input and output baud-rates in c_cflag. The table below shows symbolic names defined in <termios.h> and the baud-rate each represents:

B0	hang up
B50	50 baud
B75	75 baud
B110	110 baud
B134	134.5 baud
B150	150 baud
B200	200 baud
B300	300 baud
B600	600 baud
B1200	1200 baud
B1800	1800 baud
B2400	2400 baud
B4800	4800 baud
B9600	9600 baud
B19200	19200 baud
B38400	38400 baud

Note that the zero baud-rate, B0, is used to terminate the connection. If B0 is specified, the modem control lines are no longer asserted; normally, this discon-nects the line [see cfsetospeed(2) and tcsetattr(2)]:

The termios structure members c_iflag, c_oflag, c_cflag and c_lflag take as values the bitwise inclusive-OR of bitwise distinct masks with symbolic names defined by the <termios.h> header file [see termios(7)].

Input Modes

The input-modes field c_iflag specifies treatment of terminal input. Calling read on a terminal-device-file works as described in "Input Processing and Read-ing Data" and the value of c_iflag along with the value of c_lflag determine how to process input read from the terminal [see "Input Modes" and "Local Modes" in termios(7)].

Output Modes

The output-modes field **c_oflag** specifies treatment of terminal output. Calling **write** on a terminal-device-file works as described in "Writing Data and Output Processing" and the value of **c_oflag** determines how to process output written to the terminal [see "Output Modes" in **termios**(7)].

Control Modes

The control-modes field **c_cflag** specifies communication control for terminals. The value of **c_cflag** controls characteristics of the communications-port to a terminal-device, but the underlying hardware may fail to support all **c_cflag** values [see "Control Modes" in **termios**(7)]. A communication-port other than an asynchronous serial connection may ignore some of the control-modes; for example, if an attempt is made to set the baud-rate on a network-connection to a terminal on another host, the baud-rate may or may not be set on the connection between the terminal and the machine it is directly connected to.

Local Modes and Line Disciplines

The local-modes field **c_lflag** specifies the *line-discipline* for the terminal. The line-discipline works as described in "Canonical Mode Input Processing" and "Non-Canonical Mode Input Processing" and the value of **c_lflag** along with the value of **c_iflag** determine how the line-discipline acts on input from a terminal-device-file [see "Local Modes" and "Input Modes" in **termios**(7)].

Special Control Characters

The array **c_cc** specifies the special control-characters that affect the operation of the communication-port and the processing of terminal input and output as described in the "Special Characters" section below. For each entry of the control-character array **c_cc**, the following are typical default values:

Table 5-2: Terminal Device Control Character Array

Subscript Value	Subscript Name	Character Value	Character Description
0	VINTR	ASCII DEL	INTR character
1	VQUIT	ASCII FS	QUIT character
2	VERASE	#	ERASE character
3	VKILL	@	KILL character
4	VEOF	ASCII EOT	EOF character
5	VEOL	ASCII NUL	EOL character

Table 5-2: Terminal Device Control Character Array (continued)

Subscript Value	Subscript Name	Character Value	Character Description
6	reserved		
7	reserved		
8	VSTART	ASCII DC1	START character
9	VSTOP	ASCII DC3	STOP character
10	VSUSP	ASCII SUB	SUSP character

The subscript values are unique, except that the **VMIN** and **VTIME** subscripts may have the same value as the **VEOF** and **VEOL** subscripts respectively. The **<termios.h>** header file defines the relative positions, subscript names and default values for the control-character array **c_cc** [see "Special Control Characters" in **termios**(7)].

The NL and CR character cannot be changed. The INTR, QUIT, ERASE, KILL, EOF, EOL, SUSP, STOP and START characters can be changed as follows:

```
struct termios term;
term.c_cc[VINTR] = 'a';
term.c_cc[VQUIT] = 'b';
term.c_cc[VERASE] = 'c';
term.c_cc[VKILL] = 'd';
term.c_cc[VEOF] = 'e';
term.c_cc[VEOL] = 'f';
term.c_cc[VSUSP] = 'g';
term.c_cc[VSTOP] = 'h';
term.c_cc[VSTART] = 'i';
```

where a, b, c, d, e, f, g, h and i are the INTR, QUIT, ERASE, KILL, EOF, EOL, SUSP, STOP and START characters respectively.

Implementations which prohibit changing the START and STOP characters may ignore the character values in the **c_cc** array indexed by the **VSTART** and **VSTOP** subscripts when **tcsetattr** is called, but return the character value when **tcsetattr** is called [see **tcsetattr**(2)].

If **_POSIX_VDISABLE** is defined for the terminal-device-file, and the value of one of the changeable special control-characters equals **_POSIX_VDISABLE**, that function is disabled; that is, the special character is ignored on input and is not recognized [see "Special Characters" section below]. If **ICANON** is clear, the value of **_POSIX_VDISABLE** lacks any special meaning for the **VMIN** and **VTIME** entries of the **c_cc** array.

Opening a Terminal Device File

When a terminal-device-file is opened, it normally causes the process to wait until a connection is established. In practice, application-programs seldom open such files; instead, at system-initialization time special-programs open terminal-device-files as the *standard input*, *standard output* and *standard error* files [see **stdio**(4)].

Opening a terminal-device-file with the flag **O_NONBLOCK** clear on the **open** system call causes the process to block until the terminal-device is ready and available [see **open**(2)]. The flag **CLOCAL** can also affect the **open** system call [see "Control Modes" in **termios**(7)].

Input Processing and Reading Data

A terminal-device accessed through an open terminal-device-file ordinarily operates in full-duplex mode. This means data may arrive at any time, even while output is occurring. Each terminal-device-file has associated with it an *input-queue*, into which the system stores incoming data before the process reads that data. The system imposes a limit of **MAX_INPUT**, the maximum allowable number of bytes of input data, on the number of bytes of data that it stores in the input-queue. Data is lost only when the input-queue becomes completely full, or when an input line exceeds **MAX_INPUT**. The behavior of the system when this limit is exceeded is implementation-dependent.

In UNIX System V, if the data in the terminal-device-file input-queue exceeds **MAX_INPUT** and **IMAXBEL** is clear, all the bytes of data saved up to that point are discarded without any notice, but if **IMAXBEL** is set and the data in the terminal-device-file input-queue exceeds **MAX_INPUT**, the ASCII BEL character is echoed. Further input is not stored, and any data already present in the input-queue remains undisturbed.

Two general kinds of input processing are available, determined by whether the terminal-device-file is operating in canonical mode or non-canonical mode. These modes are described in "Canonical Mode Input Processing" and "Non-Canonical Mode Input Processing". Additionally, input is processed according to the **c_iflag** and **c_lflag** fields [see "Input Modes" and "Local Modes" in **termios**(7)]. Such processing can include *echoing*, which in general means transmitting input data bytes immediately back to the terminal when they are received from the terminal. This is useful for terminals that can operate in full-duplex mode.

The way a process reading from a terminal-device-file gets data depends on whether the terminal-device-file is operating in canonical mode or non-canonical mode. How **read** operates on a terminal-device-file also depends on how **open**(2) or **fcntl**(2) sets the flag O_NONBLOCK for the file:

- If O_NONBLOCK and O_NDELAY are clear, **read** blocks until data is available or a signal interrupts the **read** operation.

- If O_NONBLOCK is set, **read** completes, without blocking, in one of the following three ways:

  1. If enough bytes of data are available to satisfy the entire request, **read** completes successfully and returns the number of bytes it transferred.

  2. If too few bytes of data are available to satisfy the entire request, **read** completes successfully, having transferred as much data as it could, and returns the number of bytes it actually transferred.

  3. If *no* data is available, **read** returns **-1** and **errno** equals **EAGAIN**.

When data become available depends on whether the input-processing mode is canonical or non-canonical. The following sections, "Canonical Mode Input Processing" and "Non-Canonical Mode Input Processing", describe each of these input-processing modes.

Canonical Mode Input Processing

In canonical mode input processing, terminal input is processed in units of lines. A line is delimited by the new-line (**'\n'**) character, end-of-file (EOF) character or end-of-line (EOL) character [see "Special Characters" section below for more information on EOF and EOL].

Processing terminal input in units of lines means that a program attempting a **read** from a terminal-device-file is suspended until an entire line is typed, or a signal is received. Also, no matter how many bytes of data a **read** may request from a terminal-device-file, it transfers at most one line of input. It is not, however, necessary to read the entire line at once; a **read** may request any number of bytes of data, even one, without losing any data remaining in the line of input.

If **MAX_CANON** is defined for this terminal-device, it is a limit on the number of bytes in a line. The behavior of the system when this limit is exceeded is implementation-dependent. If **MAX_CANON** is not defined for this terminal-device, there is no such limit [see "Pathname Variable Values"].

It should be noted that there is a possible inherent deadlock if the program and the implementation conflict on the value of **MAX_CANON**. With both **ICANON** and **IXOFF** set when more than **MAX_CANON** characters transmitted without a line-feed, transmission is stopped, the line-feed (or carriage-return if **ICRLF** is set) never arrives, and the **read** is never satisfied.

A program should never set **IXOFF** if it is using canonical-mode unless it knows that (even in the face of a transmission error) the conditions described previously cannot be met or unless it is prepared to deal with the possible deadlock in some other way, such as time-outs.

 NOTE This would only occur if the transmitting side was a communications device (for example, an asynchronous port). This normally will not happen since the transmitting side is a user at a terminal.

It should also be noted that this can be made to happen in non-canonical-mode if the number of characters received that would cause **IXOFF** to be sent is less than **VMIN** when **VTIME** equals zero.

In UNIX System V, if the data in the line-discipline buffer exceeds **MAX_CANON** in canonical mode and **IMAXBEL** is clear, all the bytes of data saved in the buffer up to that point are discarded without any notice, but if **IMAXBEL** is set and the data in the line-discipline buffer exceeds **MAX_INPUT**, the ASCII BEL character is echoed. Further input is not stored, and any data already present in the input-queue remains undisturbed.

During input, *erase* and *kill* processing occurs whenever either of two special characters, the ERASE and KILL characters is received [see "Special Characters"]. This processing affects data in the input-queue that has yet to be delimited by a new-line, EOF or EOL character. This un-delimited data makes up the current line. The ERASE character deletes the last character (if any) in the current line; it does not erase beyond the beginning of the line. The KILL character deletes all data (if any) in the current line; it optionally outputs a new-line character. The ERASE and KILL characters have no effect if the current line lacks any data.

Both the ERASE and KILL characters operate on a key-stroke basis independently of any backspacing or tabbing. Typically, # is the default ERASE character, and @ is the default KILL character. The ERASE and KILL characters themselves are not placed in the input-queue.

Non-Canonical Mode Input Processing

In non-canonical input processing, input bytes are not assembled into lines, and erase and kill processing does not occur. The values of the MIN and TIME members of the **c_cc** array determine how to process any data received.

MIN is the minimum number of bytes of data that a **read** should return when it completes successfully. If MIN exceeds **MAX_INPUT**, the response to the request is implementation-defined. In UNIX System V, the maximum value that can be stored for MIN in **c_cc[VMIN]** is 256, less than **MAX_INPUT** which equals 512; thus, the MIN value can never exceed **MAX_INPUT**. TIME is a read-timer with a 0.10 second granularity used to time-out bursty and short-term data transmissions. The four possible interactions between MIN and TIME follow:

1. (MIN>0, TIME>0).

   Because TIME>0, it serves as an inter-byte timer activated on receipt of the first byte of data, and reset on receipt of each byte of data. MIN and TIME interact as follows:

   - As soon as a byte of data is received, the inter-byte timer starts (remember that the timer is reset on receipt of each byte)

   - If MIN bytes of data are received before the inter-byte timer expires, the **read** completes successfully.

   - If the inter-byte timer expires before MIN bytes of data are received, the **read** transfers any bytes received up until then.

   When TIME expires, a **read** transfers at least one byte of data because the inter-byte timer is enabled if and only if a byte of data was received. A program using this case must wait for at least one byte of data to be read before proceeding. In case (MIN>0, TIME>0), a **read** blocks until receiving a byte of data activates MIN and TIME, or a signal interrupts the **read**. Thus, the **read** transfers at least one byte of data.

2. (MIN>0, TIME=0).

   Because TIME=0, the timer plays no role and only MIN is significant. A **read** completes successfully only on receiving MIN bytes of data (i.e., the pending **read** blocks until MIN bytes of data are received) or a signal interrupts the **read**. Use these values only when the program cannot continue until a predetermined number of bytes of data are read. A program using this case to do record-based terminal I/O may block indefinitely in a **read**.

3. (MIN=0, TIME>0).

Because MIN=0, TIME no longer serves as an inter-byte timer, but now serves as a read-timer activated when a **read** is processed (in canon). A **read** completes successfully as soon as any bytes of data are received or the read-timer expires. A **read** does not transfer any bytes of data if the read-timer expires. If the read-timer does not expire, a **read** completes successfully if and only if some bytes of data are received. In case (MIN=0, TIME>0), the **read** does not block indefinitely waiting for a byte of data. If no bytes of data are received within TIME*0.10 seconds after the **read** starts, it returns 0 having read no data. If the buffer holds data when a **read** starts, the read-timer starts as if it received data immediately. MIN and TIME are useful when a program can assume that data is not available after a TIME interval and other processing can be done before data is available.

4. (MIN=0, TIME=0).

Without waiting for more bytes of data to be received, a **read** returns the minimum of either the number of bytes of data requested or the number of bytes of data currently available. In this case, a **read** immediately transfers any bytes of data present, or if no bytes of data are available, it returns 0 having read no data. In case (MIN=0, TIME=0), **read** operates identically to the **O_NDELAY** flag in canonical mode.

MIN/TIME interactions serve different purposes and thus do not parallel one another. In case [2]: (MIN>0, TIME=0), TIME lacks effect, but with the conditions reversed in case [3]: (MIN=0, TIME>0), both MIN and TIME play a role in that receiving a single byte satisfies the MIN criteria. Furthermore, in case [3]: (MIN=0, TIME>0), TIME represents a read-timer, while in case [1]: (MIN>0, TIME>0), TIME represents an inter-byte timer,

Cases [1] and [2], where MIN>0, handle burst mode activity (e.g., file-transfers), where programs need to process at least MIN bytes of data at a time. In case [1], the inter-byte timer acts as a safety measure; in case [2], the timer is turned off.

Cases [3] and [4] handle single byte, timed transfers like those used by screen-based programs that need to know if a byte of data is present in the input-queue before refreshing the screen. In case [3], the **read** is timed, while in case [4], it is not.

One should also note that MIN is always just a minimum, and does not define a record length. Thus, if a program tries a **read** of 20 bytes when 25 bytes of data are present and MIN is 10, the **read** returns 20 bytes of data. In the special case of MIN=0, this still applies: if more than one byte of data is available, all data is returned immediately.

Writing Data and Output Processing

When a process writes data onto a terminal-device-file, `c_oflag` controls how to process those bytes [see "Output Modes" in `termios`(7)]. UNIX System V provides buffering such that a call to `write` schedules data for transfer to the device, but has not necessarily completed the transfer when the call returns [see `write`(2) for the effects of `O_NONBLOCK` on `write`].

Closing a Terminal Device File

The last process to close a terminal-device-file causes any output remaining to be sent to the device and any input remaining to be discarded. Following these actions, if the flag `HUPCL` is set in the control-modes and the communication-port supports a disconnect function, the terminal-device does a disconnect.

Because the POSIX.1 standard is silent on whether a `close` blocks waiting for transmission to drain, or even if a `close` might flush any pending output, a program concerned about how data in terminal input and output-queues are handled should call the appropriate functions such as `tcdrain` to ensure the desired behavior [see `close`(2) and `tcdrain`(2)].

Special Characters

Certain characters have special functions on input or output or both. These functions and their typical default character values are summarized below:

INTR   (typically, rubout or ASCII DEL) sends an *interrupt* signal, `SIG-INT`, to all processes in the foreground process-group for which the terminal is the controlling-terminal. Receiving the signal `SIG-INT` normally forces a process to terminate, but a process may arrange to ignore the signal or to call a signal-catching function [see `sigaction`(2)].

                If `ISIG` is set, the INTR character is recognized and acts as a special character on input and is discarded when processed [see "Local Modes" in `termios`(7)].

QUIT   (typically, control-\ or ASCII FS) sends a *quit* signal, `SIGQUIT`, to all processes in the foreground process-group for which the terminal is the controlling-terminal. Receiving the signal `SIGQUIT` normally forces a process to terminate just as the signal `SIGINT` does except that, unless a receiving process makes other arrangements, it not only terminates but a core image file (called `CORE`) will be created in the current working directory of the process [see **sigaction**(2)].

If **ISIG** is set, the QUIT character is recognized and acts as a special character on input and is discarded when processed [see "Local Modes" in **termios**(7)].

ERASE   (typically, the character **#**) erases the most recently input character in the current line [see "Canonical Mode Input Processing"]. It does not erase beyond the start of a line.

If **ICANON** is set, the ERASE character is recognized and acts as a special character on input and is discarded when processed [see "Local Modes" in **termios**(7)].

KILL   (typically, the character **@**) deletes the entire line, as delimited by an EOF, EOL or NL character.

If **ICANON** is set, the KILL character is recognized and acts as a special character on input and is discarded when processed [see "Local Modes" in **termios**(7)].

EOF   (typically, control-**d** or ASCII EOT) generates an EOF, from a terminal. On receiving EOF, a **read** immediately passes any bytes of data it holds to the process without waiting for a new-line, and discards the EOF. If EOF occurred at the beginning of a line, a **read** holds no bytes of data, and returns a byte count of zero, the standard end-of-file indication.

If **ICANON** is set, the EOF character is recognized and acts as a special character on input and is discarded when processed [see "Local Modes" in **termios**(7)].

NL   (ASCII LF) is the normal line delimiter, (**'\n'**), which can not be changed or escaped.

If **ICANON** is set, the NL character is recognized and acts as a special character on input [see "Local Modes" in **termios**(7)].

EOL   (typically, ASCII NUL) is an additional line delimiter, like the NL character. EOL is not normally used.

If **ICANON** is set, the EOL character is recognized and acts as a special character on input [see "Local Modes" in **termios**(7)].

SUSP   (typically, control-**z** or ASCII SUB) sends an *stop* signal, **SIGTSTP**, to all processes in the foreground process-group for which the terminal is the controlling-terminal.

If job-control is supported and **ISIG** is set, the SUSP character is recognized and acts as a special character on input and is discarded when processed [see "Local Modes" in **termios**(7)].

STOP   (typically, control-**s** or ASCII DC3) temporarily suspends output. It is useful with CRT terminals to prevent output from disappearing before it can be seen. While output is suspended, STOP characters are ignored not read. The STOP character can be changed through the **c_cc** array [see "Special Control Characters" in **termios**(7)].

If **IXON** (output control) is set or **IXOFF** (input control) is set, the STOP character is recognized and acts as a special character on both input and output. If **IXON** is set, the STOP character is discarded when processed [see "Input Modes" in **termios**(7)].

START   (typically, control-**q** or ASCII DC1) resumes output suspended by a STOP character. While output is not suspended, START characters are ignored and not read. The START character can be changed through the **c_cc** array [see "Special Control Characters" in **termios**(7)].

If **IXON** (output control) is set or **IXOFF** (input control) is set, the START character is recognized and acts as a special character on both input and output. If **IXON** is set, the START character is discarded when processed [see "Input Modes" in **termios**(7)].

CR   (ASCII CR) is a line delimiter, (**'\r'**), which is translated into the NL character, and it has the same effect as the NL character if **ICANON** and **ICRNL** are set and **IGNCR** is clear.

If **ICANON** is set, the NL character is recognized and acts as a special character on input [see "Local Modes" in **termios**(7)].

MIN   controls terminal I/O during raw mode (**ICANON** off) processing [see "Non-Canonical Input Processing"].

TIME   controls terminal I/O during raw mode (**ICANON** off) processing [see "Non-Canonical Input Processing"].

The NL and CR character cannot be changed. The INTR, QUIT, ERASE, KILL, EOF, EOL, SUSP, STOP and START characters can be changed through the **c_cc** array [see "Special Control Characters" in **termios**(7)].

The ERASE, KILL and EOF characters may be entered literally (their special meaning escaped) by preceding them with the escape character (**'\'**). In this case, no special function is done and the escape character is not read as input.

The Controlling-Terminal and Process-Groups

A terminal may belong to a process as its controlling-terminal, which is a terminal uniquely associated with one session. Each process of a session with a controlling-terminal has the same controlling-terminal assigned to it. Each session may have at most one controlling-terminal associated with it and vice versa. A terminal may be assigned to at most one session as the controlling-terminal. Certain input sequences from the controlling-terminal cause signals to be sent to all processes in the process-group for the controlling-terminal [see **termios**(7)]. The controlling-terminal plays a special role in handling *quit* and *interrupt* signals [see "Special Characters"].

The controlling-terminal for a session is acquired by the session-leader, which is the process that created the session; the session-id of a session equals the process-id of the session-leader. When a session-leader acquires a controlling-terminal for its session, it thereby becomes the controlling-process of that session [see **setsid**(2)]. Should the terminal later cease to be a controlling-terminal for the session of the session-leader, the session-leader ceases to be a controlling-process.

When a session-leader without a controlling-terminal opens a terminal-device-file and the flag **O_NOCTTY** is clear on **open**, that terminal becomes the controlling-terminal assigned to the session-leader if the terminal is not already assigned to some session [see **open**(2)]. When any process other than a session-leader opens a terminal-device-file, or the flag **O_NOCTTY** is set on **open**, that terminal does not become the controlling-terminal assigned to the calling-process.

A controlling-terminal distinguishes one of the process-groups in the session assigned to it as the *foreground* process-group; all other process-groups in the session are *background* process-groups. By default, when the session-leader acquires a controlling-terminal, the process-group of the session-leader becomes the foreground process-group of the controlling-terminal. The foreground process-group plays a special role in handling signal-generating input characters [see "Special Characters" above].

A new process inherits the controlling-terminal through the **fork** operation [see **fork**(2)]. When a process calls **setsid** to create a new session, the process relinquishes its controlling-terminal; other processes remaining in the old session with that terminal as their controlling-terminal continue to have it [see **setsid**(2)]. When all file-descriptors that denote the controlling-terminal in the system are closed (whether or not it is in the current session), it is unspecified whether all processes that had that terminal as their controlling-terminal cease to have any controlling-terminal. Whether and how a session-leader can reacquire a controlling-terminal after the controlling-terminal is relinquished in this fashion is unspecified. A process does not relinquish its controlling-terminal simply by closing all of its file-descriptors that denote the controlling-terminal if other processes continue to have it open.

When a session-leader terminates, the current session relinquishes the controlling-terminal allowing a new session-leader to acquire it. Any further attempts to access the terminal by other processes in the old session may be denied and treated as if modem-disconnect was detected on the terminal.

Session Management and Job Control

If _POSIX_JOB_CONTROL is defined, UNIX System V supports job-control and command interpreter processes supporting job-control can assign the terminal to different jobs, or process-groups, by placing related processes in a single process-group and assigning the process-group with the terminal. A process may examine or change the foreground process-group of a terminal assuming the process has the required permissions [see tcgetpgrp(2) and tcsetpgrp(2)]. The termios facility aids in this assignment by restricting access to the terminal by processes outside of the foreground process-group [see "Job Control" in the chapter "Signals and Pipes" in this guide].

When there is no longer any process whose process-id or process-group-id matches the process-group-id of the foreground process-group, the terminal lacks any foreground process-group. It is unspecified whether the terminal has a foreground process-group when there is no longer any process whose process-group-id matches the process-group-id of the foreground process-group, but there is a process whose process-id matches the process-group-id of the foreground process-group. Only a successful call to tcsetpgrp or assignment of the controlling-terminal as described can make a process-group the foreground process-group of a terminal [see tcsetpgrp(2)].

Background process-groups in the session of the session-leader are subject to a job-control line-discipline when they attempt to access their controlling-terminal. Typically, they are sent a signal that causes them to stop, unless they have made other arrangements [see signal(4)]. An exception is made for processes that belong to a orphaned process-group, which is a process-group none of whose members have a parent in another process-group within the same session and thus share the same controlling-terminal. When these processes attempt to access their controlling-terminal, they return errors, because there is no process to continue them if they should stop [see "Job Control" in "Signals and Pipes"].

Improving Terminal I/O Performance

For user-level programs that read and write to terminals, the TTY subsystem in UNIX System V provides a flexible interface, known as the **termio** facility. The flexibility of the **termio** facility enables users to perform efficient TTY I/O in a wide range of applications. However, the improper use of this **termio** can result in inefficient user programs. This section discusses writing programs that use **termio** and focuses on the topics of buffer size, canonical mode, raw mode and flow control and provides several code examples.

User programs that read from terminal devices must read from TTYs in either canonical mode or raw mode.

TTY in Canonical Mode

In canonical mode, characters are read from the device and processed before being returned. This processing translates kill and erase characters. Characters are not returned until a new line (NL), end of file (EOF), or end of line (EOL) is read, which means that characters are returned a line at a time. Canonical mode is usually associated with terminals.

An important factor to consider when using canonical mode is what to do when reading from a TTY device for which characters are not available. If the **O_NDELAY** flag has been set for the TTY, then such **read**s return a **0**, indicating that no characters are available. Otherwise, **read**s will not return until a character is available. If a program can perform other processing when characters are not available from a TTY, then the **O_NDELAY** flag should be set for the TTY. This might require programs to be more complicated, but the complication are offset by an increase in efficiency.

The following function opens a TTY device for reading or writing (line 12), places it in canonical mode (line 23), and sets the **O_NDELAY** option so that **read**s are not blocked when characters are not available (line 12).

Figure 5-1: Improving TTY performance – canonical mode

```
 1   #include <fcntl.h>
 2   #include <termio.h>
 3
 4   extern struct termio old_term;
 5
 6   setup1(TTY)
 7   char *TTY;
 8   {
 9         int fid;
10         struct termio new_term;
11
12         if ((fid = open(TTY, O_RDWR|O_NDELAY)) == -1)
13         {
14                 printf("open failed.\n");
15                 exit(1);
16         }
17                 else if (ioctl(fid, TCGETA, &old_term) == -1)
18                         {
19                                 printf("ioctl get failed.\n");
20                                 exit(1);
21                         }
22         new_term = old_term;
23         new_term.c_lflag |= ICANON;
24         if (ioctl(fid, TCSETA, &new_term) == -1)
25         {
26                 printf("ioctl set failed.\n");
27                 exit(1);
28         }
29         return fid;
30   }
```

TTY in Raw Mode

In raw mode, characters are read and returned as is; that is, without being processed. Reading from a TTY device in raw mode is faster than reading from a TTY device in canonical mode. In the interest of efficiency, raw mode should be used when characters do not need to be canonically processed.

Just as in canonical mode, TTY devices that are in raw mode must deal with the problem of what to do when reading from a device for which characters are not available. The **O_NDELAY** flag only applies to TTY devices that are in canonical mode. The same function is provided by the MIN and TIME values for raw TTY devices. By choosing appropriate values of MIN and TIME, a programmer can help maximize efficiency when reading from TTY devices in raw mode.

The following function inputs a TTY that has previously been opened in raw mode and sets the MIN and TIME options to be **0** so that **read**s will not be blocked when characters are not available.

Figure 5-2: Improving TTY performance – raw mode

```
 1   #include <termio.h>
 2
 3   extern struct termio old_term;
 4
 5   setup2(fid)
 6   int fid;
 7   {
 8        struct termio new_term;
 9
10        if (ioctl(fid, TCGETA, &old_term) == -1)
11        {
12             printf("ioctl get failed.\n");
13             exit(1);
14        }
15
16        new_term = old_term;
17        new_term.c_lflag &= ~ICANON;
18        new_term.c_cc[VMIN] = 0;
19        new_term.c_cc[VTIME] = 0;
20
21        if (ioctl(fid, TCSETA, &new_term) == -1)
22        {
23             printf("ioctl set failed.\n");
24             exit(1);
25        }
26   }
```

TTY Flow Control

Flow control becomes a problem when a program that reads from a TTY device that cannot keep up with the number of characters that are coming into the TTY. If this happens, characters are over-written in the TTY input queue before they can be read by the program.

Conversely, when a program writes to a TTY, the device might not be able to keep up with the TTY. When this happens, characters that are written by a program to a TTY are not being seen by the appropriate device.

The **termio** facility provides a mechanism called software flow control to solve this problem. If a program cannot keep up with the characters coming into a TTY, the TTY sends a STOP character to the originator. The originator, upon receipt of the STOP character, stops sending characters to the TTY until it received a START character. The TTY sends the START character when the program has sufficiently emptied its input queue.

If a device cannot keep up with a TTY, the device sends a STOP character to the TTY. Upon receipt of the STOP character, the TTY stops sending characters to the terminal until it receives a START character. The terminal sends the START character when it has sufficiently emptied its input queue. The TTY then blocks **write**s to the TTY until the TTY's output has sufficiently emptied.

Three different options are provided for flow control: **IXON**, **IXOFF**, and **IXANY**. If **IXOFF** is set, then software flow control is enabled on the TTY's input queue. The TTY transmits a STOP character when the program cannot keep up with its input queue and transmits a START character when its input queue in nearly empty again.

If **IXON** is set, software flow control is enabled on the TTY's output queue. The TTY blocks **write**s by the program when the device to which it is connected cannot keep up with it. If **IXANY** is set, then any character received by the TTY from the device restarts the output that has been suspended.

The following function (see the following figure) sets the **IXANY**, **IXOFF**, and **IXANY** options for a TTY device that has previously been opened so that software flow control is enabled for both input and output.

Figure 5-3: Improving TTY performance – flow control

```
 1   #include <termio.h>
 2
 3   extern struct termio old_term;
 4
 5   setup3(fid)
 6   int fid;
 7   {
 8           struct termio new_term;
 9
10           if (ioctl(fid, TCGETA, &old_term) == -1)
11           {
12                   printf("ioctl get failed.\n");
13                   exit(1);
14           }
15
16           new_term = old_term;
17           new_term.c_iflag |= IXON | IXOFF | IXANY;
18
19           if (ioctl(fid, TCSETA, &new_term) == -1)
20           {
21                   printf("ioctl set failed.\n");
22                   exit(1);
23           }
24   }
```

When you design programs that read and write for the TTY subsystem, remember to address buffer size, canonical/raw mode and flow control concerns to ensure programming efficiency. For further information, see the following references:

■ **termio**(7) in the *System Files and Devices Reference*.

■ **open**(2), **read**(2), and **ioctl**(2) in the *Operating System API Reference*.

■ **termio(BA_ENV)** in the *System V Interface Definition*.

STREAMS-Based Terminal Subsystem

UNIX System V Release 4 implements the terminal subsystem in STREAMS. The STREAMS-based terminal subsystem (see Figure 5-4) provides many benefits:

- Reusable line discipline modules. The same module can be used in many STREAMS where the configuration of these STREAMS may be different.

- Line discipline substitution. Although UNIX System V provides a standard terminal line discipline module, another one conforming to the interface may be substituted. For example, a remote login feature may use the terminal subsystem line discipline module to provide a terminal interface to the user.

- Internationalization. The modularity and flexibility of the STREAMS-based terminal subsystem enables an easy implementation of a system that supports multiple byte characters for internationalization. This modularity also allows easy addition of new features to the terminal subsystem.

- Easy customizing. Users may customize their terminal subsystem environment by adding and removing modules of their choice.

- The pseudo-terminal subsystem. The pseudo-terminal subsystem can be easily supported.

- Merge with networking. By pushing a line discipline module on a network line, you can make the network look like a terminal line.

Figure 5-4: STREAMS-based Terminal Subsystem

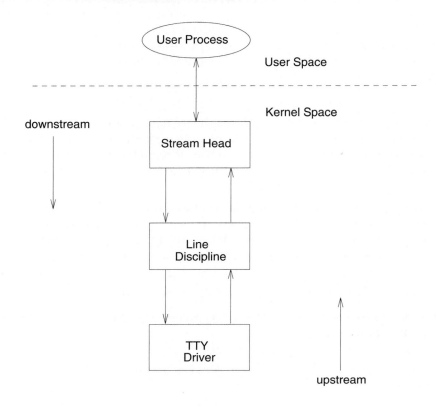

The initial setup of the STREAMS-based terminal subsystem is handled with the **ttymon**(1M) command within the framework of the Service Access Facility (SAF) or the autopush facility. The autopush facility is discussed in Appendix C.

The STREAMS-based terminal subsystem supports **termio**, the **termios** specification of the POSIX standard, multiple byte characters for internationalization, the interface to asynchronous hardware flow control and peripheral controllers for asynchronous terminals [see **termio**(7), **termios**(7) and **termiox**(7)]. XENIX and BSD compatibility can also be provided by pushing the **ttcompat** module [see **ttcompat**(7)].

To use **shl** with the STREAMS-based terminal subsystem, the **sxt** driver is implemented as a STREAMS-based driver. However, the **sxt** feature is being phased out and users are encouraged to use the job control mechanism. Note that both **shl** and job control should not be run simultaneously.

Line Discipline Module

A STREAMS line discipline module called **ldterm** [see **ldterm**(7)] is a key part of the STREAMS-based terminal subsystem. Throughout this chapter, the terms ''line discipline'' and **ldterm** are used interchangeably and refer to the STREAMS version of the standard line discipline and not the traditional character version. **ldterm** performs the standard terminal I/O processing that was traditionally done through the **linesw** mechanism.

The **termio** and **termios** specifications describe four flags that are used to control the terminal: **c_iflag** (defines input modes), **c_oflag** (defines output modes), **c_cflag** (defines hardware control modes), and **c_lflag** (defines terminal functions used by **ldterm**). To process these flags elsewhere (for example, in the firmware or in another process), a mechanism is in place to turn on and off the processing of these flags. When **ldterm** is pushed, it sends an **M_CTL** message downstream, which asks the driver which flags the driver will process. The driver sends back that message in response if it needs to change **ldterm**'s default processing. By default, **ldterm** assumes that it must process all flags except **c_cflag**, unless it receives a message telling otherwise.

Default Settings

When **ldterm** is pushed on the Stream, the open routine initializes the settings of the **termio** flags. The default settings are

```
c_iflag = BRKINT|ICRNL|IXON|ISTRIP|IXANY
c_oflag = OPOST|ONLCR|TAB3
c_cflag = 0
c_lflag = ISIG|ICANON|ECHO|ECHOK
```

In canonical mode (**ICANON** flag in **c_lflag** is turned on), **read** from the terminal file descriptor is in message nondiscard (**RMSGN**) mode [see **streamio**(7)]. This implies that in canonical mode, **read** on the terminal file descriptor always returns at most one line regardless of how many characters have been requested. In non-canonical mode, **read** is in byte-stream (**RNORM**) mode.

Open and Close Routines

The open routine of the **ldterm** module allocates space for holding state information.

The **ldterm** module establishes a controlling tty for the line when an **M_SETOPTS** message (**so_flags** is set to **SO_ISTTY**) is sent upstream. The Stream head allocates the controlling tty on the open, if one is not already allocated.

To maintain compatibility with existing application-programs that use the **O_NDELAY** flag, the **open** routine sets the **SO_NDELON** flag on in the **so_flags** field of the **stroptions** structure in the **M_SETOPTS** message.

The open routine fails if there is insufficient space for allocating the state structure, or when an interrupt occurs while the open is sleeping until memory becomes available.

The close routine frees all the outstanding buffers allocated by this Stream. It also sends an **M_SETOPTS** message to the Stream head to undo the changes made by the open routine. The **ldterm** module also sends **M_START** and **M_STARTI** messages downstream to undo the effect of any previous **M_STOP** and **M_STOPI** messages.

Read-Side Processing

The **ldterm** module's read-side processing has **put** and **service** procedures. **ldterm** can send the following messages upstream:

M_DATA, M_BREAK, M_PCSIG, M_SIG, M_FLUSH, M_ERROR, M_IOCACK, M_IOCNAK, M_HANGUP, M_CTL, M_SETOPTS, M_COPYOUT, and **M_COPYIN** (see Appendix A).

The **ldterm** module's read-side processes **M_BREAK, M_DATA, M_CTL, M_FLUSH, M_HANGUP**, and **M_IOCACK** messages. All other messages are sent upstream unchanged.

The **put** procedure scans the message for flow control characters (**IXON**), signal generating characters, and after (possible) transformation of the message, queues the message for the **service** procedure. Echoing is handled completely by the **service** procedure.

In canonical mode if the **ICANON** flag is on in **c_lflag**, canonical processing is performed. If the **ICANON** flag is off, noncanonical processing is performed [see **termio**(7) for more details]. Handling **VMIN/VTIME** in the STREAMS environment is somewhat complicated, because **read** needs to activate a timer in the **ldterm** module in some cases; hence, read notification becomes necessary. When a user issues an **ioctl** to put **ldterm** in noncanonical mode, the **ldterm** module sends an **M_SETOPTS** message to the Stream head to register read notification. Further reads on the terminal file descriptor causes the Stream head to issue an **M_READ** message downstream and data are sent upstream in response to the **M_READ** message. With read notification, buffering of raw data is performed by **ldterm**. It is possible to canonize the raw data when the user has switched from raw to canonical mode. However, the reverse is not possible.

To summarize, in noncanonical mode, the **ldterm** module buffers all data until a request for the data arrives in the form of an **M_READ** message. The number of bytes sent upstream is the argument of the **M_READ** message.

Input flow control is regulated by the **ldterm** module by generating **M_STARTI** and **M_STOPI** high-priority messages. When sent downstream, receiving drivers or modules take appropriate action to regulate the sending of data upstream. Output flow control is activated when **ldterm** receives flow control characters in its data stream. The **ldterm** module then sets an internal flag indicating that output processing is to be restarted/stopped and sends an **M_START/M_STOP** message downstream.

Write-Side Processing

Write-side processing of the **ldterm** module is performed by the write-side **put** and **service** procedures. The **ldterm** module supports the following **ioctl**s:

TCSETA, TCSETAW, TCSETAF, TCSETS, TCSETSW, TCSETSF, TCGETA, TCGETS, TCXONC, TCFLSH, TCSBRK, TIOCSWINSZ, TIOCGWINSZ, and **JWINSIZE**.

All **ioctl**s not recognized by the **ldterm** module are passed downstream to the neighboring module or driver. BSD functionality is turned off by **IEXTEN** [see **termio**(7) for more details].

The following messages can be received on the write-side:

M_DATA, M_DELAY, M_BREAK, M_FLUSH, M_STOP, M_START, M_STOPI, M_STARTI, M_READ, M_IOCDATA, M_CTL, and **M_IOCTL**.

On the write-side, the **ldterm** module processes **M_FLUSH, M_DATA, M_IOCTL**, and **M_READ** messages, and all other messages are passed downstream unchanged.

An **M_CTL** message is generated by **ldterm** as a query to the driver for an intelligent peripheral and to determine the functional split for **termio** processing. If all or part of **termio** processing is done by the intelligent peripheral, **ldterm** can turn off this processing to avoid computational overhead. This is done by sending an appropriate response to the **M_CTL** message, as follows: [see also **ldterm**(7)].

- If all the **termio** processing is done by the peripheral hardware, the driver sends an **M_CTL** message back to **ldterm** with **ioc_cmd** of the structure **iocblk** set to **MC_NO_CANON**. If **ldterm** is to handle all **termio** processing, the driver sends an **M_CTL** message with **ioc_cmd** set to **MC_DO_CANON**. Default is **MC_DO_CANON**.

- If the peripheral hardware handles only part of the **termio** processing, it informs **ldterm** in the following way:

  The driver for the peripheral device allocates an **M_DATA** message large enough to hold a **termios** structure. The driver then turns on those **c_iflag**, **c_oflag**, and **c_lflag** fields of the **termios** structure that are processed on the peripheral device by ORing the flag values. The **M_DATA** message is then attached to the **b_cont** field of the **M_CTL** message it received. The message is sent back to **ldterm** with **ioc_cmd** in the data buffer of the **M_CTL** message set to **MC_PART_CANON**.

The **ldterm** module does not check if write-side flow control is in effect before forwarding data downstream. It expects the downstream module or driver to queue the messages on its queue until flow control is lifted.

EUC Handling in ldterm

The idea of letting post-processing (the **o_flags**) happen off the host processor is not recommended unless the board software is prepared to deal with international (EUC) character sets properly. The reason for this is that post-processing must take the EUC information into account. **ldterm** knows about the screen width of characters (that is, how many columns are taken by characters from each given code set on the current physical display) and it takes this width into account when calculating tab expansions. When using multibyte characters or multicolumn characters **ldterm** automatically handles tab expansion (when **TAB3** is set) and does not leave this handling to a lower module or driver.

By default, multibyte handling by **ldterm** is turned off. When **ldterm** receives an **EUC_WSET ioctl** call, it turns multibyte processing on, if it is essential to handle properly the indicated code set. Thus, if one is using single byte 8-bit codes and has no special multicolumn requirements, the special multicolumn processing is not used at all. This means that multibyte processing does not reduce the processing speed or efficiency of **ldterm** unless it is actually used.

The following describes how the EUC handling in **ldterm** works:

First, the multibyte and multicolumn character handling is only enabled when the **EUC_WSET ioctl** indicates that one of the following conditions is met:

- Code set consists of more than one byte (including the **SS2** and/or **SS3**) of characters.

- Code set requires more than one column to display on the current device, as indicated in the **EUC_WSET** structure.

Assuming that one or more of the above conditions, EUC handling is enabled. At this point, a parallel array, used for other information, is allocated. When a byte with the high bit arrives, it is checked to see if it is **SS2** or **SS3**. If so, it belongs to code set 2 or 3. Otherwise, it is a byte that comes from code set 1. Once the extended code set flag has been set, the input processor retrieves the subsequent bytes, as they arrive, to build one multibyte character. A counter field tells the input processor how many bytes remain to be read for the current character. The parallel array holds the display width of each logical character in the canonical buffer. During erase processing, positions in the parallel array are consulted to figure out how many backspaces need to be sent to erase each logical character. (In canonical mode, one backspace of input erases one logical character, no matter how many bytes or columns that character consumes.) This greatly simplifies erase processing for EUC.

The **t_maxeuc** field holds the maximum length, in memory bytes, of the EUC character mapping currently in use. The **eucwioc** field is a substructure, which holds information about each extended code set.

The **t_eucign** field aids in output post-processing (tab expansion). When characters are output, **ldterm** keeps a column to show the current cursor column. When it sends the first byte of an extended character, it adds the number of columns required for that character to the output column. It then subtracts one from the total width in memory bytes of that character and stores the result in **t_eucign**. This field tells **ldterm** how many bytes to ignore for the purposes of column calculation. (**ldterm** calculates the appropriate number of columns when it sees the first byte of the character.)

The field **t_eucwarn** is a counter for occurrences of bad extended characters. It is mostly useful for debugging. After receiving a certain number of invalid EUC characters (perhaps because of some problem on the line or with declared values), a warning is given on the system console.

There are two relevant files for handling multibyte characters: **<euc.h>** and **<eucioctl.h>**. The **<eucioctl.h>** header contains the structure that is passed with **EUC_WSET** and **EUC_WGET** calls. The normal way to use this structure is to get **CSWIDTH** (see note below) from the locale using a mechanism such as **getwidth** or **setlocale** and then copy the values into the structure in **<eucioctl.h>**, and send the structure using an **I_STR ioctl** call. The **EUC_WSET** call informs the **ldterm** module about the number of bytes in extended characters and how many columns the extended characters from each set consume on the screen. This allows **ldterm** to treat multibyte characters as single entities for erase processing and to calculate correctly tab expansions for multibyte characters.

NOTE

LC_CTYPE (instead of CSWIDTH) should be used in the environment in UNIX System V Release 4 systems. See chrtbl(1M) for more information.

The file **<euc.h>** has the structure with fields for EUC width, screen width, and wide character width. The following functions are used to set and get EUC widths (these functions assume the environment where the **eucwidth_t** structure is needed and available):

```
#include <eucioctl.h>        /* need some other things too, like
                                stropts.h */
struct eucioc eucw;          /* for EUC_WSET/EUC_WGET to line discipline */
eucwidth_t width;            /* return struct from _getwidth() */
/*
 * set_euc        Send EUC code widths to line discipline.
 */
set_euc(e)
        set_euc(struct eucioc *e)
        {
        struct strioctl sb;

        sb.ic_cmd = EUC_WSET;
        sb.ic_timout = 15;
        sb.ic_len = sizeof(struct eucioc);
        sb.ic_dp = (char *) e;

        if (ioctl(0, I_STR, &sb) < 0)
                fail();
        }
/*
 * euclook        Get current EUC code widths from line discipline.
 */
euclook(e)
        euclook(struct eucioc *e)
        {
        struct strioctl sb;

        sb.ic_cmd = EUC_WGET;
        sb.ic_timout = 15;
        sb.ic_len = sizeof(struct eucioc);
        sb.ic_dp = (char *) e;
        if (ioctl(0, I_STR, &sb) < 0)
                fail();
        printf("CSWIDTH=%d:%d,%d:%d,%d:%d0,
                                        e->eucw[1], e->scrw[1],
                                        e->eucw[2], e->scrw[2],
                                        e->eucw[3], e->scrw[3]);
        }
```

The brief discussion of multiple byte character handling by the **ldterm** module was provided here for those interested in internationalization applications in UNIX System V.

Support of termiox

UNIX System V Release 4 includes the extended general terminal interface [see **termiox**(7)] that supplements the **termio**(7) general terminal interface by adding for asynchronous hardware flow control, isochronous flow control and clock modes, and local implementations of additional asynchronous features. **termiox**(7) is handled by hardware drivers if the board supports it.

Hardware flow control supplements the **termio**(7) **IXON, IXOFF**, and **IXANY** character flow control. The **termiox**(7) interface allows for both unidirectional and bidirectional hardware flow control. Isochronous communication is a variation of asynchronous communication where two communicating devices provide transmit and/or receive clock to each other. Incoming clock signals can be taken from the baud rate generator on the local isochronous port controller. Outgoing signals are sent on the receive and transmit baud rate generator on the local isochronous port controller.

Terminal parameters are specified in the **termiox** structure that is defined in the **<termiox.h>**.

Hardware Emulation Module

If a Stream supports a terminal interface, a driver or module that understands all **ioctl**s to support terminal semantics (specified by **termio** and **termios**) is needed. If there is no hardware driver that understands all **ioctl** commands downstream from the **ldterm** module, a hardware emulation module must be placed downstream from the **ldterm** module. The function of the hardware emulation module is to understand and acknowledge the **ioctl**s that may be sent to the process at the Stream head and to mediate the passage of control information downstream. The combination of the **ldterm** module and the hardware emulation module behaves as if there were a terminal on that Stream.

The hardware emulation module is necessary whenever there is no tty driver at the end of the Stream. For example, it is necessary in a pseudo-tty situation where there is process-to-process communication on one system and in a network situation where a **termio** interface is expected (for example, remote login) but there is no tty driver on the Stream.

Most actions taken by the hardware emulation module are the same regardless of the underlying architecture. However, some actions differ depending on whether the communication is local or remote and whether the underlying transport protocol supports the remote connection.

Each hardware emulation module has an open, close, read queue **put** procedure, and write queue **put** procedure.

The hardware emulation module does the following:

- Processes, if appropriate, and acknowledges receipt of the following `ioctl`s on its write queue by sending an **M_IOCACK** message back upstream: **TCSETA, TCSETAW, TCSETAF, TCSETS, TCSETSW, TCSETSF, TCGETA, TCGETS,** and **TCSBRK**.

- Acknowledges the Extended UNIX Code (EUC) `ioctl`s.

- If the environment supports windowing, it acknowledges the windowing `ioctl`s **TIOCSWINSZ, TIOCGWINSZ,** and **JWINSIZE**. If the environment does not support windowing, an **M_IOCNAK** message is sent upstream.

- If any other `ioctl`s are received on its write queue, it sends an **M_IOCNAK** message upstream.

- When the hardware emulation module receives an **M_IOCTL** message of type **TCSBRK** on its write queue, it sends an **M_IOCACK** message upstream and the appropriate message downstream. For example, an **M_BREAK** message could be sent downstream.

- When the hardware emulation module receives an **M_IOCTL** message on its write queue to set the baud rate to 0 (**TCSETAW** with **CBAUD** set to **B0**), it sends an **M_IOCACK** message upstream and an appropriate message downstream; for networking situations this probably is an **M_PROTO** message, which is a TPI **T_DISCON_REQ** message requesting the transport provider to disconnect.

- All other messages (**M_DATA**, and so forth) not mentioned here are passed to the next module or driver in the Stream.

The hardware emulation module processes messages in a way consistent with the driver that exists below.

Terminal Device Control

STREAMS-based Pseudo-Terminal Subsystem

The pseudo-terminal subsystem (pseudo-tty) supports a pair of STREAMS-based devices called the "master" device and "slave" device. The slave device provides processes with an interface that is identical to the terminal interface. However, where all devices that provide the terminal interface have some hardware device behind them, the slave device has another process manipulating it through the master half of the pseudo terminal. Anything written on the master device is given to the slave as an input and anything written on the slave device is presented as an input on the master-side.

Figure 5-5 illustrates the architecture of the STREAMS-based pseudo-terminal subsystem. The master driver called **ptm** is accessed through the clone driver [see **clone**(7)] and is the controlling part of the system. The slave driver called **pts** works with the **ldterm** module and the hardware emulation module to provide a terminal interface to the user process. An optional packetizing module called **pckt** is also provided. It can be pushed on the master-side to support packet mode.

The number of pseudo-tty devices that can be installed on a system depends on available memory.

Line Discipline Module

In the pseudo-tty subsystem (see Figure 5-5), the line discipline module **ldterm** is pushed on the slave side to present the user with the terminal interface.

ldterm may turn off the processing of the **c_iflag**, **c_oflag**, and **c_lflag** fields to allow processing to take place elsewhere. The **ldterm** module may also turn off all canonical processing when it receives an **M_CTL** message with the **MC_NO_CANON** command to support remote mode. Although **ldterm** passes through messages without processing them, the appropriate flags are set when a "get" **ioctl**, such as **TCGETA** or **TCGETS**, is issued to show that canonical processing is being performed.

Figure 5-5: Pseudo-tty Subsystem Architecture

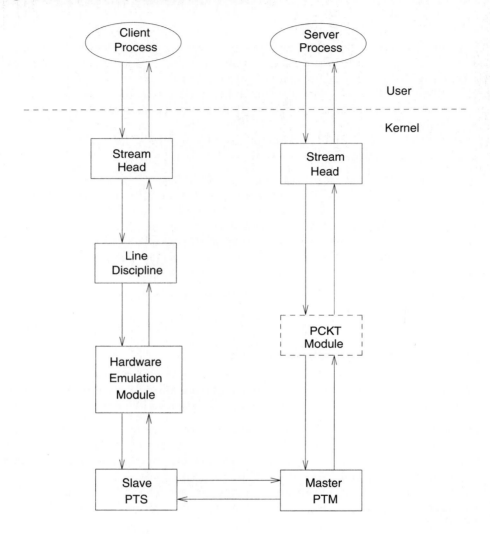

Terminal Device Control

Pseudo-tty Emulation Module — ptem

Because the pseudo-tty subsystem has no hardware driver downstream from the ldterm module to process the terminal ioctl calls, another module that understands the ioctl commands is placed downstream from the ldterm. This module, known as ptem, processes all the terminal ioctl commands and mediates the passage of control information downstream.

ldterm and ptem together behave like a real terminal. Because there is no real terminal or modem in the pseudo-tty subsystem, some of the ioctl commands are ignored and cause only an acknowledgement of the command. The ptem module keeps track of the terminal parameters set by the various "set" commands such as TCSETA or TCSETAW but does not usually perform any action. For example, if one of the "set" ioctls is called, none of the bits in the c_cflag field of termio has any effect on the pseudo-terminal except if the baud rate is set to 0. When setting the baud rate to 0, it has the effect of hanging up the pseudo-terminal.

The pseudo-terminal has no concept of parity so none of the flags in the c_iflag that control the processing of parity errors have any effect. The delays specified in the c_oflag field are not also supported.

The ptem module does the following:

- Processes, if appropriate, and acknowledges receipt of the following ioctls on its write queue by sending an M_IOCACK message back upstream:

  TCSETA, TCSETAW, TCSETAF, TCSETS, TCSETSW, TCSETSF, TCGETA, TCGETS, and TCSBRK.

- Keeps track of the window size; information needed for the TIOCSWINSZ, TIOCGWINSZ, and JWINSIZE ioctl commands.

- When it receives any other ioctl on its write queue, it sends an M_IOCNAK message upstream.

- It passes downstream the following ioctls after processing them:

  TCSETA, TCSETAW, TCSETAF, TCSETS, TCSETSW, TCSETSF, TCSBRK, and TIOCSWINSZ.

- ptem frees any M_IOCNAK messages it receives on its read queue in case the pckt module is not on the pseudo-terminal subsystem and the above ioctls get to the master's Stream head, which then sends an M_IOCNAK message.

- In its open routine, the ptem module sends an M_SETOPTS message upstream requesting allocation of a controlling tty.

- When the **ptem** module receives an **M_IOCTL** message of type **TCSBRK** on its read queue, it sends an **M_IOCACK** message downstream and an **M_BREAK** message upstream.

- When it receives an **ioctl** message on its write queue to set the baud rate to 0 (**TCSETAW** with CBAUD set to B0), it sends an **M_IOCACK** message upstream and a 0-length message downstream.

- When it receives an **M_IOCTL** of type **TIOCSIGNAL** on its read queue, it sends an **M_IOCACK** downstream and an **M_PCSIG** upstream where the signal number is the same as in the **M_IOCTL** message.

- When the **ptem** module receives an **M_IOCTL** of type **TIOCREMOTE** on its read queue, it sends an **M_IOCACK** message downstream and the appropriate **M_CTL** message upstream to enable/disable canonical processing.

- When it receives an **M_DELAY** message on its read or write queue, it discards the message and does not act on it.

- When it receives an **M_IOCTL** message with type **JWINSIZE** on its write queue and if the values in the **jwinsize** structure of **ptem** are not zero, it sends an **M_IOCACK** message upstream with the **jwinsize** structure. If the values are zero, it sends an **M_IOCNAK** message upstream.

- When it receives an **M_IOCTL** message of type **TIOCGWINSZ** on its write queue and if the values in the **winsize** structure are not zero, it sends an **M_IOCACK** message upstream with the **winsize** structure. If the values are zero, it sends an **M_IOCNAK** message upstream. It also saves the information passed to it in the **winsize** structure and sends a STREAMS signal message for signal **SIGWINCH** upstream to the slave process if the size changed.

- When the **ptem** module receives an **M_IOCTL** message with type **TIOCGWINSZ** on its read queue and if the values in the **winsize** structure are not zero, it sends an **M_IOCACK** message downstream with the **winsize** structure. If the values are zero, it sends an **M_IOCNAK** message downstream. It also saves the information passed to it in the **winsize** structure and sends a STREAMS signal message for signal **SIGWINCH** upstream to the slave process if the size changed.

- All other messages not mentioned above are passed to the next module or driver.

Remote Mode

A feature known as remote mode is available with the pseudo-tty subsystem. This feature is used for applications that perform the canonical function normally done by the `ldterm` module and tty driver. The remote mode allows applications on the master-side to turn off the canonical processing. An `ioctl TIOCREMOTE` with a nonzero parameter [`ioctl(fd, TIOCREMOTE, 1)`] is issued on the master-side to enter the remote mode. When this occurs, an `M_CTL` message with the command `MC_NO_CANON` is sent to the `ldterm` module indicating that data should be passed when received on the read-side and no canonical processing is to take place. The remote mode may be disabled by `ioctl(fd, TIOCREMOTE, 0)`.

Packet Mode

The STREAMS-based pseudo-terminal subsystem also supports a feature called packet mode. This is used to inform the process on the master-side when "state" changes have occurred in the pseudo-tty. Packet mode is enabled by pushing the `pckt` module on the master-side. Data written on the master-side is processed normally. When data is written on the slave-side or when other messages are encountered by the `pckt` module, a header is added to the message so it can be retrieved later by the master-side with a `getmsg` operation.

The `pckt` module does the following:

- When a message is passed to this module on its write queue, the module does no processing and passes the message to the next module or driver.

- The `pckt` module creates an `M_PROTO` message when one of the following messages is passed to it:

  `M_DATA`, `M_IOCTL`, `M_PROTO`/`M_PCPROTO`, `M_FLUSH`, `M_START`/`M_STOP`, `M_STARTI`/`M_STOPI`, and `M_READ`.

  All other messages are passed through. The `M_PROTO` message is passed upstream and retrieved when the user issues `getmsg(2)`.

- If the message is an `M_FLUSH` message, `pckt` does the following:

  If the flag is `FLUSHW`, it is changed to `FLUSHR` (because `FLUSHR` was the original flag before the `pts` driver changed it), packetized into an `M_PROTO` message, and passed upstream. To prevent the Stream head's read queue from being flushed, the original `M_FLUSH` message must not be passed upstream.

  If the flag is `FLUSHR`, it is changed to `FLUSHW`, packetized into an `M_PROTO` message, and passed upstream. To flush the write queues properly, an `M_FLUSH` message with the `FLUSHW` flag set is also sent upstream.

If the flag is **FLUSHRW**, the message with both flags set is packetized and passed upstream. An **M_FLUSH** message with the **FLUSHW** flag set is also sent upstream.

Pseudo-tty Drivers — ptm and pts

In order to use the pseudo-tty subsystem, a node for the master-side driver **/dev/ptmx** and N number of slave drivers must be installed. (N is determined at installation time.) The names of the slave devices are **/dev/pts/**M where M has the values 0 through N-1. A user accesses a pseudo-tty device through the master device (called **ptm**) that in turn is accessed through the clone driver [see **clone**(7)]. The master device is set up as a clone device where its major device number is the major for the clone device and its minor device number is the major for the **ptm** driver.

The master pseudo-driver is opened by the **open** system call with **/dev/ptmx** as the device to be opened. The clone open finds the next available minor device for that major device; a master device is available only if it and its corresponding slave device are not already open. There are no nodes in the file system for master devices.

When the master device is opened, the corresponding slave device is automatically locked out. No user may open that slave device until it is unlocked. A user may invoke a function **grantpt** that will change the owner of the slave device to that of the user who is running this process, change the group ID to **tty**, and change the mode of the device to **0620**. Once the permissions have been changed, the device may be unlocked by the user. Only the owner or superuser can access the slave device. The user must then invoke the **unlockpt** function to unlock the slave device. Before opening the slave device, the user must call the **ptsname** function to obtain the name of the slave device. The functions **grantpt**, **unlockpt**, and **ptsname** are called with the file descriptor of the master device. The user may then invoke the **open** system call with the name that was returned by the **ptsname** function to open the slave device.

The following example shows how a user may invoke the pseudo-tty subsystem:

```
int fdm fds;
char *slavename;
extern char *ptsname();

fdm = open("/dev/ptmx", O_RDWR);    /* open master */
grantpt(fdm);                        /* change permission of slave */
unlockpt(fdm);                       /* unlock slave */
slavename = ptsname(fdm);            /* get name of slave */
fds = open(slavename, O_RDWR);       /* open slave */
ioctl(fds, I_PUSH, "ptem");          /* push ptem */
ioctl(fds, I_PUSH, "ldterm");        /* push ldterm */
```

Unrelated processes may open the pseudo-device. The initial user may pass the
master file descriptor using a STREAMS-based pipe or a slave name to another
process to enable it to open the slave. After the slave device is open, the owner is
free to change the permissions.

 NOTE   Certain programs such as **write** and **wall** are set group-ID (**setgid**) to **tty**
and are also able to access the slave device.

After both the master and slave have been opened, the user has two file descriptors that provide full-duplex communication using two Streams. The two Streams
are automatically connected. The user may then push modules onto either side of
the Stream. The user also needs to push the **ptem** and **ldterm** modules onto the
slave-side of the pseudo-terminal subsystem to get terminal semantics.

The master and slave drivers pass all STREAMS messages to their adjacent
queues. Only the **M_FLUSH** needs some processing. Because the read queue of one
side is connected to the write queue of the other, the **FLUSHR** flag is changed to
FLUSHW flag and vice versa.

When the master device is closed, an **M_HANGUP** message is sent to the slave device
that will render the device unusable. The process on the slave-side gets the **errno**
ENXIO when attempting to write on that Stream but it will be able to read any data
remaining on the Stream head read queue. When all the data has been read, **read**
returns **0** indicating that the Stream can no longer be used.

On the last close of the slave device, a 0-length message is sent to the master
device. When the application on the master-side issues a **read** or **getmsg** and **0** is
returned, the user of the master device decides whether to issue a **close** that dismantles the pseudo-terminal subsystem. If the master device is not closed, the
pseudo-tty subsystem will be available to another user to open the slave device.

Because 0-length messages are used to indicate that the process on the slave-side has closed and should be interpreted that way by the process on the master-side, applications on the slave-side should not **write** 0-length messages. If that occurs, the **write** returns 0, and the 0-length message is discarded by the **ptem** module.

The standard STREAMS system calls can access the pseudo-tty devices. The slave devices support the **O_NDELAY** and **O_NONBLOCK** flags. Because the master-side does not act like the terminal, if **O_NONBLOCK** or **O_NDELAY** is set, **read** on the master side returns **-1** with **errno** set to **EAGAIN** if no data is available, and **write** returns **-1** with **errno** set to **EAGAIN** if there is internal flow control.

The master driver supports the **ISPTM** and **UNLKPT** **ioctl**s that are used by the functions **grantpt**, **unlockpt**, and **ptsname** [see **grantpt**(3C), **unlockpt**(3C), **ptsname**(3C)]. The **ioctl** **ISPTM** determines whether the file descriptor is that of an open master device. On success, it returns the major/minor number (type **dev_t**) of the master device that can be used to determine the name of the corresponding slave device. The **ioctl** **UNLKPT** unlocks the master and slave devices. It returns 0 on success. On failure, the **errno** is set to **EINVAL** indicating that the master device is not open.

The format of these commands is

        int ioctl (int *fd*, int *command*, int *arg*)

where *command* is either **ISPTM** or **UNLKPT** and *arg* is 0. On failure, **-1** is returned.

When data is written to the master-side, the entire block of data written is treated as a single line. The slave-side process reading the terminal receives the entire block of data. Data is not input-edited by the **ldterm** module regardless of the terminal mode. The master-side application is responsible for detecting an interrupt character and sending an interrupt signal **SIGINT** to the process in the slave-side. This can be done as follows:

        ioctl (*fd*, TIOCSIGNAL, SIGINT)

where **SIGINT** is defined in the file **<signal.h>**. When a process on the master-side issues this **ioctl**, the argument is the number of the signal that should be sent. The specified signal is then sent to the process group on the slave-side.

To summarize, the master driver and slave driver have the following characteristics:

- Each master driver has a one-to-one relationship with a slave device based on major/minor device numbers.

- Only one open is allowed on a master device. Multiple opens are allowed on the slave device according to standard file mode and ownership permissions.

- Each slave driver minor device has a node in the file system.

- An open on a master device automatically locks out an open on the corresponding slave driver.

- A slave cannot be opened unless the corresponding master is open and has unlocked the slave.

- To provide a tty interface to the user, the **ldterm** and **ptem** modules are pushed on the slave-side.

- A **close** on the master sends a hang-up to the slave and renders both Streams unusable after all data has been consumed by the process on the slave side.

- The last **close** on the slave-side sends a 0-length message to the master but does not sever the connection between the master and slave drivers.

grantpt

The **grantpt** function changes the mode and the ownership of the slave device that is associated with the given master device. Given a file descriptor *fd*, **grantpt** first checks that the file descriptor is that of the master device. If so, it obtains the name of the associated slave device and sets the user ID to that of the user running the process and the group ID to **tty**. The mode of the slave device is set to **0620**.

If the process is already running as root, the permission of the slave can be changed directly without invoking this function. The interface is

      grantpt (int *fd***)**

The **grantpt** function returns **0** on success and **-1** on failure. It fails if one or more of the following occurs: *fd* is not an open file descriptor, *fd* is not associated with a master device, the corresponding slave could not be accessed, or a system call failed because no more processes could be created.

unlockpt

The **unlockpt** function clears a lock flag associated with a **master/slave** device pair. Its interface is

      unlockpt (int *fd***)**

The **unlockpt** returns **0** on success and **-1** on failure. It fails if one or more of the following occurs: *fd* is not an open file descriptor or *fd* is not associated with a master device.

ptsname

The **ptsname** function returns the name of the slave device that is associated with the given master device. It first checks that the file descriptor is that of the master. If it is, it then determines the name of the corresponding slave device **/dev/pts/**M and returns a pointer to a string containing the null-terminated pathname. The return value points to static data whose content is overwritten by each call. The interface is

```
char *ptsname (int fd)
```

The **ptsname** function returns a non-**NULL** pathname on success and a **NULL** pointer upon failure. It fails if one or more of the following occurs: *fd* is not an open file descriptor or *fd* is not associated with the master device.

6 Internationalization

Introduction

This chapter describes the programming interface to the UNIX System V internationalization feature. Its primary audience is the application programmer in C, although it may be of interest to system programmers and, to a lesser extent, administrators. We assume that readers are experienced in the UNIX system and the C language.

The chapter consists of a discussion of the programming interface, and covers only as much of the interface as programmers will need to get started. Much of the details can be found in the manual pages of the reference set. A list of UNIX system commands that have been enhanced for internationalization is provided in this chapter.

For the most part, the discussion concentrates on the System V implementation of ANSI standard C functions. These routines are supported in turn by the X/Open consortium, of which many System V vendors are members. To provide as realistic a view as possible, we give the locations of files used by these functions as they would be installed on a System V target implementation. You should not assume that these will be their locations on other X/Open or ANSI C-conforming systems, nor should you assume that these locations are permanent even on System V installations. In other words, the path names we provide should not be hardcoded in programs intended to be portable across UNIX or C language implementations. Similarly, although some type of "extended character set" will be supported on every X/Open and ANSI C-conforming system, the discussion below of "extended UNIX code" (EUC) is specific to System V, and should not be taken to describe the character encoding elsewhere.

Of course, both System V and X/Open go beyond the ANSI C standard in various other ways, most importantly in providing facilities for handling program messages in international contexts. In this regard, note that System V offers two distinct approaches to message handling, only one of which is standard to X/Open. Although we describe both approaches below, keep in mind that the X/Open method is employed throughout much of Europe, so you can generally count on wider support for it than for the System V-specific method. By and large, System V internationalization is aligned with the X/Open *Portability Guide Issue 4*. We depart from it significantly only in not providing full support for internationalized regul ar expressions.

Discussion

This chapter describes C language functions that you can use to write UNIX applications that will process input and generate output in a user's native language or cultural environment. It shows you how to use these functions and some associated commands to create programs that make no assumptions about the language environments in which they will be run, and so are portable across these environments. We'll also look at a STREAMS module called **kbd** (for "keyboard display") that can be programmed to alter or supplement data as it flows between the physical terminal and a user process to produce language-dependent effects: for example, characters that cannot be entered from terminal keyboards, for instance, or overstriking sequences on printers.

The basic idea behind the internationalization interface is that at any time a C program has a current "locale": a collection of information on which it relies for language- or culture-dependent processing. This information is supplied by implementations and seen by the program only at run time. Because the information is stored externally to the program, applications need not make — and should not make if they mean to be portable — any assumptions about

- the *code sets* used by the implementation in which they are executed. The 7-bit US ASCII code set, for example, cannot represent every member of the Spanish character set; the 8-bit code sets used for most European languages cannot represent every ideogram and phonogram in the Japanese language.

- the *cultural and language conventions* of the application's users. The same date is formatted in the United States as **6/14/90**, in Great Britain as **14/6/90**, in Germany as **14.6.90**. Similar problems arise in formatting numeric and monetary values. By language conventions we mean, for instance, that the sharp **s** in German is collated as **ss**; the character **ch** in Spanish collated after all other character sequences starting with **c**.

- the *language of the messages* in which the program communicates with the user. Interactive applications in an English-speaking setting usually will query users at some point for a **yes** or **no** response; in a German-language setting the responses will be **ja** or **nein**; in a French one **oui** or **non**. Program error messages will differ much more widely than that across languages: **File not found**, **Fichier inexistant**, and so on.

A typical locale, then, consists of an encoding scheme; databases that describe the conventions appropriate to some nationality, culture, and language; and a file which you supply, that contains your program's message strings in whatever language the locale implements.

Organization

The discussion is organized in terms of these three elements of a locale. "Character Representation" describes the character encoding used by System V implementations that support the internationalization feature, and the ANSI C library functions that perform codeset-dependent tasks. It also discusses the sequences of bytes, or "multibyte characters," that are needed to encode Asian-language ideograms. "Cultural and Language Conventions" looks at ANSI C functions that collate strings and format cultural information in locale-dependent ways. "Message Handling" describes the functions you use to generate program messages in a user's native language. The "**kbd**" section outlines the function of the STREAMS module used as the keyboard display interface. Before we turn to this material, there's some background we need to give on how C programs determine their locales.

> **NOTE** For the relationship of System V internationalization to the ANSI C and X/Open standards, see the "Introduction" section in the beginning of this chapter.

Locales

One or more locales is provided by every UNIX system implementation that supports the internationalization feature. Each UNIX System V program begins in the **"C"** locale, which causes all library functions to behave as they have historically; any other locale will cause certain of these functions to behave in the appropriate language- or culture-dependent ways. Locales can have names that are strings — **"french"**, **"german"**, and so forth (or **"fr"** and **"de"**, following ISO conventions) — but only **"C"** and **""** are guaranteed. When given as the second argument to the ANSI C **setlocale** function, the string **""** tells the program to change its current locale to the one set by the user, or the system administrator for all users, in the UNIX system shell environment. Any other argument will cause the program to change its current locale to the one specified by the string.

Locales are partitioned into categories:

LC_CTYPE	character representation information
LC_TIME	date and time printing information
LC_MONETARY	currency printing information
LC_NUMERIC	numeric printing information
LC_COLLATE	sorting information
LC_MESSAGES	message information

In the implementation's view, these categories are files in directories named for each locale it supports; the directories themselves are usually kept in **/usr/lib/locale**. In the user's view, the categories are environment variables that can be set to given locales:

```
$ LC_COLLATE=german export LC_COLLATE
$ LC_CTYPE=french export LC_CTYPE
$ LC_MESSAGES=french export LC_MESSAGES
```

In the program's view, the categories are macros that can be passed as the first argument to **setlocale** to specify that it change the program's locale for just that category. That is,

```
setlocale(LC_COLLATE, "");
```

tells the program to use the sorting information for the locale specified in the environment, in this case, **german**, but leaves the other categories unchanged.

LC_ALL is the macro that specifies the entire locale. Given the environment setup above, the code

```
setlocale(LC_ALL, "");
```

would allow a user to work in a French interface to a program while sorting German text files. Incidentally, the **LANG** environment variable is the user equivalent of **LC_ALL**; setting it to **spanish**, for instance, causes all the categories to be set to **spanish** in the environment. **LANG** is checked after the environment variables for individual categories, so a user could set a category to **french** and use **LANG** to set the other categories to **spanish**.

setlocale, then, is the interface to the program's locale. Any program that has a need to use language or cultural conventions should put a call such as

```
#include <locale.h>
/*...*/
setlocale(LC_ALL, "");
```

early in its execution path. You'll generally want to use **""** as the second argument to **setlocale** so that your application will change locales correctly for whatever language environment in which it is run. Occasionally, though, you may want to change the locale or a portion of it for a limited duration in a way that's transparent to the user.

Suppose, for example, there are parts of your program that need only the ASCII upper- and lowercase characters guaranteed by ANSI C in the **<ctype.h>** header. In these parts, in other words, you want the program to see the character classification information in **LC_CTYPE** for the **"C"** locale. Since the user of the program in a non-ASCII environment will presumably have set **LC_CTYPE** to a locale other than **"C"**, and will not be able to change its setting mid-program, you'll have to arrange for the program to change its **LC_CTYPE** locale whenever it is in those parts. **setlocale** returns the name of the current locale for a given category and serves in an inquiry-only capacity when its second argument is a null pointer. So you might want to use code something like this:

```
char *oloc;
/*...*/
oloc = setlocale(LC_CTYPE, NULL);
if (setlocale(LC_CTYPE, "C") != 0)
{
    /* use temporarily changed locale */
    (void)setlocale(LC_CTYPE, oloc);
}
```

The **setlocale**(3C) function is described in section (3C) of the reference manual set.

Character Representation

Every System V implementation that supports the internationalization feature can represent up to four code sets concurrently in an 8-bit byte stream. The code sets are configured in a scheme called "extended UNIX code," or EUC. The primary code set (code set 0) is always 7-bit US ASCII. Each byte of any character in a supplementary code set (code sets 1,2, or 3) has the high-order bit set; code sets 2 and 3 are distinguished from code set 1 and each other by their use of a special "shift byte" before each character.

Figure 6-1: EUC Code Set Representations

Code Set	EUC Representation
0	0xxxxxxx
1	1xxxxxxx [1xxxxxxx [...]]
2	SS2 1xxxxxxx [1xxxxxxx [...]]
3	SS3 1xxxxxxx [1xxxxxxx [...]]

SS2 is represented in hexadecimal by 0x8e, SS3 by 0x8f.

EUC is provided mainly to support the huge number of ideograms needed for I/O in an Asian-language environment. To work within the constraints of usual computer architectures, these ideograms are encoded as sequences of bytes, or "multibyte characters." Because single-byte characters (the digits 0–9, say) can be intermixed with multibyte characters, the sequence of bytes needed to encode an ideogram must be self-identifying: regardless of the supplementary code set used, each byte of a multibyte character will have the high-order bit set; if code sets 2 or 3 are used, each multibyte character will also be preceded by a shift byte. In a moment, we'll take a closer look at multibyte characters and at the implementation-defined integral type **wchar_t** that lets you manipulate variable width characters as uniformly sized data objects called "wide characters." We'll also discuss the functions you use to manage multibyte and wide characters.

Of course, programmers developing applications for less complex linguistic environments need not concern themselves with the details of multibyte or wide character processing. In Europe, for instance, a single 8-bit code set can hold all the characters of the major languages. In these environments, at least one 8-bit character set will be represented in the EUC code sets, usually code sets 0 and 1. Other character sets may be represented simultaneously, in various combinations. Applications will work correctly with any standard 7- or 8-bit character set,

Internationalization

provided (1) they are "8-bit clean" — they make no assumptions about the contents of the high-order bit when processing characters; and (2) they use correctly the functions supplied by the interface for codeset-dependent tasks — character classification and conversion, in other words. We'll take a brief look at these issues now.

"8-bit Clean"

UNIX system applications written for 7-bit US ASCII environments have sometimes assumed that the high-order bit is available for purposes other than character processing. In data communications, for instance, it was often used as a parity bit. On receipt and after a parity check, the high-order bit was stripped either by the line discipline or the program to obtain the original 7-bit character:

```
char c;
/* bitwise AND with octal value 177 strips high-order bit */
c &= 0177;
```

Other programs used the high-order bit as a private data storage area, usually to test a flag:

```
char c;
/*...*/
c |= 0200;   /* bitwise OR with octal value 200 sets flag */
/*...*/
c &= 0177;   /* bitwise AND removes flag */
/*...*/
if (c & 0200)/* test if flag set */
{
/*...*/
}
c &= 0177;   /* original character */
```

Neither of these practices will work with 8-bit or larger code sets. To show you how to store data in a codeset-independent way, we'll look at code fragments from a UNIX system program before and after it was made 8-bit clean. In the first fragment, the program sets the high-order bit of characters quoted on the command line:

```
#define LITERAL '\''
#define QUOTE 0200
register int c;
register char *argp = arg->argval;

if (c == LITERAL)  /* character is a single quote */
{
        /* get next character until next single quote */
        while ((c = getc()) && c != LITERAL)
        {
                *argp++ = (c | QUOTE);
        }
}
```

In the next fragment, the same data are stored by internally placing backslashes before quoted characters in the command string:

```
#define LITERAL '\''
register int c;
register unsigned char *argp = arg->argval;

if (c == LITERAL)
{
        while ((c = getc()) && c != LITERAL)
        {
        /* precede each character within single quotes with a backslash */
                *argp++ = '\\';
                *argp++ = c;
        }
}
```

Because the data are stored in 8-bit character values rather than the high-order bit of the quoted characters, the program will work correctly with code sets other than US ASCII. Note, by the way, the use of the type **unsigned char** in the declaration of the character pointer in the second fragment. We'll discuss the reasons why you use it in the next section.

Character Classification and Conversion

The ANSI C functions declared in the `<ctype.h>` header file classify or convert character-coded integer values according to type and conversion information in the program's locale. All the classification functions except `isdigit` and `isxdigit` can return nonzero (true) for single-byte supplementary code set characters when the `LC_CTYPE` category of the current locale is other than `"C"`. In a Spanish locale, `isalpha('n')` should be true. Similarly, the case conversion functions `toupper` and `tolower` will appropriately convert any single-byte supplementary code set characters identified by the `isalpha` function.

The point of these functions is to let you determine a character's type or case without reference to its numeric value in a given code set. Whereas a program written for a US ASCII environment might test whether a character is printable with the code

```
if ( c <= 037 || c == 0177 )
```

a codeset-independent program will use `isprint`:

```
if ( !isprint(c) )
```

Similarly,

```
c = toupper(c);
```

will do the same thing as

```
if( c >= 'a' && c <= 'z')
    c += 'a' -'A';
```

without relying on the fact that upper- and lowercase characters are numerically contiguous in the US ASCII code set.

The `<ctype.h>` functions are almost always macros that are implemented using table lookups indexed by the character argument. Their behavior is changed by resetting the table(s) to the new locale's values, so there should be no performance impact. The classification functions are described on the `ctype`(3C) manual page, the conversion functions on the `conv`(3C) page. Both single- and multibyte character classification and conversion routines are declared in the `<wctype.h>` header, and described on the pages `wctype`(3W) and `wconv`(3W). Note that the multibyte routines are not part of the ANSI C standard, nor are the single-byte functions `isascii` and `toascii`.

Sign Extension

In some C language implementations, character variables that are not explicitly declared **signed** or **unsigned** are treated as nonnegative quantities with a range typically from 0 to 255. In other implementations, they are treated as signed quantities with a range typically from -128 to 127. When a signed object of type **char** is converted to a wider integer, the machine is obliged to propagate the sign, which is encoded in the high-order bit of the new integer object. If the character variable holds an eight-bit character with the high-order bit set, the sign bit will be propagated the full width of an object of type **int** or **long**, producing a negative value.

You can avoid this problem (which typically occurs with the **ctype** functions) by declaring as **unsigned** any object of type **char** that is liable to be converted to a wider integer. In the example we showed earlier, for instance, the declaration of the character pointer as of type **unsigned char** would guarantee that on any implementation the values pointed at will be nonnegative.

Characters Used as Indices

A related problem arises when characters are used as indices into arrays and tables. If a table has been defined to contain only 128 possible characters, the amount of allocated memory will be exceeded if an eight-bit character whose value is greater than 127 is used as an index. Moreover, if the character is signed, the index may be negative.

The solution, at least when dealing with 8-bit code sets, is obviously to increase the size of the table from the 7-bit maximum of 128 to the 8-bit maximum of 256. And again, to declare the object that will hold the character as type **unsigned char**.

Wide Characters

Earlier in this section we looked at the encoding scheme used for the multibyte characters that are needed to represent Asian-language ideograms. We noted that because single-byte characters can be intermixed with multibyte characters, the sequence of bytes needed to encode an ideogram must be self-identifying: regardless of the supplementary code set used, each byte of a multibyte character will have the high-order bit set. In this way, any byte of a multibyte character can always be distinguished from a member of the primary, 7-bit US ASCII code set, whose high-order bit is not set (or "0"). If code sets 2 or 3 are used, each multibyte character will also be preceded by a shift byte; that is, if code set 1 were dedicated to a single-byte character set, either of code sets 2 or 3 could be used to represent multibyte characters. Given some set of these encodings, then any program interested in the next character will be able to determine whether the next byte represents a single-byte character or the first byte of a multibyte character. If the latter, then the program will have to retrieve bytes until the character is complete.

Some of the inconvenience of handling multibyte characters would be eliminated, of course, if all characters were a uniform number of bytes. ANSI C provides the implementation-defined integral type **wchar_t** to let you manipulate variable-width characters as uniformly sized data objects called wide characters. Since there can be thousands or tens of thousands of ideograms in an Asian-language set, programs should use a 32-bit sized integral value to hold all members. **wchar_t** is defined in the headers **<stdlib.h>** and **<widec.h>** as a **typedef** declaration of **long**.

Implementations provide appropriate libraries with functions that you can use to manage multibyte and wide characters. We'll look at these functions below.

For each wide character there is a corresponding EUC representation and vice versa; the wide character that corresponds to a regular single-byte character is required to have the same numeric value as its single-byte value, including the null character. There is no guarantee that the value of the macro **EOF** can be stored in a **wchar_t**, just as **EOF** might not be representable as a **char**.

Figure 6-2: EUC and Corresponding 32-bit Wide-character Representation

Code Set	EUC Code Representation	Wide-character Representation
0	0xxxxxxx	00000000000000000000000xxxxxxx
1	1xxxxxxx	00110000000000000000000xxxxxxx
	1xxxxxxx1xxxxxxx	0011000000000000000xxxxxxxxxxxxxx
	1xxxxxxx1xxxxxxx1xxxxxxx	0011000000xxxxxxxxxxxxxxxxxxxxx
2	SS2 1xxxxxxx	00010000000000000000000xxxxxxx
	SS2 1xxxxxxx1xxxxxxx	0001000000000000000xxxxxxxxxxxxxx
	SS2 1xxxxxxx1xxxxxxx1xxxxxxx	0001000000xxxxxxxxxxxxxxxxxxxxx
3	SS3 1xxxxxxx	00100000000000000000000xxxxxxx
	SS3 1xxxxxxx1xxxxxxx	0010000000000000000xxxxxxxxxxxxxx
	SS3 1xxxxxxx1xxxxxxx1xxxxxxx	0010000000xxxxxxxxxxxxxxxxxxxxx

Most of the functions provided let you convert multibyte characters into wide characters and back again. Before we turn to the functions, we should note that most application programs will not need to convert multibyte characters to wide characters in the first place. Programs such as **diff**, for example, will read in and write out multibyte characters, needing only to check for an exact byte-for-byte match. More complicated programs such as **grep**, that use regular expression pattern matching, may need to understand multibyte characters, but only the common set of functions that manages the regular expression needs this knowledge. The program **grep** itself requires no other special multibyte character handling. Finally, note that except for **libc**, the libraries described below are archives, not shared objects. They cannot be dynamically linked with your program.

Multibyte and Wide-character Conversion

ANSI C provides five library functions that manage multibyte and wide characters:

mblen	length of next multibyte character
mbtowc	convert multibyte character to wide character
wctomb	convert wide character to multibyte character
mbstowcs	convert multibyte character string to wide character string
wcstombs	convert wide character string to multibyte character string

The first three functions are described on the **mbchar**(3C) manual page, the last two on the **mbstring**(3C) page.

Input/Output

Since most programs will convert between multibyte and wide characters just before or after performing I/O, **libc** provides routines that let you manage the conversion within the I/O function itself. **getwc**, for instance, reads bytes from a stream until a complete EUC character has been seen and returns it in its wide-character representation. **getws** does the same thing for strings; **putwc** and **putws** are the corresponding write versions. Of course, these routines and others are functionally similar to the **stdio**(3S) functions; they differ only in their handling of EUC representations. Check the 3W manual pages for details. Here is a look at how you can expect the functions to work.

Given the following declarations

```
#include <stdio.h>
#include <widec.h>

wchar_t s1[BUFSIZ]; /* declare array s1 to store wide characters */
char    s2[BUFSIZ]; /* declare array s2 of characters for EUC
                       representation */
```

a multibyte string can be input into **s1** using **getws**:

```
getws(s1);          /* read EUC string from stdin and convert
                       to process code string in s1 */
```

gets and **strtows**:

```
gets(s2);           /* read EUC string from stdin into s2 */
strtows(s1, s2);    /* convert EUC string in s2 to process
                       code string in s1 */
```

the **%ws** conversion specifier for **scanf**:

```
scanf("%ws", s1);   /* read EUC string from stdin and convert
                       to process code string in s1 */
```

the **%s** conversion specifier for **scanf** and **strtows**:

```
scanf("%s", s2);    /* read EUC string from stdin into s2 */
strtows(s1, s2);    /* convert EUC string in s2 to process
                       code string in s1 */
```

You can use **putws, wstostr**, and the **%ws** conversion specifier for **printf** in the same way for output.

Character Classification and Conversion

Single- and multibyte character classification and conversion functions are provided in **libc**. You can use these routines to test 7-bit US ASCII characters, for instance, in their wide-character representations, or to determine whether multibyte characters are ideograms, phonograms, or the like. See the **wctype**(3W) and **wconv**(3W) manual pages in the *Operating System API Reference* for details.

As noted, these routines are declared in the **<wctype.h>** header. Implementations provide another standard header, **<xctype.h>**, that can be used to define private character classification and conversion rules with the **_iswctype** and **_trwctype** routines. **<wctype.h>** includes **<xctype.h>** which contains nothing initially.

CAUTION   The header file **/usr/include/xctype.h** was originally designed to specify the definition of native language character and symbol classification and conversion routines. To avoid conflict among different locales that might share character classification functions with identical names, an application should include its locale-specific header, for example, **/usr/include/** *jctype.h* for a Japanese locale, **/usr/include/** *kctype.h* for a Korean locale, etcetera. This localized header should *not* be included in **/usr/include/wctype.h**.

USL's localization packages implement such header files.

Here is some background on what **<xctype.h>** might contain.

The **_iswctype** and **_trwctype** functions are supplied by System V to allow you to define native language character classifications and conversion rules. The rules themselves are coded into the character class table that is created by **chrtbl**(1M) and/or **wchrtbl**(1M) utility. These two functions get their information from the character class table. These functions have the following format:

```
_iswctype(c, _En)
_trwctype(c, _En)
```

_iswctype returns nonzero if **c** is a member of the set of characters specified by **_En**. **_trwctype** returns a corresponding converted character if **c** is a member of the set of characters specified by **_En**. **_En** is a bit mask defined in the specification to the **wchrtbl**(1M) command, which generates EUC character class tables. Because it is a bit mask, combinations of **_En** can be supplied to these functions.

As an example of the use of **_iswctype**, assume that the flag **_En_XYZ** is defined in the character class table as being true for the uppercase letters **X, Y** and **Z**. Similarly, assume that the flag **_En_xyz** is defined for the lowercase letters **x, y** and **z**. The following macro, when declared in **<xctype.h>**, would then return true when the parameter **c** was a member of the set { **X, x, Y, y, Z, z** }:

```
#define isXYZ_anycase(c)    _iswctype(c , _En_XYZ | _En_xyz)
```

Whereas the following macro would return true only for uppercase values:

```
#define isXYZ_upper_case(c)    _iswctype(c , _En_XYZ)
```

curses Support

32-bit versions of certain **curses** functions are provided in **libcurses** and declared in **<curses.h>**. Check the 3X manual pages in the *Operating System API Reference*, especially **curses**(3X), for some of the things you need to look out for in using these functions.

C Language Features

To give even more flexibility to the programmer in an Asian environment, ANSI C provides 32-bit wide character constants and wide string literals. These have the same form as their non-wide versions except that they are immediately prefixed by the letter **L**:

'x'	regular character constant
'¥'	regular character constant
L'x'	wide character constant
L'¥'	wide character constant
"abc¥xyz"	regular string literal
L"abc¥xyz"	wide string literal

Note that multibyte characters are valid in both the regular and wide versions. The sequence of bytes necessary to produce the ideogram ¥ is encoding-specific, but if it consists of more than one byte, the value of the character constant **'¥'** is implementation-defined, just as the value of **'ab'** is implementation-defined. A regular string literal contains exactly the bytes (except for escape sequences) specified between the quotes, including the bytes of each specified multibyte character. Of course, programs using this feature will probably not be portable.

When the compilation system encounters a wide character constant or wide string literal, each multibyte character is converted (as if by calling the **mbtowc** function) into a wide character. Thus the type of **L'¥'** is **wchar_t** and the type of **L"abc¥xyz"** is array of **wchar_t** with length eight. (Just as with regular string literals, each wide string literal has an extra zero-valued element appended, but in these cases it is a **wchar_t** with value zero.)

Just as regular string literals can be used as a short-hand method for character array initialization, wide string literals can be used to initialize **wchar_t** arrays:

```
wchar_t *wp = L"a¥z";
wchar_t x[] = L"a¥z";
wchar_t y[] = {L'a', L'¥', L'z', 0};
wchar_t z[] = {'a', L'¥', 'z', '\0'};
```

In the above example, the three arrays **x**, **y** and **z** as well as the array pointed to by **wp**, have the same length and all are initialized with identical values.

Adjacent wide string literals will be concatenated, just as with regular string literals. Adjacent regular and wide string literals produce undefined behavior.

System-defined Words

The UNIX system uses a number of special words to identify system resources, user and group names, process IDs, peripherals, and other information. The following should be specified only with characters from the primary code set:

- process ID numbers
- message queue, semaphore, and shared memory identifiers
- external symbol names and fill patterns for the **cc** and **as** commands
- layer names

Although the following can be specified with supplementary code set characters, we recommend against it:

- user names
- group names
- passwords
- names of devices, terminals, and special devices
- printer names and printer class names
- system names
- disk pack, diskette, and tape label/volume names
- names visible to other machines on a network
- environment variable names

The following can be specified with primary or supplementary code set characters, subject to length limitations imposed by the file system:

- file names
- directory names
- command names
- file system names

File name prefixes of the form `s.`, or suffixes of the form `.c`, must be specified with characters from the primary code set.

Cultural and Language Conventions

In this section we'll look at how programs interpret or print the formatted date and time, or formatted numeric and monetary values, in locale-dependent ways. We'll also look at the functions you use to collate strings according to the rules of the language the locale implements.

Date and Time

The ANSI C function **strftime** provides a **sprintf**-like formatting of the values in a **struct tm**, along with some date and time representations that depend on the **LC_CTIME** category of the current locale. (**strftime** supersedes **ctime** and **ascftime**, although, for the sake of compatibility with older systems, these routines format the date and time correctly for a given locale.) Here is how you might use **strftime** to print the current date in a locale-dependent way:

```
#include <stdio.h>
#include <locale.h>
#include <time.h>

main()
{
        time_t tval;
        struct tm *tmptr;
        char buf [BUFSIZ];

        tval = time(NULL);
        tmptr = localtime(&tval);

        setlocale(LC_ALL, "");

        strftime(buf, BUFSIZE, "%x", tmptr);
        puts(buf);
}
```

In this case, **strftime** puts characters into the array pointed to by **buf**, as controlled by the string pointed to by **%x**. **%x** is a directive that provides an implementation-defined date representation appropriate to the locale. In a Spanish locale, for example, the current date June 14, 1990, might be represented as **14 Junio 1990** or **14/6/90** or any other way the implementation deems appropriate to the locale. No particular format is guaranteed.

Use the **%X** directive to obtain the locale's appropriate time representation:

```
strftime(buf, BUFSIZE, "%x %X", tmptr)
```

or **%c** to obtain both the date and time representation. Check the **strftime**(3C) manual page in the *Operating System API Reference* for the other directives.

Although it requires a bit more work, you can control the format of the date and time for different locales by using **printf** with the message retrieval functions **gettxt** or **catgets**. Suppose, for example, you want the current date June 14, 1990, to be displayed in a British locale as **14/6/90**, in a German locale as **14.6.90**, and in a U.S. locale as **6/14/90**. What you need, in other words, is some way to switch the arguments to **printf** depending on the program's current locale. The **%n$** form of conversion specification lets you convert the *n*th argument in a **printf** argument list rather than the next unused argument. That is,

```
printf(gettxt("progmsgs:9", "%d/%d/%d\n"),
       tm->tm.mon,
       tm->tm.mday,
       tm->tm.year);
```

will produce the locale-dependent date displays we want, so long as the string whose index is **9** in the message file **progmsgs** reads, in the British locale

```
"%2$d/%1$d/%3$d\n"
```

in the German locale

```
"%2$d.%1$d.%3$d\n"
```

and in the U.S. locale

```
"%1$d/%2$d/%3$d\n" /* or simply "%d/%d/%d\n" */
```

You can use **scanf** in a similar way to interpret formatted dates in the input:

```
int month, day, year;
scanf(gettxt("progmsgs:9", "%d/%d/%d\n"),
      &month, &day, &year);
```

Note that the **%n$** form of conversion specification has a wider application than the one we've described here, as we'll show in the "Message Handling" section below. There, too, we'll take a closer look at **gettxt** and **catgets**. Detailed information concerning **printf**(3S), **scanf**(3S), **gettxt**(3C) and **catgets**(3C) can be found in the *Operating System API Reference*.

Numeric and Monetary Information

The ANSI C **localeconv** function returns a pointer to a structure containing information useful for formatting numeric and monetary information appropriate to the current locale's **LC_NUMERIC** and **LC_MONETARY** categories. (This is the only function whose behavior depends on more than one category.) For numeric values the structure describes the decimal-point (radix) character, the thousands separator, and where the separator(s) should be located. Other structure members describe how to format monetary values, as in the following, somewhat contrived example. Assuming **setlocale** has been called, the code

```
int thousands = 1;
int rest = 234;
int frac = 56;

struct lconv *lptr;
lptr = localeconv();

printf("%s%d%c%d%c%d\n",
        lptr->currency_symbol,
        thousands, lptr->mon_thousands_sep[0], rest,
        lptr->mon_decimal_point[0], frac);
```

will print **kr1.234,56** in a Norwegian locale, **F 1.234,56** in a Dutch locale, and **SFrs.1,234.56** in a Swiss locale. Check **localeconv**(3C) in the *Operating System API Reference* for details.

localeconv aside, functions that write or interpret printable floating values — **printf** and **scanf**, for example — will use a decimal-point character other than a period (**.**) when the **LC_NUMERIC** category of the current locale is other than **"C"**. There is no provision for converting numeric values to printable form with thousands separator-type characters, but when converting from a printable form to an internal form, implementations are allowed to accept such additional forms, again in other than the **"C"** locale. Functions that make use of the decimal-point character are the **printf** and **scanf** families, **atof**, and **strtod**. Functions that are allowed implementation-defined extensions for the thousands separator are **atof**, **atoi**, **atol**, **strtod**, **strtol**, **strtoul**, and the **scanf** family.

String Collation

ANSI C provides two functions for locale-dependent string compares. **strcoll** is analogous to **strcmp** except that the two strings are compared according to the **LC_COLLATE** category of the current locale. [see **strcoll**(3C) and **strcmp**(3C)]. Conceptually, collation occurs in two passes to obtain an appropriate ordering of accented characters, two-character sequences that should be treated as one (the Spanish character **ch**, for example), and single characters that should be treated as two (the sharp **s** in German, for instance). Since this comparison is not necessarily as inexpensive as **strcmp**, the **strxfrm** function is provided to transform a string into another. Therefore, any two such after-translation strings can be passed to **strcmp** to get an ordering identical to what **strcoll** would have returned if passed the two pre-translation strings. You are responsible for keeping track of the strings in their translated and printable forms. Generally, you should use **strxfrm** when a string will be compared a number of times.

The following example uses **qsort**(3C) and **strcoll**(3C) to sort lines in a text file:

```
#include <stdio.h>
#include <string.h>
#include <locale.h>

char table [ELEMENTS] [WIDTH];

main(argc, argv)
int argc;
char **argv;
{
        FILE *fp;
        int nel, i;

        setlocale(LC_ALL, "");

        if ((fp = fopen(argv[1], "r")) == NULL) {
                fprintf(stderr, gettxt("progmsgs:2",
                        "Can't open %s\n", argv[1]);
                exit(2);
        }
        for (nel = 0; nel < ELEMENTS &&
                fgets(table[nel], WIDTH, fp); ++nel);

        fclose(fp);

        if (nel >= ELEMENTS) {
                fprintf(stderr, gettxt("progmsgs:3",
                        "File too large\n");
                exit(3);
        }
        qsort(table, nel, WIDTH, strcoll);
        for (i = 0; i < nel; ++i)
                fputs(table(i), stdout);
        return(0);
}
```

The next example does the same thing with a function that uses **strxfrm**:

```
compare (s1, s2)
char *s1, *s2;
{
        char *tmp;
        int result;
        size_t n1 = strxfrm(NULL, s1, 0) + 1;
        size_t n2 = strxfrm(NULL, s2, 0) + 1;

        if ((tmp = malloc(n1 + n2)) == NULL)
                return strcmp(s1, s2);

        (void)strxfrm(tmp, s1, n1);
        (void)strxfrm(tmp + n1 + 1, s2, n2);

        result = strcmp(tmp, tmp + n1 + 1);
        free(tmp);
        return(result);
}
```

Assuming **malloc** succeeds, the return value of **compare (s1, s2)** should correspond to the return value of **strcoll(s1, s2)**. Although it is too complicated to show here, it would probably be better to hold onto the strings for subsequent comparisons rather than transforming them each time the function is called. Details of **strcoll**(3C) and **strxfrm**(3C) can be found in the *Operating System API Reference*.

Message Handling

As the examples in earlier sections may have suggested, the general approach behind the message handling feature is to separate messages from program source code, replacing hard-coded character strings with function calls that fetch the strings from a file. You supply the file, which contains your program's messages in whatever language the locale implements. You can adapt your applications to different locales, then, without having to change and recompile source code.

In this section we'll look at the System V-specific and X/Open message handling facilities as they might be used to adapt an "English-speaking" program to a French locale. The code fragment below queries the English-speaking user for an affirmative or negative response, and reads the response:

```
#include <stdio.h>

main()
{
        int yes();

        while(1)
        {
                puts("Choose (y/n)");
                if (yes())
                        puts("yes");
                else
                        puts("no");
        }
}

static int
yes()
{
        int i, b;

        i = b = getchar();
        while (b != '\n' && b != '\0' && b != EOF)
                b = getchar();
        return(i == 'y');
}
```

mkmsgs and gettxt (System V-specific)

You use the **mkmsgs** command to store the strings for a given locale in a file that can be read by the message retrieval function **gettxt**. **mkmsgs** accepts an input file consisting of text strings separated by newlines. If the file **fr.str** contains

```
Votre choix (o/n)
oui
non
```

the command

```
$ mkmsgs -o -i french fr.str progmsgs
```

will generate a file called **progmsgs** that, when installed in the directory `/usr/lib/locale/french/LC_MESSAGES`, can be read by **gettxt** such that

```
puts(gettxt("progmsgs:1", "Choose (y/n)"));
```

will display

```
Votre choix (o/n)
```

in a French locale. **gettxt** takes as its first argument the name of the file created by **mkmsgs** and the number of the string in the file, counting from 1. You hard-code the second argument, not necessarily in English, in case **gettxt** fails to retrieve the message string from the current locale, or the **"C"** locale.

exstr and srchtxt (System V-specific)

Once you have created the message files for the different locales, you can use the **exstr** command to extract the strings from the original source code and replace them with calls to **gettxt**. If the name of the source file is **prog.c**, the command

```
$ exstr -e prog.c > prog.strings
```

will produce the following output in **prog.strings**:

```
prog.c:9:8:::Choose (y/n)
prog.c:11:8:::yes
prog.c:13:8:::no
```

The first three fields in each entry are the file name, the line number in which the string appears in the file, and the character position of the string in the line. You fill in the next two fields with the name of the message file and the index of the string in the file:

```
prog.c:9:8:progmsgs:1:Choose (y/n)
prog.c:11:8:progmsgs:2:yes
prog.c:13:8:progmsgs:3:no
```

Now the command

```
$ exstr -rd prog.c < prog.strings > intl.c
```

will produce in `intl.c`

```c
#include <stdio.h>

extern char *gettxt();
main()
{
        int yes();

        while(1)
        {
                puts(gettxt("progmsgs:1", "Choose (y/n)"));
                if (yes())
                        puts(gettxt("progmsgs:2", "yes"));
                else
                        puts(gettxt("progmsgs:3", "no"));
        }
}

static int
yes()
{
        int i, b;

        i = b = getchar();
        while (b != '\n' && b != '\0' && b != EOF)
                b = getchar();
        return(i == 'y');
}
```

The completed source code would look like this:

Internationalization

```
#include <stdio.h>
#include <unistd.h>
#include <string.h>
#include <locale.h>
#define RESPLEN 16

char yesstr[RESPLEN];           /* assumed to be long enough */
extern char *gettxt();
main()
{
        int yes();

        setlocale(LC_ALL, "");

        /* save local yes string for subsequent comparisons */
        strcpy(yesstr, gettxt("progmsgs:2", "yes"));

        while(1)
        {
                puts(gettxt("progmsgs:1", "Choose (y/n)"));
                if (yes())
                        puts(yesstr);
                else
                        puts(gettxt("progmsgs:3", "no"));
        }
}

static int
yes()
{
        int i, b;

        i = b = getchar();
        while (b != '\n' && b != '\0' && b != EOF)
                b = getchar();
        return(i == (int) yesstr[0]);
}
```

The **srchtxt** command lets you display or search for text strings in message files installed in a given locale. Among other ways, you might want to use it to see how other programs have translated messages similar to yours. Details of the **mkmsgs**(1), **exstr**(1), **srchtxt**(1) and **gettxt**(3C) commands can be found in the *Operating System API Reference*.

catopen and catclose (X/Open)

As noted in the "Introduction" section at the beginning of this chapter, the X/Open messaging interface is the de facto standard throughout much of Europe, so you can generally count on wider support for it than for the System V-specific version. The principal difference between the interfaces lies in where your message files, or message catalogs, to use the X/Open terminology, are located on the target system. System V-specific message files must be installed in the standard place. X/Open message catalogs can be installed anywhere on the system, which means that programs must search their environments for the location of message catalogs at run time.

Users specify message catalog search paths with the **NLSPATH** environment variable. The value of **NLSPATH** is used by the function `catopen` to locate the message catalog named in its first argument. Users will almost always find it convenient to use the **%L** and **%N** substitution fields when setting **NLSPATH**:

```
$ NLSPATH="%L/%N" export NLSPATH
```

In this example, the value of the **LC_MESSAGES** locale category is substituted for **%L**. The value of the first argument to `catopen` is substituted for **%N**. So if the name of the catalog given to `catopen` is `progmsgs`, and if the environment variable **LC_MESSAGES** is set to `french`, then the value of **NLSPATH** would be `/usr/lib/locale/french/LC_MESSAGES/progmsgs` on a System V implementation. For more on **NLSPATH**, see the `catopen`(3C) manual page.

The call to `catopen` would look like:

```
nl_catd catd;
catd = catopen("progmsgs", 0);
```

where `catopen` and the type `nl_catd` are defined in the header `<nl_types.h>`. `catd` is a message catalog descriptor that can be passed as an argument to subsequent calls of the `catgets` and `catclose` functions. We'll look at `catgets` in the next section; `catclose` closes the message catalog identified by `catd`. The second argument to `catopen` is not used by implementations currently and should be set to `0`.

gencat and catgets (X/Open)

You use the **gencat** command to store the strings for a given locale in a catalog that can be read by the message retrieval function **catgets**. The **gencat** input file for our example would be:

```
$set
1 votre choix (o/n)
2 oui
3 non
```

The **$set** directive specifies that the three messages are members of set 1. A subsequent **$set** directive would mean that the following messages are members of set 2, and so on. The messages for each module of an application, then, can be assigned to different sets, making it easier to keep track of message numbers across source files: the messages for any given module will always be numbered consecutively from 1. Note that each message in a **gencat** input file must be numbered. For details of the input file syntax, see the **gencat**(1) manual page in the *Command Reference*.

If the **gencat** input file is named **fr.str**, the command

```
$ gencat progmsgs fr.str
```

will generate a catalog called **progmsgs** that, when installed in the appropriate directory, can be read by **catgets** such that

```
puts(catgets(catd, 1, 1, "Choose (y/n)"));
```

will display

```
Votre choix (o/n)
```

in a French locale. **catd** is the message catalog descriptor returned by the earlier call to **catopen**; the second and third arguments are the set and message numbers, respectively, of the string in the catalog. Again, you hard-code the final argument in case **catgets** fails. Details on **gencat**(1) can be found in the *Command Reference*; **catgets**(3C) and **catopen**(3C) can be found in the *Operating System API Reference*.

The X/Open version of our example follows:

```
#include <stdio.h>
#include <nl_types.h>
#include <string.h>
#include <locale.h>
#define RESPLEN 16

char yesstr[RESPLEN];          /* assumed to be long enough */
extern char *catgets();
main()
{
        int yes();
        nl_catd catd;
        setlocale(LC_ALL, "");
        catd = catopen("progmsgs", 0);

        /* save local yes string for subsequent comparisons */
        strcpy(yesstr, catgets(catd, 1, 2, "yes"));

        while(1)
        {
                puts(catgets(catd, 1, 1, "Choose (y/n)"));
                if (yes())
                        puts(yesstr);
                else
                        puts(catgets(catd, 1, 3, "no"));
        }
}

static int
yes()
{
        int i, b;
        i = b = getchar();
        while (b != '\n' && b != '\0' && b != EOF)
                b = getchar();
        return(i == (int) yesstr[0]);
}
```

%*n*$ Conversion Specifications

Earlier we noted that the %*n*$ form of conversion specification lets you convert the
*n*th argument in a **printf** or **scanf** argument list rather than the next unused
argument. We showed you how you could use the feature to control the format of
the date and time in different locales, and suggested that %*n*$ had a wider

application than that. What we had in mind were cases in which the rules of a given language were built into print statements such as

```
printf("%s %s\n",
        func == MAP ? "Can't map" : "Can't create", pathname);
```

The problem with this code is that it assumes that the verb precedes the object of the sentence, which is not the case in many languages. In other words, even if we rewrote the fragment to use **gettxt**, and stored translations of the strings in message files in the appropriate locales, we would still want to use the *%n$* conversion specification to switch the arguments to **printf** depending on the locale. That is, the **printf** format string

```
"%1$s %2$s\n"
```

in an English-language locale would be written

```
"%2$s %1$s\n"
```

in a locale in which the object of the sentence precedes the predicate.

kbd

As noted, **kbd** is a STREAMS module that can be programmed to alter or supplement data as it flows between the physical terminal and a user process to produce language-dependent effects. It translates strings in the input stream according to instructions given in tables compiled with the **kbdcomp** command. In a European environment these instructions might describe how to compose characters that cannot be entered from terminal keyboards (so-called compose and dead keys), or how to map one key to another (a German user of a **QWERTY** keyboard, for instance, will want the **y** and **z** keys swapped). In an Asian-language environment, where the number of ideograms far exceeds the number of keys on most keyboards, **kbd** might be used to implement a dictionary lookup scheme that converts single-byte input to multibyte characters.

The compiled tables are loaded with the **kbdload** command, and attached to user processes with the **kbdset** command. Public tables, which are loaded when the system is first brought up, are retained in memory across invocations and made available to all users. Private tables can be defined and loaded by users, but do not remain resident in memory. **kbd** also supports the use of external kernel-resident functions as if they were tables. These functions, which must be registered with the **alp** ("algorithm pool management") module, are needed for code set conversions that would be difficult or impossible with normal **kbd** tables.

In this section, we'll take a brief look at how you might build a **kbd** table. We provide this material for background only. Most programmers will not have occasion to use **kbd**. For more on the STREAMS facility, see the *STREAMS Modules and Drivers*. Detailed information concerning **alp**(7), **alpq**(1), **kbd**(7), **kbdcomp**(1M), **kbdload**(1M), **kbdpipe**(1), and **kbdset**(1) can be found in the reference set.

Building kbd Tables

A **kbd** table typically consists of a map declaration of the form

        map (*name*) {
                expressions
        }

The expressions we'll look at here have the forms

        keylist (*string string*)
        define (*word value*)
        word (*extension result*)

In the following example of a map for a German-language environment

```
map(german) {
        keylist(yzYZ zyZY)
        define(umlaut '\042')
        umlaut(a '\0344')
        umlaut(o '\0366')
        umlaut(u '\0374')
        define(sharp '\044)
        sharp(ss '\0315')
}
```

the **keylist** expression causes the **y** and **z** keys to be swapped by defining **y** as **z** and vice versa in the lookup table generated by **kbdcomp** for this map. The first **define** expression causes the double quote key (octal 042 in the code set being used) to be defined as a dead key such that whenever it is followed by an **a**, **o** or **u** in the input, it will produce the umlaut version of that character in the code set. The second **define** does the same thing with the sharp key and the characters **ss** to produce the German sharp **s**. Check the **kbdcomp**(1) manual page for details. The mappings are summarized below:

Input	Output
y	z
z	y
"a	a
"o	o
"u	u
#ss	β

Internationalization Facilities

Interface Standards

The functions discussed in this chapter are listed below by task. In the first table, pages describing utilities compatible with both the ANSI C and X/Open standards are denoted by an asterisk (*); pages describing utilities compatible with the X/Open standard only are denoted by a dagger (†).

Application Programming	
locale specification	**setlocale**(3C)*, **environ**(5)
character classification	**conv**(3C)*, **ctype**(3C)*
multibyte/wide character conversion	**mbchar**(3C)*, **mbstring**(3C)*
wide character handling	all (3W) †
curses wide character handling	all (3X)
date and time	**strftime**(3C)*, **strftime**(4)* **nl_langinfo**(3C) †, **langinfo**(5) † **getdate**(3C)
numeric and monetary conventions	**localeconv**(3C)* **nl_langinfo**(3C) †, **langinfo**(5) †
string collation	**strcoll**(3C)*, **strxfrm**(3C)*
formatted input/output	**printf**(3S)*, **scanf**(3S)*
message handling	**gencat**(1) †, **catgets**(3C) †, **catopen**(3C) †, **nl_types**(5) † **exstr**(1), **gettxt**(1), **mkmsgs**(1), **srchtxt**(1), **gettxt**(3C)
message management and monitoring	**lfmt**(1), **pfmt**(1), **addsev**(3C), **lfmt**(3C), **pfmt**(3C), **setcat**(3C), **setlabel**(3C)

character tables	**chrtbl**(1M), **wchrtbl**(1M)
monetary tables	**montbl**(1M)
collation tables	**colltbl**(1M)
date and time databases	**strftime**(4)
STREAMS	**alpq**(1), **kbdpipe**(1), **kbdset**(1), **pseudo**(1), **kbdcomp**(1M), **kbdload**(1M), **euctioctl**(5), **iconv**(5), **alp**(7), **kbd**(7)

Enhanced Commands

All System V commands are "8-bit clean." They make no assumptions about the contents of the high-order bit when processing characters. Accordingly, they will work correctly with any standard 7- or 8-bit character set, provided the environment variables **LC_CTYPE** or **LANG** have been set to a locale in which the character set is implemented. Similar arrangements have been made for commands that use locale-dependent date and time representations and collation.

Many of these commands have been further enhanced to process multibyte characters, again, provided the environment variables **LC_CTYPE** or **LANG** have been set to a locale in which the multibyte character set is implemented. In the manual pages, these characters are described as "supplementary code set characters" in reference to their EUC representation. Check the manual pages for the degree of multibyte support provided.

Finally, many commands have been enhanced to produce locale-specific message output, provided the environment variables **LC_MESSAGES** or **LANG** have been set to a locale in which the message output is stored. Note that commands that produce localized output messages use the System V-specific messaging interface.

Figure 6-3: Enhanced Commands

Command Name	Multibyte Support	Message Facility
accept	y	y
admin	y	y
ar		y
as		y
at		y
atq		y
atrm		y
awk	y	y
banner		y
basename		y
batch		y
bfs	y	
cal	y	y
calendar	y	y
cancel	y	y
cat	y	y
cb	y	
cc	y	y
cd		y
cflow	y	
chgrp		y
chmod		y
chown		y
cksum		y
cmp		y
col		y
comm		y
compress		y
cp		y
cpio	y	y
cron		y

Figure 6-3: Enhanced Commands (continued)

Command Name	Multibyte Support	Message Facility
crontab		y
csh	y	y
csplit	y	y
ctccpio	y	
cu	y	y
cut	y	y
cxref	y	
date	y	y
dd	y	y
delta	y	y
devattr		y
devnm		y
df		y
diff	y	y
diff3		y
dircmp	y	y
dirname		y
disable	y	
du		y
echo	y	
ed	y	y
edit	y	y
egrep	y	y
enable	y	
env	y	y
ex	y	y
expr	y	y
fgrep	y	y
file	y	y
find	y	y
fmt	y	y

Figure 6-3: Enhanced Commands (continued)

Command Name	Multibyte Support	Message Facility
fold	y	y
fsdb	y	
fuser		y
gencat		y
get		y
getopt	y	y
getopts	y	
gettxt		y
getty		y
grep	y	y
head	y	y
iconv		y
id		y
installf		y
join	y	y
jsh	y	y
kill		y
ksh	y	y
lex	y	
line		y
ln		y
logger		y
login		y
logname		y
lp	y	y
lpadmin		y
lpfilter		y
lpforms		y
lpmove		y
lpsched		y
lpshut		y

Figure 6-3: Enhanced Commands (continued)

Command Name	Multibyte Support	Message Facility
lpstat	y	y
lpusers		y
ls	y	y
m4	y	y
mail	y	y
mailx	y	y
make		y
mesg		y
mkdir		y
mkfifo		y
mkmsgs	y	y
more	y	y
mv		y
mvdir		y
nawk	y	y
newform	y	
newgrp		y
news		y
nl	y	y
nlsadmin	y	
nohup		y
od	y	y
pack		y
page	y	y
passwd		y
paste	y	y
pathchk		y
pcat		y
pg	y	y
pkgadd		y
pkgask		y

Figure 6-3: Enhanced Commands (continued)

Command Name	Multibyte Support	Message Facility
pkgchk		y
pkginfo		y
pkgmk		y
pkgparam		y
pkgproto		y
pkgrm		y
pkgtrans		y
pr	y	y
printf		y
prs		y
ps		y
pwd		y
read		y
red	y	y
regcmp	y	
reject	y	
removef		y
rfuadmin	y	
rm		y
rmdel		y
rmdir		y
rsh	y	y
sdiff	y	
sed	y	y
sh	y	y
shl	y	y
sleep		y
sort	y	y
split		y
srchtxt	y	
strip		y

Internationalization

Figure 6-3: Enhanced Commands (continued)

Command Name	Multibyte Support	Message Facility
stty		y
sttydefs		y
su		y
sum		y
sysadm	y	
tabs		y
tail	y	y
tar		y
tee		y
test	y	y
touch		y
tr	y	y
tty		y
ttyadm		y
ttymon		y
umask		y
uname		y
uncompress		y
unget		y
uniq	y	y
unpack		y
uucleanup	y	
uucp	y	y
uudecode		y
uuencode		y
uulog	y	y
uuname	y	y
uupick		y
uustat		y
uuto		y
uux	y	y

Figure 6-3: Enhanced Commands (continued)

Command Name	Multibyte Support	Message Facility
vedit	y	y
vi	y	y
view	y	y
wait		y
wall	y	y
wc	y	y
who		y
write	y	y
xargs		y
yacc	y	y
zcat		y

Internationalization

7 Directory and File Management

Introduction

UNIX System V File System functions create and remove files and directories, and inspect and modify their characteristics. Processes use these functions to access files and directories for subsequent I/O operations. One of the most important services provided by an operating system is to maintain a consistent, orderly and easily accessed file system. The UNIX System V file system contains directories of files arranged in a tree-like structure. The UNIX System V file system is simple in structure; nevertheless, it is more powerful and general than those often found even in considerably larger operating systems.

All UNIX System V files have a consistent structure to conceal physical properties of the device storing the file, such as the size of a disk track. It is not necessary, nor even possible, to preallocate space for a file. The size of a file is the number of bytes in it, with the last byte determined by the high-water mark of writes to the file. UNIX System V presents each file as a featureless, randomly addressable sequence of bytes arranged as a one-dimensional array of bytes ending with **EOF**.

The UNIX System V file system organizes files and directories into a tree-like structure of directories with files attached anywhere (and possibly multiply) into this hierarchy of directories. Files can be accessed by a "full pathname" or "relative pathname", have independent protection modes, are automatically allocated and de-allocated, and can be linked across directories.

In the hierarchically arranged directory tree-structure, each directory contains a list of names (character strings) and the associated file index, which implicitly refers to the same device as does the directory. Because directories are themselves files, the naming structure is potentially an arbitrary directed graph. Administrative rules restrict it to have the form of a tree, except that non-directory-files may have several names (entries in various directories).

The same non-directory-file may appear in several directories under possibly different names. This feature is called *linking*; a directory-entry for a file is sometimes called a *link*. UNIX System V differs from other systems in which linking is permitted in that all links to a file have equal status. That is, a file does not exist within a particular directory; the directory-entry for a file consists merely of its name and a pointer to the information actually describing the file. Thus, a file exists independently of any directory-entry, although in practice a file is removed along with the last link to it.

Structure of the File System

Types of Files

From the point of view of the user, there are three types of files:

1. regular files
2. directory files
3. special files

The user and user application programs access all three types of files simply as a string of bytes, and must interpret the file appropriately. In UNIX System V, files normally reside on a disk.

Regular Files

Regular files contain whatever information users write onto them (for example, character data, source programs or binary objects). Any file other than a special file or a directory file is a regular file. Every file is a (one-dimensional) array of bytes; UNIX System V imposes no further structure on the contents of files. A file of text consists simply of a string of characters, with the new-line character delimiting lines. Binary files are sequences of words as they appear in memory when the file executes. Some programs operate on files with more structure; for example, the assembler generates, and the loader expects, object files in a specific format. The programs that use files dictate their structure, not the system.

Directory Files

Directory files (also called "directories") provide the mapping (paths) between the names of files and the files themselves. Directories induce a tree-like structure on the file system as a whole to create a hierarchical system of files with directories as the nodes in the hierarchy. A directory is a file that catalogs the files, including directories (sub-directories), directly beneath it in the hierarchy.

Each user owns a directory of files, and may also create sub-directories to contain groups of files conveniently treated together. A directory behaves exactly like a regular file except that only the operating system can write onto it. UNIX System V controls the contents of directories; however, users with permission may read a directory just like any other file.

The operating system maintains several directories for its own use. One of these is the *root-directory*. Each file in the file system can be found by tracing a path from the root-directory through a chain of directories until the desired file is reached. Other system directories contain any programs provided for general use; that is, all *commands*; however, it is by no means necessary that a program reside in one of these directories for it to be executed.

Entries in a directory file are called *links*. A link associates a file-identifier with a filename. Each directory has at least two links, " **.** " (dot) and " **..** " (dot-dot). The link dot refers to the directory itself; while dot-dot refers to the parent of the directory in which dot-dot appears. Programs may read the current-directory using " **.** " without knowing its complete pathname.

The root-directory, which is the top-most node of the hierarchy, has itself as its parent-directory; thus, " **/** " is the pathname of both the root-directory and the parent-directory of the root-directory.

The directory structure is constrained to have the form of a rooted tree. Except for the special entries " **.** " and " **..** ", each directory must appear as an entry in exactly one other directory, which is its parent. The reason for this is to simplify the writing of programs that visit sub-trees of the directory structure, and more important, to avoid the separation of portions of the hierarchy. If arbitrary links to directories were permitted, it would be quite difficult to detect when the last connection from the root-directory to a directory was severed.

Special Files

Special files constitute the most unusual feature of the UNIX System V file system. Each supported I/O device is associated with at least one special file. Special files are read and written just like regular files, but requests to read or write result in activation of the associated device-handler (driver) rather than the normal file mechanism.

An entry for each special file resides under the directory " **/dev** ", although a link may be made to one of these files just as it may to a regular file. For example, to write on magnetic tape one may write on the file " **/dev/mt** ". Special files exist for peripheral devices such as terminal ports, communication links, disk drives, tape drives and for physical main memory. Of course, the active disks and memory special files are protected from indiscriminate access by appropriate read and write permissions.

There are several advantages to treating I/O devices this way:

■ file and device I/O are as similar as possible; all I/O is treated uniformly, and the same system calls work on all types of files.

- file and device names have the same syntax and meaning, so that a program expecting a filename as a parameter can be passed a device name.

- the same protection mechanism works on special files, directory files and regular files.

Organization of Files

The file system is made up of a set of regular files, special files, symbolic links, and directories. These components provide a way to organize, retrieve, and manage information electronically. The "File and Device Input/Output" chapter introduced some of the properties of directories and files; this section will review them briefly before discussing how to use them.

- A regular file is a collection of characters stored on a disk. It may contain text for a report or code for a program.

- A special file represents a physical device, such as a terminal or disk.

- A symbolic link is a file that points to another file.

- A directory is a collection of files and other directories (sometimes called subdirectories). Use directories to group files together on the basis of any criteria you choose. For example, you might create a directory for each product that your company sells or for each of your student's records.

The set of all the directories and files is organized into a tree shaped structure. Figure 7-1 shows a sample file structure with a directory called root (/) as its source. By moving down the branches extending from root, you can reach several other major system directories. By branching down from these, you can, in turn, reach all the directories and files in the file system.

Figure 7-1: A Sample File System

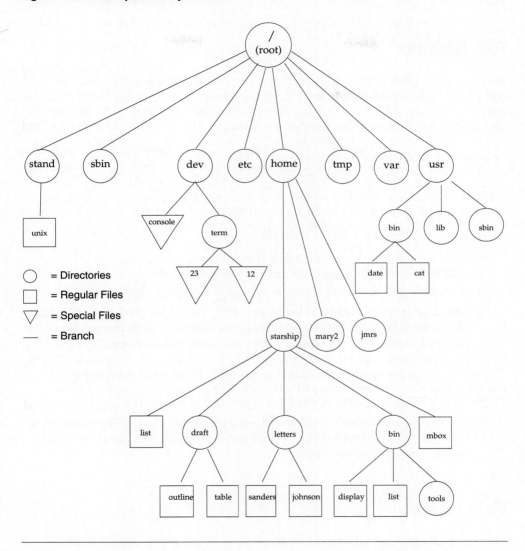

In this hierarchy, files and directories that are subordinate to a directory have what is called a parent/child relationship. This type of relationship is possible for many layers of files and directories. In fact, there is no limit to the number of files and directories you may create in any directory that you own. Neither is there a limit to the number of layers of directories that you may create. Thus, you have the capability to organize your files in a variety of ways, as shown in the preceding figure.

File Naming

Strings of 1 to **{NAME_MAX}** characters may be used to name a regular file, directory file or special file. **{NAME_MAX}** must be at least 14, and the characters may be any from the set of all character values excluding *null* and *slash*, " / ". The following are examples of legal directory or file names:

memo	MEMO	section2	ref:list
file.d	chap3+4	item1-10	outline

A regular file, special file or directory may have any name that conforms to the following rules:

- All characters other than / are legal.

- Non-printing characters including space, tab and backspace, are best avoided. If you use a space or tab in a directory or filename, you must enclose the name in quotation-marks on the command-line.

- Note that it is generally unwise to use " * ", " ? ", " ! ", " [" or "] " as part of filenames because of the special meaning given these characters for filename expansion by the command interpreter [see **system**(2)]. Other characters to avoid are the hyphen, " < ", " > ", backslash, single and double quotes, accent grave, vertical bar, caret, curly braces and parentheses.

- Avoid using a +, - or . as the first character in a filename.

- Upper case and lower case characters are distinct to the UNIX system. For example, the system considers a directory (or file) named **draft** to be different from one named **DRAFT**.

Path Names

The name of a file may take the form of a *pathname*, which is a sequence of directory names separated from one another by " / " and ending in a filename. A pathname is a null-terminated character-string starting with an optional slash, " / ", followed by zero or more directory-names separated by slashes and optionally followed by a filename.

More precisely, a pathname is a null-terminated character-string as follows:

<path_name> ::= <file_name> | <path_prefix><file_name> | / | . | ..
<path_prefix> ::= <rtprefix> | /<rtprefix> | *empty*
<rtprefix> ::= <dirname> / | <rtprefix><dirname> /

where `<file_name>` is a string of 1 to `{NAME_MAX}` significant characters (other than slash and null), and `<dirname>` is a string of 1 to `{NAME_MAX}` significant characters (other than slash and null) that names a directory. The result of names not produced by the grammar are undefined. A null string is undefined and may be considered an error. As a limiting case, the pathname " / " refers to the root-directory itself. An attempt to create or delete the pathname slash by itself is undefined and may be considered an error. The meanings of " . " and " .. " are defined earlier under the heading "Directory Files".

The sequence of directories preceding the filename is called a *path-prefix*, and if the path-prefix begins with a slash, the search begins in the root-directory. This is called a *full pathname*.

Full Pathnames

A full pathname (sometimes called an "absolute pathname") starts in the root directory and leads down through a unique sequence of directories to a particular directory or file. Because a full pathname always starts at the root of the file system, its leading character is always a / (slash). The final name in a full pathname can be either a file name or a directory name. All other names in the path must be directories. You can use a full pathname to reach any file or directory in the UNIX system in which you are working.

To understand how a full pathname is constructed and how it directs you, consider the following example. Suppose you are working in the **starship** directory, located in **/home**. You issue the **pwd** command and the system responds by printing the full pathname of your working directory: **/home/starship**.

The following figure and key diagrams the elements of this pathname:

Figure 7-2: Diagram of a Full Pathname

/ (leading)	= the slash that appears as the first character in the pathname is the root of the file system
home	= system directory one level below root in the hierarchy to which root points or branches
/ (subsequent)	= the next slash separates or delimits the directory names **home** and **starship**
starship	= current working directory

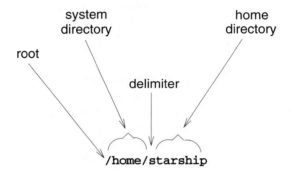

The following pathname:

> **/usr/bin/send**

causes a search of the root-directory for directory "**usr**", then a search of "**usr**" for "**bin**", finally to find "**send**" in "**bin**". The file "**send**" may be a directory, regular or special file. A null-prefix (or for that matter, any path-prefix without an initial "**/**") causes the search to begin in the current-directory of the user. Thus, the simplest form of pathname, "**alpha**", refers to a file found in the current-directory, and the pathname "**alpha/beta**" specifies the file named "**beta**" in sub-directory "**alpha**" of the current-directory. This *relative pathname* allows a user to quickly specify a sub-directory without needing to know (or input) the full pathname.

The dashed lines in Figure 7-3 trace the full path to **/home/starship**.

Figure 7-3: Full Pathname of the /home/starship Directory

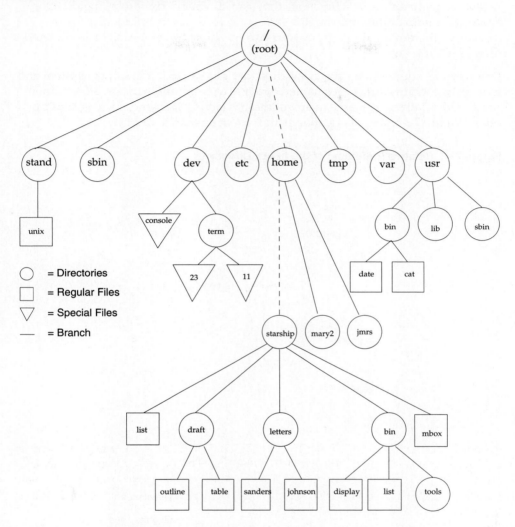

○ = Directories
□ = Regular Files
▽ = Special Files
— = Branch

Relative Pathnames

A relative pathname gives directions that start in your current working directory and lead you up or down through a series of directories to a particular file or directory. By moving down from your current directory, you can access files and directories you own.

For example, suppose you are in the directory **starship** in the sample system and **starship** contains directories named **draft**, **letters**, and **bin** and a file named **mbox**. The relative pathname to any of these is simply its name, such as **draft** or **mbox**. Figure 7-4 traces the relative path from **starship** to **draft**.

Figure 7-4: Relative Pathname of the draft Directory

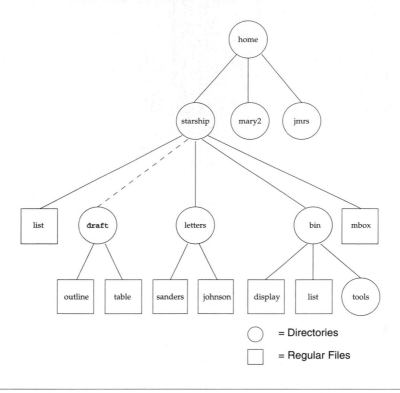

The **draft** directory belonging to **starship** contains the files **outline** and **table**. The relative pathname from **starship** to the file **outline** is **draft/outline**.

Directory and File Management

Figure 7-5 traces this relative path. Notice that the slash in this pathname separates the directory named **draft** from the file named **outline**. Here, the slash is a delimiter showing that **outline** is subordinate to **draft**; that is, **outline** is a child of its parent, **draft**.

Figure 7-5: Relative Pathname from starship to outline

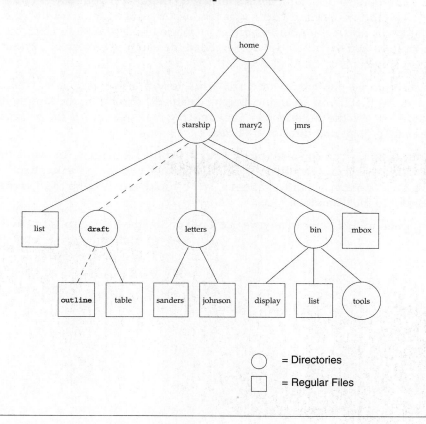

So far, the discussion of relative pathnames has covered how to specify names of files and directories that belong to, or are children of, the current directory. You can move down the system hierarchy level by level until you reach your destination. You can also, however, ascend the levels in the system structure or ascend and subsequently descend into other files and directories.

By moving up from your current directory, you pass through layers of parent directories to the grandparent of all system directories, root. From there you can move anywhere in the file system.

The relative pathname is just one of the mechanisms built into the file system to alleviate the need to use full pathnames. By convention, the path-prefix " .. " refers to the parent-directory (that is, the directory containing the current-directory), and the path-prefix " . " refers to the current-directory.

A relative pathname begins with one of the following: a directory or file name; a " . " (pronounced dot), which is a shorthand notation for your current directory; or a " .. " (pronounced dot dot), which is a shorthand notation for the directory immediately above your current directory in the file system hierarchy. The directory represented by " .. " (dot dot) is called the parent directory of . (your current directory).

To ascend to the parent of your current directory, you can use the " .. " notation. This means that if you are in the directory named " **draft** " in the sample file system, " .. " is the pathname to " **starship** ", and " **../..** " is the pathname to " **starship** "'s parent directory, " **home** ".

From " **draft** ", you can also trace a path to the file " **sanders** " by using the pathname " **../letters/sanders** ". The " .. " brings you up to " **starship** ". Then the names " **letters** " and " **sanders** " take you down through the " **letters** " directory to the " **sanders** " file.

Keep in mind that you can always use a full pathname in place of a relative one.

Figure 7-6 shows some examples of full and relative pathnames.

Figure 7-6: Example Pathnames

Path Name	Meaning
/	full pathname of the root directory
/usr/bin	full pathname of the **bin** directory that belongs to the **usr** directory that belongs to **root** (contains most executable programs and utilities)
/home/starship/bin/tools	full pathname of the **tools** directory belonging to the **bin** directory that belongs to the **starship** directory belonging to **home** that belongs to root
bin/tools	relative pathname to the file or directory **tools** in the directory **bin**
	If the current directory is **/**, then the UNIX system searches for **/usr/bin/tools**. However, if the current directory is **starship**, then the system searches the full path **/home/starship/bin/tools**.
tools	relative pathname of a file or directory **tools** in the current directory.

Moving files to the directory " **.** " moves them into the current-directory. In addition, files can be linked across directories. Linking a file to the current-directory obviates the need to supply a path-prefix when accessing the file. When created, a process has one current-directory and one root-directory associated with it, which can differ for other processes. See the chapter entitled "Process Management" for more detail on processes.

Symbolic Links

A symbolic link is a special type of file that represents another file. The data in a symbolic link consists of the pathname of a file or directory to which the symbolic link file is linked. The link that is formed is called symbolic to distinguish it from a regular (also called a hard) link such as can be created by using the ln(1) command. A symbolic link differs functionally from a regular link in three major ways: files from different file systems may be linked together; directories as well as regular files may be symbolically linked by any user; and a symbolic link can be created even if the file it represents does not exist.

In order to understand how a symbolic link works, it is necessary to understand how the UNIX operating system views files. (The following description pertains to files that belong to the standard System V file system type.) The internal representation of a file is contained in an inode, which contains a description of the layout of the file data on disk as well as information about the file, such as the file owner, the access permissions, and the access times. Every file has one inode, but a file may have several names, all of which point to the inode. Each name is called a regular (or hard) link.

When a file is created, an inode is allocated for it, the file contents are stored in data blocks, and an entry is created in a directory. A directory is a file whose data is a sequence of entries, each consisting of an inode number and the name of a file. The inode initially has a link count of one, which means that this file has one name (or one link to it).

We are now in a position to understand the difference between the creation of a regular and a symbolic link. When a user creates a regular link to a file with the ln(1) command, a new directory entry is created containing a new file name and the inode number of an existing file. The link count of the file is incremented.

In contrast, when a user creates a symbolic link both a new directory entry and a new inode are created. A data block is allocated to contain the pathname of the file to which the symbolic link refers. The link count of the referenced file is not incremented.

Symbolic links can be used to solve a variety of common problems. For example, it frequently happens that a disk partition (such as root) runs out of disk space. With symbolic links, an administrator can create a link from a directory on that file system to a directory on another file system. Such a link provides extra disk space and is, in most cases, transparent to both users and programs.

Symbolic links can also help deal with the built-in pathnames that appear in the code of many commands. Changing the pathnames would require changing the programs and recompiling them. With symbolic links, the pathnames can effectively be changed by making the original files symbolic links that point to new files.

In a shared resource environment like NFS, symbolic links can be very useful. For example, if it is important to have a single copy of certain administrative files, symbolic links can be used to help share them. Symbolic links can also be used to share resources selectively. Suppose a system administrator wants to do a remote mount of a directory that contains sharable devices. These devices must be in **/dev** on the client system, but this system has devices of its own so the administrator does not want to mount the directory onto **/dev**. Rather than do this, the administrator can mount the directory at a location other than **/dev** and then use symbolic links in the **/dev** directory to refer to these remote devices. (This is similar to the problem of built-in pathnames since it is normally assumed that devices reside in the **/dev** directory.)

Finally, symbolic links can be valuable within the context of the virtual file system (VFS) architecture. With VFS new services, such as higher performance files, events, and network IPC, may be provided on a file system basis. Symbolic links can be used to link these services to home directories or to places that make more sense to the application or user. Thus one might create a database index file in a RAM-based file system type and symbolically link it to the place where the database server expects it and manages it.

 NOTE The phrases "following symbolic links" and "not following symbolic links" as they are used in this document refer to the evaluation of the last component of a pathname. In the evaluation of a pathname, if any component other than the last is a symbolic link, the symbolic link is followed and the referenced file is used in the pathname evaluation. However, if the last component of a pathname is a symbolic link, the link may or may not be followed.

Properties of Symbolic Links

This section summarizes some of the essential characteristics of symbolic links. Succeeding sections describe how symbolic links may be used, based on the characteristics outlined here.

As we have seen above, a symbolic link is a new type of file that represents another file. The file to which it refers may be of any type; a regular file, a directory, a character-special, block-special, or FIFO-special file, or another symbolic link. The file may be on the local system or on a remote system. In fact, the file to which a symbolic link refers does not even have to exist. In particular, the file does not have to exist when the symbolic link is created or when it is removed.

Creation and removal of a symbolic link follow the same rules that apply to any file. To do either, the user must have write permission in the directory that contains the symbolic link. The ownership and the access permissions (mode) of the symbolic link are ignored for all accesses of the symbolic link. It is the ownership and access permissions of the referenced file that are used.

A symbolic link cannot be opened or closed and its contents cannot be changed once it has been created.

If **/usr/jan/junk** is a symbolic link to the file **/etc/passwd**, in effect the file name **/etc/passwd** is substituted for **junk** so that when the user executes

        cat /usr/jan/junk

it is the contents of the file **/etc/passwd** that are printed.

Similarly, if **/usr/jan/junk** is a symbolic link to the file **../junk2**, executing

        cat /usr/jan/junk

is the same as executing

        cat /usr/jan/../junk2

or

        cat /usr/junk2

When a symbolic link is followed and brings a user to a different part of the file tree, we may distinguish between where the user really is (the physical path) and how the user got there (the virtual path). The behavior of **/usr/bin/pwd**, the shell built-in **pwd**, and **..** are all based on the physical path. In practical terms this means that there is no way for the user to retrace the path which brought the user to the current position in the file tree.

 CAUTION Other shells may use the virtual path. For example, by default the Korn shell **pwd** uses the virtual path, though there is an option allowing the user to make it use the physical path.

Figure 7-7: File Tree with Symbolic Link

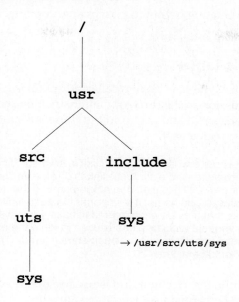

Consider the case shown in Figure 7-7 where **/usr/include/sys** is a symbolic link to **/usr/src/uts/sys**. Here if a user enters

    cd /usr/include/sys

and then enters **pwd**, the result is

    /usr/src/uts/sys

If the user then enters **cd ..** followed by **pwd**, the result is

    /usr/src/uts

Using Symbolic Links

This section discusses creating, removing, accessing, copying, and linking symbolic links.

Creating Symbolic Links

To create a symbolic link, the new system call **symlink**(2) is used and the owner must have write permission in the directory where the link will reside. The file is created with the user's user-id and group-id but these are subsequently ignored. The mode of the file is created as 0777.

 No checking is done when a symbolic link is created. There is nothing to stop a user from creating a symbolic link that refers to itself or to an ancestor of itself or several links that loop around among themselves. Therefore, when evaluating a pathname, it is important to put a limit on the number of symbolic links that may be encountered in case the evaluation encounters a loop. The variable MAXSYMLINKS is used to force the error ELOOP after MAXSYMLINKS symbolic links have been encountered. The value of MAXSYMLINKS should be at least 20.

To create a symbolic link, the **ln** command is used with the **-s** option [see **ln**(1)]. If the **-s** option is not used and a user tries to create a link to a file on another file system, a symbolic link will not be created and the command will fail.

The syntax for creating symbolic links is as follows:

> **ln -s** *sourcefile1* **[** *sourcefile2* **...** **]** *target*

With two arguments:

- *sourcefile1* may be any pathname and need not exist.

- *target* may be an existing directory or a non-existent file.

- If *target* is an existing directory, a file is created in directory *target* whose name is the last component of *sourcefile1* (` **basename** *sourcefile1* `). This file is a symbolic link that references *sourcefile1*.

- If *target* does not exist, a file with name *target* is created and it is a symbolic link that references *sourcefile1*.

- If *target* already exists and is not a directory, an error is returned.

- *sourcefile1* and *target* may reside on different file systems.

With more than two arguments:

- For each *sourcefile*, a file is created in *target* whose name is *sourcefile* or its last component (` basename *sourcefile* `) and is a symbolic link to *sourcefile*.

- If *target* is not an existing directory, an error is returned.

- Each *sourcefile* and *target* may reside on different file systems.

Examples

The following examples show how symbolic links may be created.

```
ln -s /usr/src/uts/sys  /usr/include/sys
```

In this example **/usr/include** is an existing directory. But file **sys** does not exist so it will be created as a symbolic link that refers to **/usr/src/uts/sys**. The result is that when file **/usr/include/sys/x** is accessed, the file **/usr/src/uts/sys/x** will actually be accessed.

This kind of symbolic link may be used when files exist in the directory **/usr/src/uts/sys** but programs often refer to files in **/usr/include/sys**. Rather than creating corresponding files in **/usr/include/sys** that are hard links to files in **/usr/src/uts/sys**, one symbolic link can be used to link the two directories. In this example **/usr/include/sys** becomes a symbolic link that links the former **/usr/include/sys** directory to the **/usr/src/uts/sys** directory.

```
ln -s  /etc/group  .
```

In this example the *target* is a directory (the current directory), so a file called **group** (` basename /etc/group `) is created in the current directory that is a symbolic link to **/etc/group**.

```
ln -s  /fs1/jan/abc  /var/spool/abc
```

In this example we imagine that **/fs1/jan/abc** does not exist at the time the command is issued. Nevertheless, the file **/var/spool/abc** is created as a symbolic link to **/fs1/jan/abc**. Later, **/fs1/jan/abc** may be created as a directory, regular file, or any other file type.

The following example illustrates the use of more than two arguments:

```
ln -s  /etc/group  /etc/passwd  .
```

The user would like to have the **group** and **passwd** files in the current directory but cannot use hard links because **/etc** is a different file system. When more than two arguments are used, the last argument must be a directory; here it is the current directory. Two files, **group** and **passwd**, are created in the current directory, each a symbolic link to the associated file in **/etc**.

Removing Symbolic Links

Normally, when accessing a symbolic link, one follows the link and actually accesses the referenced file. However, this is not the case when one attempts to remove a symbolic link. When the **rm**(1) command is executed and the argument is a symbolic link, it is the symbolic link that is removed; the referenced file is not touched.

Accessing Symbolic Links

Suppose **abc** is a symbolic link to file **def**. When a user accesses the symbolic link **abc**, it is the file permissions (ownership and access) of file **def** that are actually used; the permissions of **abc** are always ignored. If file **def** is not accessible (that is, either it does not exist or it exists but is not accessible to the user because of access permissions) and a user tries to access the symbolic link **abc**, the error message will refer to **abc**, not file **def**.

Copying Symbolic Links

This section describes the behavior of the **cp**(1) command when one or more arguments are symbolic links. With the **cp**(1) command, if any argument is a symbolic link, that link is followed. Then the semantics of the command are as described in the *Command Reference*. Suppose the command line is

        cp sym file3

where **sym** is a symbolic link that references a regular file **test1** and **file3** is a regular file. After execution of the command, **file3** gets overwritten with the contents of the file **test1**.

If the last argument is a symbolic link that references a directory, then files are copied to that directory. Suppose the command line is

        cp file1 sym symd

where **file1** is a regular file, **sym** is a symbolic link that references a regular file **test1**, and **symd** is a symbolic link that references a directory **DIR**. After execution of the command, there will be two new files, **DIR/file1** and **DIR/sym** that have the same contents as **file1** and **test1**.

Linking Symbolic Links

This section describes the behavior of the **ln**(1) command when one or more arguments are symbolic links. To understand the difference in behavior between this and the **cp**(1) command, it is useful to think of a copy operation as dealing with the contents of a file while the link operation deals with the name of a file.

Let us look at the case where the source argument to **ln** is a symbolic link. If the **-s** option is specified to **ln**, the command calls the **symlink** system call [see **symlink**(2)]. **symlink** does not follow the symbolic link specified by the source argument and creates a symbolic link to it. If **-s** is not specified, **ln** invokes the **link**(2) system call. **link** follows the symbolic link specified by the source argument and creates a hard link to the file referenced by the symbolic link.

For the target argument, **ln** invokes a **stat** system call [see **stat**(2)]. If **stat** indicates that the target argument is a directory, the files are linked in that directory. Otherwise, if the target argument is an existing file, it is overwritten. This means that if the second argument is a symbolic link to a directory, it is followed, but if it is a symbolic link to a regular file, the symbolic link is overwritten.

For example, if the command line is

        ln sym file1

where **sym** is a symbolic link that references a regular file **foo**, and **file1** is a regular file, **file1** is overwritten and hard-linked to **foo**. Thus a hard link to a regular file has been created.

If the command is

        ln -s sym file1

where the files are the same as in first example, **file1** is overwritten and becomes a symbolic link to **sym**.

If the command is

        ln file1 sym

where the files are the same as in the first example, **sym** is overwritten and hard-linked to **file1**.

When the last argument is a directory as in

        ln file1 sym symd

where **symd** is a symbolic link to a directory **DIR**, and **file1** and **sym** are the same as in the first example, the file **DIR/file1** is hard-linked to **file1** and **DIR/sym** is hard-linked to **foo**.

Moving Symbolic Links

This section describes the behavior of the **mv**(1) command. Like the **ln**(1) command, **mv**(1) deals with file names rather than file contents. With two arguments, a user invokes the **mv**(1) command to rename a file. Therefore, one would not want to follow the first argument if it is a symbolic link because it is the name of the file that is to be changed rather than the file contents. Suppose that **sym** is a symbolic link to **/etc/passwd** and **abc** is a regular file. If the command

        mv sym abc

is executed, the file **sym** is renamed **abc** and is still a symbolic link to **/etc/passwd**. If **abc** existed (as a regular file or a symbolic link to a regular file) before the command was executed, it is overwritten.

Suppose the command is

        mv sym1 file1 symd

where **sym1** is a symbolic link to a regular file **foo**, **file1** is a regular file, and **symd** is a symbolic link that references a directory **DIR**. When the command is executed, the files **sym1** and **file1** are moved from the current directory to the **DIR** directory so that there are two new files, **DIR/sym1**, which is still a symbolic link to **foo**, and **DIR/file1**.

In UNIX System V Release 4, the **mv**(1) command uses the **rename**(2) system call. If the first argument to **rename**(2) is a symbolic link, **rename**(2) does not follow it; instead it renames the symbolic link itself. In System V prior to Release 4, a file was moved using the **link**(2) system call followed by the **unlink**(2) system call. Since **link**(2) and **unlink**(2) do not follow symbolic links, the result of those two operations is the same as the result of a call to **rename**(2).

File Ownership and Permissions

The system calls **chmod**, **chown** and **chgrp** are used to change the mode and ownership of a file. If the argument to **chmod**, **chown** or **chgrp** is a symbolic link, the mode and ownership of the referenced file rather than of the symbolic link itself will be changed. (See the section on "Symbolic Links" that follows in this chapter). In such cases, the link is followed.

Once a symbolic link has been created, its permissions cannot be changed. By default, the **chown**(1) and **chgrp**(1) commands change the owner and group of the referenced file. However, a new **-h** option enables the user to change the owner and group of the symbolic link itself. This is useful for removing files from sticky directories.

Using Symbolic Links with NFS

When using symbolic links in an NFS environment, it is important to understand how pathnames are evaluated. The rule by which evaluations are performed is simple. Symbolic links that a client encounters on the server are interpreted in accordance with the client's view of the file tree.

Users on a server system must keep this rule in mind when they create symbolic links in order to avoid problems. The examples that follow illustrate situations in which failure to consider the client's view of the file tree can lead to problems.

Figure 7-8: Symbolic Links with NFS: Example 1

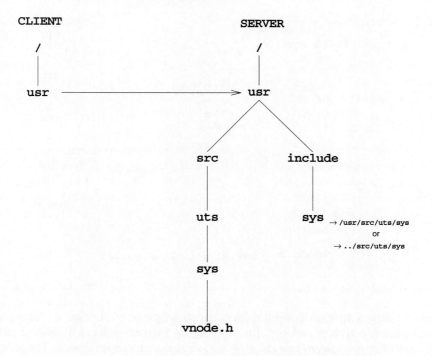

In the example shown in Figure 7-8, the server advertises its **/usr** file system as USR. If the server creates the symbolic link **/usr/include/sys** as an absolute pathname to **/usr/src/uts/sys**, evaluation of the link will work as intended as long as a client mounts USR as **/usr**. Another way of saying this is that if the file tree naming conventions are the same on the client and the server, things will work as intended. However, if the client mounts USR as **/mnt/usr**, when the symbolic link **/usr/src/uts/sys** is evaluated, the evaluation will be done with respect to the client's view of the file tree and will not cross the mount point back to the server but will remain on the client. Thus the client will not access the file intended. In this situation the server should create the symbolic link as a relative pathname, **. . /src/uts/sys**, so that evaluation will produce the desired results regardless of where the client mounts USR.

Figure 7-9: Symbolic Links with NFS: Example 2

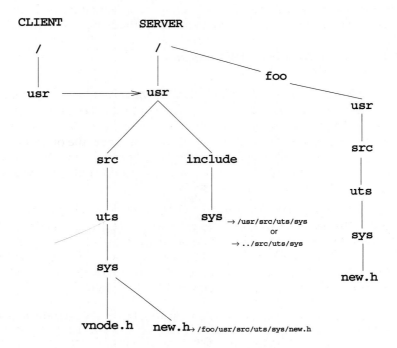

Figure 7-9 shows another potential problem situation in which the server advertises its **/usr** file system as USR. But in this case the server has a symbolic link from **/usr/src/uts/sys/new.h** to **/foo/usr/src/uts/sys/new.h**. Because the referenced file, **/foo/usr/src/uts/sys/new.h**, is outside of the advertised resource, users on the server can access this file but users on the client cannot. In this example, it would make no difference if the symbolic link was a relative rather than an absolute pathname, because the directory **/foo** on the server is not part of the client's name space. When the system evaluates the symbolic link, it will look for the file on the client and will not follow the link as intended.

Archiving Commands

The **cpio**(1) command copies file archives usually to or from a storage medium such as tape, disk, or diskette. By default, **cpio** does not follow symbolic links. unles thee **-L** option used with the **-o** and **-p** options to indicates that symbolic links should be followed. Note that this option is *not* valid with the **-i** option.

Normally, a user invokes the **find**(1) command to produce a list of filenames and pipes this into the **cpio**(1) command to create an archive of the files listed. The **find**(1) command also has a new option **-follow** to indicate that symbolic links should be followed. If a user invokes **find**(1) with the **-follow** option, then **cpio**(1) must also be invoked with its new option **-L** to indicate that it too should follow symbolic links.

When evaluating the output from **find**(1), following or not following symbolic links only makes a difference when a symbolic link to a directory is encountered. For example, if **/usr/jan/symd** is a symbolic link to the directory **../joe/test** and files **test1** and **test2** are in directory **/usr/joe/test**, the output of a **find** starting from **/usr/jan** includes the file **/usr/jan/symd** if symbolic links are not followed, but includes **/usr/jan/symd/test1** and **/usr/jan/symd/test2** as well as **/usr/jan/symd** if symbolic links are followed.

If the user wants to preserve the structure of the directories being archived, it is recommended that symbolic links not be followed on both commands. (This is the default.) When this is done symbolic links will be preserved and the directory hierarchy will be duplicated as it was. If the user is more concerned that the contents of the files be saved, then the user should use the **-L** option to **cpio**(1) and the **-follow** option to **find**(1) to follow symbolic links.

 CAUTION The user should take care not to mix modes, that is, the user should either follow or not follow symbolic links for both **cpio**(1) and **find**(1). If modes are mixed, an archive will be created but the resulting hierarchy created by **cpio -i** may exhibit unexpected and undesirable results.

The **-i** option to **cpio**(1) copies symbolic links as is. So if a user creates an archive to be read in on a pre-System V Release 4 system, it may be more useful to follow symbolic links because System V prior to Release 4 lacked symbolic links and the result of copying in a symbolic link will be a regular file containing the pathname of the referenced file.

Summary of UNIX System Files & Directories

UNIX system files are organized in a hierarchy; their structure is often described as an inverted tree. At the top of this tree is the root directory, the source of the entire file system. It is designated by a / (slash). All other directories and files descend and branch out from root, as shown in the following figure:

Figure 7-10: Directory Tree from root

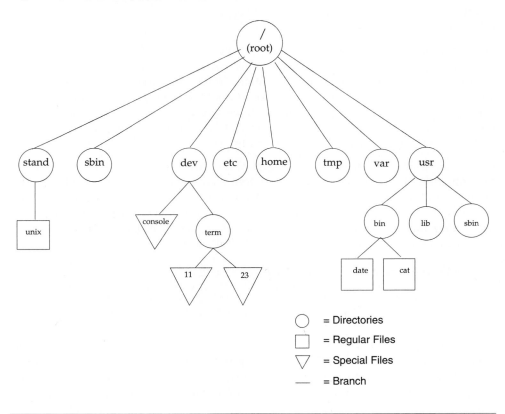

The following section provides brief descriptions of the root directory and the system directories under it, as shown in an earlier figure.

UNIX System Directories

`/`	the source of the file system (called the root directory)
`/stand`	contains programs and data files used in the booting process
`/sbin`	contains essential executables used in the booting process and in manual system recovery
`/dev`	contains special files that represent peripheral devices, such as:

`console`	console
`lp`	line printer
`term/*`	user terminal(s)
`dsk/*`	disks

`/etc`	contains machine-specific administrative configuration files and system administration databases
`/home`	the root of a subtree for user directories
`/tmp`	contains temporary files, such as the buffers created for editing a file
`/var`	the root of a subtree for varying files such as log files
`/usr`	contains other directories, including `lib` and `bin`
`/usr/bin`	contains many executable programs and utilities, including the following:

```
cat
date
login
grep
mkdir
who
```

`/usr/lib`	contains libraries for programs and languages

Directories and Files

This section describes:

- Directories and files that are important for administering a system

- Directories that are new for this software release

- The reorganization of the directory structure introduced in this release

- The new organization of the root file system, and significant directories mounted on root

 CAUTION To maintain a secure environment, do not change the file or directory permissions from those assigned at the time of installation.

Directory and File Relocations

For this software release, many commands and directories have been relocated. This section lists the commands that have been moved, the locations of these commands in UNIX System V Release 4, and the locations of the same commands in earlier releases of the UNIX system. UNIX System V Release 4.0 provides symbolic links between the old and new locations. However, in future software releases, these links may be removed. The asterisk (*) means that all files in the directory indicated have been moved to the new location.

 NOTE Depending on the operating system release and the packages installed, all of these files may not be included on your system. For example, RFS and RFS files (such as `/usr/lib/rfs/nserve`) are not included in SVR4.2 MP.

Pre-Release 4 Location	Release 4 Location
`/bin/*`	`/usr/bin/*`
`/etc/bcheckrc`	`/sbin/bcheckrc`
`/etc/chroot`	`/usr/sbin/chroot`
`/etc/crash`	`/usr/sbin/crash`
`/etc/cron`	`/usr/sbin/cron`

Pre-Release 4 Location	Release 4 Location
/etc/dcopy	/usr/sbin/dcopy
/etc/devnm	/usr/sbin/devnm
/etc/dfsck	/usr/sbin/dfsck
/etc/ff	/usr/sbin/ff
/etc/fsck	/sbin/fsck
/etc/fsdb	/sbin/fsdb
/etc/fstyp	/sbin/fstyp
/etc/fuser	/usr/sbin/fuser
/etc/getty	/usr/sbin/getty
/etc/grpck	/usr/sbin/grpck
/etc/init	/sbin/init
/etc/install	/usr/sbin/install
/etc/killall	/usr/sbin/killall
/etc/labelit	/sbin/labelit
/etc/ldsysdump	/usr/sbin/ldsysdump
/etc/link	/usr/sbin/link
/etc/log/*	/var/adm/log/*
/etc/mkfs	/sbin/mkfs
/etc/mknod	/sbin/mknod
/etc/mount	/sbin/mount
/etc/mountall	/sbin/mountall
/etc/mvdir	/usr/sbin/mvdir
/etc/ncheck	/usr/sbin/ncheck
/etc/prfdc	/usr/sbin/prfdc
/etc/prfld	/usr/sbin/prfld
/etc/prfpr	/usr/sbin/prfpr
/etc/prfsnap	/usr/sbin/prfsnap
/etc/prfstat	/usr/sbin/prfstat
/etc/prtvtoc	/sbin/prtvtoc
/etc/pwck	/usr/sbin/pwck
/etc/rc0	/sbin/rc0
/etc/rc1	/sbin/rc1
/etc/rc2	/sbin/rc2
/etc/rc3	/sbin/rc3
/etc/rc6	/sbin/rc0
/etc/rmount	/usr/sbin/rmount
/etc/rmountall	/usr/sbin/rmountall
/etc/rumountall	/usr/sbin/rumountall

Pre-Release 4 Location	Release 4 Location
/etc/setclk	/sbin/setclk
/etc/setmnt	/sbin/setmnt
/etc/shutdown	/sbin/shutdown
/etc/swap	/usr/sbin/swap
/etc/sysdef	/usr/sbin/sysdef
/etc/telinit	/sbin/init
/etc/termcap	/usr/share/lib/termcap
/etc/uadmin	/sbin/uadmin
/etc/umount	/sbin/umount
/etc/umountall	/sbin/umountall
/etc/unlink	/usr/sbin/unlink
/etc/utmp	/var/adm/utmp
/etc/volcopy	/usr/sbin/volcopy
/etc/wall	/usr/sbin/wall
/etc/whodo	/usr/sbin/whodo
/etc/wtmp	/var/adm/wtmp
/lib/*	/usr/lib/*
/shlib/*	/usr/lib/*
/unix	/stand/unix
/usr/adm/*	/var/adm/*
/usr/bin/fumount	/usr/sbin/fumount
/usr/bin/fusage	/usr/sbin/fusage
/usr/bin/nlsadmin	/usr/sbin/nlsadmin
/usr/bin/powerdown	/usr/sbin/powerdown
/usr/bin/sadp	/usr/sbin/sadp
/usr/bin/strace	/usr/sbin/strace
/usr/bin/strclean	/usr/sbin/strclean
/usr/bin/strerr	/usr/sbin/strerr
/usr/lib/cron/*	/etc/cron.d/*
/usr/lib/spell/hlista	/usr/share/lib/spell/hlista
/usr/lib/spell/hstop	/usr/share/lib/spell/hstop
/usr/lib/terminfo/*	/usr/share/lib/terminfo/*
/usr/lib/uucp/Devconfig	/etc/uucp/Devconfig
/usr/lib/uucp/Devices	/etc/uucp/Devices

Directory and File Management

Pre-Release 4 Location	Release 4 Location
/usr/lib/uucp/Dialcodes	/etc/uucp/Dialcodes
/usr/lib/uucp/Dialers	/etc/uucp/Dialers
/usr/lib/uucp/Permissions	/etc/uucp/Permissions
/usr/lib/uucp/Poll	/etc/uucp/Poll
/usr/lib/uucp/Sysfiles	/etc/uucp/Sysfiles
/usr/lib/uucp/Systems	/etc/uucp/Systems
/usr/mail/*	/var/mail/*
/usr/man/*	/usr/share/man/*
/usr/net/nls/dbfconv	/usr/lib/saf/dbfconv
/usr/net/nls/listen	/usr/lib/saf/listen
/usr/nserve/*	/etc/rfs/*
/usr/nserve/nserve	/usr/lib/rfs/nserve
/usr/nserve/rfudaemon	/usr/lib/rfs/rfudaemon
/usr/nserve/TPnserve	/usr/lib/rfs/TPnserve
/usr/pub/*	/usr/share/lib/*
/usr/spool/*	/var/spool/*
/usr/tmp/*	/var/tmp/*

There are some additional directories in root that did not appear in previous software releases. These directories are:

```
/export    /opt    /sbin    /stand    /var
/home      /proc
```

The root directories are explained in the next section. Important administrative files and subdirectories are explained later.

Directories in root

The / (root) file system contains executables and other files necessary to boot and run the system. The directories of the root file system are explained next.

/bck

The **/bck** directory is used to mount a backup file system for restoring files.

/boot

The **/boot** directory contains configurable object files created by the **/usr/sbin/mkboot** program (see **mkboot**(1M)).

/conf

The **/conf** directory contains files that define the hardware drivers, software drivers, and system parameters used to build the UNIX system file **/stand/unix**.

/dev

The **/dev** directory contains block and character special files that are usually associated with hardware devices or STREAMS drivers.

/dgn

The **/dgn** directory contains diagnostic programs.

/etc

The **/etc** directory contains machine-specific configuration files and system administration databases.

/export

The **/export** directory contains the default root of the exported file system tree.

/home

The **/home** directory contains user directories.

/install

The **/install** directory is used by the packaging commands to mount add-on packages for installation and removal (**/install** file system).

/lost+found

The **/lost+found** directory is used by **fsck** to save disconnected files and directories.

/mnt

The **/mnt** directory is used to mount file systems for temporary use.

/opt

The **/opt** directory is the mount point from which add-on application packages are installed.

/proc

The **/proc** directory is the mount point of the **proc** file system which provides information on the system's processes.

/save

The **/save** directory is used by packaging commands for saving data on floppy diskettes.

/sbin

The **/sbin** directory contains executables used in the booting process and in manual recovery from a system failure.

/stand

The **/stand** directory is used as the mount point for the boot file system, which contains the standalone (bootable) programs and data files necessary for the system boot procedure.

/tmp

The **/tmp** directory contains temporary files.

/usr

The **/usr** directory is the mount point of the **usr** file system.

/var

The **/var** directory is the mount point of the **var** file system. It contains those files and directories that vary from machine to machine, such as **tmp**, **spool** and **mail**. The **/var** file system also contains administrative directories such as **/var/adm** and **/var/opt**, the latter is installed by application packages.

Directories in /etc

This section describes the directories under the **/etc** directory, which contain machine-specific configuration files and system administration databases.

/etc/bkup

This directory contains machine-specific files and directories for the extended backup and restore operations. Also contained here are files and directories that allow restore operations to be performed from single-user mode (system state 1).

/etc/bkup/method

This directory contains files that describe all the extended backup and restore methods currently used on your computer.

/etc/cron.d

This directory contains administrative files for controlling and monitoring **cron** activities.

/etc/default

This directory contains files that assign default values to certain system parameters.

/etc/init.d

This directory contains executable files used in upward and downward transitions to all system states. These files are linked to files beginning with **S** (start) or **K** (stop) in **/etc/rc**n**.d**, where n is the appropriate system state. Files are executed from the **/etc/rc**n**.d** directories.

/etc/lp

This directory contains the configuration files and interface programs for the LP print service.

/etc/mail

This directory contains files used in administering the electronic mail system.

/etc/mail/lists

This directory contains files, each of which contains a mail alias. The name of each file is the name of the mail alias that it contains. (See the **mailx**(1) command for a description of the mail alias format.)

/etc/rc.d

This directory contains executable files that perform the various functions needed to initialize the system to system state 2. The files are executed when **/usr/sbin/rc2** is run. (Files contained in this directory before UNIX System V Release 3.0 were moved to **/etc/rc2.d**. This directory is maintained only for compatibility reasons.)

/etc/rc0.d

This directory contains files executed by **/usr/sbin/rc0** for transitions to system states 0, 5, and 6. Files in this directory are linked from the **/etc/init.d** directory, and begin with either a **K** or an **S**. **K** shows processes that are stopped, and **S** shows processes that are started when entering system states 0, 5, or 6.

/etc/rc1.d

This directory contains files executed by **/usr/sbin/rc1** for transitions to system state 1. Files in this directory are linked from the **/etc/init.d** directory, and begin with either a **K** or an **S**. **K** shows processes that should be stopped, and **S** shows processes that should be started when entering system state 1.

/etc/rc2.d

This directory contains files executed by **/usr/sbin/rc2** for transitions to system state 2. Files in this directory are linked from the **/etc/init.d** directory, and begin with either a **K** or an **S**. **K** shows processes that should be stopped, and **S** shows processes that should be started when entering system state 2.

/etc/rc3.d

This directory contains files executed by **/usr/sbin/rc3** for transitions to system state 3 (multi-user mode). Files in this directory are linked from the **/etc/init.d** directory, and begin with either a **K** or an **S**. **K** shows processes that should be stopped, and **S** shows processes that should be started when entering system state 3.

`/etc/saf`

This directory contains files and subdirectories used by the Service Access Facility. The following commands in **/usr/sbin** use **/etc/saf** subdirectories for data storage and retrieval: **nlsadmin, pmadm** and **sacadm**. The following files are included:

_sactab	A list of port monitors to be started by the Service Access Controller (SAC). Each port monitor listed in this table has a **_pmtab** file in the **/etc/saf/** *pmtag* directory, where *pmtag* is the tag of this port monitor (such as **/etc/saf/starlan** for the starlan port monitor).
_sysconfig	The configuration script used to modify the environment for the Service Access Facility.

`/etc/save.d`

This directory contains files used by the **sysadm** command for backing up data on floppy diskettes. The following files are included:

except	A list of the directories and files that should not be copied as part of a backup is maintained in this file.
timestamp/ . . .	The date and time of the last backup (volume or incremental) is maintained for each file system in the **/etc/save.d/timestamp** directory.

`/etc/shutdown.d`

This directory is maintained only for compatibility reasons. The files contained in this directory prior to UNIX System V Release 3.0 were executable files that invoked the various functions required during the transition to the single-user mode (system states 1, s, or S). These files are now located in **/etc/rc0.d**.

Files in /etc

The following files are used in machine-specific configuration and system administration databases.

`/etc/bkup/bkexcept.tab`

This file contains a list of files to be excluded from an incremental backup.

`/etc/bkup/bkhist.tab`

This file contains information about the success of all backup attempts.

`/etc/bkup/bkreg.tab`

This file contains instructions to the system for performing backup operations on your computer.

`/etc/bkup/bkstatus.tab`

This file contains the status of backup operations currently taking place.

`/etc/bkup/rsmethod.tab`

This file contains descriptions of the types of objects that may be restored using the full or partial restore method.

`/etc/bkup/rsnotify.tab`

This file contains the electronic mail address of the operator to be notified whenever restore requests require operator intervention.

`/etc/bkup/rsstatus.tab`

This file contains a list of all restore requests made by users of your computer.

`/etc/bkup/rsstrat.tab`

This file specifies a strategy for selecting archives when handling restore requests. In completing restore operations for these requests, the backup history log is used to navigate through the backup tape to find the desired files and or directories.

`/etc/d_passwd`

This file contains a list of programs that will require dial-up passwords when run from **login**. Each line in the file is formatted as

> *program*:*encrypted_password*:

where *program* is the full path to any programs into which a user can log in and run. The password referred to in the *encrypted_password* is the one that will be used by the dial-up password program. This password must be entered before the user is given the login prompt. It is used in conjunction with the file `/etc/dialups`.

`/etc/default/cron`

This file contains the default status (**enable** or **disable**) for the **CRONLOG** operation.

`/etc/default/login`

This file may contain the following parameters that define a user's login environment:

ALTSHELL   Alternate shell status available to users (**yes** or **no**).

Directory and File Management

CONSOLE	Root login allowed only at the console terminal.
HZ	Number of clock ticks per second.
IDLEWEEKS	Number of weeks a password may remain unchanged before the user is denied access to the system.
PASSREQ	Password requirement on logins (**yes** or **no**).
PATH	User's default **PATH**.
SUPATH	Root's default **PATH**.
TIMEOUT	Number of seconds allowed for logging in before a timeout occurs.
TIMEZONE	Time zone used within the user's environment.
ULIMIT	File size limit (**ulimit**).
UMASK	User's value for **umask**.

/etc/default/passwd

This file contains the following information about the length and aging of user passwords:

MINWEEKS	Minimum number of weeks before a password can be changed.
MAXWEEKS	Maximum number of weeks a password can be unchanged.
PASSLENGTH	Minimum number of characters in a password.
WARNWEEKS	Number of weeks before a password expires that the user is to be warned.

/etc/default/su

This file contains values for the following parameters affecting the work of privileged users:

SULOG	A pathname that identifies a file in which a log of all **su** attempts may be created.
CONSOLE	Pathnames of the console on which are broadcast messages notifying you whenever someone attempts to **su root**.
PATH	**PATH** used for **su** users.
SUPATH	**PATH** used for **su root** users.

/etc/device.tab

This file is the device table. It lists the device alias, path to the vnode, and special attributes of every device connected to the computer.

/etc/devlock.tab

This file is created at run time and lists the reserved (locked) devices. Device reservations do not remain intact across system reboots.

/etc/saf/*pmtag***/_config**

This file contains a configuration script used to customize the environment for the port monitor tagged as *pmtag* (such as **/etc/saf/starlan/_config** for the starlan port monitor). Port monitor configuration scripts are optional.

/etc/dgroup.tab

This file lists the group or groups to which a device belongs.

/etc/dialups

This file contains a list of terminal devices that cannot be accessed without a dial-up password. It is used in conjunction with the file **/etc/d_passwd**.

/etc/group

This file describes each user group to the system. An entry is added for each new group with the **groupadd** command.

/etc/inittab

This file contains instructions for the **/sbin/init** command. The instructions define the processes created or stopped for each initialization state. Initialization states are called system states or run states. By convention, system state 1 (or S or s) is single-user mode; system states 2 and 3 are multi-user modes. (See **inittab**(4) in the *System Files and Devices Reference* for additional information.)

/etc/mail/mailcnfg

This file permits per-site customizing of the mail subsystem. See the **mailcnfg**(4) manual page in the *System Files and Devices Reference* and the ''Administering the Mail Subsystem'' chapter in the *System Administration*.

/etc/mail/mailsurr

This file lists actions to be taken when mail containing particular patterns is processed by **mail**. This can include routing translations and logging. See the **mailsurr**(4) manual page in the *System Files and Devices Reference*.

/etc/mail/mailx.rc

This file contains defaults for the **mailx** program. It may be added by the system administrator. See **mailx**(1).

/etc/mail/notify and **/etc/mail/notify.sys**

These files are used by the **notify** program to determine the location of users in a networked environment and to establish systems to use in case of file error.

/etc/motd

This file contains the message of the day. The message of the day is displayed on a user's screen after that user has successfully logged in. (The commands that produce this output on the screen are in the **/etc/profile** file.) This message should be kept short and to the point. The **/var/news** files should be used for lengthy messages.

/etc/passwd

This file identifies each user to the system. An entry is automatically added for each new user with the **useradd** command, removed with the **userdel** command, and modified with the **usermod** command.

/etc/profile

This file contains the default profile for all users. The standard (default) environment for all users is established by the instructions in the **/etc/profile** file. The system administrator can change this file to set options for the **root** login. For example, the six lines of code shown in Figure 7-11 can be added to the **/etc/profile**. This code defines the erase character, automatically identifies the terminal type, and sets the **TERM** variable when the login ID is **root**.

Figure 7-11: Excerpt from /etc/profile

```
1  if [ ${LOGNAME} = root ]
2      then
3          stty echoe
4          echo "Terminal: 5          export TERM
6      fi
```

/etc/dfs/dfstab

This file specifies the distributed file system resources from your machine that are automatically shared to remote machines when entering system state 3. Each entry in this file should be a **share**(1M) command line.

/etc/saf/_pmtag_**/_pmtab**

This is the administrative file for the port monitor tagged as _pmtag_. It contains an entry for each service available through the _pmtag_ port monitor.

`/etc/saf/_sactab`

This file contains information about all port monitors for which the Service Access Controller (SAC) is responsible.

`/etc/saf/_sysconfig`

This file contains a configuration script to customize the environments for all port monitors on the system. This per-system configuration file is optional.

`/etc/TIMEZONE`

This file sets the time zone shell variable **TZ**. The **TZ** variable is initially established for the system via the **sysadm setup** command. The **TZ** variable in the **TIMEZONE** file is changed by the **sysadm timezone** command. The **TZ** variable can be redefined on a user (login) basis by setting the variable in the associated **.profile**. The **TIMEZONE** file is executed by **/usr/sbin/rc2**. (See **timezone**(4) in the *System Files and Devices Reference* for more information.)

`/etc/ttydefs`

This file contains information used by ttymon port monitor to set the terminal modes and baud rate for a TTY port.

`/etc/vfstab`

This file provides default values for file systems and remote resources. The following information can be stored in this file:

- The block and character devices on which file systems reside

- The resource name

- The location where a file system is usually mounted

- The file system type

- Information on special mounting procedures

These defaults do not override command line arguments that have been entered manually. (See **mountall**(1M) in the *Command Reference* for additional information.) Figure 7-12 shows a sample of this file.

Figure 7-12: Sample `/etc/vfstab` **File**

```
1  #special              fsckdev              mountp    fstype fsckpass automnt mntflags
2  /dev/SA/diskette1     /dev/rdiskette       /install  s5     -        no      -
3  /dev/diskette         /dev/rdiskette       /install  s5     -        no      -
4  /dev/dsk/c1d0s3       /dev/rdsk/c1d0s3     /stand    bfs    1        yes     -
5  /dev/dsk/c1d0s8       /dev/rdsk/c1d0s8     /usr2     s5     1        yes     -
6  /dev/dsk/c1d1s2       /dev/rdsk/c1d1s2     /usr      s5     1        yes     -
7  /dev/dsk/c1d1s8       /dev/rdsk/c1d1s8     /home     s5     1        yes     -
8  /dev/root             /dev/root            -         s5     -        no      -
9  /proc                 -                    /proc     proc   -        no      -
```

Directories in /usr

This section describes the directories in the **/usr** file system. The **/usr** file system contains architecture-dependent and architecture-independent files and system administration databases that can be shared.

/usr/bin

This directory contains public commands and system utilities.

/usr/include

This directory contains public header files for C programs.

/usr/lib

This directory contains public libraries, daemons, and architecture dependent databases.

/usr/lib/lp

This directory contains the directories and files used in processing requests to the LP print service.

/usr/lib/mail

This directory contains directories and files used in processing mail.

/usr/lib/mail/surrcmd

This directory contains programs necessary for mail surrogate processing.

/usr/sadm/bkup

This directory contains executables for the extended backup and restore services.

`/usr/sbin`

This directory contains executables used for system administration.

`/usr/share`

This directory contains architecture independent files that can be shared.

`/usr/share/lib`

This directory contains architecture independent databases.

`/usr/sadm/skel`

This directory contains the files and directories built when using the **useradd** command with the **-m** argument. All directories and files under this location are built under the **$HOME** location for the new user.

`/usr/ucb`

This directory contains binaries from the BSD Compatibility Package.

`/usr/ucbinclude`

This directory contains header files from the BSD Compatibility Package.

`/usr/ucblib`

This directory contains libraries from the BSD Compatibility Package.

Files in /usr

This section describes the files in the **/usr** directories, which contain architecture-dependent and architecture-independent files and system administrative data-bases that can be shared.

`/usr/sbin/rc0`

This file contains a shell script executed by **/usr/sbin/shutdown** for transitions to single-user state, and by **/sbin/init** for transitions to system states 0, 5, and 6. Files in the **/etc/shutdown.d** and **/etc/rc0.d** directories are executed when **/usr/sbin/rc0** is run. The file **K00ANNOUNCE** in **/etc/rc0.d** prints the message **System services are now being stopped**. Any task that you want executed when the system is taken to system states 0, s, 5, or 6 is done by adding a file to the **/etc/rc0.d** directory.

`/usr/sbin/rc1`

This file contains a shell script executed by **/sbin/init** for transitions to system state 1 (single-user state). Executable files in the **/etc/rc.d** directory and any executable files beginning with **S** or **K** in the **/etc/rc1.d** directories are executed when **/usr/sbin/rc1** is run. All files in **rc1.d** are linked from files in the **/etc/init.d** directory. Other files may be added to the **/etc/rc1.d** directory as a function of adding hardware or software to the system.

Directory and File Management

/usr/sbin/rc2

This file contains a shell script executed by **/sbin/init** for transitions to system state 2 (multi-user state). Executable files in the **/etc/rc.d** directory and any executable files beginning with **S** or **K** in the **/etc/rc2.d** directories are executed when **/usr/sbin/rc2** is run. All files in **rc2.d** are linked from files in the **/etc/init.d** directory. Other files may be added to the **/etc/rc2.d** directory as a function of adding hardware or software to the system.

/usr/sbin/rc3

This file is executed by **/sbin/init**. It executes the shell scripts in **/etc/rc3.d** for transitions to a distributed file system mode (system state 3).

/usr/sbin/rc6

This shell script is run for transitions to system state 6 (for example, using **shutdown -i6**). If the kernel needs reconfiguring, the **/sbin/buildsys** script is run. If reconfiguration succeeds, **/usr/sbin/rc6** reboots without running diagnostics. If reconfiguration fails, it spawns a shell.

/usr/sbin/shutdown

This file contains a shell script to shut down the system gracefully in preparation for a system backup or scheduled downtime. After stopping all nonessential processes, the **shutdown** script executes files in the **/etc/shutdown.d** directory by calling **/usr/sbin/rc0** for transitions to system state 1 (single-user state). For transitions to other system states, the **shutdown** script calls **/sbin/init**.

/usr/share/lib/mailx/mailx.help and /usr/share/lib/mailx/mailx.help.

Help files for **mailx**. The file **mailx.help.~** contains help messages for **mailx**'s tilde commands. See **mailx**(1) in the *Command Reference*.

Directories in /var

This section describes the directories of the **/var** directory, which contain files and directories that vary from machine to machine.

/var/adm

This directory contains system logging and accounting files.

/var/cron

This directory contains the **cron** log file.

/var/lp

This directory contains log files for the LP print service.

/var/mail

This directory contains subdirectories and mail files that users access with the **mail**(1) and **mailx**(1) commands.

/var/mail/:saved

This directory contains temporary storage for mail messages while **mail** is running. Files are named with the user's ID while they are in **/var/mail**.

/var/news

This directory contains news files. The file names are descriptive of the contents of the files; they are analogous to headlines. When a user reads the news, using the **news** command, an empty file named **.news_time** is created in his or her login directory. The date (time) of this file is used by the **news** command to determine if a user has read the latest news file(s).

/var/opt

This directory is created and used by application packages.

/var/options

This directory contains a file (or symbolic link to a file) that identifies each utility installed on the system. This directory also contains information created and used by application packages (such as temporary files and logs).

/var/preserve

This directory contains backup files for **vi** and **ex**.

/var/sadm

This directory contains logging and accounting files for the backup and restore services, software installation utilities, and package management facilities.

/var/sadm/pkg

This directory contains data directories for installed software packages.

/var/saf

This directory contains log files for the Service Access Facility.

/var/spool

This directory contains temporary spool files.

/var/spool/cron/crontabs

This directory contains **crontab** files for the **adm**, **root** and **sys** logins. Users whose login IDs are in the **/etc/cron.d/cron.allow** file can establish their own **crontab** file using the **crontab** command. If the **cron.allow** file does not exist, the **/etc/cron.d/cron.deny** file is checked to determine if the user should be denied the use of the **crontab** command.

As **root**, you can use the **crontab** command to make the desired entries. Revisions to the file take effect at the next reboot. The file entries support the **calendar** reminder service and the Basic Networking Utilities. Remember, you can use the **cron** command to decrease the number of tasks you perform with the **sysadm** command; include recurring and habitual tasks in your **crontab** file. (See **crontab**(1) in the *Command Reference* for additional information.)

/var/spool/lp

This directory contains temporary print job files.

/var/spool/smtpq

This directory contains Simple Mail Transfer Protocol (SMTP) directories and log files. Directories named *host* contain messages spooled to be sent to that host. Files named **LOG.** *n* contain the logs from the past seven days (Sunday's log is called **log.0**). The current day's log is simply **LOG**.

/var/spool/uucp

This directory contains files to be sent by **uucp**.

/var/spool/uucppublic

This directory contains files received by **uucp**.

/var/tmp

This directory contains temporary files.

/var/uucp

This directory contains logging and accounting files for **uucp**.

Files in /var

This section describes the files in the **/var** directories, which contain information that varies from machine to machine.

/var/adm/spellhist

If the Spell Utility is installed, this file contains a history of all words that the **spell** command fails to match. Periodically, this file should be reviewed for words that you can add to the dictionary. Clear the **spellhist** file after reviewing it. (Refer to **spell**(1) in the *Command Reference* for information on adding words to the dictionary, cleaning up the **spellhist** file, and other commands that can be used with the Spell Utility.)

/var/adm/utmp

This file contains information on the current system state. This information is accessed with the **who** command.

/var/adm/utmpx

This file contains information similar to that in the **/var/adm/utmp** file, along with a record of the remote host.

/var/adm/wtmp

This file contains a history of system logins. The owner and group of this file must be **adm**, and the access permissions must be 664. Each time **login** is run this file is updated. As the system is accessed, this file increases in size. Periodically, this file should be cleared or truncated. The command line **>/var/adm/wtmp** when executed by **root** creates the file with nothing in it. The following command lines limit the size of the **/var/adm/wtmp** file to the last 3600 characters in the file:

```
# tail -3600c /var/adm/wtmp > /var/tmp/wtmp
# mv /var/tmp/wtmp /var/adm/wtmp
#
```

The **/usr/sbin/cron**, **/usr/sbin/rc0**, or **/usr/sbin/rc2** command can be used to clean up the **wtmp** file. You can add the appropriate command lines to the **/var/spool/cron/crontabs/root** file or add shell command lines to directories such as **/etc/rc2.d**, **/etc/rc3.d**, and so on.

/var/adm/wtmpx

This file contains information similar to that in the **/var/adm/wtmp** file, along with a record of the remote host.

/var/adm/loginlog

If this file exists, it is a text file that contains one entry for each group of five consecutive unsuccessful attempts to log in to the system.

/var/adm/sulog

This file contains a history of substitute user (**su**) command usage. As a security measure, this file should not be readable by **others**. The **/var/adm/sulog** file should be truncated periodically to keep the size of the file within a reasonable limit. The **/usr/sbin/cron**, the **/usr/sbin/rc0**, or the **/usr/sbin/rc2** command can be used to clean up the **sulog** file. You can add the appropriate command lines to the **/var/spool/cron/crontabs/root** file or add shell command lines to directories such as **/etc/rc2.d**, **/etc/rc3.d**, and so on. The following command lines limit the size of the log file to the last 100 lines in the file:

```
# tail -100 /var/adm/sulog > /var/tmp/sulog
# mv /var/tmp/sulog /var/adm/sulog
#
```

`/var/cron/log`

This file contains a history of all actions taken by **/usr/sbin/cron**. The **/var/cron/log** file should be truncated periodically to keep the size of the file within a reasonable limit. The **/usr/sbin/cron, /usr/sbin/rc0,** or **/usr/sbin/rc2** command can be used to clean up the **/var/cron/log** file. You can add the appropriate command lines to the **/var/spool/cron/crontabs/root** file or add shell command lines in the following directories (as applicable): **/etc/rc2.d, /etc/rc3.d,** (and so on). The following command lines limit the size of the log file to the last 100 lines in the file:

```
# tail -100 /var/cron/log > /var/tmp/log
# mv /var/tmp/log /var/cron/log
#
```

/var/sadm/bkup/logs/bklog

This file contains a process log used when troubleshooting a backup operation.

/var/sadm/bkup/logs/bkrs

This file contains a process log used when troubleshooting a backup or restore operation for which a method was not specified.

/var/sadm/bkup/logs/rslog

This file contains a process log used when troubleshooting a restore operation.

/var/sadm/bkup/toc

This file contains table of contents entries created by a backup method.

File Access Controls

When the `ls -l` command displays the contents of a directory, the first column of output describes the "mode" of the file. This information tells you not only what type of file it is, but who has permission to access it. This first field is 10 characters long. The first character defines the file type and can be one of the following types:

Figure 7-13: File Types

Type	Symbol
Text, programs, etc.	-
Directories	d
Character special	c
Block special	b
FIFO (named pipe) special	p
Symbolic links	l

Using this key to interpret the previous screen, you can see that the **starship** directory contains three directories and two regular disk files.

The next several characters, which are either letters or hyphens, identify who has permission to read and use the file or directory. (Permissions are discussed in the description of the **chmod** function under "Accessing and Manipulating Files" later in this chapter.)

The following number is the link count. For a file, this equals the number of users linked to that file. For a directory, this number shows the number of directories immediately under it plus two (for the directory itself and its parent directory).

Next, the login name of the file's owner appears (here it is **starship**), followed by the group name of the file or directory (**project**).

The following number shows the length of the file or directory entry measured in units of information (or memory) called bytes. The month, day, and time that the file was last modified is given next. Finally, the last column shows the name of the directory or file.

Figure 7-14 identifies each column in the rows of output from the `ls -l` command.

Figure 7-14: Description of Output Produced by the `ls -l` **Command**

```
                    number of        owner              length of
                    blocks used      name               file in bytes


                        number       group                                   name
                        of links     name


              total 30
          d   rwxr-xr-x 3 starship proj     96 Oct 27 08:16   bin
          d   rwxr-xr-x 2 starship proj     64 Nov  1 14:19   draft
 File     d   rwxr-xr-x 2 starship proj     80 Nov  8 08:41   letters
 type     -   rwx------ 2 starship proj 12301 Nov  2 10:15   list
          -   rw------- 1 starship proj     40 Oct 27 10:00   mbox


              permissions                     time/date last
                                              modified
```

File Protection

Because the UNIX operating system is a multi-user system, you usually do not work alone in the file system. System users can follow pathnames to various directories and read and use files belonging to one another, as long as they have permission to do so.

If you own a file, you can decide who has the right to read it, write in it (make changes to it), or, if it is a program, to execute it. You can also restrict permissions for directories. When you grant execute permission for a directory, you allow the specified users to change directory to it and list its contents with the **ls** command [see **ls**(1)]. Only the owner or a privileged user can define the following:

- which users have permission to access data

- which types of permission they have (that is, how they are allowed to use the data)

This section introduces access-permissions for files and discusses file protection.

File Permissions

UNIX System V defines access-control and privilege mechanisms to allow for extended-security-controls that implement security policies different from those in UNIX System V, but which avoid altering or overriding the defined semantics of any functions in UNIX System V. Although quite simple, the access-control scheme has some unusual features. Each UNIX System V user has a unique user-identification (user-id) number, as well as a shared group-identification (group-id) number. A file is tagged with the user-id and group-id of its owner, and a set of access-permission-bits when created by **open**, **creat**, **mkdir**, **mknod** and **mkfifo** [see **open**(2), **creat**(2), **mkdir**(2), **mknod**(2) and **mkfifo**(2)]. UNIX System V file-access-control uses the access-permission-bits to specify independent read, write and execute permissions for the *owner* of the file, for any members of the owner's *group* and for any *other* users. For directories, execute permission means *search* permission. These access-permission-bits are changed by **chmod**, and are read by **stat** and **fstat** [see **chmod**(2), **stat**(2) and **fstat**(2)].

When a process requests file-access-permission for read, write or execute/search, access is determined as follows:

1. If the effective-user-id of the process is a user with appropriate access-permissions (such as a privileged user).

   a. If read, write or directory search permission is requested, access is granted.

   b. If execute permission is requested, access is granted if execute permission is granted to at least one user by the file-permission-bits or by an alternate-access-control mechanism; otherwise, access is denied.

2. Otherwise:

   a. The read, write and execute/search access-permissions on a file are granted to a process if one or more of the following are true [see **chmod**(2)]:

- The appropriate access-permission-bit of the *owner* portion of the file-mode is set and the effective-user-id of the process matches the user-id of the owner of the file

- The appropriate access-permission-bit of the *group* portion of the file-mode is set, the effective-group-id of the process matches the group-id of the file and the effective-user-id of the process fails to match the user-id of the owner of the file.

- The appropriate access-permission-bit of the *other* portion of the file-mode is set, the effective-group-id of the process fails to match the group-id of the file and the effective-user-id of the process fails to match the user-id of the owner of the file.

Otherwise, the corresponding access-permissions on a file are denied to the process.

b. Access is granted if an alternate-access-control mechanism is not enabled and the requested access-permission-bit is set for the class to which the process belongs, or if an alternate-access-control mechanism is enabled and it allows the requested access; otherwise, access is denied.

Implementations may provide additional-file-access-control or alternate-file-access-control mechanisms, or both. An additional-access-control mechanism only further restricts the file-access-permissions defined by the file-permission-bits. An alternate-access-control mechanism shall:

1. specify file-permission-bits for the file-owner-class, file-group-class and file-other-class of the file, corresponding to the access-permissions, that **stat** and **fstat** return.

2. Be enabled only by explicit user action, on a per-file basis by the file-owner or a user with the appropriate-privilege.

3. Be disabled for a file after the file-permission-bits are changed for that file with **chmod**. The disabling of the alternate mechanism need not disable any additional mechanisms defined by an implementation.

UNIX System V recognizes one particular user-id, the "super-user", as exempt from the usual constraints on file access; thus, for example, programs may be written to dump and reload the file system without unwanted interference from the protection system. A process is recognized as a super-user process and is granted special privileges if its effective-user-id is 0.

Setting Default Permissions

When a file is created its default permissions are set. These default settings may be changed by placing an appropriate **umask** command in the system profile (`/etc/profile`).

Figure 7-15: umask(1) **Settings for Different Security Levels**

Level of Security	umask	Disallows
Permissive	0002	w for others
Moderate	0027	w for group, rwx for others
Severe	0077	rwx for group and others

How to Determine Existing Permissions

You can determine what permissions are currently in effect on a file or a directory by using **ls -l** to produce a long listing of a directory's contents.

In the first field of the **ls -l** output, the next nine characters are interpreted as three sets of three bits each. The first set refers to the owner's permissions; the next to permissions of members in the file's group; and the last to all others. Within each set, the three characters show permission to read, to write, and to execute the file as a program, respectively. For a directory, "execute" permission is interpreted to mean permission to search the directory for a specified file. For example, typing **ls -l** while in the directory named **starship/bin** in the sample file system produces the following output:

```
$ ls -l
total 35
-rwxr-xr-x   1 starship      project      9346  Nov 1  08:06  display
-rw-r--r--   1 starship      project      6428  Dec 2  10:24  list
drwx--x--x   2 starship      project        32  Nov 8  15:32  tools
$
```

Permissions for the **display** and **list** files and the **tools** directory are shown on the left of the screen under the line **total 35**, and appear in this format:

    -rwxr-xr-x   (for the display file)
    -rw-r--r--   (for the list file))
    drwx--x--x   (for the tools directory)

After the initial character, which describes the file type (for example, a - (dash) symbolizes a regular file and a **d** a directory), the other nine characters that set the permissions comprise three sets of three characters. The first set refers to permissions for the *owner*, the second set to permissions for *group* members, and the last set to permissions for all *other* system users. Within each set of characters, the **r**, **w** and **x** show the permissions currently granted to each category. If a dash appears instead of an **r**, **w** or **x** permission to read, write or execute is denied.

The following diagram summarizes this breakdown for the file named **display**.

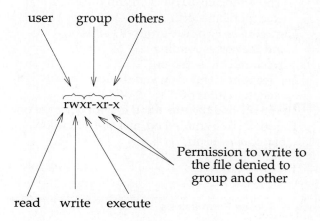

As you can see, the owner has **r**, **w**, and **x** permissions and members of the group and other system users have **r** and **x** permissions.

There are two exceptions to this notation system. Occasionally the letter **s** or the letter **l** may appear in the permissions line, instead of an **r**, **w** or **x**. The letter **s** (short for set user ID or set group ID) represents a special type of permission to execute a file. It appears where you normally see an **x** (or -) for the user or group (the first and second sets of permissions). From a user's point of view it is equivalent to an **x** in the same position; it implies that execute permission exists. It is significant only for programmers and system administrators. (See the *System Administration* guide for details about setting the user or group ID.) The letter **l** indicates that locking will occur when the file is accessed. It does not mean that the file has been locked. The permissions are as follows:

Figure 7-16: File Access Permissions

Symbol	Explanation
r	The file is readable.
w	The file is writable.
x	The file is executable.
-	This permission is *not* granted.
l	Mandatory locking will occur during access. (The set-group-ID bit is on and the *group* execution bit is off.)
s	The set-user-ID or set-group-ID bit is on, and the corresponding *user* or *group* execution bit is also on.
S	The set-user-ID bit is on and the *user* execution bit is off.
t	The sticky and the execution bits for *other* are on.
T	The sticky bit is turned on, and the execution bit for *other* is off.

Figure 7-17: Directory Access Permissions

Symbol	Explanation
r	The directory is readable.
w	The directory may be altered (files may be added or removed).
x	The directory may be searched. (This permission is required to **cd** to the directory.)
t	File removal from a writable directory is limited to the owner of the directory or file unless the file is writable.

How to Change Existing Permissions

After you have determined what permissions are in effect, you can change them by calling the **chmod** command in the following format:

chmod *who+permission file(s)*

Directory and File Management

or

    chmod *who=permission file(s)*

The following list defines each component of this command line.

chmod	name of the program
who	one of three user groups (**u**, **g** or **o**)
	u = user
	g = group
	o = others
+ or **-**	instruction that grants (**+**) or denies (**-**) permission
permission	any combination of three authorizations (**r**, **w** and **x**)
	r = read
	w = write
	x = execute
file(s)	file (or directory) name(s) listed; assumed to be branches from your current directory, unless you use full pathnames.

NOTE   The **chmod** command will not work if you type a space(s) between *who*, the instruction that gives (**+**) or denies (**-**) permission, and the *permission*.

The following examples show a few possible ways to use the **chmod** command. As the owner of **display**, you can read, write, and run this executable file. You can protect the file against being accidentally changed by denying yourself write (**w**) permission. To do this, type the command line:

    chmod u-w display

After receiving the prompt, type **ls -l** and press the RETURN key to verify that this permission has been changed, as shown in the following screen.

```
$ chmod u-w display
$ ls -l
total 35
-r-xr-xr-x   1 starship     project       9346  Nov 1  08:06  display
rw-r--r--    1 starship     project       6428  Dec 2  10:24  list
drwx--x--x   2 starship     project         32  Nov 8  15:32  tools
$
```

As you can see, you no longer have permission to write changes into the file. You will not be able to change this file until you restore write permission for yourself.

Now consider another example. Notice that permission to write into the file **display** has been denied to members of your group and other system users. However, they do have read permission. This means they can copy the file into their own directories and then make changes to it. To prevent all system users from copying this file, you can deny them read permission by typing:

> chmod go-r display

The **g** and **o** stand for group members and all other system users, respectively, and the **-r** denies them permission to read or copy the file. Check the results with the **ls -l** command.

```
$ chmod go-r display
$ ls -l
total 35
-rwx--x--x   1 starship      project        9346  Nov 1  08:06  display
rw-r--r--    1 starship      project        6428  Dec 2  10:24  list
drwx--x--x   2 starship      project          32  Nov 8  15:32  tools
$
```

For more information, refer to **ls**(1) and **chmod**(1) in the *Command Reference*.

A Note on Permissions and Directories

You can use the **chmod** command to grant or deny permission for directories as well as files. Simply specify a directory name instead of a file name on the command line.

However, consider the impact on various system users of changing permissions for directories. For example, suppose you grant read permission for a directory to yourself (**u**), members of your group (**g**), and other system users (**o**). Every user who has access to the system will be able to read the names of the files contained in that directory by running the **ls -l** command. Similarly, granting write permission allows the designated users to create new files in the directory and remove existing ones. Granting permission to execute the directory allows designated users to move to that directory (and make it their current directory) by using the **cd** command.

An Alternative Method

There are two methods by which the **chmod** command can be executed. The method described above, in which symbols such as **r**, **w** and **x** are used to specify permissions, is called the symbolic method.

An alternative method is the octal method. Its format requires you to specify permissions using three octal numbers, ranging from 0 to 7. (The octal number system is different from the decimal system that we typically use on a day-to-day basis.) To learn how to use the octal method, see the **chmod**(1) entry in the *Command Reference*.

Security Considerations

This section gives the software developer information on various security features and their impact on writing applications. While many of the security features, like Mandatory Access Control, are available only if the Enhanced Security Utilities are installed and running, it is to your advantage to program your application so that it will run on UNIX System V Release 4 with and without the Enhanced Security Utilities installed. This way, you can avoid programming the same application for each environment.

What Security Means to Programmers

As a programmer on UNIX System V Release 4, you need a general understanding of how security affects you and protects your files on the computer system. You also need to understand the difference between basic security and enhanced security. Finally, you need to understand the term Trusted Computing Base (TCB), an all-encompassing term which describes the mechanisms used to enforce Enhanced Security.

What Is Security?

Security for a computing system means that the information on the system is protected from unauthorized disclosure or modification. If each user had a personal non-networked computing system that was kept locked up, each user's files would be secure. But isolation and physical security are not practical in most circumstances.

On a computer system that many people share, the simplest security mechanism would be to allow only the owner of a file to access that file. That would be inconvenient, however, since one of the benefits of a computer system is the sharing of resources. For example, it would be wasteful for each user to have a private copy of each command. Commands are usually shared, but users often want to restrict access to the contents of data files.

On a secure system, each user has a unique identity and a level of authorization associated with that identity. For security to work, the computer system must have some way of identifying users, their level of authorization, and their files. For the most part, while you are logged in, all data you enter, create, and process belongs to you. Data is stored in named files on the computer system. Each file you own is kept separate from the rest of your files and from the files belonging to other users.

As a programmer, you are also concerned with the impact of security on users who run your programs.

A secure computer system must have a mechanism that makes access decisions, that is, one that decides who can access what, based upon user identity and authorization.

There are many ways in which the security of a computer system can be violated. Unauthorized access to read or write files can be the result of:

- the abuse of privileges by administrators

- malicious programs that gain privileges or access to files

- idle browsing of files that are inadequately protected

Most computer systems provide some degree of basic security.

How Basic Security Works

An operating system stores and processes information in the form of electronic data. In doing so, it provides an interface between you, the user of the computer, and the computer. An operating system provides you with commands, library routines, functions, and programs that allow you to tell the computer how to store and process the information that belongs to you.

A computer system enforces basic security by making access decisions, that is, by deciding who can access what. In order to make access decisions, a computer system uniquely identifies each user on the system and stores information in named files, each of which belongs to a single user on the system. It would be a potential violation of security if users could access any files at will.

UNIX System V supplies basic security through the use of the **login** and **passwd** (password) mechanisms, which identify you to the system and put you in control of your data. Also included in basic security are **access mode bits,** which give users some control over what other users can access their files. It is not a violation of basic security for users to have the ability to share individual files with specific other users.

Privileges

Privilege, in the simplest terms, is the ability to override system restrictions on the actions of users. All operating systems allow users to exercise special privilege, under certain conditions, to perform sensitive system operations. Sensitive system operations are those which affect the configuration of the system or its availability to users.

Most users cannot, for example, execute commands affecting the hardware or software configuration of the system. Activities such as mounting and checking file systems, adding users, modifying user profiles, adding and removing peripherals, installing application software, password administration, and administration of the user terminal lines, are restricted to certain users.

In UNIX System V Release 4.0 and previous releases, the restriction of privilege is implemented by designating a special user identifier (UID) of 0; the login name historically associated with this UID is **root**.

When a person logs in as **root**, that person has unrestricted access to every file on the system, and the ability to alter system operation. Commands that execute sensitive system operations check to see whether the effective UID of the process requesting the operation is 0. If it is, the user process is given unlimited access to the system.

The **root** login in UNIX System V Release 4.0 and previous releases possesses, in effect, the one privilege necessary to override all system restrictions on command execution and access: the superuser privilege.

UNIX System V Release 4.2 (SVR4.2) supplements this privilege mechanism with a more flexible mechanism to suit the needs of the user community. Now, rather than investing the power to issue any command on the system to one user, you can give partial super-user power to several users. By assigning privileges linked to specific tasks, you essentially assign a role to each such user.

This privilege mechanism is actually a combination of the old UID functionality supported in the UNIX operating system for over 20 years, and new, discrete privilege functionality.

The most important advantage of this privilege mechanism over the pure UID-based privilege mechanism is the fine granularity with which it can apportion system privileges to executing processes. For example, you might assign someone to the role of mail administrator. That person would have all the privileges necessary to oversee maintenance and troubleshooting of the mail subsystem, but no others; he or she wouldn't be able to add and delete user accounts, reorganize file systems, or do any other administrative work unrelated to electronic mail.

The superuser privilege can be replaced by a list of discrete privileges based on the categorization of sensitive system operations into groups of operations exercising the same kind of privilege. In other words, many different commands might need to override discretionary read access restrictions on files to perform their functions; defining a privilege such as P_DACREAD, and designating it as one of the possible privileges a command can have allows for a more controlled propagation of privileges by processes than the superuser privilege.

This means that there are two ways to acquire privilege with the superuser module (SUM) provided in SVR4.2: first, when the effective UID of a new process is equal to the tunable parameter PRIVID, and also, when an executable with fixed privileges is executed. With PRIVID set equal to 0, this behavior preserves the omnipotence of a process with effective uid 0. The system is delivered with PRIVID equal to 0.

It is important to recognize that the list of system privileges, and fixed privileges on files, are all part of the basic privilege mechanism provided by the operating system.

Privileges Associated with a File

For every executable file there may be a set of privileges that are acquired when that program is executed via an **exec** system call. This set of privileges is known as fixed privileges: they are always given to the new program, independent of the privileges of the parent or calling-process. Each executable file can have two sets of privileges associated with it that are propagated when that program is executed via an **exec** system call:

- Fixed privileges are always given to the new program, independent of the calling or parent process's privileges.

- Inheritable privileges will exist in the new program only if they existed in the previous program. Inheritable privileges are given to the new program only if they exist in the calling process's privilege set; inheritable privileges are only used by the LPM privilege module, not by the SUM privilege module. (See "Privilege Policy Modules" below.)

These sets are disjoint, that is, a privilege can not be defined as both fixed and inheritable for the same file. If an executable file does not require any privileges then this set is empty.

CAUTION Privileges associated with a file are removed when the validity information for the file changes (for example, when the file is opened for writing or when the modes of the file change). This removes the file from the Trusted Computing Base; the privileges must be set again in order for the command to run with privilege.

Manipulating File Privileges

Use the **filepriv** system call to set, retrieve, or count the privileges associated with a file [see **filepriv**(2)]. An administrative command also provides these same basic functions [see **filepriv**(1M)].

The **filepriv** system call has three command types:

- **PUTPRV** sets the privileges associated with a file. This is an absolute setting; the specified privileges replace any previously existing privileges for the file.

- **GETPRV** retrieves the privileges associated with a file.

- **CNTPRV** returns the number of privileges associated with a file.

privilege(5) lists the names of the privileges as well as some other important items. **priv**(5) lists some functions used to easily indicate to **filepriv** the particular privilege set to which a privilege belongs.

Some of the above command types require a list of privileges or return such a list. **PUTPRV** requires an array of privilege descriptors that lists the privileges to be set. A privilege descriptor is an integral data type that is assigned a value defining the privilege and the set it is in. Functions have been defined to make this task simpler. Use **pm_inher** to indicate an inheritable privilege. For example, **pm_fixed(P_DACREAD)** would indicate the **P_DACREAD** privilege in the fixed set. Similarly **pm_inher(P_MACREAD)** would indicate the **P_MACREAD** privilege in the inheritable set.

Figure 7-18 shows a code fragment that sets file privileges. Some of the privilege sets indicated in this example may or may not exist or be valid for your particular system.

Figure 7-18: Setting File Privileges

```
#include <priv.h>

priv_t privd[3];
/*
 * Set P_DACREAD and P_DACWRITE as inheritable and
 * P_SETUID as fixed for file /sbin/testprog.
 * This process must have P_SETFPRIV, P_DACREAD, P_DACWRITE, and
 * P_SETUID in its maximum set.
 */
privd[0] = pm_inher(P_DACREAD);
privd[1] = pm_inher(P_DACWRITE);
privd[2] = pm_fixed(P_SETUID);
if (filepriv("/sbin/testprog", PUTPRV, privd, 3) == -1) {
        /* Some error occurred, display the error and exit. */
        perror("filepriv PUTPRV error");
        exit(1);
}
```

In this example, privileges are being set for the executable file **/sbin/testprog**.
The privileges **P_DACREAD** and **P_DACWRITE** are made inheritable, while **P_SETUID**
is made fixed. **pm_inher** and **pm_fixed** are used to assign values to the privilege
descriptors; the **pm_inher** function marks **P_DACREAD** and **P_DACWRITE** as inheritable while **pm_fixed** marks **P_SETUID** as fixed. The call to **filepriv** using
PUTPRV will set the indicated privileges for the file. If an error occurred, **perror** is
called to display an error message [see **perror**(3C)] and the program terminates.

NOTE — A privilege that is being set for a file must exist in the maximum set of the process making the **filepriv** system call.

NOTE — Since the **PUTPRV** command for **filepriv** is a privileged operation, a process
using this system call must have the appropriate privilege in its working set.
See intro(2) for a list of privileges.

Use the **GETPRV** command for the **filepriv** system call to determine the
privileges associated with a file. This command also requires a pointer to an array
of privilege descriptors. You must ensure that the array is large enough to contain
all the privileges associated with the file.

Figure 7-19 shows a code fragment that will retrieve the privileges associated with a file.

Figure 7-19: Retrieving File Privileges

```
#include <priv.h>

priv_t *privp;
int cnt;
/*
 * Determine the number of privileges for /sbin/testprog.
 */
if ((cnt = filepriv("/sbin/testprog", CNTPRV, (priv_t *)0, 0)) == -1) {
        /* filepriv failed; display error and exit. */
        perror("filepriv CNTPRV error");
        exit(1);
}
if (cnt > 0) {
        /*
         * malloc some memory and get the privileges.
         */
        if ((privp = (priv_t *)malloc(cnt * sizeof(priv_t)) == NULL) {
                exit(1);    /* Couldn't malloc so exit. */
        }
        if (filepriv("/sbin/testprog", GETPRV, privp, cnt) == -1) {
                /* filepriv failed; display error and exit. */
                perror("filepriv GETPRV error");
                exit(1);
        }
}
```

In this example, the **CNTPRV** command is used to determine the number of privileges. This number is then used to determine the amount of memory to request when calling **malloc** for an array large enough to contain all the privileges. [see **malloc**(3C)]. **filepriv** is then called with the **GETPRV** command to retrieve the actual privileges.

Privileges Associated with a Process

After a **fork**, the privileges of the parent and child processes are identical. However, when an **exec** system call is performed, the privileges of the new program are determined from those of the program performing the **exec** and from the privileges associated with the executable file.

Each process has three sets of privileges:

- The maximum set contains all the privileges granted to the process.

- The working set contains all the privileges currently being used by the process.

- The saved set contains all privileges acquired by executing files with fixed privileges.

How the privileges for a new process are determined is specific to the privilege (policy) module installed.

Manipulating Process Privileges

Use the **procpriv** system call to add, put, remove, retrieve, or count privileges associated with the calling process. This system call has five command types:

- **SETPRV** adds the requested privileges to the working set for the current process. Privileges already in the working set are not affected; they remain in the set. Requested privileges not in the current maximum set are ignored.

- **PUTPRV** sets the working and maximum sets for the current process. This is an absolute setting; the specified privileges replace the current working and maximum sets. Privileges requested which are not in the current maximum set are ignored.

- **CLRPRV** removes the requested privileges from either the working or maximum set. If a privilege is removed from the maximum set, it is also removed from the working set if it exists there, since the working set is always a subset of the maximum set.

- **GETPRV** retrieves the working and maximum privilege sets for the current process.

- **CNTPRV** returns the number of privileges associated with the current process.

Figure 7-20 shows a code fragment that does a **setuid** and uses **procpriv** to set and clear the appropriate privilege as needed.

Figure 7-20: Adding and Clearing Process Privileges

```
#include <priv.h>

priv_t privd[2];
int uid;

privd[0] = pm_work(P_SETUID);
privd[1] = pm_max(P_SETUID);
/*
 * Add P_SETUID to the working set of the current process.  P_SETUID
 * must be in the maximum working set to be successful.
 */
if (procpriv(SETPRV, privd, 1) == -1) {
        /* It failed, so display error and exit. */
        perror("procpriv SETPRV error");
        exit(1);
}
/*
 * Change to user id "uid" (previously initialized)
 */
if (setuid(uid) == -1) {
        /*
         * It failed, perhaps P_SETUID wasn't in our maximum working
         * set.  Display error and exit.
         */
        perror("setuid error");
        exit(1);
}
/*
 * We don't need P_SETUID any more so remove it from the working
 * and maximum sets.
 */
if (procpriv(CLRPRV, privd, 2) == -1) {
        /*
         * It failed, so display error and exit.
         */
        perror("procpriv CLRPRV error");
        exit(1);
}
```

The first call to **procpriv** sets the **P_SETUID** privilege in the process's working set. Note that the count of 1 in the system call indicates that only one (the first) element of the array **privd** is to be used. Once the privilege is in the working set, **setuid** is called. Since **P_SETUID** will not be required by the program any more, **procpriv** is again called, this time with the **CLRPRV** command.

Directory and File Management

Note in this case that the count of 2 indicates that both elements of array **privd** are to be used, thus removing the privilege from both the maximum and working sets. Note that if the privilege had only been removed from the maximum set, the system would have also removed it from the working set, since the working set must be a subset of the maximum set, that is, the working set can not contain privileges which are not in the maximum set.

Use the **PUTPRV** command for **procpriv** similarly to **SETPRV,** but remember that the setting is absolute, that is, the indicated privileges replace both the current working and maximum sets. The privileges you request must exist in the current maximum set.

Figure 7-21 shows a code fragment that uses the **PUTPRV** command to set the maximum and working sets.

Figure 7-21: Setting Process Privileges Using PUTPRV

```
#include <priv.h>

priv_t privd[2];

privd[0] = pm_max(P_SETUID);
/*
 * Set the maximum set to P_SETUID.  The working set is empty since
 * it is not set here.
 */
if (procpriv(PUTPRV, privd, 1) == -1) {
        /* It failed, so display error and exit. */
        perror("procpriv PUTPRV error");
        exit(1);
}
```

In this example, the privilege descriptor is set to **P_SETUID** in the maximum set. If **P_SETUID** is already in the maximum set, **procpriv** causes the new maximum set to contain only **P_SETUID**. The new working set will be empty, since no privileges are defined for it.

The **GETPRV** and **CNTPRV** commands work in a manner similar to their counterparts in the **filepriv** system call. Figure 7-22 shows a code fragment that will retrieve the privileges associated with a process.

Figure 7-22: Retrieving Process Privileges

```
#include <priv.h>

priv_t *privp;
int cnt;

/*
 * Determine the number of privileges for this process.
 */
if ((cnt = procpriv(CNTPRV, (priv_t *)0, 0)) == -1) {
        /* procpriv failed; display error and exit. */
        perror("procpriv CNTPRV error");
        exit(1);
}
if (cnt > 0) {
        /*
         * malloc some memory and get the privileges.
         */
        if ((privp = (priv_t *)malloc(cnt * sizeof(priv_t)) == NULL) {
                /* Couldn't malloc so exit. */
                exit(1);
        }
        if (procpriv(GETPRV, privp, cnt) == -1) {
                /* procpriv failed; display error and exit. */
                perror("procpriv GETPRV error");
                exit(1);
        }
}
```

In this example, the number of privileges returned by the **CNTPRV** command to **procpriv** is used to determine the amount of memory to request when calling **malloc**. **procpriv** is then called with the **GETPRV** command to retrieve the actual privileges.

With proper use, the privilege mechanism provides a way to restrict execution of sensitive system functions and improves the security of the system. See "Guidelines for Writing Trusted Software" in this guide.

8 Signals, Job Control and Pipes

Table of Contents

Introduction

The UNIX kernel provides several means by which processes can communicate with each other. This chapter provides a detailed discussion on three of these facilities: signals, pipes, and job control.

Signals are a communications mechanism between processes and the kernel. They notify a process that a certain event has occurred, and they can be sent to a process or a group of processes. Based on the type of signal received, a process might take some necessary action. Included in this chapter is a discussion on the types of signals, signal handlers, how signals are sent, and the signal stack feature.

Job control provides a means of managing processes during a login session. The discussion here includes an overview of job control, and STREAMS-based job control.

Also included in this chapter is a section devoted to pipes, and one on STREAMS-based pipes and FIFOs. Pipes are a mechanism which provide a means of passing information from one running process to another. As of UNIX System V Release 4, pipes and FIFOs have become STREAMS-based for network applications. For completeness, a discussion of this subject has also been included.

Signals

A *signal* is an asynchronous notification of an event, and is said to be *generated for* (or *sent to*) a process when the event that causes the signal first occurs. A signal may be sent to a process by another process, from the terminal or by the system itself. A signal can be generated several ways, including:

- An error during a system call.

- Some condition raised at the controlling-terminal of a process (such as break or hangup).

- An explicit system call to **kill**(2), **sigsend**(2), or **raise**(3C).

- Expiration of the alarm clock timer or the generation of the trap signal during process tracing.

Signals are the most frequently used means to notify a process of the occurrence of some event that may have an impact on that process. In some circumstances, the same event generates signals for multiple processes. All signals have the same *priority*. If multiple signals are pending simultaneously, the order in which they are delivered to a process is implementation-specific.

Multithreading brings additional complexity and additional capabilities to signal management. Signal semantics for multithreaded applications are described in the chapter entitled, ''Programming with the Threads Library.'' That chapter also describes the recommended paradigm for signal management in multithreaded programs.

Signal Types

There are two categories of signals, those generated externally, such as a break from a terminal, and those generated internally (a process fault). Both types are treated identically. The file **/usr/include/signal.h** defines the signals that may be delivered to a process.

UNIX System V supports the following signals required by POSIX.1:

Symbolic Name	Signal Event Description
SIGABRT	Abnormal termination [see abort(2)]
SIGALRM	Alarm time out [see alarm(2)]
SIGFPE	Floating-Point Exception / Erroneous Arithmetic Operation
SIGHUP	Hangup on controlling-terminal [see termios(2)]
SIGILL	Illegal hardware instruction / Invalid function image
SIGINT	Interactive attention – *interrupt* [see termios(2)]
SIGKILL	Termination (cannot be caught or ignored)
SIGPIPE	Write onto pipe without readers [see write(2)]
SIGQUIT	Interactive termination – *quit* [see termios(2)]
SIGSEGV	Invalid memory (segmentation) reference
SIGTERM	Termination
SIGUSR1	Reserved as application-defined signal 1
SIGUSR2	Reserved as application-defined signal 2

UNIX System V supports the following job control signals:

Symbolic Name	Signal Event Description
SIGCHLD	Child Status Changed
SIGCONT	Continue process execution
SIGSTOP	Stop process execution
SIGTSTP	Interactive stop [see termios(2)]
SIGTTIN	Stop tty input [see termios(2)]
SIGTTOU	Stop tty output [see termios(2)]

UNIX System V supports the following additional signals:

Symbolic Name	Signal Event Description
SIGBUS	Bus Error
SIGEMT	Emulation Trap
SIGPOLL	Pollable Event [see streamio(7)]
SIGPWR	Power Fail / Restart
SIGSYS	Bad System Call
SIGTRAP	Trace / Breakpoint Trap
SIGWINCH	Window Size Change
SIGXCPU	CPU time limit exceeded [see getrlimit(2)]
SIGXFSZ	File size limit exceeded [see getrlimit(2)]
SIGWAITING	All LWPs blocked
SIGLWP	Virtual interprocessor interrupt for the Threads Library
SIGAIO	Asynchronous I/O

The signals fall into one of the following classes:

- hardware conditions
- software conditions
- input/output notification
- job control
- resource control

Hardware signals are derived from exceptional conditions which may occur during execution. Such signals include SIGBUS for accesses that result in hardware-related errors, SIGFPE representing floating-point and other arithmetic exceptions, SIGILL for invalid instruction execution, and SIGSEGV for addresses outside the currently assigned area of memory or for accesses that violate memory protection constraints. Other, more CPU-specific hardware signals such as SIGABRT, SIGEMT and SIGTRAP may be defined by a specific implementation.

Software signals reflect interrupts generated by user request: SIGINT for the normal interrupt signal; SIGQUIT for the more powerful quit signal that normally causes a core image to be generated; SIGHUP and SIGTERM that cause graceful process termination, either because a user has *hung up*, or by user or program request; and SIGKILL, a more powerful termination signal that a process cannot catch or ignore. Programs may define their own asynchronous events using SIGUSR1 and SIGUSR2. Other software signals, such as SIGALRM, SIGVTALRM, SIGPROF, indicate the expiration of interval timers.

A process can request notification via the signal SIGPOLL when input or output is possible on a file descriptor, or when a *non-blocking* operation completes. A process may request to receive the signal SIGURG when an urgent condition arises.

A process may be *stopped* by a signal sent to it or the members of its process group [see "Terminal Device Control" and termios(2)]. The signal SIGSTOP is a powerful stop signal, because it cannot be caught. Other stop signals SIGTSTP, SIGTTIN and SIGTTOU are used when a user request, input request, or output request respectively is the reason for stopping the process. The signal SIGCONT is sent to a process when it is continued from a stopped state. Processes may receive notification with the signal SIGCHLD when a child process changes state, either by stopping or by terminating [see wait(2)].

Exceeding resource limits may cause signals to be generated. SIGXCPU occurs when a process nears its CPU time limit and SIGXFSZ warns that the limit on file size limit has been reached.

Three system signals, `SIGLWP`, `SIGWAITING`, and `SIGAIO`, are generated by the operating system for internal use by the Threads Library.

Signal Actions

Signals interrupt the normal flow of control in a process. Signals do not direct the execution of a process; but rather, request that the process take some action. For most signals, a process can arrange to respond in one of the following ways:

- terminate on receipt of the signal

- ignore it completely

- catch it and act on it in some way defined by the user process.

The chosen response for each signal is known as the signal's *disposition*.

For example, an interrupt signal may be sent by pressing an appropriate key on the terminal (*delete*, *break* or *rubout*). The action taken depends on the requirements of the specific program being executed. For example:

- The shell invokes most commands in such a way that they stop executing immediately (die) when an interrupt is received. For example, the **pr** (print) command normally dies, allowing the user to stop unwanted output.

- The shell itself ignores interrupts when reading from the terminal because the shell should continue execution even when the user stops a command like **pr**.

- The editor **ed** chooses to catch interrupts so that it can halt its current action (especially printing) without allowing itself to be terminated.

A signal is said to be *delivered* to a process when the process receives the signal and takes the action established for it. Signal delivery resembles the occurrence of a hardware interrupt: the signal is normally blocked from further occurrence, the current process context is saved, and a new one is built.

Signal Handlers

A process calls **sigaction**(2) to set the disposition for a signal. If the signal is to be caught, a process specifies the *handler* function, which will be called when the signal occurs. Alternatively, a process can specify that the signal is to be *blocked* or *ignored*, or it may specify that the *default* action is to be taken when the signal occurs.

For each signal, the **<signal.h>** header file establishes the default signal action to be one of the following:

Abort   On receipt of the signal, the receiving process terminates abnormally with all the consequences outlined in **exit**(2). In addition, a core image file is created, which contains the current memory image of the process for use in post-mortem debugging.

Exit   On receipt of the signal, the receiving process terminates normally with all the consequences outlined in **exit**(2).

Ignore   On receipt of the signal, the receiving process ignores it.

Stop   On receipt of the signal, the receiving process stops.

As the default action for a signal typically is to terminate a process, a process wanting to continue processing after a signal must use the function **sigaction** to arrange alternative handling of the signal [see **sigaction**(2)]. To control the way a signal is delivered, a process calls **sigaction** to associate a handler with that signal. The call

```
#include <signal.h>

sigaction(signo, sa, osa)
        int signo;
        struct sigaction *sa;
        struct sigaction *osa;
```

assigns the address of the interrupt handler specified by **sa** to the signal specified by **signo**. If **osa** is non-zero, **sigaction** stores the previous signal action at that address.

The first argument to the function **sigaction** is just an integer code number that represents a signal. The **<signal.h>** header file defines symbolic names for the signal numbers and must always be included when signals are used.

The second and third arguments to **sigaction** are pointers to the **sigaction** structure defined by the **<signal.h>** header file to contain the following members [see **signal**(2)]:

```
void        (*sa_handler)();
sigset_t    sa_mask;
int         sa_flags;
```

The member **sa_handler** specifies what action to take on receipt of the signal. Assigning one of the following values to **sa_handler** establishes the signal action as follows:

SIG_IGN   ignore the signal

SIG_DFL   take the default action for the signal

a pointer to a signal handler
         handle the signal by calling a function

The **<signal.h>** header file defines the special values used to request that the signal be ignored (**SIG_IGN**) or that the default action for the signal be taken (**SIG_DFL**) each of which the **<signal.h>** header file expands into a distinct constant expression of the type **(void(*)())**, whose value matches no declarable function.

The **sa_handler** routine is called by a C call of the form

```
(*sa_handler)(signo, infop, ucp);
        int signo;
        siginfo_t *infop;
        ucontext_t *ucp;
```

signo gives the number of the signal that occurred. **infop** is either equal to 0, or points to a structure that contains information detailing the reason why the signal was generated. This information must be explicitly asked for when the signal's action is specified. The **ucp** parameter is a pointer to a structure containing the process's context prior to the delivery of the signal, and will be used to restore the process's context upon return from the signal handler.

sa_mask specifies the set of signals to be masked when the signal handler is invoked; it implicitly includes the signal which invoked the signal handler. When a signal condition arises for a process, the signal is added to a set of signals pending for the process. If the signal is not currently blocked by the process then it is delivered. The process of signal delivery adds the signal to be delivered and those signals specified in the **sa_mask** for the associated signal handler to a set of those masked for the process, saves the current process context, and places the process in the context of the signal-handling routine. The call is arranged so that if the signal-handling routine exits normally, the signal mask is restored and the process resumes execution in the original context. Should the process wish to resume in a different context, it must arrange to restore the signal mask itself.

Signal masks are usually constructed with the following routines [see **sigsetops**(3C)]:

sigemptyset	empty a set
sigfillset	fill a set with every signal currently supported
sigaddset	add specified signals to a set
sigdelset	delete specified signals from a set
sigismember	test membership in a set

Signal sets should always be initialized with a call to **sigemptyset** or **sigfillset**.

The mask of blocked signals is independent of signal handlers for delays. It delays the delivery of signals much as a raised hardware interrupt priority level delays hardware interrupts. Preventing an interrupt from occurring by changing the handler is analogous to disabling a device from further interrupts.

The member **sa_flags** specifies special properties of the signal, such as whether system calls should be restarted if the signal handler returns, if the signal action should be reset to **SIG_DFL** when it is caught, and whether the signal handler should operate on the normal run-time stack or a special signal stack [see "Signal Stacks" below and **sigaction**(2)].

Initially, all signals are set to **SIG_DFL** or **SIG_IGN** prior to entry of the function **main** [see **exec**(2)]. Once an action is established for a specific signal, it usually remains established until another action is explicitly established by a call to either **signal**(2), **sigset**(2), **sigignore**(2), or **sigaction**(2) explicitly establishes another action, or until the process calls **fork**(2) or an **exec**(2) function. A child process inherits the actions of the parent for the defaulted and ignored signals. Caught signals are reset to the default action in the child process. This is necessary since the address linkage for signal-handling routines specified in the parent are no longer appropriate in the child. When a process **execs**, all signals set to catch the signal are reset to **SIG_DFL**. Alternatively, a process may request that the action for a signal automatically be reset to **SIG_DFL** after catching it [see **signal**(2) and **sigaction**(2)].

In the following example, the first call to **sigaction** causes interrupts to be ignored; while the second call to **sigaction** restores the default action for interrupts, which is to terminate the process. In both cases, **sigaction** returns the previous signal action in the final argument **old_act**.

```
#include <signal.h>

main() {
    struct sigaction new_act, old_act;

    new_act.sa_handler = SIG_IGN;
    sigaction(SIGINT, &new_act, &old_act);

    /* do processing */

    new_act.sa_handler = SIG_DFL;
    sigaction(SIGINT, &new_act, &old_act);
}
```

Instead of the special values **SIG_IGN** or **SIG_DFL**, the second argument to **sigac-tion** may specify a signal-handling routine; in which case, the specified function is called when the signal occurs. Most commonly this facility is used to allow the program to clean up unfinished business before terminating, for example to delete a temporary file, as in the following example:

Figure 8-1: Signal programming example

```
#include <signal.h>

main() {
    struct sigaction new_act, old_act;
    void on_intr();

    new_act.sa_handler = SIG_IGN;
    sigaction(SIGINT, &new_act, &old_act);

    if (old_act.sa_handler != SIG_IGN) {
        new_act.sa_handler = on_intr;
        sigaction(SIGINT, &new_act, &old_act);
    }

    /* do processing */

    exit(0);        /* exit with normal status */
}

void on_intr() {

    unlink(tempfile);

    exit(1);        /* exit with interrupted status */
}
```

Before establishing **on_intr** as the signal handler for **SIGINT**, the program tests the state of interrupt handling, and continues to ignore interrupts if they are already being ignored. This is needed because **SIGINT** is sent to *all* processes started from a specific terminal. Accordingly, when a program is initiated with "**&**" to run without any interaction in the background, the shell turns off interrupts for it so it won't be stopped by interrupts intended for foreground processes. If this program began by setting **on_intr** to catch all interrupts regardless, that would undo the shell's efforts to protect it when run in the background. The solution, shown above, is to call **sigaction** for **SIGINT** first to get the signal action currently established for the interrupt signal, which is returned in the third argument to **sigaction**. If interrupt signals were already being ignored, the process should continue to ignore them; otherwise, they should be caught. In that case, the second call to **sigaction** for **SIGINT** establishes a new signal action which specifies **on_intr** as the signal handler.

A more sophisticated program may wish to intercept and interpret **SIGINT** as a request to stop what it is doing and return to its own command processing loop. Think of a text editor: interrupting a long printout should not cause it to terminate and lose the work already done. The outline of the code for this case is probably best written as follows:

Figure 8-2: Signal programming example

```
#include <signal.h>
#include <setjmp.h>
jmp_buf sjbuf;

main() {
    struct sigaction new_act, old_act;
    void on_intr();

    new_act.sa_handler = SIG_IGN;
    sigaction(SIGINT, &new_act, &old_act);

    setjmp(sjbuf);    /* save current stack position */

    if (old_act.sa_handler != SIG_IGN) {
        new_act.sa_handler = on_intr;
        sigaction(SIGINT, &new_act, &old_act);
    }
/*
 * main command processing loop
 */
    exit(0)
}
void on_intr() {
    printf("\nInterrupt\n");    /* print message */

    longjmp(sjbuf);    /* return to saved state */
}
```

The `<setjmp.h>` header file declares the type `jmp_buf` for a buffer in which the state can be saved, and the program above declares `sjbuf` to be of type `jmp_buf` which is an array of some type. The function `setjmp` saves the current context of the user process in `sjbuf`. When an interrupt occurs, a call to the function `on_intr` is forced, which prints a message and could set flags or do something else. The function `longjmp` takes as argument an object stored into by `setjmp`, and restores control to the location after the call to `setjmp`, so control (and the stack level) pops back to place in the program **main** where the signal is set up and the main loop entered. Notice, by the way, that the signal gets set again after an interrupt occurs. This is necessary; most signals are automatically reset to their default action when they occur.

Some programs that want to detect signals simply can't be stopped at an arbitrary point, for example in the middle of updating a linked list. If the function called on occurrences of a signal sets a flag and then returns instead of calling **exit** or `longjmp`, execution resumes at the exact point it was interrupted. The interrupt flag can then be tested later.

This approach has the following difficulty. Suppose the program is reading the terminal when the interrupt is sent. The specified function is duly called; it sets its flag and returns. If it were really true, as said earlier, that "execution resumes at the exact point it was interrupted," the program would continue reading the terminal until the user typed another line. This behavior might well be confusing, since the user might not know the program is reading, and presumably would prefer to have the signal take effect instantly. The method chosen to resolve this difficulty is to terminate the **read** from the terminal when execution resumes after the signal, with **read** returning an error code (**EINTR**) which indicates the interruption.

As a consequence, programs which catch and resume execution after signals should be prepared for 'errors' caused by interrupted system calls. (The ones to watch out for in particular are **wait** and **pause** as well as any **read** from the terminal).

A program whose **on_intr** function just sets **intflag**, resets the interrupt signal, and returns, should usually include code like the following when it reads the standard input or directly from a terminal device.

```
if (getchar() == EOF)
    if (intflag)
        /* EOF caused by interrupt */
    else
        /* actual end-of-file */
```

A final subtlety to keep in mind becomes important when signal handling is combined with execution of other programs. Suppose a program handles interrupts, and also includes a method (like " ! " in the editor) whereby other programs can be executed. Then the code should look something like this:

```
if (fork() == 0)
    exec( ... );

new_act.sa_handler = SIG_IGN;   /* ignore interrupts */
sigaction(SIGINT, &new_act, &old_act);

wait(&status);                  /* until the child completes */

new_act.sa_handler = on_intr;   /* restore interrupts */
sigaction(SIGINT, &new_act, &old_act);
```

Why is this? Again, its not obvious but not really difficult. Suppose the program called catches its own interrupts. When this subprogram gets interrupted, it receives the signal, returns to its main loop and probably tries to read the terminal. But the calling program also pops out of its wait for the subprogram and tries to read the terminal. Two processes trying to read the terminal is very unfortunate, since the system randomly decides which should get each line of input. A simple solution is for the parent to ignore interrupts until the child completes.

This reasoning is reflected in the function **system** as follows:

Figure 8-3: `system()` – **Signal programming example**

```
#include <signal.h>

system(cmd_str) /* run command string */
    char *cmd_str;
{
    int status;
    pid_t wpid, xpid;
    struct sigaction sig_act, i_stat, q_stat;

    if ((xpid=fork()) == 0) {
        execl("/bin/sh", "sh", "-c", cmd_str, 0);
        _exit(127);
    }

    sig_act.sa_handler = SIG_IGN;
    sigaction(SIGINT, &sig_act, &i_stat);

    sig_act.sa_handler = SIG_IGN;
    sigaction(SIGQUIT, &sig_act, &q_stat);

    while ( ((wpid=wait(&status)) != xpid) && (wpid != -1) )
        ;
    if (wpid == -1)
        status = -1;

    sigaction(SIGINT, &i_stat, &sig_act);
    sigaction(SIGQUIT, &q_stat, &sig_act);

    return(status);
}
```

Protecting Critical Sections

Signal-handling routines normally execute with the signal that caused their invocation to be *blocked*, but other signals may yet occur. Mechanisms are provided whereby *critical-sections* of code may protect themselves against the occurrence of specified signals.

To block a section of code against one or more signals, a call to **sigprocmask** may be used to add a set of signals to the existing mask and return the old mask:

```
sigprocmask ( SIG_BLOCK ,
        sigset_t *new_mask ,
        sigset_t *old_mask )
```

The old mask can then be restored later with **sigprocmask**, as follows:

```
sigprocmask ( SIG_UNBLOCK ,
        sigset_t *new_mask ,
        sigset_t *old_mask )
```

The function **sigprocmask** can be used to read the current mask without changing it by specifying a null-pointer as its second argument.

It is possible to check conditions with some signals blocked and then to pause waiting for a signal and restoring the mask, by using:

```
sigsuspend (
        sigset_t *sig_mask )
```

Signal Stacks

Applications that maintain complex or fixed-size stacks can use the call

```
struct sigaltstack {
        caddr_t       ss_sp;
        int    ss_size;
        int    ss_flags;
};

sigaltstack(ss, oss)
        struct sigaltstack *ss;
        struct sigaltstack *oss;
```

to provide the system with a stack based at **ss_sp** of size **ss_size** for delivery of signals. The system automatically adjusts for direction of stack growth. The member **ss_flags** indicates whether the process is currently on the signal stack and whether the signal stack is disabled.

When a signal is to be delivered and the process has requested that it be delivered on the alternate stack, the system checks whether the process is on a signal stack [see **sigaction**(2)]. If it is not, then the process is switched to the signal stack for delivery, with the return from the signal arranged to restore the previous stack.

If the process wishes to take a non-local exit from the signal-handling routine or run code from the signal stack that uses a different stack, a **sigaltstack** call should be used to reset the signal stack [see **sigaltstack**(2)].

Sending Signals

A process can send a signal to another process or group of processes using either
kill(2) or sigsend(2):

```
kill(pid, signo);
        int pid, signo;

sigsend(idtype, id, signo);
        idtype_t idtype;
        id_t id;
```

Unless the process sending the signal is privileged, its real or effective user- ID
must be equal to the receiving process's real or saved user- ID.

A process can send a signal to itself using the function **raise** as follows [see
raise(3C)]:

```
raise ( int sig_val );
```

Signals can also be sent from a terminal device to the process group or session
leader associated with the terminal [see **termio**(7).

Job Control and Session Management

An overview of Job Control is provided here for completeness and because it interacts with the STREAMS-based terminal subsystem. This section describes how to use a Stream as a controlling terminal. More information on Job Control can be obtained from the following manual pages: **exit**(2), **getpgid**(2), **getpgrp**(2), **getsid**(2), **kill**(2), **setpgid**(2), **setpgrp**(2), **setsid**(2), **sigaction**(2), **signal**(2), **sigsend**(2), **termios**(2), **waitid**(2), **waitpid**(3C), **signal**(5), and **termio**(7).

Overview of Job Control

Job Control is a feature supported by the BSD UNIX operating system. It is also an optional part of the IEEE P1003.1 POSIX standard. Job Control breaks a login session into smaller units called jobs. Each job consists of one or more related and cooperating processes. One job, the foreground job, is given complete access to the controlling terminal. The other jobs, called background jobs, are denied read access to the controlling terminal and given conditional write and **ioctl** access to it. The user may stop an executing job and resume the stopped job either in the foreground or in the background.

Under Job Control, background jobs do not receive events generated by the terminal and are not informed with a hangup indication when the controlling process exits. Background jobs that linger after the login session has been dissolved are prevented from further access to the controlling terminal, and do not interfere with the creation of new login sessions.

If **_POSIX_JOB_CONTROL** is defined, UNIX System V supports job-control and command interpreter processes supporting job-control can assign the terminal to different jobs, or process-groups, by placing related processes in a single process-group and assigning the process-group with the terminal. A process may examine or change the foreground process-group of a terminal assuming the process has the required permissions [see **tcgetpgrp**(2) and **tcsetpgrp**(2)]. The **termios** facility aids in this assignment by restricting access to the terminal by processes outside of the foreground process-group [see "Terminal Access Control"].

When there is no longer any process whose process-id or process-group-id matches the process-group-id of the foreground process-group, the terminal lacks any foreground process-group. It is unspecified whether the terminal has a foreground process-group when there is no longer any process whose process-group-id matches the process-group-id of the foreground process-group, but there is a process whose process-id matches the process-group-id of the foreground process-group. Only a successful call to **tcsetpgrp** or assignment of the controlling terminal as described can make a process-group the foreground process-group of a terminal [see **tcsetpgrp**(2)].

Background process-groups in the session of the session-leader are subject to a job-control line-discipline when they attempt to access their controlling terminal. Typically, they are sent a signal that causes them to stop, unless they have made other arrangements [see **signal**(4)]. An exception is made for processes that belong to a orphaned process-group, which is a process-group none of whose members have a parent in another process-group within the same session and thus share the same controlling terminal. When these processes attempt to access their controlling terminal, they return errors, because there is no process to continue them if they should stop [see "Terminal Access Control"].

Job Control Terminology

The following defines terms associated with Job Control:

- Background Process-group — a process-group that is a member of a session that established a connection with a controlling terminal and is not the foreground process-group.

- Controlling Process — a session leader that established a connection to a controlling terminal.

- Controlling Terminal — a terminal that is associated with a session. Each session may have at most one controlling terminal associated with it and a controlling terminal may be associated with at most one session. Certain input sequences from the controlling terminal cause signals to be sent to the process-groups in the session associated with the controlling terminal.

- Foreground Process Group — each session that establishes a connection with a controlling terminal distinguishes one process-group of the session as a foreground process-group. The foreground process-group has certain privileges that are denied to background process-groups when accessing its controlling terminal.

- Orphaned Process Group — a process-group in which the parent of every member in the group is either a member of the group, or is not a member of the process-group's session.

- Process Group — each process in the system is a member of a process-group that is identified by a process-group ID. Any process that is not a process-group leader may create a new process-group and become its leader. Any process that is not a process-group leader may join an existing process-group that shares the same session as the process. A newly created process joins the process-group of its creator.

- Process Group Leader — a process whose process ID is the same as its process group ID.

- Process Group Lifetime — a time period that begins when a process-group is created by its process-group leader and ends when the last process that is a member in the group leaves the group.

- Process ID — a positive integer that uniquely identifies each process in the system. A process ID may not be reused by the system until the process lifetime, process-group lifetime, and session lifetime ends for any process ID, process-group ID, and session ID sharing that value.

- Process Lifetime — a time period that begins when the process is forked and ends after the process exits, when its termination has been acknowledged by its parent process.

- Session — each process-group is a member of a session that is identified by a session ID.

- Session ID — a positive integer that uniquely identifies each session in the system. It is the same as the process ID of its session leader.

- Session Leader — a process whose session ID is the same as its process and process-group ID.

- Session Lifetime — a time period that begins when the session is created by its session leader and ends when the lifetime of the last process-group that is a member of the session ends.

Job Control Signals

The following signals manage Job Control [see also **signal**(5)]:

SIGCONT	Sent to a stopped process to continue it.
SIGSTOP	Sent to a process to stop it. This signal cannot be caught or ignored.
SIGTSTP	Sent to a process to stop it. It is typically used when a user requests to stop the foreground process.
SIGTTIN	Sent to a background process to stop it when it attempts to read from the controlling terminal.
SIGTTOU	Sent to a background process to stop it when one attempts to write to or modify the controlling terminal.

The Controlling Terminal and Process-Groups

A session may be allocated a controlling terminal. For every allocated controlling terminal, Job Control elevates one process group in the controlling process's session to the status of foreground process group. The remaining process-groups in the controlling process's session are background process-groups. A controlling terminal gives a user the ability to control execution of jobs within the session. Controlling-terminals play a central role in Job Control. A user may cause the foreground job to stop by typing a predefined key on the controlling terminal. A user may inhibit access to the controlling terminal by background jobs. Background jobs that attempt to access a terminal that has been so restricted will be sent a signal that typically causes the job to stop. (See the section titled "Accessing the Controlling Terminal" later in this chapter.)

Terminal Access Control

If a process is in the foreground process-group of its controlling terminal, **read** works as described in "Input Processing and Reading Data". If any process in a background process-group attempts to read from its controlling terminal when job-control is supported, the signal **SIGTTIN** is sent to its process-group unless one of these special cases apply:

- If the reading process either ignores or blocks the signal **SIGTTIN** or if the reading process is a member of an orphaned process-group, attempting to read the controlling terminal fails without sending the signal **SIGTTIN**, the **read** returns **-1** and **errno** equals **EIO**.

The default action of the signal **SIGTTIN** is to stop the process to which it is sent [see **signal**(4)].

If a process is in the foreground process-group of its controlling terminal, **write** works as described in "Writing Data and Output Processing". If any process in a background process-group attempts to write onto its controlling terminal when the flag **TOSTOP** is set in the **c_lflag** field of the **termios** structure, the signal **SIGTTOU** is sent to the process-group unless one of these special cases apply:

- If the writing process either ignores or blocks the signal **SIGTTOU**, attempting to write the controlling terminal proceeds without sending the signal **SIGTTOU**.

- If the writing process neither ignores nor blocks the signal **SIGTTOU** and if the writing process is a member of an orphaned process-group, attempting to write the controlling terminal fails without sending the signal **SIGTTOU**, the **write** returns **-1** and **errno** equals **EIO**.

If the flag **TOSTOP** is clear, attempting to write the controlling terminal proceeds without sending the signal **SIGTTOU**.

Certain calls that set terminal parameters are treated the same as **write** calls, except that the flag **TOSTOP** is ignored; thus, the effect is the same as terminal **write** calls when the flag **TOSTOP** is set [see **tcgetattr**(2) and **tcsetattr**(2)].

If the implementation supports job-control, unless otherwise noted, processes in a background process-group are restricted in their use of the terminal-control-functions [see **tcdrain**(2), **tcflow**(2), **tcflush**(2), **tcgetattr**(2), **tcgetpgrp**(2), **tcsendbreak**(2), **tcsetattr**(2), **tcsetsid**(2), **tcsetpgrp**(2)]. Attempts to perform these functions cause the process-group to be sent the signal **SIGTTOU**. If the calling process either ignores or blocks the signal **SIGTTOU**, attempting to perform a control-function proceeds without sending the signal **SIGTTOU**.

The default action of the signal **SIGTTOU** is to stop the process to which it is sent [see **signal**(4)].

All terminal-control-functions operate on an open file-descriptor and they affect the underlying terminal-device-file denoted by the file-descriptor, not the open-file-description that represents it.

If a member of a background process-group attempts to invoke an **ioctl** on its controlling terminal, and that **ioctl** modifies terminal parameters (e.g., **TIOCSPGRP**, **TCSETA**, **TCSETAW** or **TCSETAF**) its process-group is sent **SIGTTOU**, which normally causes the members of that process-group to stop.

- If the calling process either ignores or blocks the signal **SIGTTOU**, attempting to perform a terminal-control-function on the controlling terminal proceeds without sending the signal **SIGTTOU**.

- If the calling process neither ignores nor blocks the signal **SIGTTOU** and if the calling process is a member of an orphaned process-group, attempting to perform a terminal-control-function on the controlling terminal fails without sending the signal **SIGTTOU**, the **ioctl** returns **-1** and **errno** equals **EIO**.

The terminal access controls described in this section apply only to a process accessing its controlling terminal because these controls are for the purpose of job-control, not security, and job-control relates only to a controlling terminal for a process. Normal file-access-permissions handle security. A process accessing a terminal other than the controlling terminal is effectively treated the same as a member of the foreground process-group.

If a process in a background orphaned process-group calls **read** or **write**, stopping the process-group is undesirable, as it is no longer under the control of a job-control shell that can put it into foreground again. Accordingly, calls to **read** and **write** by such processes receive an immediate return error.

The terminal-driver must repeatedly do a foreground/background/orphaned process-group check until either the process-group of the calling process is orphaned or the calling process moves into the foreground. If a calling process is in the background and should receive a job-control signal, the terminal-driver sends the appropriate signal (**SIGTTIN** or **SIGTTOU**) to every process in the process-group of the calling process then lets the calling process receive the signal immediately, usually by blocking the process so it reacts to the signal right away. Note, however, that after the process catches the signal and the terminal-driver regains control, the driver must repeat the foreground/background/orphaned process-group check. The process may still be in the background, either because a job-control shell continued the process in the background, or because the process caught the signal and did nothing.

The terminal-driver repeatedly does the foreground/background/orphaned process-group check whenever a process tries to access the terminal. For **write** or the line-control functions, the check is done on entering the function. For **read**, the check is done not only on entering the function but also after blocking the process to wait for input data (if necessary). If the process calling **read** is in the foreground, the terminal-driver tries to get data from the input-queue, and if the queue is empty, blocks the process to wait for data. When data are input and the terminal-driver regains control, it must repeat the foreground/background/orphaned process-group check again because the process may have moved to the background from the foreground while it blocked to wait for input data. [see "job-control" in the "Glossary"].

Modem Disconnect

The following arrangements are made to allow processes that read from a terminal-device-file and test for end-of-file to terminate appropriately when a modem-disconnect is detected on the terminal-device:

- All processes with that terminal as the controlling terminal receive a hang-up signal, **SIGHUP**, if **CLOCAL** is clear in the **c_cflags** for the terminal [see "Control Modes" in **termios**(4)]. Unless other arrangements are made, the signal **SIGHUP** forces the processes to terminate [see **signal**(4) and **sigaction**(2)]. If the signal **SIGHUP** is ignored or caught by a signal-catching function, any subsequent **read** returns **0** to indicate end-of-file until the terminal-device-file is closed [see **read**(2)].

- If the controlling process is not in the foreground process group of the terminal, the signal **SIGTSTP** is sent to all processes in the foreground process group for which the terminal is the controlling terminal. Unless other arrangements are made, the signal **SIGTSTP** forces the processes to terminate [see **signal**(4) and **sigaction**(2)].

- Processes in background process groups that try a **read** or a **write** of the controlling terminal after a modem-disconnect while the terminal is still assigned to the session receive the appropriate signal, **SIGTTIN** or **SIGTTOU** respectively [see **read**(2) and **write**(2)]. Unless other arrangements are made, the signal **SIGTTIN** or **SIGTTOU** forces the processes to terminate [see **signal**(4) and **sigaction**(2)].

STREAMS-based Job Control

Job Control requires support from a line discipline module on the controlling terminal's Stream. The **TCSETA**, **TCSETAW**, and **TCSETAF** commands of **termio**(7) allow a process to set the following line discipline values relevant to Job Control:

SUSP character	A user defined character that, when typed, causes the line discipline module to request that the Stream head sends a **SIGTSTP** signal to the foreground process with an **M_PCSIG** message, which by default stops the members of that group. If the value of **SUSP** is zero, the **SIGTSTP** signal is not sent, and the **SUSP** character is disabled.
TOSTOP flag	If **TOSTOP** is set, background processes are inhibited from writing to their controlling terminal.

A line discipline module must record the **SUSP** suspend character and notify the Stream head when the user has typed it, and record the state of the **TOSTOP** bit and notify the Stream head when the user has changed it.

Allocation and Deallocation

A Stream is allocated as a controlling terminal for a session if

- The Stream is acting as a terminal

- The Stream is not already allocated as a controlling terminal

- The Stream is opened by a session leader that does not have a controlling terminal.

Drivers and modules can inform the Stream head to act as a terminal Stream by sending an **M_SETOPTS** message with the **SO_ISTTY** flag set upstream. This state may be changed by sending an **M_SETOPTS** message with the **SO_ISNTTY** flag set upstream.

Controlling-terminals are allocated with the **open**(2) system call. A Stream head must be informed that it is acting as a terminal by an **M_SETOPTS** message sent upstream before or while the Stream is being opened by a potential controlling process. If the Stream head is opened before receiving this message, the Stream is not allocated as a controlling terminal.

Hung-up Streams

When a Stream head receives an **M_HANGUP** message, it is marked as hung-up. Streams that are marked as hung-up are allowed to be reopened by their session leader if they are allocated as a controlling terminal, and by any process if they are not allocated as a controlling terminal. This way, the hangup error can be cleared without forcing all file descriptors to be closed first.

If the reopen is successful, the hung-up condition is cleared.

Hangup Signals

When the **SIGHUP** signal is generated by an **M_HANGUP** message (instead of an **M_SIG** or **M_PCSIG** message), the signal is sent to the controlling process instead of the foreground process-group, since the allocation and deallocation of controlling terminals to a session is the responsibility of that process-group.

Accessing the Controlling Terminal

If a process attempts to access its controlling terminal after it has been deallocated, access is denied. If the process is not holding or ignoring **SIGHUP**, it is sent a **SIGHUP** signal. Otherwise, the access fails with an **EIO** error.

Members of background process-groups have limited access to their controlling terminals:

- If the background process is ignoring or holding the **SIGTTIN** signal or is a member of an orphaned process-group, an attempt to read from the controlling terminal fails with an **EIO** error. Otherwise, the process is sent a **SIGTTIN** signal, which by default stops the process.

- If the process is attempting to write to the terminal and if the terminal's **TOSTOP** flag is clear, the process is allowed access.

  The **TOSTOP** flag is set on reception of an **M_SETOPTS** message with the **SO_TOSTOP** flag set in the **so_flags** field. It is cleared on reception of an **M_SETOPTS** message with the **SO_TONSTOP** flag set.

- If the terminal's **TOSTOP** flag is set and a background process is attempting to write to the terminal, the write succeeds if the process is ignoring or holding **SIGTTOU**. Otherwise, the process stops except when it is a member of an orphaned process-group, in which case, it is denied access to the terminal and it is returned an **EIO** error.

- If a background process is attempting to perform a destructive `ioctl` (an `ioctl` that modifies terminal parameters), the `ioctl` call succeeds if the process is ignoring or holding **SIGTTOU**. Otherwise, the process will stop except when the process is a member of the orphaned process-group. In that case, the access to the terminal is denied and an **EIO** error is returned.

Signals, Job Control and Pipes

Basic Interprocess Communication – Pipes

The system call **pipe** creates a *pipe*, a type of unnamed FIFO (First In First Out) file used as an I/O channel between two cooperating processes: one process writes onto the pipe, while the other reads from it. Most pipes are created by the shell, as in:

```
ls | pr
```

which connects the standard output of **ls** to the standard input of **pr**. Sometimes, however, it is most convenient for a process to set up its own plumbing; this section illustrates how to establish and use the pipe connection.

Since a pipe is both for reading and writing, **pipe** returns two file-descriptors as follows:

```
int  fd[2];

stat = pipe(fd);
if (stat == -1)
     /* there was an error ... */
```

where **fd** is an array of two file-descriptors, with **fd[0]** for the read end of the pipe and **fd[1]** for the write end of the pipe. These may be used in **read**, **write** and **close** calls just like any other file-descriptors.

Implementation of pipes consists of implied **lseek** operations before each **read** or **write** in order to implement first-in-first-out. The system looks after buffering the data and synchronizing the two processes to prevent the writer from grossly out-producing the reader and to prevent the reader from overtaking the writer. If a process reads a pipe which is empty, it will wait until data arrive; if a process writes into a pipe which is full, it will wait until the pipe empties somewhat. If the write end of the pipe is closed, a subsequent **read** will encounter end-of-file.

To illustrate the use of pipes in a realistic setting, consider a function **popen**(*cmd*, *mode*), which creates a process *cmd*, and returns a file-descriptor that will either read or write that process, according to *mode*; thus, the call

```
fout = popen("pr", WRITE);
```

creates a process that executes the **pr** command; subsequent **write** calls using the file-descriptor **fout** send data to that process through the pipe.

Figure 8-4: popen

```
#include <stdio.h>

#define   READ   0
#define   WRITE  1
#define   tst(a, b)  (mode == READ ? (b) : (a))
static    int popen_pid;

popen(cmd, mode)
    char *cmd;
    int  mode;
{
    int p[2];

    if (pipe(p) < 0)
        return(NULL);

    if ((popen_pid = fork( )) == 0) {
        close(tst(p[WRITE], p[READ]));
        close(tst(0, 1));
        dup(tst(p[READ], p[WRITE]));
        close(tst(p[READ], p[WRITE]));
        execl("/bin/sh", "sh", "-c", cmd, 0);
        _exit(1) /* disaster occurred if we got here */
    }
    if (popen_pid == -1)
        return(NULL);

    close(tst(p[READ], p[WRITE]));
    return(tst(p[WRITE], p[READ]));
}
```

The function **popen** first calls **pipe** to create a pipe, then calls **fork** to create two copies of itself. The child decides whether it is supposed to read or write, closes the other end of the pipe, then calls the shell (via **execl**) to run the desired process. The parent likewise closes the end of the pipe it does not use. These **close** operations are necessary to make end-of-file tests work properly. For example, if a child that intends to read fails to close the write end of the pipe, it will never encounter the end-of-file on the pipe, just because there is one writer potentially active. The sequence of **close** operations in the child is a bit tricky. Suppose that the task is to create a child process that will read data from the parent. Then the first **close** closes the write end of the pipe, leaving the read end open.

To associate a pipe with the standard input of the child, use the following:

```
close(tst(0, 1));
dup(tst(p[READ], p[WRITE]));
```

The **close** call closes file-descriptor **0**, the standard input, then the **dup** call returns a duplicate of the open file-descriptor. File-descriptors are assigned in increasing order and **dup** returns the first available one, so the **dup** call effectively copies the file-descriptor for the pipe (read end) to file-descriptor **0** making the read end of the pipe the standard input. (Although somewhat tricky, it's a standard idiom.) Finally, the old read end of the pipe is closed. A similar sequence of operations takes place when the child process must write to the parent process instead of reading from it. To finish the job we need a function **pclose** to close a pipe created by **popen**.

Figure 8-5: `pclose`

```
#include <signal.h>
pclose(fd)      /* close pipe descriptor */
    int fd;
{
    struct sigaction o_act, h_act, i_act, q_act;
    extern pid_t popen_pid;
    pid_t c_pid;
    int   c_stat;

    close(fd);

    sigaction(SIGINT, SIG_IGN, &i_act);
    sigaction(SIGQUIT, SIG_IGN, &q_act);
    sigaction(SIGHUP, SIG_IGN, &h_act);

    while ((c_pid=wait(&c_stat))!=-1 && c_pid!=popen_pid);
    if (c_pid == -1)
        c_stat = -1;

    sigaction(SIGINT, &i_act, &o_act);
    sigaction(SIGQUIT, &q_act, &o_act);
    sigaction(SIGHUP, &h_act, &o_act);

    return(c_stat);
}
```

The main reason for using a separate function rather than **close** is that it is desirable to wait for the termination of the child process. First, the return value from **pclose** indicates whether the process succeeded. Equally important when a process creates several children is that only a bounded number of unwaited-for children can exist, even if some of them have terminated; performing the **wait** lays the child to rest. The calls to **sigaction** make sure that no interrupts, etc., interfere with the waiting process [see **sigaction**(2)].

The routine as written has the limitation that only one pipe may be open at once, because of the single shared variable **popen_pid**; it really should be an array indexed by file-descriptor. A **popen** function, with slightly different arguments and return value is available as part of the Standard I/O Library [see **stdio**(3S)].

STREAMS-Based Pipes and FIFOs

A pipe in the UNIX system is a mechanism that provides a communication path between multiple processes. Before Release 4, UNIX System V had "standard" pipes and named pipes (also called FIFOs). With standard pipes, one end was opened for reading and the other end for writing, thus data flow was unidirectional. FIFOs had only one end; typically, one process opened the file for reading and another process opened the file for writing. Data written into the FIFO by the writer could then be read by the reader.

To provide greater support and development flexibility for networked applications, pipes and FIFOs have become STREAMS-based in UNIX System V Release 4. The basic interface remains the same but the underlying implementation has changed. Pipes now provide a bidirectional mechanism for process communication. When a pipe is created by the **pipe** system call, two Streams are opened and connected together, thus providing a full-duplex mechanism. Data flow is on a FIFO basis. Previously, pipes were associated with character devices and the creation of a pipe was limited to the capacity and configuration of the device. STREAMS-based pipes and FIFOs are not attached to STREAMS-based character devices, eliminating configuration constraints and the number of opened pipes to the number of file descriptors for that process.

 NOTE The remainder of this chapter uses the terms "pipe" and "STREAMS-based pipe" interchangeably.

Creating and Opening Pipes and FIFOs

FIFOs, which are created by **mknod**(2) or **mkfifo**(3C) behave like regular file system nodes but are distinguished from other file system nodes by the **p** in the first column when the **ls -l** command is executed. Data written to the FIFO or read from the FIFO flow up and down the Stream in STREAMS buffers. Data written by one process can be read by another process.

FIFOs are opened in the same way as other file system nodes using the **open** system call. Any data written to the FIFO can be read from the same file descriptor in a FIFO manner. Modules can also be pushed on the FIFO. See **open**(2) for the restrictions that apply when opening a FIFO.

A STREAMS-based pipe is created by the **pipe** system call that returns two file descriptors, **fd[0]** and **fd[1]**. Both file descriptors are opened for reading and writing. Data written to **fd[0]** becomes data read from **fd[1]** and vice versa.

Each end of the pipe has knowledge of the other end through internal data structures. Subsequent reads, writes, and closes are aware of whether the other end of the pipe is open or closed. When one end of the pipe is closed, the internal data structures provide a way to access the Stream for the other end so that an **M_HANGUP** message can be sent to its Stream head.

After successful creation of a STREAMS-based pipe, **0** is returned. If **pipe** is unable to create and open a STREAMS-based pipe, it will fail with **errno** set as follows:

ENFILE	File table is overflowed.
EMFILE	Cannot allocate more file descriptors for the process.
ENOSR	Could not allocate resources for both Stream heads.
EINTR	Signal was caught while creating the Stream heads.

STREAMS modules can be added to a STREAMS-based pipe with the **ioctl** **I_PUSH**. A module can be pushed onto one or both ends of the pipe (see Figure 8-6). However, a pipe maintains the concept of a midpoint so that if a module is pushed onto one end of the pipe, that module cannot be popped from the other end.

Figure 8-6: Pushing Modules on a STREAMS-based Pipe

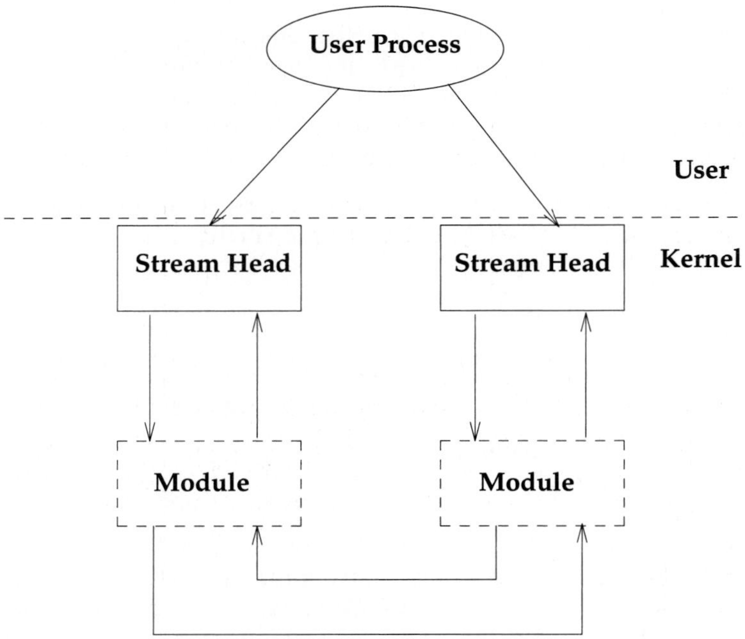

Accessing Pipes and FIFOs

STREAMS-based pipes and FIFOs can be accessed through the operating system routines **read**(2), **write**(2), **ioctl**(2), **close**(2), **putmsg**(2), **getmsg**(2), and **poll**(2). If FIFOs, **open** is also used.

Reading from a Pipe or FIFO

The **read** [or **getmsg**] system call is used to read from a pipe or FIFO. A user reads data from a Stream (not from a data buffer as was done prior to Release 4). Data can be read from either end of a pipe.

On success, the **read** returns the number of bytes read and placed in the buffer. When the end of the data is reached, the **read** returns 0.

When a user process attempts to read from an empty pipe (or FIFO), the following will happen:

- If one end of the pipe is closed, **0** is returned indicating the end of the file.

- If no process has the FIFO open for writing, **read** returns **0** to indicate the end of the file.

- If some process has the FIFO open for writing, or both ends of the pipe are open, and **O_NDELAY** is set, **read** returns **0**.

- If some process has the FIFO open for writing, or both ends of the pipe are open, and **O_NONBLOCK** is set, **read** returns **-1** and sets **errno** to **EAGAIN**.

- If **O_NDELAY** and **O_NONBLOCK** are not set, the **read** call blocks until data is written to the pipe, until one end of the pipe is closed, or the FIFO is no longer open for writing.

Writing to a Pipe or FIFO

When a user process calls the **write** system call, data is sent down the associated Stream. If the pipe or FIFO is empty (no modules pushed), data written is placed on the read queue of the other Stream for STREAMS-based pipes, and on the read queue of the same Stream for FIFOs. Because the size of a pipe is the number of unread data bytes, the written data is reflected in the size of the other end of the pipe.

Zero Length Writes If a user process issues **write** with **0** as the number of bytes to send down a STREAMS-based pipe or FIFO, **0** is returned, and by default no message is sent down the Stream. However, if a user requires that a 0-length message be sent downstream, an **ioctl** call may be used to change this default behavior. The flag **SNDZERO** supports this. If **SNDZERO** is set in the Stream head, **write** requests of *L0*l bytes generate a 0-length message and send the message down the Stream. If **SNDZERO** is not set, no message is generated and **0** is returned to the user.

To toggle the **SNDZERO** bit, the **ioctl I_SWROPT** is used. If *arg* in the **ioctl** call is set to **SNDZERO** and the **SNDZERO** bit is off, the bit is turned on. If *arg* is set to **0** and the **SNDZERO** bit is on, the bit is turned off.

The **ioctl I_GWROPT** is used to return the current write settings.

Atomic Writes If multiple processes simultaneously write to the same pipe, data from one process can be interleaved with data from another process, if modules are pushed on the pipe or the write is greater than **PIPE_BUF**. The sequence of data written is not necessarily the sequence of data read. To ensure that writes of less than **PIPE_BUF** bytes are not be interleaved with data written from other processes, any modules pushed on the pipe should have a maximum packet size of at least **PIPE_BUF**.

NOTE

PIPE_BUF is an implementation-specific constant that specifies the maximum number of bytes that are atomic in a write to a pipe. When writing to a pipe, write requests of **PIPE_BUF** or less bytes are not interleaved with data from other processes doing writes on the same pipe. However, write requests greater than **PIPE_BUF** bytes may have data interleaved on arbitrary byte boundaries with writes by other processes whether the O_NONBLOCK or O_NDELAY flag is set.

If the module packet size is at least the size of **PIPE_BUF**, the Stream head packages the data in such a way that the first message is at least **PIPE_BUF** bytes. The remaining data may be packaged into smaller or larger blocks depending on buffer availability. If the first module on the Stream cannot support a packet of **PIPE_BUF**, atomic writes on the pipe cannot be guaranteed.

Closing a Pipe or FIFO

The **close** system call closes a pipe or FIFO and dismantles its associated Streams. On the last close of one end of a pipe, an **M_HANGUP** message is sent upstream to the other end of the pipe. Later **read** or **getmsg** calls on that Stream head return the number of bytes read and **0** when there is no more data. Later **write** or **putmsg** requests will fail with **errno** set to **EIO**. If the pipe has been mounted using **fattach**, the pipe must be unmounted before calling **close**; otherwise, the Stream will not be dismantled. If the other end of the pipe is mounted, the last close of the pipe will force it to be unmounted.

Flushing Pipes and FIFOs

When the flush request is initiated from a user **ioctl** or from a **flushq** routine, the **FLUSHR** and/or **FLUSHW** bits of an **M_FLUSH** message have to be switched. The point of switching the bits is the point where the **M_FLUSH** message is passed from a write queue to a read queue. This point is also known as the midpoint of the pipe.

The midpoint of a pipe is not always easily detectable, especially if there are numerous modules pushed on either end of the pipe. In that case, there needs to be a mechanism to intercept all messages passing through the Stream. If the message is an **M_FLUSH** message and it is at the Streams midpoint, the flush bits need to switched.

This bit switching is handled by the **pipemod** module. **pipemod** should be pushed onto a pipe or FIFO where flushing of any kind takes place. The **pipemod** module can be pushed on either end of the pipe. The only requirement is that it is pushed onto an end that previously did not have modules on it. That is, **pipemod** must be the first module pushed onto a pipe so that it is at the midpoint of the pipe itself.

The **pipemod** module handles only **M_FLUSH** messages. All other messages are passed on to the next module by the **putnext** utility routine. If an **M_FLUSH** message is passed to o **pipemod** and the **FLUSHR** and **FLUSHW** bits are set, the message is not processed but is passed to the next module by the **putnext** routine. If only the **FLUSHR** bit is set, the **FLUSHR** bit is turned off and the **FLUSHW** bit is set. The message is then passed to the next module by **putnext**. Similarly, if the **FLUSHW** bit is the only bit set in the **M_FLUSH** message, the **FLUSHW** bit is turned off and the **FLUSHR** bit is turned on. The message is then passed to the next module on the Stream.

The **pipemod** module can be pushed on any Stream that desires the bit switching. It must be pushed onto a pipe or FIFO if any form of flushing must take place.

Named Streams

Some applications may want to associate a Stream or STREAMS-based pipe with an existing node in the file system name space. For example, a server process may create a pipe, name one end of the pipe, and allow unrelated processes to communicate with it over that named end.

fattach

A STREAMS file descriptor can be named by attaching that file descriptor to a node in the file system name space. The routine **fattach** [see also **fattach**(3C)] is used to name a STREAMS file descriptor. **fattach**(3C). Its format is

```
int fattach (int fildes, char *fildes)
```

where *fildes* is an open file descriptor that refers to either a STREAMS-based pipe or a STREAMS device driver (or a pseudo device driver), and *path* is an existing node in the file system name space (for example, regular file, directory, character special file, and so forth).

The *path* cannot have a Stream already attached to it. It cannot be a mount point for a file system nor the root of a file system. A user must be an owner of the *path* with write permission or a user with the appropriate privileges to attach the file descriptor.

If the *path* is in use when the routine **fattach** is executed, those processes accessing the *path* are not interrupted and any data associated with the *path* before the call to the **fattach** routine will continue to be accessible by those processes.

After a Stream is named, all subsequent operations [for example, **open**(2)] on the *path* operate on the named Stream. Thus, it is possible that a user process has one file descriptor pointing to the data originally associated with the *path* and another file descriptor pointing to a named Stream.

Once the Stream has been named, the **stat** system call on *path* shows information for the Stream. If the named Stream is a pipe, the **stat**(2) information shows that *path* is a pipe. If the Stream is a device driver or a pseudo-device driver, *path* appears as a device. The initial modes, permissions, and ownership of the named Stream are taken from the attributes of the *path*. The user can issue the system calls **chmod** and **chown** to alter the attributes of the named Stream and not affect the original attributes of the *path*, nor the original attributes of the STREAMS file.

The size represented in the **stat** information reflects the number of unread bytes of data currently at the Stream head. This size is not necessarily the number of bytes written to the Stream.

A STREAMS-based file descriptor can be attached to many different *path*s at the same time (that is, a Stream can have many names attached to it). The modes, ownership, and permissions of these *path*s may vary, but operations on any of these *path*s access the same Stream.

Named Streams can have modules pushed on them, be polled, be passed as file descriptors, and be used for any other STREAMS operation.

fdetach

A named Stream can be disassociated from a file with the **fdetach** routine [see also **fdetach**(3C)], which has the following format:

        int fdetach (char *path)

where *path* is the name of the previously named Stream. Only the owner of *path* or the user with the appropriate privileges may disassociate the Stream from its name. The Stream may be disassociated from its name while processes are accessing it. If these processes have the named Stream open at the time of the **fdetach** call, the processes do not get an error, and continue to access the Stream. However, after the disassociation, later operations on *path* access the underlying file rather than the named Stream.

If only one end of the pipe is named, the last close of the other end causes the named end to be automatically detached. If the named Stream is a device and not a pipe, the last close does not cause the Stream to be detached.

If there is no named Stream or the user does not have access permissions on *path* or on the named Stream, **fdetach** returns **–1** with **errno** set to **EINVAL**. Otherwise, **fdetach** returns **0** for success.

A Stream remains attached with or without an active server process. If a server aborted, the only way a named Stream is cleaned up is if the server executed a clean up routine that explicitly detached and closed down the Stream.

If the named Stream is that of a pipe with only one end attached, clean up occurs automatically. The named end of the pipe is forced to be detached when the other end closes down. If there are no other references after the pipe is detached, the Stream is deallocated and cleaned up. Thus, a forced detach of a pipe end occurs when the server is aborted.

If both ends of the pipe are named, the pipe remains attached even after all processes have exited. In order for the pipe to become detached, a server process has to explicitly invoke a program that executes the **fdetach** routine.

To eliminate the need for the server process to invoke the program, the **fdetach**(1M) command can be used. This command accepts a pathname that is a path to a named Stream. When the command is invoked, the Stream is detached from the path. If the name is the only reference to the Stream, the Stream is also deallocated.

A user invoking the **fdetach**(1M) command must be an owner of the named Stream or a user with the appropriate permissions.

isastream

The function **isastream** [see also **isastream**(3C)] may be used to determine if a file descriptor is associated with a STREAMS device. Its format is

```
int isastream (int fildes)
```

where *fildes* refers to an open file. **isastream** returns 1 if *fildes* represents a STREAMS file, and 0 if not. On failure, **isastream** returns −1 with **errno** set to **EBADF**.

This function is useful for client processes communicating with a server process over a named Stream to check whether the file has been overlaid by a Stream before sending any data over the file.

File Descriptor Passing

Named Streams are useful for passing file descriptors between unrelated processes. A user process can send a file descriptor to another process by invoking the **ioctl I_SENDFD** on one end of a named Stream. This sends a message containing a file pointer to the Stream head at the other end of the pipe. Another process can retrieve that message containing the file pointer by invoking the **ioctl I_RECVFD** on the other end of the pipe.

Unique Connections

With named pipes, client processes may communicate with a server process by using a module called **connld** that enables a client process to gain a unique, non-multiplexed connection to a server. The **connld** module can be pushed onto the named end of the pipe. If **connld** is pushed on the named end of the pipe and that end is opened by a client, a new pipe is created. One file descriptor for the new pipe is passed back to a client (named Stream) as the file descriptor from the **open** call and the other file descriptor is passed to the server. The server and the client may now communicate through a new pipe.

Figure 8-7 illustrates a server process that has created a pipe and pushed the **connld** module on the other end. The server then invokes the **fattach** routine to name the other end **/usr/toserv**.

Figure 8-7: Server Sets Up a Pipe

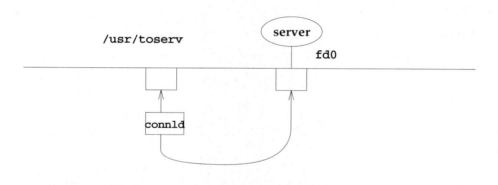

When process X (**procx**) opens **/usr/toserv**, it gains a unique connection to the server process that was at one end of the original STREAMS-based pipe. When process Y (**procy**) does the same, it also gains a unique connection to the server. Figure 8-8 shows that the server process has access to three separate STREAMS-based pipes using three file descriptors.

connld is a STREAMS-based module that has an **open**, **close**, and **put** procedure. **connld** is opened when the module is pushed onto the pipe for the first time and whenever the named end of the pipe is opened. The **connld** module distinguishes between these two opens with the **q_ptr** field of its read queue. On the first **open**, this field is set to **1** and the routine returns without further processing. On later **open**s, the field is checked for **1** or **0**. If the **1** is present, the **connld** module creates a pipe and sends the file descriptor to a client and a server. When the named Stream is opened, the open routine of **connld** is called. The **connld** open fails if

- The pipe ends cannot be created.

- A file pointer and file descriptor cannot be allocated.

- The Stream head cannot stream the two pipe ends.

- A failure occurs while sending the file descriptor to the server.

The open is not complete until the server process receives the file descriptor using the **ioctl I_RECVFD**.

The setting of the **O_NDELAY** or **O_NONBLOCK** flag has no affect on the open.

The **connld** module does not process messages. All messages are passed to the next object in the Stream. The read and write **put** routines call **putnext** to send the message up or down the Stream.

Figure 8-8: Processes X and Y Open /usr/toserv

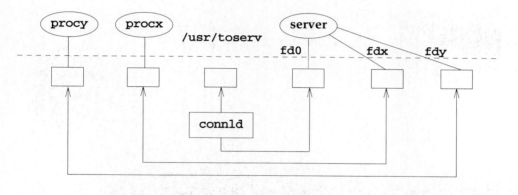

9 Programming with the Threads Library

Introduction

This chapter introduces the Threads Library, which provides facilities for concurrent programming. Before describing the routines included in the Threads Library, this chapter first discusses concepts and terminology of concurrent programming in general and of the Threads Library in particular.

The Threads Library provides two classes of routines: thread management routines and synchronization routines. The thread management routines are discussed in "Basic Threads Management". These include routines to create threads, terminate threads, wait for threads, and adjust threads' scheduling characteristics. In addition, this section discusses how signals interact with multithreaded programs, how threads are scheduled, and the relationship between threads and lightweight processes. The synchronization routines are discussed in "Synchronizing Threads". This includes an overview of the various types of locks, semaphores, barriers, and condition variables, used to synchronize threads that are sharing data.

The section entitled, "Development Environment", discusses the compilation environment and facilities for tracing multithreaded programs. Finally, "Examples" gets you started with some basic threads programs.

This chapter is not intended to replicate all the information covered on the reference manual pages for the threads library routines. Please refer to the individual pages in the *Operating System API Reference* for details such as error returns. The overview pages, **thread**(3thread) and **synch**(3synch) list all the available routines.

What is Concurrent Programming?

Historically, most programs are examples of *sequential programming*. That is, they consist of a series of operations that are carried out one at a time. With *concurrent programming* the programmer can specify sets of instructions that *potentially* can be executed in parallel and still provide correct results.

The advantages of this style of programming are:

- A powerful programming paradigm

  Programs are often written to emulate or respond to events in the real world. In the real world, concurrency is common and purely sequential events are the exception. Modeling such behavior is facilitated if the programming environment supports the notion of concurrency.

- Possible performance improvement

  If multiple processors are available, the program might be executed in less real time (than sequential execution) if more than one processor is working simultaneously. This is called *true concurrency*.

  Even on uniprocessor machines, there may be some performance gain from designing greater concurrency into the program. While one activity is blocked, others might still be executing.

  Thus, there is an advantage to concurrent programming even if the resources (processors) are not available to provide *true concurrency* and the application is only *logically concurrent*.

Concurrent programming has been available in the UNIX System since its inception via the *process model*. In the UNIX System problems are solved not just by running programs but by running sets of programs (a running program is called a *process*) — sometimes pre-existing *tools* or *commands*; sometimes specifically written programs — that work together (often concurrently) to solve the problem. Processes can communicate and synchronize with each other by mechanisms that include:

- pipes (named and unnamed)
- files and file/record locks
- signals

- messages
- shared memory (IPC style shared memory or mapped files)
- semaphores (IPC style)

What are Threads?

UNIX System V Release 4.2 MP (SVR4.2 MP) provides vastly expanded capabilities for concurrent programming via the Threads Library. These capabilities include:

- Facilities to define multiple *threads of control* to be run concurrently within a single process. Each *thread* is a set of instructions that is itself sequential but can be executed concurrently with other threads.

- A new, rich set of software mechanisms for coordinating and synchronizing the activities of the process' threads. These include:

  - mutual exclusion locks (*mutexes*); both recursive and not; both blocking and spinning.

  - reader-writer locks

  - counting semaphores (*not* the IPC semaphore system calls)

  - condition variables

  - barriers

- Features to control the level of concurrency and the scheduling of threads.

- Underlying operating system kernel support that enables the library to provide true concurrency (on multi-processor architectures), not just logical concurrency for threads.

 NOTE The interfaces provided by the Threads Library are a semantic superset of those specified in the *IEEE POSIX 1003.4a Extensions for Portable Operating Systems Standard (DRAFT)*, with the exception of mutex scheduling options.

General characteristics of threads programming:

- Each thread starts executing at a programmer-specified address of a function.

  - A given, common function can be the starting point for several unique threads.

- A thread has many features that are analogous to process features. For example,

  - Each thread is an individually schedulable entity.

  - Threads can be preempted; consequently, a thread cannot assume uninterrupted access to common data unless special synchronizing arrangements (for example, locking) are made.

  - Threads execute logically in parallel, exhibit logical concurrency and possibly true concurrency.

  - A thread will go through many states during its lifetime such as:

    - executing

    - ready to run but not currently executing

    - waiting for some resource

    - terminated thread with unreported exit status

    - stopped from running

  - Threads can receive signals; consequently, asynchronous programming is still possible. (See the section below on "Threads and Signals".)

  - In this implementation, most of the features of the Threads Library are implemented by user-level library code that is dynamically linked with the application program at run time. The underlying operating system kernel is not aware of the threads of a process.

  - The operating system kernel supports a scheduling abstraction called the *lightweight process* (LWP). An LWP is not the same as a thread. It is a facility that is used by the Threads Library to provide true concurrency for threads. (See the section below on "Managing Threads Concurrency".)

Each thread of the process has access to all of the resources of the process including:

  - The entire address space.

    Any thread can access any memory location in the process. By using threads for concurrency, the programmer sacrifices the address space protection that the operating system maintains (with support of hardware features) between processes. A wild pointer in one thread can easily corrupt another.

On the other hand, thread-to-thread data sharing is easy and efficient. By default, all data is available to all threads. Thread-to-thread communication avoids the system call overhead and typical data copying of process-to-process communications.

- Resources maintained by the operating system, including:

    - Open files, file pointer offsets, file/record locks, and current directory.

    - Access rights (to files, IPC facilities, and so on) and Enhanced Security privileges.

    - Resource limits such as *ulimit*, *umask*, and file descriptor limit.

- Process identity (such as process ID number, parent process ID, process group number)

The features that are unique to each thread include:

- Program context (that is, register values)

- Stack

- Scheduling information (such as scheduling class, current priority)

- Timers

- Signal handling

    Actually, some signal handling features are maintained per thread and some are maintained at the process level. The relationship between the two (and how to use them) will be discussed later. (See the section below on "Threads and Signals".)

- Thread ID number and thread-private data.

On the whole, there is a much more intimate relationship between the threads of a process than between processes of an application. This gives the programmer much greater flexibility and potentially better performance.

- With this intimacy there is a greater potential for introducing subtle errors and that implies a greater demand on the programmer's skill to produce correct code.

- Moreover, the proper design of a concurrent program requires certain disciplines that do not often arise in sequential programming. For example, inappropriate use of the Threads Library facilities for synchronizing threads may result in a program that is incorrect, inefficient, or both.

Programming with the Threads Library

The facilities of the Threads Library are well-suited for medium- to coarse-grained concurrency. It may be inappropriate to use the facilities of the Threads Library if:

- the scale of concurrent tasks cannot be efficiently expressed in terms of a function.

- the task to be performed concurrently is an entire program (perhaps an existing program) then use fork(2)/exec(2) (or even the shell).

- the task to be performed concurrently is extremely small scale (loop level) the Threads Library entail too much overhead. Parallelizing compilers exist for this scale of concurrency.

Threads Illustrated

Figure 9-1 illustrates the relation of threads to LWPs to processes to processors. The terms *multiplexed* threads and *bound* threads will be discussed later in this chapter.

Figure 9-1: Overview of Threads

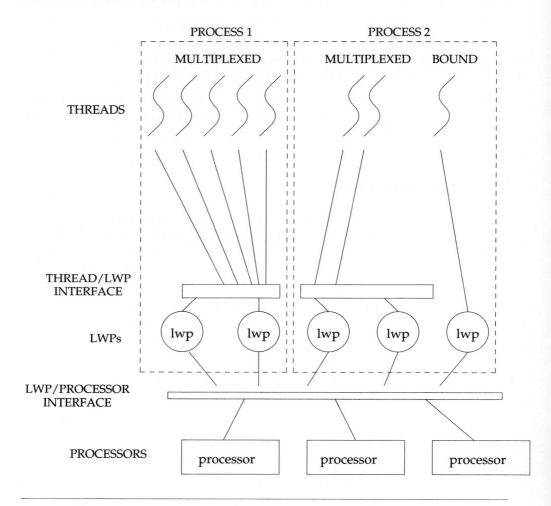

Basic Threads Management

The basic operations on threads are *conceptually* similar to certain operations on processes.

Operation	Process Method	Thread Method
Creation	**fork**(2)/**exec**(2)	**thr_create**(3thread)
Termination	**exit**(2)	**thr_exit**(3thread)
Synchronization	**wait**(2)	**thr_join**(3thread)

Creating a New Thread

In UNIX System V Release 4.2 MP (SVR4.2 MP) processes are single-threaded when they start running new programs [that is, on entry to **main**, following a successful call to **exec**(2)]. The thread created to execute **main** is known as the *initial thread*. If no additional threads are created, a process can continue to execute with the same semantics as the traditional UNIX process.

New threads can be created via the **thr_create**(3thread) routine

```
int thr_create(
        void      *stack_address,
        size_t    stack_size,
        void      *(*start_routine)(void *arg),
        void      *arg,
        long      flags,
        thread_t  *new_thread
);
```

which takes the following parameters:

stack_address and *stack_size*

> These define the stack space for the new thread. (This space is used for function call transactions and for automatic variables in functions called by the thread.)
>
> The stack of the traditional UNIX process has *autogrow* support by the operating system. That is, if the stack grows beyond its initial size the operating system automatically increases its size as needed (or until it runs into some other defined segment). However, threads (other than the initial thread) use stacks that do not have autogrow support; consequently, the stacks should be allocated to meet the maximum needs of the thread.

As a convenience, the Threads Library will implicitly allocate a reasonably-sized stack (twice the page size or 16K bytes, whichever is greater) if *stack_address* and *stack_size* are set to **NULL** and **0**, respectively,

- The programmer can specify other sizes if needed. The value must not be less than that returned by **thr_minstack**(3thread). Note that *stack_address* should point to the base address (lowest) of the allocated space.

- In this implementation, the Threads Library manages the process address space so that stack overflows will result in an addressing error (**SIGSEGV**). For most applications, this is a desirable behavior. It is better to discover such errors as soon as they occur rather than have one stack corrupt another.

start_routine and *arg*

These parameters define the starting condition of the newly created thread. *start_routine* is the function address where the new thread's execution will begin and *arg* is the argument that *start_routine* will receive.

start_routine takes a single parameter of type (**void ***) and returns a value of the same type. These values can be used (with type casts) to pass values (or aggregations of values in structures) of any type.

NOTE	For portability, do *not* cast an **int** to (**void ***), and then cast it back to **int**. These values should only be used as pointers; otherwise, information can be lost.

Of course, a thread need not be entirely defined by a single function. That initial function will typically call other functions (hence the thread's need for a separate stack).

flags

These flags will be discussed as their respective topics arise later in this chapter. These flags are not mutually exclusive; they can be combined with a bitwise inclusive OR. For each flag, the relevant section is shown:

Programming with the Threads Library

THR_SUSPENDED	"Managing Thread Scheduling"
THR_BOUND	"Managing Concurrency Level"
THR_DETACHED	"Waiting for Thread Termination"
THR_INCR_CONC	"Managing Concurrency Level"
THR_DAEMON	"Terminating a Thread"

new_thread   The *thread ID* of the newly created thread is delivered to the creator thread at this address.

- This value can be used in other functions to influence that thread.

- The scope of the value is limited to the enclosing process; it is not relevant to threads in other processes.

- A thread can learn its own thread ID number by the **thr_self**(3thread) function.

NOTE   **thr_create**(3thread) and the other functions in the Threads Library return 0 on success. On failure, instead of setting the **errno** global variable, they *return* the error code as the function's value.

The creation of one thread by another is conceptually similar but not identical to the creation of a new process by another process via the **fork**(2) system call. Some differences are:

- After a **fork**(2) system call both the creator (parent) and created (child) processes resume from the same point of computation — the return from **fork**(2).

  In contrast, a new thread starts execution at the *start_function* specified by the creator [in some respects similar to the **exec**(2) system call], while the creating thread returns from **thr_create**(3thread).

- The operating system maintains a parent/child relationship between creating and created processes that affects later interactions at process termination [for example, **wait**(2) semantics]. In contrast, there is no innate hierarchy among threads. Each is a *sibling* of the other. Thus, the creator might wait for the newly created thread to terminate or, just as easily, the new thread can wait for its creator to terminate. [See discussion of **thr_join**(3thread) below.]

Terminating a Thread

A thread can terminate itself by using the **thr_exit**(3thread) function

```
void thr_exit(
        void *status
);
```

where

status   is the address returned to another thread that has called **thr_join**(3thread).

The call to **thr_exit**(3thread) initiates automatic clean-up for thread resources:

- Recovery of stack allocated by the Threads Library (see above).

 NOTE   The stack for a non-daemon thread will not be recovered until after another thread calls **thr_join** to obtain the *status* for the thread, which is stored on the stack. Likewise, an explicitly-allocated stack should not be recovered until after another thread calls **thr_join**.

- Invocation of the *destructor* function for each *key value* that the thread has used. (See section below on "Thread-Specific Data".)

The Threads Library arranges for a simple return from the *start_routine* to be equivalent to a call to **thr_exit**(3thread) (except for the initial thread, see "Termination of the Process," below).

The **thr_exit**(3thread) function allows one thread to return a value called *status* to another; however, this mechanism is more general than the exit status returned by a child process to its parent. The argument to **exit**(2) is limited to a small range of integers. The *status* returned by **thr_exit**(3thread) is a general pointer that can be used (with type casts) to direct the receiver to objects of greater complexity such as structures, arrays, and linked lists. Of course, both the terminating and receiving threads should be coded to employ the same convention.

Termination of the Process

The termination of the last *non-daemon thread* of the process will terminate the process [with *status* used as **exit**(2) status to the parent process].

- The Threads Library categorizes a thread as either a *daemon thread* or a *non-daemon thread*. In practice, daemon threads are used to provide services for other threads. Although they can terminate themselves or be terminated, there is no need to do so. By being distinguished as daemons, they will be implicitly terminated when there are no other threads (non-daemons) that might need their services.

A thread is categorized as a daemon thread at the time of its creation by use of the **THR_DAEMON** flag to **thr_create**(3thread).

■ There are some special semantics for the initial thread. If the initial thread executes a **return** statement or if it implicitly returns from **main**, the process will be terminated. However, a **thr_exit**(3thread) by the initial thread will terminate only the initial thread. The process continues to execute as long as there are other non-daemon threads.

■ Finally, any thread can terminate the process by calling the **exit**(2) system call.

Waiting for Thread Termination

One thread can suspend itself to wait for the termination of another thread with the **thr_join**(3thread) function

```
int thr_join(
        thread_t  wait_for,
        thread_t  *departed,
        void      **status
);
```

where the parameters have the following meaning:

wait_for   The ID of the thread of interest, that is, the thread whose termination the caller will await. A **(thread_t)0** indicates interest in the next thread to terminate (or one that has already terminated, but has not been joined), whatever its ID happens to be.

departed   **thr_join**(3thread) will deposit the thread ID of the terminated thread at this address.

status   **thr_join**(3thread) will deposit at this address the value given as an argument by the terminated thread when it called **thr_exit**(3thread). That value should be the address at which the terminated thread left its return value (exit status).

If the thread of interest has already terminated, **thr_join**(3thread) will return immediately; otherwise, the calling thread will block.

If there is more than one thread waiting for the termination of some particular thread:

■ The thread of interest will be joined to only one of the waiting threads. The choice is not predictable.

- All other waiting threads will return with the **ESRCH** error code.

If a thread receives a catchable signal while blocked in **thr_join**(3thread):

- The signal is handled.

- The **thr_join**(3thread) function is transparently restarted.

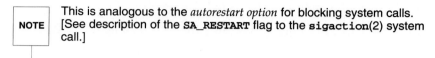

> **NOTE** This is analogous to the *autorestart option* for blocking system calls. [See description of the **SA_RESTART** flag to the **sigaction**(2) system call.]

The resources of the terminated thread (for example, a stack allocated by the Threads Library) will not be fully recovered by the Threads Library until some other thread has called **thr_join**(3thread) and received the terminated thread's exit status.

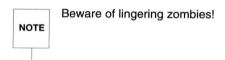

> **NOTE** Beware of lingering zombies!

Detached Threads

If the programmer knows at thread creation time that no other thread will use **thr_join**(3thread) to wait for the new thread, the **THR_DETACHED** flag to **thr_create**(3thread) should be used. When a *detached thread* terminates, its resources may be recovered immediately. In fact, it is not valid to use **thr_join**(3thread) on a detached thread.

By default, new threads are not detached threads.

Thread-Specific Data

Historically, programs have used the **static** or **extern** storage classes to save data that must be preserved between function calls. This practice is no longer valid when many threads in the same process may run a given function concurrently and reference one **static** or **extern** variable by name. Values will not be preserved across function calls if one thread modifies a value left by another.

NOTE In contrast, since each thread gets a unique stack, variables of the `auto` storage class are implicitly unique.

The facility for *thread-specific* data provides a solution to this problem.

- Data can be stored and retrieved by a *key* value.

- The same key value can be used to store data by many threads.

- *Implicit* in the access functions [`thr_setspecific`(3thread) and `thr_getspecific`(3thread)] is a disambiguation of the key by the thread ID.

- Thus, the key is a *virtual variable name* that will resolve to the correct data for the calling thread.

NOTE Analogously, the file name `/dev/tty` can be used by any process to access its particular controlling terminal.

- The data is specific to each thread but, as with any other part of the process address space, the data is not protected from access or change by other threads.

The access functions have the following syntax:

```
int  thr_setspecific(thread_key_t key, void *data);
void *thr_getspecific(thread_key_t key);
```

A key value must be created by the **thr_keycreate**(3thread) function

```
int thr_keycreate(
        thread_key_t *key,
        void          (*destructor)(void *data)
);
```

where

key   This is the address where the newly valid key value will be deposited.

destructor   specifies a function that will be called on the exit of any thread that has used the key for data storage. This function should recover any space that has been used to store thread-specific data. When called, this function receives one argument, the *data* address that the thread gave as the second argument to **thr_setspecific**(3thread).

NOTE

The key can be created (or later removed) by threads other than those that use the key for data storage. The using threads need only have access to the key value by function argument, global variable, or other means.

If a particular key value is needed for only a particular phase of a program (perhaps initialization) it can be deallocated by **thr_keydelete**(3thread).

For efficiency, it is best to minimize the number of keys used in an application.

Threads and Signals

When a process receives a signal of some type (for example, **SIGINT** type) the process can either take the default response, ignore the signal (the kernel does not actually deliver the signal), or catch the signal. When the signal is caught, the system will call a handler function when the signal is delivered. This response is called the *disposition* for the signal type. In UNIX System V Release 4.2 MP (SVR4.2 MP), that disposition is common to all of the threads of a process.

If the disposition for a signal type is

termination   Such signals will terminate all threads, and the process will terminate.

ignore   Such signals will be ignored by all threads.

catch   Any thread responding to such signals will enter the same handler function.

Moreover, if any thread changes the disposition [say by calling **sigaction**(2)] the new disposition is in effect for all threads.

NOTE

System signal types **SIGLWP** and **SIGWAITING** are used internally by the Threads Library. The Threads Library prevents modification of the disposition or masking of those signal types.

On the other hand, *signal masks* (the set of signal types being blocked) are maintained per thread.

A thread inherits the signal mask of its creating thread. A thread can alter its mask with the **thr_sigsetmask**(3thread) routine.

```
int thr_sigsetmask(
        int          how,
        const sigset_t *set,
                sigset_t *oset
);
```

where

set　　　　　　Defines a set of signal types.

how　　　　　　Specifies how *set* will be used. *how* can be one of the following:

　　　　　　SIG_SETMASK　Discard the old mask; make *set* the new mask

　　　　　　SIG_BLOCK　　Add the types in *set* to the existing mask

　　　　　　SIG_UNBLOCK　Remove the types in *set* from the existing mask

oset　　　　　　Can be used to save the prior value of the thread's signal mask.

NOTE The syntax of **thr_sigsetmask**(3thread) is nearly identical to that of the **sig-procmask**(2) system call.

Signals can be categorized as being asynchronously generated or synchronously generated. A *synchronously-generated signal* is one that arises from the action of a particular thread or process. For example, alarm signals, signals resulting from an illegal memory reference, and signals resulting from an illegal arithmetic operation are all synchronously-generated signals. An *asynchronously-generated* signal is one that is sent from outside the thread (or process); its delivery is unpredictable. Interruptions and termination signals are usually an asynchronously generated.

Asynchronously-Generated Signals

When a signal is delivered to a process, if it is being caught, it will be handled by one, and only one, of the threads meeting either of the following conditions:

1. A thread blocked in a **sigwait**(2) system call whose argument *does* include the type of the caught signal.

2. A thread whose signal mask *does not* include the type of the caught signal.

Additional considerations:

■ A thread blocked in **sigwait**(2) is given preference over a thread not blocking the signal type.

- If more than one thread meets these requirements [perhaps two threads are calling **sigwait**(2)], then one of them will be chosen by the Threads Library. This choice is not predictable by application programs.

- If no thread is eligible, the signal will remain *pending* at the process level until some thread becomes eligible.

Asynchronously-Generated Signals — Paradigm

One useful paradigm for managing signals originating outside of the process is to have *all* threads include the caught signals in their signal mask and specifically create one daemon thread to handle the signals. If that thread uses the **sigwait**(2) system call, the signals can be handled in a synchronous style.

```
thr_sigsetmask(mask);
while( (signo = sigwait(mask)) > 0){
        handle signal type signo
}
```

Note that it is not only valid to wait for masked signals with **sigwait**, but it is important to mask out the signal types of interest before calling **sigwait**. Otherwise, the arrival of one such signal between calls to **sigwait** will be handled according to the current process disposition. By default, that will terminate the entire process. **sigwait** effectively unmasks any masked signals while blocked, then masks them again before returning.

Even if a handler function is specified, it will not be executed if a signal is delivered to a thread blocked in **sigwait**; **sigwait** bypasses any handler.

Since all threads are masking out the same set of signals, one can predict that the signals in that set will be handled by the single thread using **sigwait**. This paradigm is advantageous because:

- It reduces the complexity of the program.

- Only one thread need allocate stack space for signal handling. If there are several eligible threads, each must have sufficient stack for the handler.

 NOTE Alternate signal handling stacks [see **sigaltstack**(2)] are not supported by the Threads Library.

- Signals are handled in a synchronous style, which is usually easier to write and understand than an asynchronous style.

NOTE   The thread that handles the signals should be a *bound* thread. Bound threads are introduced in a later section, under "Managing Concurrency Level".

Synchronously-Generated Signals

A caught, non-masked signal that is caused by a particular thread will be handled by that thread. Examples include:

- Signals arising from an invalid memory reference or illegal arithmetic operation. This allows the offending thread to correct its error.

- Alarm or timer signals requested by the thread.

    The Threads Library arranges for such signals to always be delivered to the requesting thread even if that (*multiplexed*) thread is no longer held by the same LWP as at the time of the request.

     NOTE   Multiplexed threads are formally introduced in the section titled "Managing Concurrency Level".

Each thread will use the common handler function.

Thread-to-Thread Signaling

One thread can signal another thread with the **thr_kill**(3thread) function:

```
int thr_kill(
        thread_t  tid,
        int       signo
);
```

where

tid   The thread ID of the target thread.

signo   The type of signal to send.

A thread catching a signal cannot distinguish between a signal originating from another thread of the process or from outside of the process.

The process disposition for the sent signal type (*signo*) is also applied for thread-to-thread signaling. As usual, the response will be to ignore the signal, to call the handler function, or to take the default response (usually, process termination).

This facility allows one thread to influence (perhaps "reset" or terminate) another thread asynchronously.

Threads Concurrency Level

Lightweight Processes

The UNIX System V Release 4.2 MP (SVR4.2 MP) operating system kernel is not aware of the multithreading of any process using the Threads Library. The kernel supports an entity known as a *lightweight process* (LWP).

- There may be many LWPs associated with a single process.

- Each LWP of a process shares the process address space with its *sibling* LWPs.

- Each LWP has its own scheduling context.

- On multiprocessor machines, several LWPs of a process might be running on different processors simultaneously (true concurrency).

- Each LWP has access to all of the resources of the process such as open file descriptors, access rights and privileges, and resource limits.

Many of these are features of threads as well. This is no coincidence. Threads have many of these features because a thread only executes once it has been *picked up* by an LWP. However, a process typically has more threads than LWPs.

Conceptually, an LWP is a dearer resource than a thread. The Threads Library will typically maintain a pool of LWPs that are shared by the set of runnable threads in a process.

 NOTE Analogously, the operating system arranges for the sharing of a relatively small number of (hardware) processors among a much greater number of processes or LWPs.

Multiplexed Threads

The Threads Library *multiplexes* threads among the pool of available LWPs for the process.

- An LWP can pick up and run only one thread at a time.

- After a time the LWP will *put down* (stop running) its current thread and pick up another.

- Some time later the thread will be picked up again; not necessarily by the previous LWP.

- The algorithm by which a thread is associated with an LWP and later preempted is covered in the section on "Multiplexed Thread Scheduling" below.

- On multiprocessor systems, a larger number of LWPs implies a greater *chance* that different threads of the process will be executed simultaneously (that is, true, not logical concurrency).

Managing Threads Concurrency

The size of the pool of available LWPs (the *actual concurrency level*) will vary over time. The Threads Library manages the size of this pool automatically and dynamically according to rules outlined below. The programmer can influence the algorithm by changing the *requested concurrency level* (with `thr_setconcurrency`, see below); at times, the actual concurrency level may be either greater than or less than the requested level.

The rules governing implicit changes to the actual concurrency level are:

- Initially, for each program, there is a single LWP available for execution of threads.

- The size of the pool is incremented when a thread is created with the `THR_INCR_CONC` flag to `thr_create`(3thread). This may increase the actual level of concurrency above the current requested level of concurrency.

 NOTE The newly created thread is not necessarily picked up by that newly created LWP. In fact, the new LWP is created asynchronously by a *housekeeping* thread that the Threads Library creates for each process.

- If all of the LWPs of a process are blocked in system calls, then the process cannot execute any threads. However, the kernel sends a `SIGWAITING` type signal to the process when this condition occurs. Additional LWPs are created if there are additional runnable threads.

- The number of LWPs should not exceed the number of threads — at least not for long — that would be wasteful. An LWP that remains unassigned to a thread for a certain time (5 minutes) is said to have *aged* and will be terminated [`_lwp_exit`(2)]. Aging will terminate LWPs until the size of the pool equals the lesser of

□ requested level of concurrency

□ number of active (running or runnable) threads

Thus, if there are few threads, the actual number of LWPs may be less than the requested level.

A thread can use the **thr_setconcurrency**(3thread) function to change the requested concurrency level mentioned in the algorithm above. The syntax is:

```
int thr_setconcurrency(
        int new_level
);
```

This request is serviced asynchronously.

The rules governing the explicit changes in actual concurrency by **thr_setconcurrency**(3thread) are:

- When the level is increased, the number of LWPs is increased asynchronously by a housekeeping thread.

  One implication is that certain errors (for example, **EAGAIN** — system limit on user [for LWPs] exceeded) may not be reported because they occur after **thr_setconcurrency** returns.

- A request to lower the level of concurrency does not have an immediate effect: no LWP is terminated, nor is any thread preempted. Instead, the actual level of concurrency becomes lower by the LWP aging described above.

- Setting *new_level* to 0 requests the default level of concurrency.

- The programmer can retrieve the current value of the requested level of concurrency with the **thr_getconcurrency**(3thread) function.

- There is no mechanism to return the current, actual level of concurrency.

Bound Threads

A thread may become runnable at a time when all LWPs of the process are already executing threads. That thread will be made runnable and enqueued until an LWP becomes available. This implies some latency (time lag) between thread awakening and execution. There may be circumstances where this behavior is not acceptable. (Perhaps the thread must respond to a signal in a timely manner.)

If a thread is created with the **THR_BOUND** flag to **thr_create**(3thread) then

- Both a thread and a new LWP are created.

- The new LWP picks up the new thread.

- That association remains in effect for the life of the thread.

- Such threads are called *bound threads*.

Bound threads are not counted in the algorithm that manages the level of concurrency.

NOTE Bound threads are not guaranteed to gain processor time whenever they are ready to execute; the LWP on which a bound thread runs must be scheduled to run on a processor by the system scheduler. See "Bound Thread Scheduling." Nevertheless, bound threads have a performance advantage over multiplexed threads.

Thread Scheduling

Thread scheduling governs the competition among threads for various system resources.

- Multiplexed threads vie for a limited number of LWPs.

    □ Bound threads are spared this competition; each maintains its association with its LWP for its lifetime.

- LWPs are, in turn, assigned by the kernel to a limited number of (hardware) processors for execution.

- To coordinate their activities, threads often make use of various synchronization mechanisms. At times there may be more than one thread waiting for a given event (for example, the unlocking of a semaphore). The Threads Library must decide which thread will receive the resource.

    This last category of thread scheduling will be covered in the section entitled "Synchronizing Threads".

Multiplexed Thread Scheduling

Multiplexed threads are subjected to two levels of scheduling:

- Threads Library Scheduling: The Threads Library scheduler assigns multiplexed threads to LWPs for execution and, at times, preempts them so the LWP can pick up another thread.

- System Scheduling: The kernel assigns LWPs to (hardware) processors and later preempts them.

The Threads Library maintains a *priority level* for each multiplexed thread. This value plays a role in the selection of a thread for assignment to an LWP. The priority value of a multiplexed thread can be modified with the **thr_setprio**(3thread) function.

```
int thr_setprio(
        thread_t tid,
        int      prio
);
```

Runnable, multiplexed threads are scheduled for execution in a round-robin manner within each priority level.

- A thread with a higher priority value will be scheduled to run before a thread with a lower value.

- The valid range of priorities is **0** to **MAXINT-1**; however, the Threads Library is optimized for a maximum priority of **126** (or less).

The Threads Library must select a thread for assignment to an LWP on the following occasions:

- When an LWP becomes available, a runnable multiplexed thread will be assigned to it.

    For example, an LWP becomes available when a thread exits, or when a multiplexed thread blocks on a thread synchronization mechanism (discussed later), or when the concurrency level is increased.

- When a multiplexed thread becomes runnable (perhaps a mutex has been released by one thread and acquired by another), it can preempt a multiplexed thread of a lower priority.

- When an executing thread calls **thr_yield**(3thread), it deliberately surrenders its LWP to a higher priority thread (if any).

Threads Library scheduling and system scheduling are independent of each other.

- The Threads Library can assign a thread to an LWP but cannot say when that LWP will actually execute.

- The kernel is unaware that the Threads Library is using LWPs to implement (user-level) threads. The kernel maintains its own scheduling context (for example, current priority, *nice value*, priority class) that is separate from similar features that the Threads Library maintains for threads.

The interaction of these two levels of scheduling can produce some interesting effects:

- LWPs of the time-sharing priority class will have their kernel priority adjusted dynamically according to processor usage and other factors.

 NOTE See the `priocntl`(2) manual page for further details of the time-sharing priority class. Note that using the `priocntl`(2) system call directly from a multiplexed thread should be avoided because it may interfere with thread scheduling by the Threads Library.

Consequently, a thread picked up by an LWP may run with a kernel priority determined by the activity of the *prior* thread on that LWP.

- It is possible for a thread of high priority from the point of view of the Threads Library to be picked up by an LWP of relatively low priority to the kernel.

Additional points to consider:

- A thread that is blocked in a system call will remain with its LWP until that system call returns. The Threads Library is unaware of such suspensions.

- Each LWP in the pool used for multiplexed LWPs is of the same kernel scheduling class (that is, time-sharing or fixed priority). That class is determined by the scheduling class (that is, time-sharing or fixed priority) of the LWP running the initial thread of the program.

- One part of associating a thread with an LWP is to make the signal mask of the LWP agree with that of the thread. On each thread context switch there is a check for agreement. If the mask of the new thread differs from that of the prior thread, there is a system call to update the mask of the LWP. One implication of this is that using threads with a wide variety of signal masks can add to the cost of switching threads.

Bound Thread Scheduling

The semantics of bound thread scheduling differs considerably from that for multiplexed threads.

- Bound threads are permanently attached to their LWPs; consequently, they are exempt from that level of scheduling by the Threads Library.

- A bound thread executes whenever the kernel schedules its underlying LWP.

- The Threads Library supports the concept of *scheduling policy* as well as *priority level* for bound threads. When the programmer specifies these characteristics, the Threads Library applies them to the LWP holding the thread.

  These characteristics can be modified with the **thr_setscheduler**(3thread) function.

- The available scheduling policies for bound threads are:

  SCHED_TS or **SCHED_OTHER**
  > The two values are synonymous. The bound thread is run by an LWP of the kernel time-sharing scheduling class.

   NOTE Technically, multiplexed threads are also categorized as having the **SCHED_TS** policy even though they are not necessarily run by LWPs in the kernel time sharing class. The Threads Library algorithm for scheduling multiplexed threads (round robin) bears a closer resemblance to the kernel's fixed priority class than the kernel's time sharing class.

  SCHED_FIFO or **SCHED_RR**
  > The thread will be run on an LWP of the fixed-priority scheduling class. **SCHED_FIFO** means that the LWP will have an infinite time quantum (not preempted) whereas **SCHED_RR** (round-robin) uses a fixed priority with a finite time slice.
  >
  > The **SCHED_FIFO** and **SCHED_RR** policies can be used only by bound threads.

   NOTE Appropriate privilege is required to set the policy of a thread to SCHED_FIFO or SCHED_RR. See **priocntl**(2).

A bound thread with real-time constraints can further improve response time by using **processor_bind**(2) to bind its LWP to a processor. It can use **_lwp_self**(2) to find the ID of the LWP to which it is bound, and pass that as an argument to **processor_bind**.

NOTE Multiplexed threads should not use `processor_bind`.

Managing Thread Scheduling

The initial thread of a newly executing program [a process returning from **exec**(2)] is always a multiplexed thread running under the **SCHED_TS** policy. The scheduling characteristics of new threads are generally derived from the creator thread. [There are some interesting variations when a bound thread creates a multiplexed thread and *vice versa*. See the **thr_create**(3thread) manual page for details.]

To create a thread with different scheduling characteristics the programmer can:

1. Create a new thread with **thr_create**(3thread) using the **THR_SUSPENDED** flag. This will create a new thread but not allow it to execute.

2. Use the returned thread ID to change the characteristics of the new thread with the **thr_setprio**(3thread) or **thr_setscheduler**(3thread) functions.

3. Use the **thr_continue**(3thread) function to make the new thread runnable.

Alternatively, a thread can use **thr_setscheduler**(3thread) or **thr_setprio**(3thread) to modify its own scheduling class or priority.

Synchronizing Threads

In general, each thread must take special care in using resources that might be concurrently used by another thread.

 NOTE The definition of *resource* will vary with applications. Typically, *resources* are manifested as some organization of data relevant to the application in process memory (perhaps a linked list or other data structure) or in files.

Unless their actions are synchronized, threads may encounter logically inconsistent linked lists or partially updated structures in common process memory. Synchronization may also be needed for concurrent actions on commonly held external resources such as file descriptors and message queues.

- There is no automatic, implicit mechanism to protect each thread from the actions of other threads. The correctness of a multithreaded program must be incorporated into the design by having each thread cooperate with the others.

- The Threads Library provides a suite of functions with several categories of synchronization semantics. The categories are:

  □ Locks

  □ Semaphores

  □ Barriers

  □ Condition Variables

  Most of these categories contain several variants.

- The programmer has the responsibility to:

  □ use the correct number and type of synchronization mechanism(s)

  □ use them where needed

  □ enforce synchronization on *every* thread using the common resource

  □ avoid deadlock and starvation conditions

- Other than programmer discipline, there is nothing to stop any thread from using common resources without obeying the synchronization protocol being used by the others.

- The general procedure for using these mechanisms is:

    1. Allocate a synchronization data structure for the resource to be protected (for example, to use a mutual exclusion lock, allocate a structure of type **mutex_t**). The address of that structure becomes an argument for all subsequent operations on this instance of the mechanism.

    2. Initialize the mechanism.

    3. Use the mechanism.

    4. Deallocate the mechanism when it is no longer needed — perhaps when the resource being protected is deallocated.

Locks

The semantics of a *lock* allow the resource to be used by only one thread at a time. The Threads Library supports several types of locks:

- mutual exclusion locks (*mutexes*)
- spin locks
- recursive mutual exclusion locks (*rmutexes*)
- reader-writer locks (these allow non-exclusive access for readers)

A thread that successfully locks a resource is said to *hold the lock* or to *have acquired the lock*. Unlocking is also known as *releasing the lock*.

Mutual Exclusion Locks

A *mutual exclusion lock*, or *mutex*, allows only one thread at any time to access the resource being protected. The lock is acquired by the **mutex_lock**(3synch) function.

```
int mutex_lock(
        mutex_t *mutex
);
```

If the lock is already held by some other thread, the calling thread will block in **mutex_lock**(3synch).

When the thread holding the lock calls **mutex_unlock**(3synch), some waiting thread (if any) will be made runnable.

```
int mutex_unlock(
        mutex_t *mutex
);
```

The Threads Library does not enforce any notion of ownership of a lock by a thread. The thread unlocking a mutex need not be the same thread that locked the mutex.

Spin Locks

A spin lock is also used for mutually exclusive access to some resource. The **_spin_lock**(3synch) function differs from **mutex_lock**(3synch) in implementation. If a spin lock is not available, the calling thread is not blocked, instead the caller busy waits (or *spins*) until the lock becomes available.

```
_spin_lock(  spin_t *lock);
_spin_unlock(spin_t *lock);
```

Considerations for the use of spin locks:

- The busy waiting prevents the LWP from being used by another thread.

- This facility is intended for use when the delay is expected to be smaller than the time to context switch to another thread and back.

- Use of this facility is not recommended on uniprocessor machines or if only one processor of a multiprocessor machine might be available. In those circumstances the spinning thread prevents the possible execution of the thread that is holding the lock, thereby delaying, possibly deadlocking, itself.

 NOTE Extreme care should be exercised in using spin locks. The minimally safe environment for using spin locks may be bound threads running on a system with more than one processor. However, deadlocks are always possible.

Recursive Mutual Exclusion

The regular mutex lock (shown earlier) will deadlock the calling thread on attempts to re-lock a lock that it already holds. A recursive mutually exclusive lock (recursive mutex or rmutex) allows the holder of a lock to re-lock without deadlock; other threads will block normally.

```
int rmutex_lock(   rmutex_t *rmutex);
int rmutex_unlock(rmutex_t *rmutex);
```

Considerations for the use of recursive mutex locks:

- The holder must unlock the lock for each time it was locked.

- This facility is useful for

  □ The implementation of recursive algorithms.

  □ Situations where the code locking a resource cannot know which locks
    have already been acquired. This may arise in the implementation of
    library functions where generally the activities of the callers are not
    known.

- Recursive mutexes only prevent deadlock of a thread with itself for a single
  resource. It is still possible for a thread to become deadlocked even with
  recursive mutexes. Two (or more) threads can deadlock by each acquiring
  multiple locks in an unfortunate order.

- Recursive mutexes provide exclusivity but they sacrifice *atomicity*. A
  resource protected by an rmutex will be used by only one thread at a time;
  however, that use must be designed to be reentrant because that thread
  might reacquire the resource in the midst of using it.

Reader-Writer Locks

Whereas the locks for mutual exclusion allow only one thread to use a resource at
a time, the reader-writer facility supports a more complicated model of resource
use. Mutual exclusion is needed only when the resource is being modified; otherwise, access need not be denied to multiple threads.

Such locks can be held in either *read mode* (a read lock) or *write mode* (a write lock).

- In read mode, there is no limit on the number of threads using the resource.
  By convention, each thread with such a lock assumes that the resource is
  stable while the lock is held. That assumption is reasonable provided no
  thread will modify the resource until it acquires a write lock and that is not
  possible while at least one read lock is being held. As usual, these assumptions are not enforced by any mechanism other than programming discipline.

- In practice, a lock held in read mode should bar only writers while a lock
  held in write mode should bar all readers and all other writers. Read and
  write locks are acquired by the **rw_rdlock**(3synch) and **rw_wrlock**(3synch)

functions, respectively.

```
int rw_rdlock(rwlock_t *rwlock);
int rw_wrlock(rwlock_t *rwlock);
```

If one or more threads are blocked waiting for a write lock, then any threads requesting read locks will be blocked to wait for the writer. This prevents a sequence of readers from indefinitely blocking a waiting writer.

- The order of access is strictly first-in-first-out (FIFO). This ordering is obeyed even if the readers have higher priority than the writer. This is an exception to the algorithm used to awaken threads by the other thread synchronization mechanisms. [See the section on "Further Considerations for Synchronization Mechanisms".]

- It is not possible to promote in place a read lock to a write lock. The read lock must be released and a write lock acquired in a separate operation.

Semaphores

Semaphores are a facility well-suited to managing the allocation and deallocation of identical resources.

- The semaphore can be initialized to the number of resources.

- A thread needing a resource should atomically decrement the associated semaphore with the **sema_wait**(3synch) function.

- If the resource is not available (semaphore count non-positive) the caller will block in **sema_wait**(3synch) until one becomes available.

```
int sema_wait(
        sema_t *sema
);
```

- When a resource is no longer in use, the thread releasing the resource should increment the associated semaphore with the **sema_post**(3synch) function.

```
int sema_post(
        sema_t *sema
);
```

- If any threads are blocked on that semaphore, the call to **sema_post** will make one runnable so that it can (implicitly) decrement the semaphore and return from **sema_wait**(3synch).

Additional considerations:

- This mechanism lacks the following features of the IPC style semaphore facility:

  - Increment/decrement by values greater than **1**.

  - Operations on semaphore sets.

  - The ability to, "block while count is non-zero" instead of the usual rule, "block only when count is zero."

  - The ability to automatically release semaphores on termination (**SEM_UNDO** flag).

- A semaphore initialized to **1** is almost equivalent to a mutex. In such cases, use the mutex facilities; they are more efficient, having been optimized for that case.

   NOTE However, if the design of the application calls for signal handlers to use the synchronization operations, then use semaphores, which are *asynchronous-safe*, and can be used to communicate between signal handlers and base level code. For example, a signal handler can safely call **sema_post**, but it should not try to lock or unlock a mutex used in the base code.

- The **sema_post**(3synch) function can validly be used to increase a semaphore count above that defined by **sema_init**(3synch).

Barriers

In a sense, a barrier is the logical inverse of a lock. Whereas a lock allows only one thread at a time to proceed (to use a resource), a barrier allows no thread to proceed until an entire group of them are ready to proceed.

- The number of threads expected to gather at a barrier is specified in the barrier structure when it is initialized with **barrier_init**(3synch). (See "Initialization of Synchronization Mechanisms" below.)

- A thread declares its arrival at the barrier with the **barrier_wait**(3synch) function.

```
int barrier_wait(
        barrier_t *barrier
);
```

- The barrier mechanism has no facility to authenticate the threads calling **barrier_wait**; it simply counts the arriving threads.

- If the number of threads at the barrier is less than the initialized value, the thread calling **barrier_wait** is suspended.

- If the arriving thread brings the count to the requisite value, all of the waiting threads are made runnable and eventually return from **barrier_wait**.

- When the threads are released, the count of threads at the barrier is reset to zero. That same barrier can be reused without re-initialization.

- A barrier should not be re-initialized while there are waiting threads.

- There is also a "spinning" variant of barriers called **_barrier_spin**(3synch). The considerations for usage are similar to those for spin locks given above.

Condition Variables

Condition variables are a general mechanism by which one thread can delay its execution until some *condition* is true and another thread can announce when some condition is true.

NOTE The semantics of condition variables are analogous to those of the *sleep-wakeup* idiom historically used in kernel and device driver code.

The condition variable (of type **cond_t**) is part of the mechanism by which this synchronization occurs but that variable is not the *condition* itself. This *condition* is a somewhat abstract concept (as is *resource*) that is represented by other code in the program. Some hypothetical examples of conditions are:

- A message has arrived.

- Data is available for processing.

- Space is available to buffer output.

The association between *condition* and the condition variable arises from the programmer's usage of the feature.

One distinguishing feature of the conditional variable mechanism is that two different types of data structures are employed, not just one. A mutual exclusion lock (type `mutex_t`) *must* be used in concert with the condition variable (type `cond_t`) itself. By convention, a thread that evaluates or modifies or acts on the *condition* must acquire the associated mutex lock beforehand and release that lock afterward.

The following pseudo-code shows the protocol for a thread that is making some *condition* true and announcing the change.

```
mutex_lock(&mutex);
```
make condition true;
```
cond_signal(&cond);
```
awaken thread (if any) waiting for condition
```
mutex_unlock(&mutex);
```

When the thread announces the change of the condition (to being true), it has a choice of awakening either a single thread waiting for that condition or all threads waiting for that condition. The syntax is:

```
int cond_signal(     cond_t *cond);
```
awaken one thread
```
int cond_broadcast(cond_t *cond);
```
awaken all threads

In either case, there is no problem if there happen to be no waiting threads at the time of announcement.

NOTE Do not confuse the term *signal* in the sense of calling `cond_signal`(3synch) and *signal* in the sense of `thr_kill`(3thread). They are different mechanisms with different semantics. (The latter provides asynchronous influence, the former does not.)

A thread wanting to delay itself until the *condition* is true must first acquire the associated mutex before evaluating the condition. If the condition is true, there is no need for delay and the thread can proceed; otherwise, the thread must call `cond_wait`(3synch) to wait for the condition to become true. The following pseudo-code illustrates the programming idiom.

```
mutex_lock(&mutex)
while(condition is false)
        cond_wait(&cond, &mutex);
act on the condition; possibly invalidate it
mutex_unlock(&mutex);
```

The mutex and condition variable used here must be the same data structures as those used in the places where the *condition* is made true.

If the *condition* is true when **cond_wait** is called, it returns immediately. If the *condition* is false, **cond_wait** will:

- Implicitly unlock the specified mutex.

  If the mutex remained locked (and the stated conventions were obeyed) no thread could enter the critical section to make the condition true.

- Block the calling thread until some other thread makes the condition true and announces that change with **cond_signal**(3synch) or **cond_broadcast**(3synch).

- Implicitly re-acquire the specified mutex before returning.

  If this were not done, the thread could neither validly re-evaluate the condition (part of the **while** loop), nor validly act on the condition.

The semantics of condition variables require that a thread re-test the *condition* on any return from **cond_wait**(3synch).

- The calling of either **cond_signal**(3synch) or **cond_broadcast**(3synch) implies that the *condition* was set true at some time.

- A thread (or threads) waiting for that condition are made runnable but there may be some delay until they actually execute and return from **cond_wait**(3synch).

- During that delay some other thread may be chosen to return from **cond_wait**(3synch) and invalidate the *condition*. This other thread might be:

  □ Another thread in the "gang" awakened by **cond_broadcast**(3synch).

  □ A thread of higher priority that concurrently called **cond_wait**(3synch).

- Consequently, for correctness every thread must re-test the *condition* on return from **cond_wait**(3synch).

Other features of condition variables are:

- Blocked threads can be awakened by signals. The handler will be called and cond_wait(3synch) returns with an **EINTR** condition.

- There is a time-limited variant of **cond_wait** called cond_timedwait(3synch).

- The separateness of the variable (type **cond_t**) used for signaling and for mutual exclusion (type **mutex_t**) means that several different conditions can be managed within one critical section.

Awakening Threads for Synchronization Mechanisms

When only one thread is to be awakened for a newly available synchronization mechanism, the selection is made by the following general rule.

1. Preference is given to bound threads over multiplexed threads.

2. If there is still more than one candidate for awakening, the thread with the highest (Threads Library) *priority* is chosen.

3. If there is still more than one candidate for awakening, the thread that blocked first is selected.

    - FIFO ordering of threads of the same priority is generally true but not guaranteed. In this implementation, there are race conditions in which the ordering is not strictly FIFO.

There are some exceptions to this algorithm:

- For a broadcast on a condition variable and for barriers, more than one thread is awakened. Conceptually, these are awakened simultaneously.

- For reader-writer locks, the order of awakening is strictly FIFO, regardless of priority or other factors.

Further Considerations for Synchronization Mechanisms

- There is no protection against *priority inversion*. When a thread holds a lock, it keeps its priority even if a higher priority thread is waiting for that lock. Therefore, a low priority thread can prevent a thread of higher priority from running.

- **thr_exit**(3thread) does not release any locks a thread may have acquired.

- There is no automatic protection from deadlock (except for the limited protection provided by recursive mutexes).

- If a caught signal is received by a thread while blocked on a synchronization mechanism (other than a condition variable):

  - The signal handler is called.

  - The blocked function call is transparently re-started.

  - The function does not return with **EINTR**.

  - Condition variables are the single exception. A call to **cond_wait** or **cond_timedwait** will be abnormally terminated on receipt of a signal, and **EINTR** will be returned.

- Each mechanism (except barriers) has a conditional **_try** variant that will not block when the resource is unavailable; error condition **EBUSY** is returned instead.

Initialization of Synchronization Mechanisms

Some general characteristics of the initialization functions are:

- The first argument is a pointer to the locking structure to be initialized.

- The *type* argument can take on the values of either:

USYNC_THREAD	thread-to-thread synchronization
USYNC_PROCESS	interprocess synchronization. For such use, the synchronization data structures must reside in memory that is shared between the processes, using either IPC shared memory or the mapped file feature.

  The *type* argument is not available for the two spinning type locks.

- Two mechanism types (barriers and semaphore) require an initial value (*count*).

- The last argument is of type (**void ***), is reserved for future use, and should be set to **NULL** for future compatibility.

The syntax of these functions is given below.

```
int sema_init(           sema_t          *sema,    int count, int type, void *arg);
int barrier_init(        barrier_t       *barrier, int count, int type, void *arg);
int _barrier_spin_init(  barrier_spin_t  *barrier, int count,           void *arg);
int _spin_init(          spin_t          *lock,                         void *arg);
int cond_init(           cond_t          *cond,               int type, void *arg);
int mutex_init(          mutex_t         *mutex,              int type, void *arg);
int rmutex_init(         rmutex_t        *rmutex,             int type, void *arg);
int rwlock_init(         rwlock_t        *rwlock,             int type, void *arg);
```

Alternative Initialization

In this implementation, it is valid to use statically initialized (zero-filled) data structures for the synchronization mechanisms.

For most of the mechanisms, a zero-filled data structure is taken to be unlocked and of type **USYNC_THREAD**. The mechanisms that take a count argument have the following additional interpretations:

- A zero-filled *sema_t* structure represents zero available resources. A **sema_wait**(3synch) on that structure will block.

- A zero-filled **barrier_t** structure is valid but meaningless.

This technique is *not* recommended for re-initialization of synchronization structures. In general, it is incorrect to re-initialize a synchronization structure while in use. Some of the initialization functions (shown above) return **EBUSY** if called for an active data structure (one on which threads are blocked). Zero-filling the data structure bypasses that check.

Invalidation of Synchronization Mechanisms

The syntax of the functions that invalidate synchronization structures is even more regular than that of the initializing functions.

- The first and only argument is a pointer to the mechanism-specific structure to be invalidated.

The syntax is:

```
int sema_destroy(          sema_t      *sema);
int _spin_destroy(         spin_t      *lock);
int barrier_destroy(       barrier_t   *barrier);
int _barrier_spin_destroy(barrier_spin_t *barrier);
int cond_destroy(          cond_t      *cond);
int mutex_destroy(         mutex_t     *mutex);
int rmutex_destroy(        rmutex_t    *rmutex);
int rwlock_destroy(        rwlock_t    *rwlock);
```

Each function can fail as follows:

EINVAL   Invalid argument specified.

EBUSY   Mechanism currently in use.

The effect of these functions is:

- To mark the structure as being invalid for further use (unless re-initialized).

- To allow the recovery of any Threads Library internal resources that may have been allocated when the synchronization mechanism was initialized.

- Though these _destroy functions recover underlying resources, the space for the synchronization structure itself remains. If the space is to be recovered (say the structure will no longer be used) that must be done separately. For example, a space acquired from malloc(3C) should be recovered with free(3C).

Development Environment

Compilation Environment

Source code that uses Threads Library functions should include the following line:

```
#include      <thread.h>
```

and should be compiled with the following command line options:

```
cc [options] -D_REENTRANT file -lthread
```

The **-lthread** flag links in the Threads Library. The **-D_REENTRANT** flag is needed for an application to be thread-safe, and to access reentrant routines in standard libraries (see below).

Source code that uses the synchronization routines in the Threads Library should include the following line:

```
#include      <synch.h>
```

Error Returns

None of the thread management or synchronization routines in the Threads Library set **errno** to indicate an error; most return an error number if an error is encountered.

- The error numbers returned correspond to **errno** numbers.

- This discourages use of **errno**, which is not reentrant and is inefficient in a multithreaded environment.

- The Threads Library does not guarantee preservation of **errno** across calls.

NOTE | The asynchronous I/O routines, which are included in the Threads Library, do set **errno**. See the **aio** reference manual pages in the *Operating System API Reference*.

However, threads may call routines that do set **errno**. If all threads in a process accessed a global **errno**, no thread could be sure that the global value resulted from a system call it had made, it might have resulted from another system call made by another thread. Therefore, the Threads Library maintains a private copy of **errno** for each thread. When a thread references **errno**, it will get the value of its private copy, not the global variable.

There is one exception: the initial thread (the thread running **main**) accesses the global **errno** via its private copy. Therefore, the initial thread can safely call into non-reentrant code (such as an old object file compiled before UNIX System V Release 4.2 MP (SVR4.2 MP)), and have correct **errno** semantics. Threads other than the initial thread should not make calls into old object files that set **errno**. The mixing of reentrant and non-reentrant object files is discouraged, and should only be done as an interim measure until applications are made reentrant.

Applications that reference **errno** should include the following line:

```
#include     <errno.h>
```

Thread-Safe Libraries

In previous releases of the UNIX System, libraries freely used global and static data. In a multithreaded program, different sibling threads running concurrently could corrupt global or static data. Therefore, in UNIX System V Release 4.2 MP (SVR4.2 MP), standard libraries have been made thread-safe. When an application is compiled with the **-D_REENTRANT** flag to **cc**(1), standard libraries will synchronize threads' use of global and static data. (As this synchronization has a performance cost to single-threaded applications, it is only enabled when the **-D_REENTRANT** flag is used.)

In addition, new, reentrant versions of some library routines have been added. The names of these routines are suffixed with **_r**. For example, the reentrant version of **strtok**(3S) is **strtok_r**(3S). Multithreaded applications should use the reentrant versions of library routines. See the *Operating System API Reference* for details.

UNIX System V Release 4.2 MP (SVR4.2 MP) supplies thread-safe versions of the following libraries:

- libc
- libm
- libnsl
- libsocket
- libresolv
- resolv
- tcpip
- straddr

Applications using other libraries that have not been made thread-safe must synchronize access to global data.

System Call Wrappers

The Threads Library provides *wrappers* for the system calls and library routines listed below. A wrapper is a routine with the same name and interface as another routine, in this case a standard system call or library routine. Wrappers usually do something to modify the behavior of the standard routine, then call the standard routine, and perhaps do something further when the standard routine returns. Many of the Threads Library wrappers cause the system call to affect a single thread instead of the entire process or LWP. See the reference manual pages for these routines in the *Operating System API Reference* for details.

When you compile with **-D_REENTRANT** and **-lthread**, references to these routines will automatically access the Threads Library wrapper versions.

- getcontext(2)
- setcontext(2)
- sigaction(2)
- sighold(2)
- sigignore(2)
- signal(2)
- sigpause(2)
- sigpending(2)
- sigprocmask(2)
- sigrelse(2)
- sigset(2)
- sigsuspend(2)
- sigwait(2)
- alarm(2)
- getitimer(3C)
- setitimer(3C)
- sleep(2)
- forkall(2)
- fork(2)

NOTE
The wrappers for the `fork` and `forkall` system calls do not change the behavior of those system calls for an application linked with `libthread`. They perform some housekeeping only when tracing is enabled (that is, when the application is linked with `libthreadT`). See the section, "Tracing Multithreaded Programs", below.

Timers

The Threads Library provides facilities that allow multiplexed threads to use alarms and real interval timers without requiring that the threads tie up LWPs between the initiation and expiration of the call. For this purpose, the Threads Library supplies wrappers for `alarm`(2), `getitimer`(3C), `setitimer`(3C), and `sleep`(2). When a bound thread calls one of these routines, it has access to the full functionality as described on the reference manual page. However, when a multiplexed thread calls one of these functions, it will use the Threads Library version of the function, and in some cases the functionality will be limited. For example, a multiplexed thread can only use real timers, not virtual or profiling timers.

In addition, the wrapper versions of these functions have per-thread semantics rather than per-LWP semantics. For example, `alarm`(2) sets an alarm clock. When the set time expires, the caller receives a `SIGALRM` signal. The wrapper function ensures that the `SIGALRM` is delivered to the calling thread (rather than the calling LWP), regardless of whether the calling thread is running on the same LWP on which it was running when it issued the call to `alarm`.

See the reference manual pages for these routines in the *Operating System API Reference* for details.

Debugging Multithreaded Programs

The graphical debugger, `debug`(1), can be used to debug multithreaded programs. See the chapters on debugging in *Programming in Standard C* for guidance on using `debug`.

Tracing Multithreaded Programs

The Threads Library provides a mechanism for tracing library events. Calls to all Threads Library routines can be traced. Significant information, such as arguments, return values, lock contention, and duration of execution is recorded. Using tracing facilities, you can find the latency time for obtaining a lock, for example, or the number of acquisition attempts on a lock.

To avoid a performance penalty on the Threads Library, a separate library, `libthreadT.so`, contains the tracing routines. To obtain trace data, the application must be linked to `libthreadT.so` instead of `libthread.so`. Use the following command:

> `cc` [*options*] `-D_REENTRANT` *file* `-lthreadT`

Trace Data Files

Trace data is collected for each LWP and stored in a separate file, by default in the current working directory. The files are named:

> `tr.`*xxxxxxx*`.`*yyy*

where *xxxxxxx* is the seven least significant hexadecimal digits of the process ID associated with the LWP and *yyy* is the three least significant hexadecimal digits of the LWP ID.

When a traced application completes execution, one trace file will exist for each LWP that existed in the life of that application. The logical way to begin to use this data is to merge all the trace files into one file with all events sorted chronologically, by thread ID, or by event. Then you can use tools to summarize the data in useful ways.

Because trace output files have not yet been standardized, no tools are provided to analyze these files, but you can construct your own using standard UNIX System tools, such as `awk`(1), `sort`(1), and `sed`(1).

Format of the Trace Data Files

Each line in the files is a trace record in the following format:

> *time1* : *time2* : *lwpid* : *pid* : *tid* : *event1* : *event2* : *which* : *a1* : *a2* : *a3* : *a4* : *a5*

The meaning of each field in the record is shown in the following table:

Table 9-1: Meaning of Trace Record Fields

Field	Meaning
time1	current time in seconds
time2	current time in nanoseconds
lwpid	LWP ID of calling thread
pid	process ID of calling thread
tid	thread ID of calling thread
event1	general category of event (type of routine called)
event2	specific event (name of routine called)
which	0 for a single record associated with this event, 1 for the first of two records, or 2 for the second or two records
a1	depends on event
a2	depends on event
a3	depends on event
a4	depends on event
a5	depends on event

The first two fields record the time, the next three fields record information about the caller, the next three fields identify the event (the routine that was called), and the remaining fields record specific details about the event, such as the arguments passed to the routine in question.

Further details about the contents of trace data files are given on the **thread_trace**(4) page in the *System Files and Devices Reference*. **thread_trace**(4) also describes environment variables that can be set to change the default trace data collection. For example, you can specify a subset of events to trace or specify the directory where trace files should be created.

Merging Trace Files

The individual trace files for each LWP will already be sorted chronologically. The following use of **sort**(1) will efficiently merge the trace files in their current format.

```
sort -m -n -o mergefilename -t: +0 -4 tracefiles
```

where *mergefilename* represents the name of the merge file to be created and *tracefiles* represents the names of the trace files to be merged (or a regular expression that identifies them). The resulting *mergefile* will be sorted chronologically, and further sorted by LWP ID and process ID.

Using Trace File Data

Once the trace data files are merged, translating the event category and event number fields into event names is an obvious next step. These are the sixth and seventh fields of each trace record. The following **awk** script will read the file specified by the first argument, translate the event fields into the associated event name, and write the output into the file specified by the second argument.

```
awk '
BEGIN { FS=":"
        OFS=":"
}
FILENAME == "/tmp/tracemap.h" {
        map[$1]=$2
        next
}
{       OUT=map[$6"_"$7]
        print $1" "$2" "$3" "$4" "$5" "OUT" \
                "$8" "$9" "$10" "$11" "$12" "$13
}' MAPPING $1 > $2
```

This script assumes that **tracemap.h** is located in **/tmp** and that it maps event names to the values in the *event1* and *event2* fields of the trace record with entries of the form:

```
1_1:thr_create
1_2:thr_exit
1_3:thr_join
1_4:thr_self
1_5:thr_minstack
     .
     .
     .
9_1:_spin_init
9_2:_spin_lock
9_3:_spin_trylock
9_4:_spin_unlock
9_5:_spin_destroy
```

where the number before the underscore on each line is the category number of the event and the number after the underscore on each line is the event number of the event listed on that line.

You can write additional **awk** scripts and **sort** commands to further consolidate your data as needed to analyze the behavior of your application.

Examples

This section presents several small programs to illustrate use of the Threads Library.

hello, world

Figure 9-2: hello, world

```
#include <stdio.h>
#include <stdlib.h>
#include <thread.h>
static void        *print(void*);
int main()
{
        int        okend = EXIT_SUCCESS;
        (void)thr_create(0,0, print, (void *)"hello, ",  0L,0);
        (void)thr_create(0,0, print, (void *)"world.\n", 0L,0);
        thr_exit(&okend);
        /*NOTREACHED*/
}
static void *print(void *s)
{
        (void)printf(s);
        return NULL;
}
```

Figure 9-2 shows the traditional first program written when one enters a new regime of the UNIX programming environment. In this example, we create one thread to output **"hello, "** and a separate thread to output **"world.\n"** Despite its brevity, this example illustrates several points about programming with the Threads Library:

- The argument types and the return type of the **printf**(3S) function disqualify it as the starting point of a thread. A *wrapper* function (**print**) had to be devised.

- There is no need for the initial thread to wait for the completion of the two threads running **print**. The process is automatically terminated after both of the printing threads complete.

> **NOTE** The use of `thr_exit`(3thread) is important. The use of `return` from `main` or allowing `main` to run off the closing brace is translated to a call to the `exit`(2) system call. That system call generally terminates the process before the printing threads can produce their output.

■ The order of the output is not guaranteed. In most cases the thread that is created first will be able to output **"hello, "** before the following thread outputs **"world.\n"** Occasionally, the order is reversed.

Basic Threads Management

Figure 9-3: `sometask`

```
#include <stdio.h>
#include <stdlib.h>
#include <unistd.h>
#include <time.h>
#include <thread.h>
#define  RANGE     10
/* ARGSUSED */
void *sometask(void *dummy)
{
        thread_t thrID    = thr_self();
        unsigned seed     = getpid() * time(NULL) * (thrID + 1);
        unsigned naptime=
                (unsigned)(1 + RANGE*((double)rand_r(&seed)/(double)RAND_MAX));
        setbuf(stdout,NULL);
        (void)printf("thread %ld entering sometask\n", thrID);
        (void)printf("thread %ld naptime %d\n",                thrID, naptime);
        (void)sleep(naptime);
        (void)printf("thread %ld leaving  sometask\n", thrID);
        return NULL;
}
```

The following examples on threads management will use (either explicitly or implicitly) the function **sometask** that appears in Figure 9-3. This function will call **sleep**(3C) to represent some arbitrary activity by the thread. Features to note in this example are:

■ The simulated action for each thread will be different since each sleeps for a different, random period of time. The seed for the random number generator depends on current process ID, current time, and thread ID.

- The activity period is at least one second plus a random component between zero and nine seconds.

- The random number is generated with **rand_r**(3C), the thread-safe version of **rand**(3C).

- Calls to **sleep**(3C) by each thread will put only the calling thread to sleep, as arranged by the wrapper version of **sleep** provided by the Threads Library.

Figure 9-4: Multiple Threads

```
#include <stdio.h>
#include <stdlib.h>
#include <thread.h>
extern void         *sometask(void *);
main(int argc, char **argv)
{
    int Nthreads, i; thread_t threadID;
    if(argc != 2){
        (void)fprintf( stderr,"%s: usage: %s Nthreads\nwhere Nthreads > 0\n",
                            argv[0], argv[0]);
        return 1;
    }
    if( (Nthreads = atoi(argv[1])) <= 0 ){
        (void)fprintf( stderr,"%s: usage: %s Nthreads\nwhere Nthreads > 0\n",
                            argv[0], argv[0]);
        return 1;
    }
    for(i = 0; i < Nthreads; i++)
        (void)thr_create(NULL, 0, sometask, NULL, 0, NULL);
    for(i = 0; i < Nthreads; i++){
        (void)thr_join(0, &threadID, NULL);
        (void)printf("thread %ld is gone\n", threadID);
    }
    return 0;
}
```

The program in Figure 9-4 creates one or more threads as follows:

- The number of threads to be created is determined by a (validated) command line parameter.

- Each new thread runs **sometask**.

- The initial thread waits for the termination of each thread that it creates.

Figure 9-5: `barrier_wait`

```
#include <stdio.h>
#include <stdlib.h>
#include <thread.h>
#include <synch.h>
extern void       *sometask (void *);
static void       *repeatask(void *);
static barrier_t   common_wall;
main(int argc, char **argv)
{
        int           Nthreads, i;
        if(argc != 2){
                (void)fprintf(    stderr,"%s: usage: %s Nthreads\nwhere Nthreads > 0\n",
                                  argv[0], argv[0]);
                return 1;
        }
        if((Nthreads = atoi(argv[1]))>0){
                (void)barrier_init(&common_wall, Nthreads, USYNC_THREAD, NULL);
        } else {
                (void)fprintf(    stderr,"%s: usage: %s Nthreads\nwhere Nthreads > 0\n",
                                  argv[0], argv[0]);
                return 1;
        }
        for(i = 0; i < Nthreads; i++)
                (void)thr_create(NULL, 0, repeatask, NULL, 0, NULL);
        thr_exit(NULL);
        /*NOTREACHED*/
}
/* ARGSUSED */
static void *repeatask(void *dummy)
{
        for(;;){
                        (void)printf("thread %ld at wall\n", thr_self());
                        (void)barrier_wait(&common_wall);
                        (void)sometask(NULL);
        }
}
```

The example in Figure 9-5 is a variation of that in Figure 9-4. In this case:

- Each thread that is created (running **repeatask**) calls **sometask** repeatedly.

- The created threads coordinate their activity into cycles by the barrier facility of the Threads Library.

- Output of this program shows a flurry of activity as the barrier count is reached and the set of threads is unleashed for the next cycle.

- There is no need for the initial thread to persist; consequently, the initial thread terminates itself with **thr_exit**(3thread). The process continues until the user terminates it manually.

Dining Philosophers

Figure 9-6: Dining Philosophers

```
#include <stdio.h>
#include <thread.h>
#include <synch.h>
#define   NPHIL     5
static sema_t        forks[NPHIL];
typedef struct {
        int       id, left_fork, right_fork;
} philo_t;
static philo_t       philo_args[NPHIL];
static void          *philo(void*);
extern void          *sometask(void*);
main()
{
        int     i;
        for(i = 0; i < NPHIL; i++){
                (void)sema_init(&forks[i], i, USYNC_THREAD, NULL);
                philo_args[i].id    = i;
                philo_args[i].left_fork    = i;
                philo_args[i].rght_fork    = (i+1)%NPHIL;
        }
        for(i = 0; i < NPHIL; i++)
                (void)thr_create(NULL, 0, philo, &philo_args[i], 0, NULL);
        thr_exit(NULL);
        /*NOTREACHED*/
}
static void *philo(void *philo_arg)
{
        philo_t   *argp    = (philo_t *)philo_arg;
        int       id       = argp->id;
        int       left     = argp->left_fork;
        int       rght     = argp->rght_fork;
        (void)printf("thrID %ld id %d left %d rght %d\n",
                        thr_self(), id, left, rght);
        for(;;){
                (void)sema_wait(&forks[left]);
```

(continued on next page)

Programming with the Threads Library

Figure 9-6: Dining Philosophers (continued)

```
                    (void)sema_wait(&forks[rght]);
                    (void)printf("philo %d eating w. %d and %d\n", id, left, rght);
                    (void)sometask(NULL); /* eating */
                    (void)printf("philo %d done   w. %d and %d\n", id, left, rght);
                    (void)sema_post(&forks[left]);
                    (void)sema_post(&forks[rght]);
                    (void)sometask(NULL); /* think */
            } /* NOTREACHED */
    }
```

The program in Figure 9-6 shows an implementation of the classic *dining philoso-*
phers problem using the facilities of the Threads Library.

In this problem there are N philosophers sitting at a round table eating and thinking. Each has a plate of spaghetti and there is a single fork (a total of N forks)
between each pair. Each philosopher must use two forks to eat the spaghetti.
Each philosopher puts down both forks to think. This simple problem illustrates
many of the issues in concurrent programming, such as the need for synchronization to prevent deadlock. The philosophers represent processes that require
shared resources (the forks).

Some features of this program are:

- Each philosopher is represented by a thread.

- Each fork is represented by a semaphore.

- Each thread runs the same code (**philo**) but needs different arguments.
  That is each philosopher being simulated will follow the same rules but is
  assigned to use a distinct pair of forks. The example shows how to assemble
  several items of information into a structure and inform the thread of where
  to find its arguments.

- This implementation can deadlock. If each philosopher picks up his or her
  left fork before any picks up his or her right fork, they will deadlock, waiting to pick up their right forks. One way to solve this deadlock would be to
  allow no more than $N-1$ philosophers to eat at the same time. That way,
  one of the philosophers will always be able to pick up two forks.

- As in other examples, there is no need for the initial thread to persist. The
  simulation continues until manually terminated.

Producer/Consumer

Figure 9-7: Producer/Consumer

```
#include         <stdio.h>
#include         <stdlib.h>
#include         <string.h>
#include         <thread.h>
#include         <synch.h>
#define TRUE      1
#define FALSE     0
static   void    *producer(void*);
static   void    *consumer(void*);
static   char    Buff[BUFSIZ];
static   cond_t  Buff_cond;
static   mutex_t Buff_mutex;
static   int     DataInBuff = FALSE;
main()
{
        (void)mutex_init(&Buff_mutex, USYNC_THREAD,  NULL);
        (void)cond_init (&Buff_cond,  USYNC_THREAD,  NULL);
        (void)thr_create(NULL, 0, producer, NULL, 0, NULL);
        (void)thr_create(NULL, 0, consumer, NULL, 0, NULL);
        thr_exit(NULL);
        /*NOTREACHED*/
}
/*ARGSUSED*/
static void *producer(void *dummy)
{
        (void)mutex_lock(&Buff_mutex);
        for(;;){
                while(DataInBuff == TRUE)
                        cond_wait(&Buff_cond, &Buff_mutex);
                  /* At this point,
                   * the buffer is empty (contents have been output).
                   * (Re)fill the buffer.
                   */
                if(fgets(Buff, sizeof(Buff), stdin) == NULL)
                        exit(EXIT_SUCCESS);
                DataInBuff = TRUE;
                cond_signal (&Buff_cond);
        }
        /*NOTREACHED*/
}
/*ARGSUSED*/
static void *consumer(void *dummy)
{
        (void)mutex_lock(&Buff_mutex);
        for(;;){
                while(DataInBuff == FALSE)
```

(continued on next page)

Programming with the Threads Library

Figure 9-7: Producer/Consumer (continued)

```
                        cond_wait(&Buff_cond, &Buff_mutex);
                    /* At this point,
                     * the buffer has data to be output
                     */
                    (void)fputs(Buff, stdout);
                    DataInBuff = FALSE;
                    cond_signal(&Buff_cond);
            }
            /*NOTREACHED*/
    }
```

The program in Figure 9-7 shows a simple producer/consumer example implemented using the condition variables facilities of the Threads Library.

■ There are two threads, each running different functions. One runs **producer**, the other runs **consumer**.

■ The item being produced and consumed is data in a common buffer.

   □ The producer obtains that data with **fgets**(3C) and places the data in the common buffer.

   □ The consumer reads the data from the buffer. That data is output with **fputs**(3S) so that its actions can be confirmed.

■ The actions of producer and consumer threads are coordinated by the condition variable facility so that they run in strict alternation.

   □ Nothing will be output (consumed) until something is placed in the buffer (produced).

   □ Data in the buffer will not be overwritten until it is output.

■ Note that this example differs from the pseudo-code shown earlier. The use of the condition variables are *not* bracketed by calls to **mutex_lock**(3thread) and **mutex_unlock**(3thread).

   □ This curiosity arises because the actions of each of these threads is organized in a loop.

- The semantics of **cond_wait**(3synch) guarantee that the named *mutex* will be released while a thread is waiting and reacquired before return from that function.

- The condition (**DataInBuff**) is tested (for different values) by each thread only when the thread holds the *mutex* and the use of **cond_wait** by each threads allows the other to acquire the *mutex*.

■ The initial calls to **mutex_lock**(3thread) by each thread and the initial state of **DataInBuff** are organized so that:

- Proper conditions are achieved for the initial pass by each thread.

- The program will work correctly no matter which thread acquires the *mutex* on the first pass.

■ The producer thread terminates the process with the **exit**(2) system call when it can obtain no more data from **fgets**(3S).

10 Interprocess Communication

Introduction

UNIX System V provides several mechanisms that allow processes to exchange data and synchronize execution. The simpler of these mechanisms are pipes, named pipes, and signals. These are limited, however, in what they can do. For instance,

- Pipes do not allow unrelated processes to communicate.

- Named pipes allow unrelated processes to communicate, but they cannot provide private channels for pairs of communicating processes; that is, any process with appropriate permission may read from or write to a named pipe.

- Sending signals, via the **kill** system call, allows arbitrary processes to communicate, but the message consists only of the signal number.

UNIX System V also provides an InterProcess Communication (IPC) package that supports three, more versatile types of interprocess communication. For example,

- Messages allow processes to send formatted data streams to arbitrary processes.

- Semaphores allow processes to synchronize execution.

- Shared memory allows processes to share parts of their virtual address space.

When implemented as a unit, these three mechanisms share common properties such as

- each mechanism contains a "get" system call to create a new entry or retrieve an existing one

- each mechanism contains a "control" system call to query the status of an entry, to set status information, or to remove the entry from the system

- each mechanism contains an "operations" system call to perform various operations on an entry

This chapter describes the system calls for each of these three forms of IPC.

This information is for programmers who write multiprocess applications. These programmers should have a general understanding of what semaphores are and how they are used.

Information from other sources would also be helpful. See the manual pages **ipcs**(1) and **ipcrm**(1) in the *Command Reference* and the following manual pages in the *Operating System API Reference*:

intro(2)	**msgget**(2)	**msgctl**(2)
msgop(2)	**semget**(2)	**semctl**(2)
semop(2)	**shmget**(2)	**shmctl**(2)
shmop(2)		

Included in this chapter are several example programs that show the use of these IPC system calls. Since there are many ways to accomplish the same task or requirement, keep in mind that the example programs were written for clarity and not for program efficiency. Usually, system calls are embedded within a larger user-written program that makes use of a particular function provided by the calls.

Messages

The message type of IPC allows processes (executing programs) to communicate through the exchange of data stored in buffers. This data is transmitted between processes in discrete portions called messages. Processes using this type of IPC can send and receive messages.

Before a process can send or receive a message, it must have the UNIX operating system generate the necessary software mechanisms to handle these operations. A process does this using the **msgget** system call. In doing this, the process becomes the owner/creator of a message queue and specifies the initial operation permissions for all processes, including itself. Subsequently, the owner/creator can relinquish ownership or change the operation permissions using the **msgctl** system call. However, the creator remains the creator as long as the facility exists. Other processes with permission can use **msgctl** to perform various other control functions.

Processes which have permission and are attempting to send or receive a message can suspend execution if they are unsuccessful at performing their operation. That is, a process which is attempting to send a message can wait until it becomes possible to post the message to the specified message queue; the receiving process isn't involved (except indirectly, for example, if the consumer isn't consuming, the queue space will eventually be exhausted) and vice versa. A process which specifies that execution is to be suspended is performing a "blocking message operation." A process which does not allow its execution to be suspended is performing a "nonblocking message operation."

A process performing a blocking message operation can be suspended until one of three conditions occurs:

- It is successful.

- It receives a signal.

- The message queue is removed from the system.

System calls make these message capabilities available to processes. The calling process passes arguments to a system call, and the system call either successfully or unsuccessfully performs its function. If the system call is successful, it performs its function and returns applicable information. Otherwise, a known error code (-1) is returned to the process, and an external error number variable, **errno**, is set accordingly.

Using Messages

Before a message can be sent or received, a uniquely identified message queue and data structure must be created. The unique identifier is called the message queue identifier (**msqid**); it is used to identify or refer to the associated message queue and data structure. This identifier is accessible by any process in the system, subject to normal access restrictions.

The message queue is used to store (header) information about each message being sent or received. This information, which is for internal use by the system, includes the following for each message:

- pointer to the next message on queue
- message type
- message text size
- message text address

There is one associated data structure for the uniquely identified message queue. This data structure contains the following information related to the message queue:

- operation permissions data (operation permission structure)
- pointer to first message on the queue
- pointer to last message on the queue
- current number of bytes on the queue
- number of messages on the queue
- maximum number of bytes on the queue
- process identification (PID) of last message sender
- PID of last message receiver
- last message send time
- last message receive time
- last change time

NOTE All `include` files discussed in this chapter are located in the `/usr/include` or `/usr/include/sys` directories.

The definition for the associated message-queue data structure **msqid_ds** includes the following members:

```
struct msqid_ds
{
        struct ipc_perm  msg_perm;      /* operation permission struct */
        struct msg       *msg_first;    /* ptr to first message on q */
        struct msg       *msg_last;     /* ptr to last message on q */
        ulong            msg_cbytes;    /* current # bytes on q */
        ulong            msg_qnum;      /* # of messages on q */
        ulong            msg_qbytes;    /* max # of bytes on q */
        pid_t            msg_lspid;     /* pid of last msgsnd */
        pid_t            msg_lrpid;     /* pid of last msgrcv */
        time_t           msg_stime;     /* last msgsnd time */
        time_t           msg_rtime;     /* last msgrcv time */
        time_t           msg_ctime;     /* last change time */
};
```

In UNIX System V Release 4.0, the value of **MSG_PAD** equals **4**. In UNIX System V Release 4.1, **MSG_PAD** is a symbolic constant.

The C programming language data structure definition for the message-queue data structure **msqid_ds** is located in the **sys/msg.h** header file.

Note that the **msg_perm** member of this structure uses **ipc_perm** as a template. The figure below breaks out the operation permissions data structure. In UNIX System V Release 4.0, the definition of the **ipc_perm** data structure is as follows:

Figure 10-1: `ipc_perm` **Data Structure**

```
struct ipc_perm
{
        uid_t           uid;            /* owner's user id */
        gid_t           gid;            /* owner's group id */
        uid_t           cuid;           /* creator's user id */
        gid_t           cgid;           /* creator's group id */
        mode_t          mode;           /* access modes */
        ulong           seq;            /* slot usage sequence number */
        key_t           key;            /* key */
        long            pad[4];         /* reserve area */
};
```

The C programming language data structure definition for the interprocess communication permissions data structure **ipc_perm** is located in the **sys/ipc.h** header file and is common to all IPC facilities.

The **msgget** system call is used to perform one of two tasks:

- to get a new message queue identifier and create an associated message queue and data structure for it

- to return an existing message queue identifier that already has an associated message queue and data structure

Both tasks require a **key** argument passed to the **msgget** system call. For the first task, if the **key** is not already in use for an existing message queue identifier, a new identifier is returned with an associated message queue and data structure created for the **key**.

There is also a provision for specifying a **key** of value zero, known as the private **key** (**IPC_PRIVATE**). When specified, a new identifier is always returned with an associated message queue and data structure created for it unless a system-tunable parameter would be exceeded. The **ipcs** command will show the **key** field for the **msqid** as all zeros.

For the second task, if a message queue identifier exists for the **key** specified, the value of the existing identifier is returned. If you do not want to have an existing message queue identifier returned, a control command (**IPC_EXCL**) can be specified (set) in the **msgflg** argument passed to the system call (see "Using msgget" for how to use this system call).

When performing the first task, the process that calls **msgget** becomes the owner/creator, and the associated data structure is initialized accordingly. Remember, ownership can be changed but the creating process always remains the creator. The message queue creator also determines the initial operation permissions for it.

Once a uniquely identified message queue and data structure are created, **msgop** (message operations) and **msgctl** (message control) can be used.

Message operations, as mentioned before, consist of sending and receiving messages. The **msgsnd** and **msgrcv** system calls are provided for each of these operations (see "Operations for Messages" for details of the **msgsnd** and **msgrcv** system calls.

The **msgctl** system call permits you to control the message facility in the following ways:

- by retrieving the data structure associated with a message queue identifier (**IPC_STAT**)

- by changing operation permissions for a message queue (**IPC_SET**)

- by changing the size (**msg_qbytes**) of the message queue for a particular message queue identifier (**IPC_SET**)

- by removing a particular message queue identifier from the UNIX operating system along with its associated message queue and data structure (**IPC_RMID**)

See the section "Controlling Message Queues" for details of the **msgctl** system call.

Getting Message Queues

This section describes how to use the **msgget** system call. The accompanying program illustrates its use.

Using msgget

The synopsis found in the **msgget**(2) entry in the *Operating System API Reference* is as follows:

```
#include   <sys/types.h>
#include   <sys/ipc.h>
#include   <sys/msg.h>

int   msgget (key_t key, int msgflg);
```

All of these **include** files are located in the **/usr/include/sys** directory of the UNIX operating system.

The following line in the synopsis:

```
int msgget (key_t key, int msgflg);
```

informs you that **msgget** is a function that returns an integer-type value. It also declares the types of the two formal arguments: **key** is of type **key_t**, and **msgflg** is of type **int**. **key_t** is defined by a **typedef** in the **sys/types.h** header file to be an integral type.

The integer returned from this function upon successful completion is the message queue identifier that was discussed earlier. Upon failure, the external variable **errno** is set to indicate the reason for failure, and the value **-1** (which is not a valid **msqid**) is returned.

As declared, the process calling the **msgget** system call must supply two arguments to be passed to the formal **key** and **msgflg** arguments.

A new **msqid** with an associated message queue and data structure is provided if either

- **key** is equal to **IPC_PRIVATE**,

or

- **key** is a unique integer and the control command **IPC_CREAT** is specified in the **msgflg** argument.

The value passed to the **msgflg** argument must be an integer-type value that will specify the following:

- operations permissions
- control fields (commands)

Operation permissions determine the operations that processes are permitted to perform on the associated message queue. "Read" permission is necessary for receiving messages or for determining queue status by means of a **msgctl** **IPC_STAT** operation. "Write" permission is necessary for sending messages.

The following figure reflects the numeric values (expressed in octal notation) for the valid operation permissions codes.

Table 10-1: Operation Permissions Codes

Operation Permissions	Octal Value
Read by User	00400
Write by User	00200
Read by Group	00040
Write by Group	00020
Read by Others	00004
Write by Others	00002

A specific value is derived by adding or bitwise ORing the octal values for the operation permissions wanted. That is, if read by user and read/write by others is desired, the code value would be 00406 (00400 plus 00006). There are constants located in the **sys/msg.h** header file which can be used for the user operations permissions. They are as follows:

```
MSG_W  0200   /* write permissions by owner */

MSG_R  0400   /* read permissions by owner */
```

Control flags are predefined constants (represented by all upper-case letters). The flags which apply to the **msgget** system call are **IPC_CREAT** and **IPC_EXCL** and are defined in the **sys/ipc.h** header file.

The value for **msgflg** is therefore a combination of operation permissions and control commands. After determining the value for the operation permissions as previously described, the desired flag(s) can be specified. This is accomplished by adding or bitwise ORing (|) them with the operation permissions; the bit positions and values for the control commands in relation to those of the operation permissions make this possible.

The **msgflg** value can easily be set by using the flag names in conjunction with the octal operation permissions value:

```
msqid = msgget (key, (IPC_CREAT | 0400));

msqid = msgget (key, (IPC_CREAT | IPC_EXCL | 0400));
```

As specified by the **msgget**(2) entry in the *Operating System API Reference*, success or failure of this system call depends upon the argument values for **key** and **msgflg** or system-tunable parameters. The system call will attempt to return a new message queue identifier if one of the following conditions is true:

- **key** is equal to **IPC_PRIVATE**

- **key** does not already have a message queue identifier associated with it and (**msgflg** and **IPC_CREAT**) is "true" (not zero).

The **key** argument can be set to **IPC_PRIVATE** like this:

```
msqid = msgget (IPC_PRIVATE, msgflg);
```

The system call will always be attempted. Exceeding the **MSGMNI** system-tunable parameter always causes a failure. The **MSGMNI** system-tunable parameter determines the systemwide number of unique message queues that may be in use at any given time.

IPC_EXCL is another control command used in conjunction with **IPC_CREAT**. It will cause the system call to return an error if a message queue identifier already exists for the specified **key.** This is necessary to prevent the process from thinking that it has received a new identifier when it has not. In other words, when both **IPC_CREAT** and **IPC_EXCL** are specified, a new message queue identifier is returned if the system call is successful.

Refer to the **msgget**(2) manual page in the *Operating System API Reference* for specific, associated data structure initialization for successful completion. The specific failure conditions and their error names are contained there also.

Example Program

Figure 10-2 is a menu-driven program. It allows all possible combinations of using the **msgget** system call to be exercised.

From studying this program, you can observe the method of passing arguments and receiving return values. The user-written program requirements are pointed out.

This program begins (lines 4-8) by including the required header files as specified by the **msgget**(2) entry in the *Operating System API Reference*. Note that the **sys/errno.h** header file is included as opposed to declaring **errno** as an external variable; either method will work.

Variable names have been chosen to be as close as possible to those in the synopsis for the system call. Their declarations are self explanatory. These names make the programs more readable are perfectly valid since they are local to the program.

The variables declared for this program and what they are used for are as follows:

key	used to pass the value for the desired **key**
opperm	used to store the desired operation permissions
flags	used to store the desired control commands (flags)
opperm_flags	used to store the combination from the logical ORing of the **opperm** and **flags** variables; it is then used in the system call to pass the **msgflg** argument
msqid	used for returning the message queue identification number for a successful system call or the error code (**-1**) for an unsuccessful one.

The program begins by prompting for a hexadecimal **key**, an octal operation permissions code, and finally for the control command combinations (flags) which are selected from a menu (lines 15-32). All possible combinations are allowed even though they might not be viable. This allows errors to be observed for invalid combinations.

Next, the menu selection for the flags is combined with the operation permissions, and the result is stored in the **opperm_flags** variable (lines 36-51).

The system call is made next, and the result is stored in the **msqid** variable (line 53).

Since the **msqid** variable now contains a valid message queue identifier or the error code (**-1**), it is tested to see if an error occurred (line 55). If **msqid** equals **-1**, a message indicates that an error resulted, and the external **errno** variable is displayed (line 57).

If no error occurred, the returned message queue identifier is displayed (line 61).

The example program for the **msgget** system call follows. We suggest you name the program file **msgget.c** and the executable file **msgget**.

Figure 10-2: `msgget` **System Call Example**

```
1     /*This is a program to illustrate
2     **the message get, msgget(),
3     **system call capabilities.*/
4     #include    <stdio.h>
5     #include    <sys/types.h>
6     #include    <sys/ipc.h>
7     #include    <sys/msg.h>
8     #include    <errno.h>
9     /*Start of main C language program*/
10    main()
11    {
12        key_t key;
13        int opperm, flags;
14        int msqid, opperm_flags;
15        /*Enter the desired key*/
16        printf("Enter the desired key in hex = ");
17        scanf("%x", &key);
18        /*Enter the desired octal operation
19          permissions.*/
20        printf("\nEnter the operation\n");
21        printf("permissions in octal = ");
22        scanf("%o", &opperm);
23        /*Set the desired flags.*/
24        printf("\nEnter corresponding number to\n");
25        printf("set the desired flags:\n");
26        printf("No flags                = 0\n");
27        printf("IPC_CREAT               = 1\n");
28        printf("IPC_EXCL                = 2\n");
29        printf("IPC_CREAT and IPC_EXCL  = 3\n");
30        printf("          Flags         = ");
31        /*Get the flag(s) to be set.*/
32        scanf("%d", &flags);
33        /*Check the values.*/
34        printf ("\nkey =0x%x, opperm = 0%o, flags = 0%o\n",
35            key, opperm, flags);
36        /*Incorporate the control fields (flags) with
37          the operation permissions*/
38        switch (flags)
39        {
40        case 0:    /*No flags are to be set.*/
41            opperm_flags = (opperm | 0);
42            break;
43        case 1:    /*Set the IPC_CREAT flag.*/
44            opperm_flags = (opperm | IPC_CREAT);
45            break;
46        case 2:    /*Set the IPC_EXCL flag.*/
```

(continued on next page)

Figure 10-2: msgget **System Call Example** (continued)

```
47                    opperm_flags = (opperm | IPC_EXCL);
48                    break;
49          case 3:    /*Set the IPC_CREAT and IPC_EXCL flags.*/
50                    opperm_flags = (opperm | IPC_CREAT | IPC_EXCL);
51          }
52          /*Call the msgget system call.*/
53          msqid = msgget (key, opperm_flags);
54          /*Perform the following if the call is unsuccessful.*/
55          if(msqid == -1)
56          {
57              printf ("\nThe msgget call failed, error number = %d\n", errno);
58          }
59          /*Return the msqid upon successful completion.*/
60          else
61              printf ("\nThe msqid = %d\n", msqid);
62          exit(0);
63      }
```

Controlling Message Queues

This section describes how to use the **msgctl** system call. The accompanying program illustrates its use.

Using msgctl

The synopsis found in the **msgctl**(2) entry in the *Operating System API Reference* is as follows:

```
#include <sys/types.h>
#include <sys/ipc.h>
#include <sys/msg.h>

int msgctl (msqid, cmd, buf)
int msqid, cmd;
struct msqid_ds *buf;
```

The **msgctl** system call requires three arguments to be passed to it; it returns an integer-type value.

When successful, it returns a zero value; when unsuccessful, it returns a **-1**.

The **msqid** variable must be a valid, non-negative, integer value. In other words, it must have already been created by using the **msgget** system call.

The **cmd** argument can be any one of the following values:

IPC_STAT   return the status information contained in the associated data structure for the specified message queue identifier, and place it in the data structure pointed to by the **buf** pointer in the user memory area.

IPC_SET   for the specified message queue identifier, set the effective user and group identification, operation permissions, and the number of bytes for the message queue to the values contained in the data structure pointed to by the **buf** pointer in the user memory area.

IPC_RMID   remove the specified message queue identifier along with its associated message queue and data structure.

To perform an **IPC_SET** or **IPC_RMID** control command, a process must have:

- an effective user id of OWNER/CREATOR, or
- an effective user id of **root** (if the system is running with the SUM privilege module), or
- the **P_OWNER** privilege.

Read permission is required to perform the **IPC_STAT** control command.

The details of this system call are discussed in the following example program. If you need more information on the logic manipulations in this program, read the **msgget**(2) entry in the *Operating System API Reference*; it goes into more detail than would be practical for this document.

Example Program

Figure 10-3 is a menu-driven program. It allows all possible combinations of using the **msgctl** system call to be exercised.

From studying this program, you can observe the method of passing arguments and receiving return values. The user-written program requirements are pointed out.

This program begins (lines 5-9) by including the required header files as specified by the **msgctl**(2) entry in the *Operating System API Reference*. Note in this program that **errno** is declared as an external variable, and therefore, the **sys/errno.h** header file does not have to be included.

Variable and structure names have been chosen to be as close as possible to those in the synopsis for the system call. Their declarations are self explanatory. These names make the program more readable and are perfectly valid since they are local to the program.

The variables declared for this program and what they are used for are as follows:

uid	used to store the **IPC_SET** value for the effective user identification
gid	used to store the **IPC_SET** value for the effective group identification
mode	used to store the **IPC_SET** value for the operation permissions
bytes	used to store the **IPC_SET** value for the number of bytes in the message queue (**msg_qbytes**)
rtrn	used to store the return integer value from the system call
msqid	used to store and pass the message queue identifier to the system call
command	used to store the code for the desired control command so that subsequent processing can be performed on it
choice	used to determine which member is to be changed for the **IPC_SET** control command
msqid_ds	used to receive the specified message queue identifier's data structure when an **IPC_STAT** control command is performed
buf	a pointer passed to the system call which locates the data structure in the user memory area where the **IPC_STAT** control command is to place its return values or where the **IPC_SET** command gets the values to set

Note that the **msqid_ds** data structure in this program (line 16) uses the data structure, located in the **sys/msg.h** header file of the same name, as a template for its declaration.

The next important thing to observe is that although the **buf** pointer is declared to be a pointer to a data structure of the **msqid_ds** type, it must also be initialized to contain the address of the user memory area data structure (line 17). Now that all of the required declarations have been explained for this program, this is how it works.

First, the program prompts for a valid message queue identifier which is stored in the **msqid** variable (lines 19, 20). This is required for every **msgctl** system call.

Then the code for the desired control command must be entered (lines 21-27) and stored in the command variable. The code is tested to determine the control command for subsequent processing.

If the **IPC_STAT** control command is selected (code 1), the system call is performed (lines 37, 38) and the status information returned is printed out (lines 39-46); only the members that can be set are printed out in this program. Note that if the system call is unsuccessful (line 106), the status information of the last successful call is printed out. In addition, an error message is displayed and the **errno** variable is printed out (line 108). If the system call is successful, a message indicates this along with the message queue identifier used (lines 110-113).

If the **IPC_SET** control command is selected (code 2), the first thing is to get the current status information for the message queue identifier specified (lines 50-52). This is necessary because this example program provides for changing only one member at a time, and the system call changes all of them. Also, if an invalid value happened to be stored in the user memory area for one of these members, it would cause repetitive failures for this control command until corrected. The next thing the program does is to prompt for a code corresponding to the member to be changed (lines 53-59). This code is stored in the choice variable (line 60). Now, depending upon the member picked, the program prompts for the new value (lines 66-95). The value is placed into the appropriate member in the user memory area data structure, and the system call is made (lines 96-98). Depending upon success or failure, the program returns the same messages as for **IPC_STAT** above.

If the **IPC_RMID** control command (code 3) is selected, the system call is performed (lines 100-103), and the **msqid** along with its associated message queue and data structure are removed from the UNIX operating system. Note that the **buf** pointer is ignored in performing this control command, and its value can be zero or NULL. Depending upon the success or failure, the program returns the same messages as for the other control commands.

The example program for the **msgctl** system call follows. We suggest that you name the source program file **msgctl.c** and the executable file **msgctl**.

Figure 10-3: `msgctl` **System Call Example**

```
 1    /*This is a program to illustrate
 2    **the message control, msgctl(),
 3    **system call capabilities.
 4    */
 5    /*Include necessary header files.*/
 6    #include    <stdio.h>
 7    #include    <sys/types.h>
 8    #include    <sys/ipc.h>
 9    #include    <sys/msg.h>
10    /*Start of main C language program*/
11    main()
12    {
13        extern int errno;
14        int uid, gid, mode, bytes;
15        int rtrn, msqid, command, choice;
16        struct msqid_ds msqid_ds, *buf;
17        buf = &msqid_ds;
18        /*Get the msqid, and command.*/
19        printf("Enter the msqid = ");
20        scanf("%d", &msqid);
21        printf("\nEnter the number for\n");
22        printf("the desired command:\n");
23        printf("IPC_STAT    =  1\n");
24        printf("IPC_SET     =  2\n");
25        printf("IPC_RMID    =  3\n");
26        printf("Entry       =  ");
27        scanf("%d", &command);
28        /*Check the values.*/
29        printf ("\nmsqid =%d, command = %d\n",
30            msqid, command);
31        switch (command)
32        {
33        case 1:    /*Use msgctl() to duplicate
34             the data structure for
35                     msqid in the msqid_ds area pointed
36                     to by buf and then print it out.*/
37            rtrn = msgctl(msqid, IPC_STAT,
38                buf);
39            printf ("\nThe USER ID = %d\n",
40                buf->msg_perm.uid);
41            printf ("The GROUP ID = %d\n",
42                buf->msg_perm.gid);
43            printf ("The operation permissions = 0%o\n",
44                buf->msg_perm.mode);
45            printf ("The msg_qbytes = %d\n",
46                buf->msg_qbytes);
47            break;
```

(continued on next page)

Figure 10-3: `msgctl` **System Call Example** (continued)

```
48        case 2:    /*Select and change the desired
49                      member(s) of the data structure.*/
50           /*Get the original data for this msqid
51               data structure first.*/
52           rtrn = msgctl(msqid, IPC_STAT, buf);
53           printf("\nEnter the number for the\n");
54           printf("member to be changed:\n");
55           printf("msg_perm.uid   = 1\n");
56           printf("msg_perm.gid   = 2\n");
57           printf("msg_perm.mode  = 3\n");
58           printf("msg_qbytes     = 4\n");
59           printf("Entry          = ");

60           scanf("%d", &choice);
61           /*Only one choice is allowed per
62             pass as an invalid entry will
63                 cause repetitive failures until
64             msqid_ds is updated with
65                 IPC_STAT.*/
66           switch(choice){
67           case 1:
68               printf("\nEnter USER ID = ");
69               scanf ("%ld", &uid);
70               buf->msg_perm.uid =(uid_t)uid;
71               printf("\nUSER ID = %d\n",
72                   buf->msg_perm.uid);
73               break;
74           case 2:
75               printf("\nEnter GROUP ID = ");
76               scanf("%d", &gid);
77               buf->msg_perm.gid = gid;
78               printf("\nGROUP ID = %d\n",
79                   buf->msg_perm.gid);
80               break;
81           case 3:
82               printf("\nEnter MODE = ");
83               scanf("%o", &mode);
84               buf->msg_perm.mode = mode;
85               printf("\nMODE = 0%o\n",
86                   buf->msg_perm.mode);
87               break;
88           case 4:
89               printf("\nEnter msq_bytes = ");
90               scanf("%d", &bytes);
91               buf->msg_qbytes = bytes;
92               printf("\nmsg_qbytes = %d\n",
93                   buf->msg_qbytes);
94               break;
95           }
```

(continued on next page)

Figure 10-3: `msgctl` **System Call Example** (continued)

```
 96              /*Do the change.*/
 97              rtrn = msgctl(msqid, IPC_SET,
 98                   buf);
 99              break;
100      case 3:     /*Remove the msqid along with its
101                      associated message queue
102                      and data structure.*/
103              rtrn = msgctl(msqid, IPC_RMID, (struct msqid_ds *) NULL);
104      }
105      /*Perform the following if the call is unsuccessful.*/
106      if(rtrn == -1)
107      {
108          printf ("\nThe msgctl call failed, error number = %d\n", errno);
109      }
110      /*Return the msqid upon successful completion.*/
111      else
112          printf ("\nMsgctl was successful for msqid = %d\n",
113              msqid);
114      exit (0);
115  }
```

Operations for Messages

This section describes how to use the **msgsnd** and **msgrcv** system calls. The accompanying program illustrates their use.

Using Message Operations: msgsnd and msgrcv

The synopsis found in the **msgop**(2) entry in the *Operating System API Reference* is as follows:

```
#include <sys/types.h>
#include <sys/ipc.h>
#include <sys/msg.h>

int msgsnd (msqid, msgp, msgsz, msgflg)
int msqid;
struct msgbuf *msgp;
int msgsz, msgflg;

int msgrcv (msqid, msgp, msgsz, msgtyp, msgflg)
int msqid;
struct msgbuf *msgp;
int msgsz;
long msgtyp;
int msgflg;
```

Sending a Message

The **msgsnd** system call requires four arguments to be passed to it. It returns an integer value.

When successful, it returns a zero value; when unsuccessful, **msgsnd** returns a **-1**.

The **msqid** argument must be a valid, non-negative, integer value. In other words, it must have already been created by using the **msgget** system call.

The **msgp** argument is a pointer to a structure in the user memory area that contains the type of the message and the message to be sent.

The **msgsz** argument specifies the length of the character array in the data structure pointed to by the **msgp** argument. This is the length of the message. The maximum **size** of this array is determined by the **MSGMAX** system-tunable parameter.

The **msgflg** argument allows the "blocking message operation" to be performed if the **IPC_NOWAIT** flag is not set ((**msgflg** and **IPC_NOWAIT**)= = 0); the operation would block if the total number of bytes allowed on the specified message queue are in use (**msg_qbytes** or **MSGMNB**), or the total system-wide number of messages on all queues is equal to the system- imposed limit (**MSGTQL**). If the **IPC_NOWAIT** flag is set, the system call will fail and return a **-1**.

The value of the **msg_qbytes** data structure member can be lowered from **MSGMNB** by using the **msgctl IPC_SET** control command, but only the **root** (if the SUM privilege module is installed) can raise it afterwards.

Further details of this system call are discussed in the following program. If you need more information on the logic manipulations in this program, read "Using msgget". It goes into more detail than would be practical for every system call.

Receiving Messages

The **msgrcv** system call requires five arguments to be passed to it; it returns an integer value.

When successful, it returns a value equal to the number of bytes received; when unsuccessful it returns a **-1**.

The **msqid** argument must be a valid, non-negative, integer value. In other words, it must have already been created by using the **msgget** system call.

The **msgp** argument is a pointer to a structure in the user memory area that will receive the message type and the message text.

The **msgsz** argument specifies the length of the message to be received. If its value is less than the message in the array, an error can be returned if desired (see the **msgflg** argument below).

The **msgtyp** argument is used to pick the first message on the message queue of the particular type specified. If it is equal to zero, the first message on the queue is received; if it is greater than zero, the first message of the same type is received; if it is less than zero, the lowest type that is less than or equal to its absolute value is received.

The **msgflg** argument allows the "blocking message operation" to be performed if the **IPC_NOWAIT** flag is not set ((**msgflg** and **IPC_NOWAIT**) == 0); the operation would block if there is not a message on the message queue of the desired type (**msgtyp**) to be received. If the **IPC_NOWAIT** flag is set, the system call will fail immediately when there is not a message of the desired type on the queue. **msgflg** can also specify that the system call fail if the message is longer than the **size** to be received; this is done by not setting the **MSG_NOERROR** flag in the **msgflg** argument ((**msgflg** and **MSG_NOERROR**)) == 0). If the **MSG_NOERROR** flag is set, the message is truncated to the length specified by the **msgsz** argument of **msgrcv**.

Further details of this system call are discussed in the following program. If you need more information on the logic manipulations in this program, read "Using msgget". It goes into more detail than would be practical for every system call.

Example Program

Figure 10-4 is a menu-driven program. It allows all possible combinations of using the **msgsnd** and **msgrcv** system calls to be exercised.

From studying this program, you can observe the method of passing arguments and receiving return values. The user-written program requirements are pointed out.

This program begins (lines 5-9) by including the required header files as specified by the **msgop**(2) entry in the *Operating System API Reference*. Note that in this program **errno** is declared as an external variable; therefore, the **sys/errno.h** header file does not have to be included.

Variable and structure names have been chosen to be as close as possible to those in the synopsis. Their declarations are self explanatory. These names make the program more readable and are perfectly valid since they are local to the program.

The variables declared for this program and what they are used for are as follows:

sndbuf	used as a buffer to contain a message to be sent (line 13); it uses the **msgbuf1** data structure as a template (lines 10-13). The **msgbuf1** structure (lines 10-13) is a duplicate of the **msgbuf** structure contained in the **sys/msg.h** header file, except that the size of the character array for **mtext** is tailored to fit this application. The **msgbuf** structure should not be used directly because **mtext** has only one element that would limit the size of each message to one character. Instead, declare your own structure. It should be identical to **msgbuf** except that the size of the **mtext** array should fit your application.
rcvbuf	used as a buffer to receive a message (line 13); it uses the **msgbuf1** data structure as a template (lines 10-13)
msgp	used as a pointer (line 13) to both the **sndbuf** and **rcvbuf** buffers
i	used as a counter for inputing characters from the keyboard, storing them in the array, and keeping track of the message length for the **msgsnd** system call; it is also used as a counter to output the received message for the **msgrcv** system call
c	used to receive the input character from the **getchar** function (line 50)
flag	used to store the code of **IPC_NOWAIT** for the **msgsnd** system call (line 61)

flags	used to store the code of the **IPC_NOWAIT** or **MSG_NOERROR** flags for the **msgrcv** system call (line 117)
choice	used to store the code for sending or receiving (line 30)
rtrn	used to store the return values from all system calls
msqid	used to store and pass the desired message queue identifier for both system calls
msgsz	used to store and pass the **size** of the message to be sent or received
msgflg	used to pass the value of flag for sending or the value of flags for receiving
msgtyp	used for specifying the message type for sending or for picking a message type for receiving.

Note that a **msqid_ds** data structure is set up in the program (line 21) with a pointer initialized to point to it (line 22); this will allow the data structure members affected by message operations to be observed. They are observed by using the **msgctl** (**IPC_STAT**) system call to get them for the program to print them out (lines 80-92 and lines 160-167).

The first thing the program prompts for is whether to send or receive a message. A corresponding code must be entered for the desired operation; it is stored in the choice variable (lines 23-30). Depending upon the code, the program proceeds as in the following **msgsnd** or **msgrcv** sections.

msgsnd

When the code is to send a message, the **msgp** pointer is initialized (line 33) to the address of the send data structure, **sndbuf**. Next, a message type must be entered for the message; it is stored in the variable **msgtyp** (line 42), and then (line 43) it is put into the **mtype** member of the data structure pointed to by **msgp**.

The program now prompts for a message to be entered from the keyboard and enters a loop of getting and storing into the **mtext** array of the data structure (lines 48-51). This will continue until an end-of-file is recognized which, for the **getchar** function, is a CTRL-d immediately following a carriage return (RETURN).

The message is immediately echoed from the **mtext** array of the **sndbuf** data structure to provide feedback (lines 54-56).

The next and final thing that must be decided is whether to set the **IPC_NOWAIT** flag. The program does this by requesting that a code of a 1 be entered for yes or anything else for no (lines 57-65). It is stored in the flag variable. If a 1 is entered, **IPC_NOWAIT** is logically ORed with **msgflg**; otherwise, **msgflg** is set to zero.

The **msgsnd** system call is performed (line 69). If it is unsuccessful, a failure message is displayed along with the error number (lines 70-72). If it is successful, the returned value is printed and should be zero (lines 73-76).

Every time a message is successfully sent, three members of the associated data structure are updated. They are:

msg_qnum   represents the total number of messages on the message queue; it is incremented by one.

msg_lspid   contains the process identification (PID) number of the last process sending a message; it is set accordingly.

msg_stime   contains the time in seconds since January 1, 1970, Greenwich Mean Time (GMT) of the last message sent; it is set accordingly.

These members are displayed after every successful message send operation (lines 79-92).

msgrcv

When the code is to receive a message, the program continues execution as in the following paragraphs.

The **msgp** pointer is initialized to the **rcvbuf** data structure (line 99).

Next, the message queue identifier of the message queue from which to receive the message is requested; it is stored in **msqid** (lines 100-103).

The message type is requested; it is stored in **msgtyp** (lines 104-107).

The code for the desired combination of control flags is requested next; it is stored in flags (lines 108-117). Depending upon the selected combination, **msgflg** is set accordingly (lines 118-131).

Finally, the number of bytes to be received is requested; it is stored in **msgsz** (lines 132-135).

The **msgrcv** system call is performed (line 142). If it is unsuccessful, a message and error number is displayed (lines 143-145). If successful, a message indicates so, and the number of bytes returned and the **msg** type returned (because the value returned may be different from the value requested) is displayed followed by the received message (lines 150-156).

When a message is successfully received, three members of the associated data structure are updated. They are:

`msg_qnum`	contains the number of messages on the message queue; it is decremented by one.
`msg_lrpid`	contains the PID of the last process receiving a message; it is set accordingly.
`msg_rtime`	contains the time in seconds since January 1, 1970, Greenwich Mean Time (GMT) that the last process received a message; it is set accordingly.

Figure 10-4 shows the **msgop** system calls. We suggest that you put the program into a source file called **msgop.c** and then compile it into an executable file called **msgop**.

Figure 10-4: msgop **System Call Example**

```
1     /*This is a program to illustrate
2     **the message operations, msgop(),
3     **system call capabilities.
4     */
5     /*Include necessary header files.*/
6     #include    <stdio.h>
7     #include    <sys/types.h>
8     #include    <sys/ipc.h>
9     #include    <sys/msg.h>
10    struct msgbuf1 {
11        long    mtype;
12        char    mtext[8192];
13    } sndbuf, rcvbuf, *msgp;
14    /*Start of main C language program*/
15    main()
16    {
17        extern int errno;
18        int i, c, flag, flags, choice;
19        int rtrn, msqid, msgsz, msgflg;
20        long mtype, msgtyp;
21        struct msqid_ds msqid_ds, *buf;
22        buf = &msqid_ds;
23        /*Select the desired operation.*/
24        printf("Enter the corresponding\n");
25        printf("code to send or\n");
26        printf("receive a message:\n");
27        printf("Send          = 1\n");
28        printf("Receive       = 2\n");
29        printf("Entry         = ");
30        scanf("%d", &choice);
31        if(choice == 1) /*Send a message.*/
```

(continued on next page)

Figure 10-4: msgop **System Call Example** (continued)

```
32          {
33              msgp = &sndbuf; /*Point to user send structure.*/
34              printf("\nEnter the msqid of\n");
35              printf("the message queue to\n");
36              printf("handle the message = ");
37              scanf("%d", &msqid);

38              /*Set the message type.*/
39              printf("\nEnter a positive integer\n");
40              printf("message type (long) for the\n");
41              printf("message = ");
42              scanf("%ld", &msgtyp);
43              msgp->mtype = msgtyp;

44              /*Enter the message to send.*/
45              printf("\nEnter a message: \n");

46              /*A control-d (^d) terminates as
47                EOF.*/

48              /*Get each character of the message
49                and put it in the mtext array.*/
50              for(i = 0; ((c = getchar()) != EOF); i++)
51                  sndbuf.mtext[i] = c;

52              /*Determine the message size.*/
53              msgsz = i;

54              /*Echo the message to send.*/
55              for(i = 0; i < msgsz; i++)
56                  putchar(sndbuf.mtext[i]);

57              /*Set the IPC_NOWAIT flag if
58                desired.*/
59              printf("\nEnter a 1 if you want \n");
60              printf("the IPC_NOWAIT flag set:  ");
61              scanf("%d", &flag);
62              if(flag == 1)
63                  msgflg = IPC_NOWAIT;
64              else
65                  msgflg = 0;

66              /*Check the msgflg.*/
67              printf("\nmsgflg = 0%o\n", msgflg);

68              /*Send the message.*/
69              rtrn = msgsnd(msqid, (const void*) msgp, msgsz, msgflg);
70              if(rtrn == -1)
71              printf("\nMsgsnd failed.  Error = %d\n",
72                      errno);
73              else {
74                  /*Print the value of test which
75                      should be zero for successful.*/
76                  printf("\nValue returned = %d\n", rtrn);

77                  /*Print the size of the message
```

(continued on next page)

Figure 10-4: msgop **System Call Example** (continued)

```
78              sent.*/
79              printf("\nMsgsz = %d\n", msgsz);
80              /*Check the data structure update.*/
81              msgctl(msqid, IPC_STAT, buf);
82              /*Print out the affected members.*/
83              /*Print the incremented number of
84                 messages on the queue.*/
85              printf("\nThe msg_qnum = %d\n",
86                  buf->msg_qnum);
87              /*Print the process id of the last sender.*/
88              printf("The msg_lspid = %d\n",
89                  buf->msg_lspid);
90              /*Print the last send time.*/
91              printf("The msg_stime = %d\n",
92                  buf->msg_stime);
93          }
94      }
95      if(choice == 2)   /*Receive a message.*/
96      {
97          /*Initialize the message pointer
98             to the receive buffer.*/
99          msgp = &rcvbuf;
100         /*Specify the message queue which contains
101                the desired message.*/
102         printf("\nEnter the msqid = ");
103         scanf("%d", &msqid);
104         /*Specify the specific message on the queue
105                by using its type.*/
106         printf("\nEnter the msgtyp = ");
107         scanf("%ld", &msgtyp);
108         /*Configure the control flags for the
109                desired actions.*/
110         printf("\nEnter the corresponding code\n");
111         printf("to select the desired flags: \n");
112         printf("No flags                    = 0\n");
113         printf("MSG_NOERROR                 = 1\n");
114         printf("IPC_NOWAIT                  = 2\n");
115         printf("MSG_NOERROR and IPC_NOWAIT  = 3\n");
116         printf("            Flags           = ");
117         scanf("%d", &flags);
118         switch(flags) {
119         case 0:
120             msgflg = 0;
121             break;
122         case 1:
123             msgflg = MSG_NOERROR;
124             break;
```

(continued on next page)

Figure 10-4: msgop **System Call Example** (continued)

```
125              case 2:
126                  msgflg = IPC_NOWAIT;
127                  break;
128              case 3:
129                  msgflg = MSG_NOERROR | IPC_NOWAIT;
130                  break;
131              }
132              /*Specify the number of bytes to receive.*/
133              printf("\nEnter the number of bytes\n");
134              printf("to receive (msgsz) = ");
135              scanf("%d", &msgsz);
136              /*Check the values for the arguments.*/
137              printf("\nmsqid =%d\n", msqid);
138              printf("\nmsgtyp = %ld\n", msgtyp);
139              printf("\nmsgsz = %d\n", msgsz);
140              printf("\nmsgflg = 0%o\n", msgflg);
141              /*Call msgrcv to receive the message.*/
142              rtrn = msgrcv(msqid, (void*), msgp, msgsz, msgtyp, msgflg);
143              if(rtrn == -1)  {
144                  printf("\nMsgrcv failed., Error = %d\n", errno);
145              }
146              else {
147                  printf ("\nMsgctl was successful\n");
148                  printf("for msqid = %d\n",
149                      msqid);
150                  /*Print the number of bytes received,
151                    it is equal to the return
152                    value.*/
153                  printf("Bytes received = %d\n", rtrn);
154                  /*Print the received message.*/
155                  for(i = 0; i<rtrn; i++)
156                      putchar(rcvbuf.mtext[i]);
157              }
158              /*Check the associated data structure.*/
159              msgctl(msqid, IPC_STAT, buf);
160              /*Print the decremented number of messages.*/
161              printf("\nThe msg_qnum = %d\n", buf->msg_qnum);
162              /*Print the process id of the last receiver.*/
163              printf("The msg_lrpid = %d\n", buf->msg_lrpid);
164              /*Print the last message receive time*/
165              printf("The msg_rtime = %d\n", buf->msg_rtime);
166          }
167      }
```

Semaphores

The semaphore type of IPC allows processes (executing programs) to communicate through the exchange of semaphore values. Since many applications require the use of more than one semaphore, the UNIX operating system has the ability to create sets or arrays of semaphores. A semaphore set can contain one or more semaphores up to a limit set by the system administrator. The tunable parameter, **SEMMSL**, has a default value of 25. Semaphore sets are created by using the **semget** (semaphore get) system call.

The process performing the **semget** system call becomes the owner/creator, determines how many semaphores are in the set, and sets the initial operation permissions for all processes, including itself. This process can subsequently relinquish ownership of the set or change the operation permissions using the **semctl** (semaphore control) system call. The creating process always remains the creator as long as the facility exists. Other processes with permission can use **semctl** to perform other control functions.

Any process can manipulate the semaphore(s) if the owner of the semaphore grants permission.

Each semaphore within a set can be incremented and decremented with the **semop** system call (documented in the *Operating System API Reference*).

To increment a semaphore, an integer value of the desired magnitude is passed to the **semop** system call. To decrement a semaphore, a minus (-) value of the desired magnitude is passed.

The UNIX operating system ensures that only one process can manipulate a semaphore set at any given time. Simultaneous requests are performed sequentially in an arbitrary manner.

A process can test for a semaphore value to be greater than a certain value by attempting to decrement the semaphore by one more than that value. If the process is successful, then the semaphore value is greater than that certain value. Otherwise, the semaphore value is not. While doing this, the process can have its execution suspended (**IPC_NOWAIT** flag not set) until the semaphore value would permit the operation (other processes increment the semaphore), or the semaphore facility is removed.

The ability to suspend execution is called a "blocking semaphore operation." This ability is also available for a process which is testing for a semaphore equal to zero; only read permission is required for this test; it is accomplished by passing a value of zero to the **semop** (semaphore operation) system call.

On the other hand, if the process is not successful and did not request to have its execution suspended, it is called a "nonblocking semaphore operation." In this case, the process is returned a known error code (-1), and the external **errno** variable is set accordingly.

The blocking semaphore operation allows processes to communicate based on the values of semaphores at different points in time. Remember also that IPC facilities remain in the UNIX operating system until removed by a permitted process or until the system is reinitialized.

Operating on a semaphore set is done by using the **semop** system call.

When a set of semaphores is created, the first semaphore in the set is semaphore number zero. The last semaphore number in the set is numbered one less than the total in the set.

A single system call can be used to perform a sequence of these "blocking/nonblocking operations" on a set of semaphores. When performing a sequence of operations, the blocking/nonblocking operations can be applied to any or all of the semaphores in the set. Also, the operations can be applied in any order of semaphore number. However, no operations are done until they can all be done successfully. For example, if the first three of six operations on a set of ten semaphores could be completed successfully, but the fourth operation would be blocked, no changes are made to the set until all six operations can be performed without blocking. Either the operations are successful and the semaphores are changed, or one ("nonblocking") operation is unsuccessful and none are changed. In short, the operations are "atomically performed."

Remember, any unsuccessful nonblocking operation for a single semaphore or a set of semaphores causes immediate return with no operations performed at all. When this occurs, an error code (-1) is returned to the process, and the external variable **errno** is set accordingly.

System calls (documented in the *Operating System API Reference*) make these semaphore capabilities available to processes. The calling process passes arguments to a system call, and the system call either successfully or unsuccessfully performs its function. If the system call is successful, it performs its function and returns the appropriate information. Otherwise, a known error code (-1) is returned to the process, and the external variable **errno** is set accordingly.

Using Semaphores

Before semaphores can be used (operated on or controlled) a uniquely identified data structure and semaphore set (array) must be created. The unique identifier is called the semaphore set identifier (**semid**); it is used to identify or refer to a particular data structure and semaphore set. This identifier is accessible by any process in the system, subject to normal access restrictions.

The semaphore set contains a predefined number of structures in an array, one structure for each semaphore in the set. The number of semaphores (**nsems**) in a semaphore set is user selectable. The following members are in each structure within a semaphore set:

- semaphore value
- PID performing last operation
- number of processes waiting for the semaphore value to become greater than its current value
- number of processes waiting for the semaphore value to equal zero

There is one associated data structure for the uniquely identified semaphore set. This data structure contains the following information related to the semaphore set:

- operation permissions data (operation permissions structure)
- pointer to first semaphore in the set (array)
- number of semaphores in the set
- last semaphore operation time
- last semaphore change time

The definition for the semaphore set (array member) **sem** is as follows:

```
struct sem
{
        ushort   semval;         /* semaphore value */
        pid_t    sempid;         /* pid of last operation */
        ushort   semncnt;        /* # awaiting semval > cval */
        ushort   semzcnt;        /* # awaiting semval = 0 */
};
```

Likewise, the definition for the associated semaphore data structure **semid_ds** contains the following members:

```
struct semid_ds
{
        struct ipc_perm sem_perm;   /* operation permission struct */
        struct sem      *sem_base;  /* ptr to first semaphore in set */
        ushort          sem_nsems;  /* # of semaphores in set */
        time_t          sem_otime;  /* last semop time */
        time_t          sem_ctime;  /* last change time */
};
```

In UNIX System V Release 4.0, the value of **SEM_PAD** equals **4**. In UNIX System V Release 4.1, **SEM_PAD** is a symbolic constant.

The C programming language data structure definition for the semaphore set (array member) and for the **semid_ds** data structure are located in the **sys/sem.h** header file.

Note that the **sem_perm** member of this structure uses **ipc_perm** as a template. The figure entitled "**ipc_perm** Data Structure" breaks out the operation permissions data structure.

The **ipc_perm** data structure is the same for all IPC facilities; it is located in the **sys/ipc.h** header file and is shown in the "Messages" section.

The **semget** system call is used to perform two tasks:

- to get a new semaphore set identifier and create an associated data structure and semaphore set for it
- to return an existing semaphore set identifier that already has an associated data structure and semaphore set

The task performed is determined by the value of the **key** argument passed to the **semget** system call. For the first task, if the **key** is not already in use for an existing **semid** and the **IPC_CREAT** flag is set, a new **semid** is returned with an associated data structure and semaphore set created for it provided no system tunable parameter would be exceeded.

There is also a provision for specifying a **key** of value zero (0), which is known as the private **key** (**IPC_PRIVATE**). When this **key** is specified, a new identifier is always returned with an associated data structure and semaphore set created for it, unless a system-tunable parameter would be exceeded. The **ipcs** command will show the **key** field for the **semid** as all zeros.

When performing the first task, the process which calls **semget** becomes the owner/creator, and the associated data structure is initialized accordingly. Remember, ownership can be changed, but the creating process always remains the creator (see "Controlling Semaphores"). The creator of the semaphore set also determines the initial operation permissions for the facility.

For the second task, if a semaphore set identifier exists for the **key** specified, the value of the existing identifier is returned. If you do not want to have an existing semaphore set identifier returned, a control command (**IPC_EXCL**) can be specified (set) in the **semflg** argument passed to the system call. The system call will fail if it is passed a value for the number of semaphores (**nsems**) that is greater than the number actually in the set; if you do not know how many semaphores are in the set, use 0 for **nsems**. (see "Using semget" for how to use this system call).

Once a uniquely identified semaphore set and data structure are created, **semop** (semaphore operations) and **semctl** (semaphore control) can be used.

Semaphore operations consist of incrementing, decrementing, and testing for zero. The **semop** system call is used to perform these operations (see "Operations On Semaphores" for details of the **semop** system call.

The **semctl** system call permits you to control the semaphore facility in the following ways:

- by returning the value of a semaphore (**GETVAL**)

- by setting the value of a semaphore (**SETVAL**)

- by returning the PID of the last process performing an operation on a semaphore set (**GETPID**)

- by returning the number of processes waiting for a semaphore value to become greater than its current value (**GETNCNT**)

- by returning the number of processes waiting for a semaphore value to equal zero (**GETZCNT**)

- by getting all semaphore values in a set and placing them in an array in user memory (**GETALL**)

- by setting all semaphore values in a semaphore set from an array of values in user memory (**SETALL**)

- by retrieving the data structure associated with a semaphore set (**IPC_STAT**)

- by changing operation permissions for a semaphore set (**IPC_SET**)

- by removing a particular semaphore set identifier from the UNIX operating system along with its associated data structure and semaphore set (**IPC_RMID**)

See the section "Controlling Semaphores" for details of the **semctl** system call.

Getting Semaphores

This section describes how to use the **semget** system call. The accompanying program illustrates its use.

Using semget

The synopsis found in the **semget**(2) entry in the *Operating System API Reference* is as follows:

```
#include  <sys/types.h>
#include  <sys/ipc.h>
#include  <sys/sem.h>

int  semget (key, nsems, semflag)
key_t  key;
int nsems, semflag;
```

The following line in the synopsis:

```
int semget (key, nsems, semflg)
```

informs you that **semget** is a function with three formal arguments that returns an integer-type value. The next two lines:

```
key_t  key;
int nsems, semflg;
```

declare the types of the formal arguments. **key_t** is defined by a **typedef** in the **sys/types.h** header file to be an integer.

The integer returned from this system call upon successful completion is the semaphore set identifier that was discussed above.

The process calling the **semget** system call must supply three actual arguments to be passed to the formal **key**, **nsems**, and **semflg** arguments.

A new **semid** with an associated semaphore set and data structure is created if either

- **key** is equal to **IPC_PRIVATE**,

or

- **key** is a unique integer and **semflg** ANDed with **IPC_CREAT** is "true."

The value passed to the **semflg** argument must be an integer that will specify the following:

- operation permissions
- control fields (commands)

Table 10-2 reflects the numeric values (expressed in octal notation) for the valid operation permissions codes.

Table 10-2: Operation Permissions Codes

Operation Permissions	Octal Value
Read by User	00400
Alter by User	00200
Read by Group	00040
Alter by Group	00020
Read by Others	00004
Alter by Others	00002

A specific value is derived by adding or bitwise ORing the values for the operation permissions wanted. That is, if read by user and read/alter by others is desired, the code value would be 00406 (00400 plus 00006). There are constants **#define**'d in the **sys/sem.h** header file which can be used for the user (OWNER). They are as follows:

```
SEM_A    0200    /* alter permission by owner */
SEM_R    0400    /* read permission by owner */
```

Control flags are predefined constants (represented by all upper-case letters). The flags that apply to the **semget** system call are **IPC_CREAT** and **IPC_EXCL** and are defined in the **sys/ipc.h** header file.

The value for **semflg** is, therefore, a combination of operation permissions and control commands. After determining the value for the operation permissions as previously described, the desired flag(s) can be specified. This specification is accomplished by adding or bitwise ORing (|) them with the operation permissions; the bit positions and values for the control commands in relation to those of the operation permissions make this possible.

The **semflg** value can easily be set by using the flag names in conjunction with the octal operation permissions value:

```
semid = semget (key, nsems, (IPC_CREAT | 0400));
semid = semget (key, nsems, (IPC_CREAT | IPC_EXCL | 0400));
```

As specified by the **semget**(2) entry in the *Operating System API Reference*, success or failure of this system call depends upon the actual argument values for **key**, **nsems**, and **semflg**, and system-tunable parameters. The system call will attempt to return a new semaphore set identifier if one of the following conditions is true:

- **key** is equal to **IPC_PRIVATE**

- **key** does not already have a semaphore set identifier associated with it and (**semflg** & **IPC_CREAT**) is "true" (not zero).

The **key** argument can be set to **IPC_PRIVATE** like this:

```
semid = semget(IPC_PRIVATE, nsems, semflg);
```

Exceeding the **SEMMNI**, **SEMMNS**, or **SEMMSL** system-tunable parameters will always cause a failure. The **SEMMNI** system-tunable parameter determines the maximum number of unique semaphore sets (**semid**'s) that may be in use at any given time. The **SEMMNS** system-tunable parameter determines the maximum number of semaphores in all semaphore sets system wide. The **SEMMSL** system-tunable parameter determines the maximum number of semaphores in each semaphore set.

IPC_EXCL is another control command used in conjunction with IPC_CREAT. It will cause the system call to return an error if a semaphore set identifier already exists for the specified **key** provided. This is necessary to prevent the process from thinking that it has received a new (unique) identifier when it has not. In other words, when both IPC_CREAT and IPC_EXCL are specified, a new semaphore set identifier is returned if the system call is successful. Any value for **semflg** returns a new identifier if the **key** equals zero (IPC_PRIVATE) and no system-tunable parameters are exceeded.

Refer to the **semget**(2) manual page in the *Operating System API Reference* for specific associated data structure initialization for successful completion. The specific failure conditions and their error names are contained there also.

Example Program

Figure 10-5 is a menu-driven program. It allows all possible combinations of using the **semget** system call to be exercised.

From studying this program, you can observe the method of passing arguments and receiving return values. The user-written program requirements are pointed out.

This program begins (lines 4-8) by including the required header files as specified by the **semget**(2) entry in the *Operating System API Reference*. Note that the **sys/errno.h** header file is included as opposed to declaring **errno** as an external variable; either method will work.

Variable names have been chosen to be as close as possible to those in the synopsis. Their declarations are self explanatory. These names make the program more readable and are perfectly valid since they are local to the program.

The variables declared for this program and what they are used for are as follows:

key	used to pass the value for the desired key
opperm	used to store the desired operation permissions
flags	used to store the desired control commands (flags)
opperm_flags	used to store the combination from the logical ORing of the **opperm** and **flags** variables; it is then used in the system call to pass the **semflg** argument
semid	used for returning the semaphore set identification number for a successful system call or the error code (-1) for an unsuccessful one.

The program begins by prompting for a hexadecimal **key**, an octal operation permissions code, and the control command combinations (flags) which are selected from a menu (lines 15-32). All possible combinations are allowed even though they might not be viable. This allows observing the errors for invalid combinations.

Next, the menu selection for the flags is combined with the operation permissions; the result is stored in **opperm_flags** (lines 36-52).

Then, the number of semaphores for the set is requested (lines 53-57); its value is stored in **nsems**.

The system call is made next; the result is stored in the **semid** (lines 60, 61).

Since the **semid** variable now contains a valid semaphore set identifier or the error code (**-1**), it is tested to see if an error occurred (line 63). If **semid** equals **-1**, a message indicates that an error resulted and the external **errno** variable is displayed (line 65). Remember that the external **errno** variable is only set when a system call fails; it should only be examined immediately following system calls.

If no error occurred, the returned semaphore set identifier is displayed (line 69).

The example program for the **semget** system call follows. We suggest that you name the source program file **semget.c** and the executable file **semget**.

Figure 10-5: semget **System Call Example**

```
1     /*This is a program to illustrate
2     **the semaphore get, semget(),
3     **system call capabilities.*/
4     #include    <stdio.h>
5     #include    <sys/types.h>
6     #include    <sys/ipc.h>
7     #include    <sys/sem.h>
8     #include    <errno.h>
9     /*Start of main C language program*/
10    main()
11    {
12        key_t key;      /*declare as long integer*/
13        int opperm, flags, nsems;
14        int semid, opperm_flags;
15        /*Enter the desired key*/
16        printf("\nEnter the desired key in hex = ");
17        scanf("%x", &key);
18        /*Enter the desired octal operation
19               permissions.*/
```

(continued on next page)

Figure 10-5: semget **System Call Example** (continued)

```
20          printf("\nEnter the operation\n");
21          printf("permissions in octal = ");
22          scanf("%o", &opperm);
23          /*Set the desired flags.*/
24          printf("\nEnter corresponding number to\n");
25          printf("set the desired flags:\n");
26          printf("No flags                = 0\n");
27          printf("IPC_CREAT               = 1\n");
28          printf("IPC_EXCL                = 2\n");
29          printf("IPC_CREAT and IPC_EXCL  = 3\n");
30          printf("          Flags         = ");
31          /*Get the flags to be set.*/
32          scanf("%d", &flags);

33          /*Error checking (debugging)*/
34          printf ("\nkey =0x%x, opperm = 0%o, flags = %d\n",
35              key, opperm, flags);
36          /*Incorporate the control fields (flags) with
37              the operation permissions.*/
38          switch (flags)
39          {
40          case 0:    /*No flags are to be set.*/
41              opperm_flags = (opperm | 0);
42              break;
43          case 1:     /*Set the IPC_CREAT flag.*/
44              opperm_flags = (opperm | IPC_CREAT);
45              break;
46          case 2:     /*Set the IPC_EXCL flag.*/
47              opperm_flags = (opperm | IPC_EXCL);
48              break;
49          case 3: /*Set the IPC_CREAT and IPC_EXCL
50                      flags.*/
51              opperm_flags = (opperm | IPC_CREAT | IPC_EXCL);
52          }

53          /*Get the number of semaphores for this set.*/
54          printf("\nEnter the number of\n");
55          printf("desired semaphores for\n");
56          printf("this set (25 max) = ");
57          scanf("%d", &nsems);

58          /*Check the entry.*/
59          printf("\nNsems = %d\n", nsems);

60          /*Call the semget system call.*/
61          semid = semget(key, nsems, opperm_flags);

62          /*Perform the following if the call is unsuccessful.*/
63          if(semid == -1)
64          {
65              printf("The semget call failed, error number = %d\n", errno);
66          }
```

(continued on next page)

Figure 10-5: semget **System Call Example** (continued)

```
67          /*Return the semid upon successful completion.*/
68          else
69              printf("\nThe semid = %d\n", semid);
70          exit(0);
71      }
```

Controlling Semaphores

This section describes how to use the **semctl** system call. The accompanying program illustrates its use.

Using semctl

The synopsis found in the **semctl**(2) entry in the *Operating System API Reference* is as follows:

```
#include <sys/types.h>
#include <sys/ipc.h>
#include <sys/sem.h>

int semctl (semid, semnum, cmd, arg)
int semid, cmd;
int semnum;
union semun
{
        int val;
        struct semid_ds *buf;
        ushort *array;
} arg;
```

The **semctl** system call requires four arguments to be passed to it, and it returns an integer value.

The **semid** argument must be a valid, non-negative, integer value that has already been created by using the **semget** system call.

The **semnum** argument is used to select a semaphore by its number. This relates to sequences of operations (atomically performed) on the set. When a set of semaphores is created, the first semaphore is number 0, and the last semaphore is numbered one less than the total in the set.

The **cmd** argument can be replaced by one of the following values:

GETVAL	return the value of a single semaphore within a semaphore set
SETVAL	set the value of a single semaphore within a semaphore set
GETPID	return the PID of the process that performed the last operation on the semaphore within a semaphore set
GETNCNT	return the number of processes waiting for the value of a particular semaphore to become greater than its current value
GETZCNT	return the number of processes waiting for the value of a particular semaphore to be equal to zero
GETALL	return the value for all semaphores in a semaphore set
SETALL	set all semaphore values in a semaphore set
IPC_STAT	return the status information contained in the associated data structure for the specified **semid**, and place it in the data structure pointed to by the **buf** pointer in the user memory area; **arg.buf** is the union member that contains pointer
IPC_SET	for the specified semaphore set (**semid**), set the effective user/group identification and operation permissions
IPC_RMID	remove the specified semaphore set (**semid**) along with its associated data structure.

To perform an **IPC_SET** or **IPC_RMID** control command, a process must have:

■ an effective user id of OWNER/CREATOR, or

■ an effective user id of **root** (if the system is running with the SUM privilege module), or

■ the **P_OWNER** privilege,

The remaining control commands require either read or write permission, as appropriate.

The **arg** argument is used to pass the system call the appropriate union member for the control command to be performed. For some of the control commands, the **arg** argument is not required and is simply ignored.

- **arg.val** required: **SETVAL**

- **arg.buf** required: **IPC_STAT**, **IPC_SET**

- **arg.array** required: **GETALL**, **SETALL**

- **arg** ignored: **GETVAL, GETPID, GETNCNT, GETZCNT, IPC_RMID**

The details of this system call are discussed in the following program. If you need more information on the logic manipulations in this program, read "Using semget". It goes into more detail than would be practical for every system call.

Example Program

Figure 10-6 is a menu-driven program. It allows all possible combinations of using the **semctl** system call to be exercised.

From studying this program, you can observe the method of passing arguments and receiving return values. The user-written program requirements are pointed out.

This program begins (lines 5-9) by including the required header files as specified by the **semctl**(2) entry in the *Operating System API Reference*. Note that in this program **errno** is declared as an external variable, and therefore the **sys/errno.h** header file does not have to be included.

Variable, structure, and union names have been chosen to be as close as possible to those in the synopsis. Their declarations are self explanatory. These names make the program more readable and are perfectly valid since they are local to the program.

The variables declared for this program and what they are used for are as follows:

semid_ds   used to receive the specified semaphore set identifier's data structure when an **IPC_STAT** control command is performed

c   used to receive the input values from the **scanf** function (line 119) when performing a **SETALL** control command

i   used as a counter to increment through the union **arg.array** when displaying the semaphore values for a **GETALL** (lines 98-100) control command, and when initializing the **arg.array** when performing a **SETALL** (lines 117-121) control command

`length`	used as a variable to test for the number of semaphores in a set against the **i** counter variable (lines 98, 117)
`uid`	used to store the **IPC_SET** value for the user identification
`gid`	used to store the **IPC_SET** value for the group identification
`mode`	used to store the **IPC_SET** value for the operation permissions
`retrn`	used to store the return value from the system call
`semid`	used to store and pass the semaphore set identifier to the system call
`semnum`	used to store and pass the semaphore number to the system call
`cmd`	used to store the code for the desired control command so that subsequent processing can be performed on it
`choice`	used to determine which member (**uid, gid, mode**) for the **IPC_SET** control command is to be changed
`semvals[]`	used to store the set of semaphore values when getting (**GETALL**) or initializing (**SETALL**)
`arg.val`	used to pass the system call a value to set, or to store a value returned from the system call, for a single semaphore (union member)
`arg.buf`	a pointer passed to the system call which locates the data structure in the user memory area where the **IPC_STAT** control command is to place its return values, or where the **IPC_SET** command gets the values to set (union member)
`arg.array`	a pointer passed to the system call which locates the array in the user memory where the **GETALL** control command is to place its return values, or when the **SETALL** command gets the values to set (union member)

Note that the **semid_ds** data structure in this program (line 14) uses the data structure located in the **sys/sem.h** header file of the same name as a template for its declaration.

Note that the **semvals** array is declared to have 25 elements (0 through 24). This number corresponds to the maximum number of semaphores allowed per set (**SEMMSL**), a system-tunable parameter.

Now that all of the required declarations have been presented for this program, this is how it works.

First, the program prompts for a valid semaphore set identifier, which is stored in the **semid** variable (lines 24-26). This is required for all **semctl** system calls.

Then, the code for the desired control command must be entered (lines 17-42), and the code is stored in the **cmd** variable. The code is tested to determine the control command for subsequent processing.

If the **GETVAL** control command is selected (code 1), a message prompting for a semaphore number is displayed (lines 48, 49). When it is entered, it is stored in the **semnum** variable (line 50). Then, the system call is performed, and the semaphore value is displayed (lines 51-54). Note that the **arg** argument is not required in this case, and the system call will simply ignore it. If the system call is successful, a message indicates this along with the semaphore set identifier used (lines 197, 198); if the system call is unsuccessful, an error message is displayed along with the value of the external **errno** variable (lines 194, 195).

If the **SETVAL** control command is selected (code 2), a message prompting for a semaphore number is displayed (lines 55, 56). When it is entered, it is stored in the **semnum** variable (line 57). Next, a message prompts for the value to which the semaphore is to be set; it is stored as the **arg.val** member of the union (lines 58, 59). Then, the system call is performed (lines 60, 62). Depending upon success or failure, the program returns the same messages as for **GETVAL** above.

If the **GETPID** control command is selected (code 3), the system call is made immediately since all required arguments are known (lines 63-66), and the PID of the process performing the last operation is displayed. Note that the **arg** argument is not required in this case, and the system call will simply ignore it. Depending upon success or failure, the program returns the same messages as for **GETVAL** above.

If the **GETNCNT** control command is selected (code 4), a message prompting for a semaphore number is displayed (lines 67-71). When entered, it is stored in the **semnum** variable (line 73). Then, the system call is performed and the number of processes waiting for the semaphore to become greater than its current value is displayed (lines 73-76). Note that the **arg** argument is not required in this case, and the system call will simply ignore it. Depending upon success or failure, the program returns the same messages as for **GETVAL** above.

If the **GETZCNT** control command is selected (code 5), a message prompting for a semaphore number is displayed (lines 77-80). When it is entered, it is stored in the **semnum** variable (line 81). Then the system call is performed and the number of processes waiting for the semaphore value to become equal to zero is displayed (lines 82-85). Depending upon success or failure, the program returns the same messages as for **GETVAL** above.

If the **GETALL** control command is selected (code 6), the program first performs an **IPC_STAT** control command to determine the number of semaphores in the set (lines 87-93). The length variable is set to the number of semaphores in the set (line 93). The **arg.array** union member is set to point to the **semvals** array where the system call is to store the values of the semaphore set (line 96). Now, a loop is entered which displays each element of the **arg.array** from zero to one less than the value of length (lines 98-104). The semaphores in the set are displayed on a single line, separated by a space. Depending upon success or failure, the program returns the same messages as for **GETVAL** above.

If the **SETALL** control command is selected (code 7), the program first performs an **IPC_STAT** control command to determine the number of semaphores in the set (lines 107-110). The length variable is set to the number of semaphores in the set (line 113). Next, the program prompts for the values to be set and enters a loop which takes values from the keyboard and initializes the **semvals** array to contain the desired values of the semaphore set (lines 115-121). The loop puts the first entry into the array position for semaphore number zero and ends when the sema- phore number that is filled in the array equals one less than the value of length. The **arg.array** union member is set to point to the **semvals** array from which the system call is to obtain the semaphore values. The system call is then made (lines 122-125). Depending upon success or failure, the program returns the same mes- sages as for **GETVAL** above.

If the **IPC_STAT** control command is selected (code 8), the system call is performed (line 129), and the status information returned is printed out (lines 130-141); only the members that can be set are printed out in this program. Note that if the sys- tem call is unsuccessful, the status information of the last successful one is printed out. In addition, an error message is displayed, and the **errno** variable is printed out (line 194).

If the **IPC_SET** control command is selected (code 9), the program gets the current status information for the semaphore set identifier specified (lines 145-149). This is necessary because this example program provides for changing only one member at a time, and the **semctl** system call changes all of them. Also, if an invalid value happened to be stored in the user memory area for one of these members, it would cause repetitive failures for this control command until corrected. The next thing the program does is to prompt for a code corresponding to the member to be changed (lines 150-156). This code is stored in the **choice** variable (line 157). Now, depending upon the member picked, the program prompts for the new value (lines 158-181). The value is placed into the appropri- ate member in the user memory area data structure, and the system call is made (line 184). Depending upon success or failure, the program returns the same mes- sages as for **GETVAL** above.

If the **IPC_RMID** control command (code 10) is selected, the system call is performed (lines 186-188). The semaphore set identifier along with its associated data structure and semaphore set is removed from the UNIX operating system. Depending upon success or failure, the program returns the same messages as for the other control commands.

The example program for the **semctl** system call follows. We suggest that you name the source program file **semctl.c** and the executable file **semctl**.

Figure 10-6: semctl **System Call Example**

```
1     /*This is a program to illustrate
2     **the semaphore control, semctl(),
3     **system call capabilities.
4     */
5     /*Include necessary header files.*/
6     #include     <stdio.h>
7     #include     <sys/types.h>
8     #include     <sys/ipc.h>
9     #include     <sys/sem.h>
10    /*Start of main C language program*/
11    main()
12    {
13        extern int errno;
14        struct semid_ds semid_ds;
15        int c, i, length;
16        int uid, gid, mode;
17        int retrn, semid, semnum, cmd, choice;
18        ushort semvals[25];
19        union semun  {
20            int val;
21            struct semid_ds *buf;
22            ushort *array;
23        } arg;
24        /*Enter the semaphore ID.*/
25        printf("Enter the semid = ");
26        scanf("%d", &semid);
27        /*Choose the desired command.*/
28        printf("\nEnter the number for\n");
29        printf("the desired cmd:\n");
30        printf("GETVAL       =  1\n");
31        printf("SETVAL       =  2\n");
32        printf("GETPID       =  3\n");
33        printf("GETNCNT      =  4\n");
34        printf("GETZCNT      =  5\n");
35        printf("GETALL       =  6\n");
36        printf("SETALL       =  7\n");
37        printf("IPC_STAT     =  8\n");
```

(continued on next page)

Figure 10-6: `semctl` **System Call Example** (continued)

```
38        printf("IPC_SET    =  9\n");
39        printf("IPC_RMID   =  10\n");
40        printf("Entry      =  ");
41        scanf("%d", &cmd);

42        /*Check entries.*/
43        printf ("\nsemid =%d, cmd = %d\n\n",
44            semid, cmd);

45        /*Set the command and do the call.*/
46        switch (cmd)
47        {

48        case 1: /*Get a specified value.*/
49            printf("\nEnter the semnum = ");
50            scanf("%d", &semnum);
51            /*Do the system call.*/
52            retrn = semctl(semid, semnum, GETVAL, arg);
53            printf("\nThe semval = %d", retrn);
54            break;
55        case 2: /*Set a specified value.*/
56            printf("\nEnter the semnum = ");
57            scanf("%d", &semnum);
58            printf("\nEnter the value = ");
59            scanf("%d", &arg.val);
60            /*Do the system call.*/
61            retrn = semctl(semid, semnum, SETVAL, arg);
62            break;
63        case 3: /*Get the process ID.*/
64            retrn = semctl(semid, 0, GETPID, arg);
65            printf("\nThe sempid = %d", retrn);
66            break;
67        case 4: /*Get the number of processes
68            waiting for the semaphore to
69            become greater than its current
70            value.*/
71            printf("\nEnter the semnum = ");
72            scanf("%d", &semnum);
73            /*Do the system call.*/
74            retrn = semctl(semid, semnum, GETNCNT, arg);
75            printf("\nThe semncnt = %d", retrn);
76            break;

77        case 5: /*Get the number of processes
78            waiting for the semaphore
79            value to become zero.*/
80            printf("\nEnter the semnum = ");
81            scanf("%d", &semnum);
82            /*Do the system call.*/
83            retrn = semctl(semid, semnum, GETZCNT, arg);
84            printf("\nThe semzcnt = %d", retrn);
```

(continued on next page)

Figure 10-6: `semctl` **System Call Example** (continued)

```
85              break;
86          case 6: /*Get all of the semaphores.*/
87              /*Get the number of semaphores in
88                the semaphore set.*/
89              arg.buf = &semid_ds;
90              retrn = semctl(semid, 0, IPC_STAT, arg);
91              if(retrn == -1)
92                  goto ERROR;
93              length = arg.buf->sem_nsems;
94              /*Get and print all semaphores in the
95                specified set.*/
96              arg.array = semvals;
97              retrn = semctl(semid, 0, GETALL, arg);
98              for (i = 0; i < length; i++)
99              {
100                 printf("%d", semvals[i]);
101                 /*Separate each
102                   semaphore.*/
103                 printf(" ");
104             }
105             break;
106         case 7: /*Set all semaphores in the set.*/
107             /*Get the number of semaphores in
108               the set.*/
109             arg.buf = &semid_ds;
110             retrn = semctl(semid, 0, IPC_STAT, arg);
111             if(retrn == -1)
112                 goto ERROR;
113             length = arg.buf->sem_nsems;
114             printf("Length = %d\n", length);
115             /*Set the semaphore set values.*/
116             printf("\nEnter each value:\n");
117             for(i = 0; i < length ; i++)
118             {
119                 scanf("%d", &c);
120                 semvals[i] = c;
121             }
122             /*Do the system call.*/
123             arg.array = semvals;
124             retrn = semctl(semid, 0, SETALL, arg);
125             break;
126         case 8: /*Get the status for the semaphore set.*/
127             /*Get and print the current status values.*/
128             arg.buf = &semid_ds;
129             retrn = semctl(semid, 0, IPC_STAT, arg);
130             printf ("\nThe USER ID = %d\n",
131                 arg.buf->sem_perm.uid);
132             printf ("The GROUP ID = %d\n",
```

(continued on next page)

Figure 10-6: `semctl` **System Call Example** (continued)

```
133                      arg.buf->sem_perm.gid);
134              printf ("The operation permissions = 0%o\n",
135                      arg.buf->sem_perm.mode);
136              printf ("The number of semaphores in set = %d\n",
137                      arg.buf->sem_nsems);
138              printf ("The last semop time = %d\n",
139                      arg.buf->sem_otime);
140              printf ("The last change time  = %d\n",
141                      arg.buf->sem_ctime);
142              break;
143          case 9:    /*Select and change the desired
144                         member of the data structure.*/
145              /*Get the current status values.*/
146              arg.buf = &semid_ds;
147              retrn = semctl(semid, 0, IPC_STAT, arg.buf);
148              if(retrn == -1)
149                  goto ERROR;
150              /*Select the member to change.*/
151              printf("\nEnter the number for the\n");
152              printf("member to be changed:\n");
153              printf("sem_perm.uid  = 1\n");
154              printf("sem_perm.gid   = 2\n");
155              printf("sem_perm.mode  = 3\n");
156              printf("Entry           = ");
157              scanf("%d", &choice);
158              switch(choice){

159              case 1: /*Change the user ID.*/
160                  printf("\nEnter USER ID = ");
161                  scanf ("%d", &uid);
162                  arg.buf->sem_perm.uid = uid;
163                  printf("\nUSER ID = %d\n",
164                      arg.buf->sem_perm.uid);
165                  break;

166              case 2: /*Change the group ID.*/
167                  printf("\nEnter GROUP ID = ");
168                  scanf("%d", &gid);
169                  arg.buf->sem_perm.gid = gid;
170                  printf("\nGROUP ID = %d\n",
171                      arg.buf->sem_perm.gid);
172                  break;

173              case 3: /*Change the mode portion of
174                   the operation
175                              permissions.*/
176                  printf("\nEnter MODE in octal = ");
177                  scanf("%o", &mode);
178                  arg.buf->sem_perm.mode = mode;
179                  printf("\nMODE = 0%o\n",
```

(continued on next page)

Figure 10-6: `semctl` **System Call Example** (continued)

```
180                      arg.buf->sem_perm.mode);
181                   break;
182               }
183               /*Do the change.*/
184               retrn = semctl(semid, 0, IPC_SET, arg);
185               break;
186           case 10:    /*Remove the semid along with its
187                        data structure.*/
188               retrn = semctl(semid, 0, IPC_RMID, arg);
189           }
190           /*Perform the following if the call is unsuccessful.*/
191           if(retrn == -1)
192           {
193   ERROR:
194               printf ("\nThe semctl call failed!, error number =  %d\n", errno);
195               exit(0);
196           }
197           printf ("\n\nThe semctl system call was successful\n");
198           printf ("for semid = %d\n", semid);
199           exit (0);
200       }
```

Operations On Semaphores

This section describes how to use the **semop** system call. The accompanying program illustrates its use.

Using semop

The synopsis found in the **semop**(2) entry in the *Operating System API Reference* is as follows:

```
#include <sys/types.h>
#include <sys/ipc.h>
#include <sys/sem.h>

int semop (semid, sops, nsops)
int semid;
struct sembuf *sops;
unsigned nsops;
```

The **semop** system call requires three arguments to be passed to it and returns an integer value which will be zero for successful completion or **-1** otherwise.

The **semid** argument must be a valid, non-negative, integer value. In other words, it must have already been created by using the **semget** system call.

The **sops** argument points to an array of structures in the user memory area that contains the following for each semaphore to be changed:

- the semaphore number (**sem_num**)

- the operation to be performed (**sem_op**)

- the control flags (**sem_flg**)

The ***sops** declaration means that either an array name (which is the address of the first element of the array) or a pointer to the array can be used. **sembuf** is the *tag* name of the data structure used as the template for the structure members in the array; it is located in the **sys/sem.h** header file.

The **nsops** argument specifies the length of the array (the number of structures in the array). The maximum size of this array is determined by the **SEMOPM** system-tunable parameter. Therefore, a maximum of **SEMOPM** operations can be performed for each **semop** system call.

The semaphore number (**sem_num**) determines the particular semaphore within the set on which the operation is to be performed.

The operation to be performed is determined by the following:

- if **sem_op** is positive, the semaphore value is incremented by the value of **sem_op**

- if **sem_op** is negative, the semaphore value is decremented by the absolute value of **sem_op**

- if **sem_op** is zero, the semaphore value is tested for equality to zero

The following operation commands (flags) can be used:

- **IPC_NOWAIT**—this operation command can be set for any operations in the array. The system call will return unsuccessfully without changing any semaphore values at all if any operation for which **IPC_NOWAIT** is set cannot be performed successfully. The system call will be unsuccessful when trying to decrement a semaphore more than its current value, or when testing for a semaphore to be equal to zero when it is not.

- **SEM_UNDO**—this operation command is used to tell the system to undo the process's semaphore changes automatically when the process exits; it allows processes to avoid deadlock problems. To implement this feature, the system maintains a table with an entry for every process in the system. Each entry points to a set of undo structures, one for each semaphore used by the process. The system records the net change.

Example Program

Figure 10-7 is a menu-driven program. It allows all possible combinations of using the **semop** system call to be exercised.

From studying this program, you can observe the method of passing arguments and receiving return values. The user-written program requirements are pointed out.

This program begins (lines 5-9) by including the required header files as specified by the **shmop**(2) entry in the *Operating System API Reference*. Note that in this program **errno** is declared as an external variable; therefore, the **sys/errno.h** header file does not have to be included.

Variable and structure names have been chosen to be as close as possible to those in the synopsis. Their declarations are self explanatory. These names make the program more readable and are perfectly valid since they are local to the program.

The variables declared for this program and what they are used for are as follows:

sembuf[10]   used as an array buffer (line 14) to contain a maximum of ten
             sembuf type structures; ten is the standard value of the tun-
             able parameter **SEMOPM**, the maximum number of operations
             on a semaphore set for each **semop** system call

sops   used as a pointer (line 14) to the **sembuf** array for the system
             call and for accessing the structure members within the array

string[8]   used as a character buffer to hold a number entered by the
             user

rtrn   used to store the return value from the system call

flags   used to store the code of the **IPC_NOWAIT** or **SEM_UNDO** flags
             for the **semop** system call (line 59)

sem_num   used to store the semaphore number entered by the user for
             each semaphore operation in the array

i   used as a counter (line 31) for initializing the structure
             members in the array, and used to print out each structure in
             the array (line 78)

semid   used to store the desired semaphore set identifier for the sys-
             tem call

nsops   used to specify the number of semaphore operations for the
             system call; must be less than or equal to **SEMOPM**

First, the program prompts for a semaphore set identifier that the system call is to
perform operations on (lines 18-21). **semid** is stored in the **semid** variable (line
22).

A message is displayed requesting the number of operations to be performed on
this set (lines 24-26). The number of operations is stored in the **nsops** variable
(line 27).

Next, a loop is entered to initialize the array of structures (lines 29-76). The semaphore number, operation, and operation command (flags) are entered for each
structure in the array. The number of structures equals the number of semaphore
operations (**nsops**) to be performed for the system call, so **nsops** is tested against
the **i** counter for loop control. Note that **sops** is used as a pointer to each element
(structure) in the array, and **sops** is incremented just like **i**. **sops** is then used to
point to each member in the structure for setting them.

After the array is initialized, all of its elements are printed out for feedback (lines 77-84).

The **sops** pointer is set to the address of the array (lines 85, 86). **sembuf** could be used directly, if desired, instead of **sops** in the system call.

The system call is made (line 88), and depending upon success or failure, a corresponding message is displayed. The results of the operation(s) can be viewed by using the **semctl** **GETALL** control command.

The example program for the **semop** system call follows. We suggest that you name the source program file **semop.c** and the executable file **semop**.

Figure 10-7: **semop** **System Call Example**

```
1      /*This is a program to illustrate
2      **the semaphore operations, semop(),
3      **system call capabilities.
4      */

5      /*Include necessary header files.*/
6      #include     <stdio.h>
7      #include     <sys/types.h>
8      #include     <sys/ipc.h>
9      #include     <sys/sem.h>
10     /*Start of main C language program*/
11     main()
12     {
13         extern int errno;
14         struct sembuf sembuf[10], *sops;
15         char string[8];
16         int retrn, flags, sem_num, i, semid;
17         unsigned nsops;

18         /*Enter the semaphore ID.*/
19         printf("\nEnter the semid of\n");
20         printf("the semaphore set to\n");
21         printf("be operated on = ");
22         scanf("%d", &semid);
23         printf("\nsemid = %d", semid);

24         /*Enter the number of operations.*/
25         printf("\nEnter the number of semaphore\n");
26         printf("operations for this set = ");
27         scanf("%d", &nsops);
28         printf("\nnsops = %d", nsops);

29         /*Initialize the array for the
30           number of operations to be performed.*/
31         for(i = 0, sops = sembuf; i < nsops; i++, sops++)
```

(continued on next page)

Interprocess Communication

Figure 10-7: semop **System Call Example** (continued)

```
32          {

33              /*This determines the semaphore in
34                the semaphore set.*/
35              printf("\nEnter the semaphore\n");
36              printf("number (sem_num) = ");
37              scanf("%d", &sem_num);
38              sops->sem_num = sem_num;
39              printf("\nThe sem_num = %d", sops->sem_num);

40              /*Enter a (-)number to decrement,
41                an unsigned number (no +) to increment,
42                or zero to test for zero.  These values
43                are entered into a string and converted
44                to integer values.*/
45              printf("\nEnter the operation for\n");
46              printf("the semaphore (sem_op) = ");
47              scanf("%s", string);
48              sops->sem_op = atoi(string);
49              printf("\nsem_op = %d\n", sops->sem_op);

50              /*Specify the desired flags.*/
51              printf("\nEnter the corresponding\n");
52              printf("number for the desired\n");
53              printf("flags:\n");
54              printf("No flags                = 0\n");
55              printf("IPC_NOWAIT              = 1\n");
56              printf("SEM_UNDO                = 2\n");
57              printf("IPC_NOWAIT and SEM_UNDO = 3\n");
58              printf("                 Flags  = ");
59              scanf("%d", &flags);

60              switch(flags)
61              {
62              case 0:
63                  sops->sem_flg = 0;
64                  break;
65              case 1:
66                  sops->sem_flg = IPC_NOWAIT;
67                  break;
68              case 2:
69                  sops->sem_flg = SEM_UNDO;
70                  break;
71              case 3:
72                  sops->sem_flg = IPC_NOWAIT | SEM_UNDO;
73                  break;
74              }
75              printf("\nFlags = 0%o\n", sops->sem_flg);
76          }
77          /*Print out each structure in the array.*/
```

(continued on next page)

Figure 10-7: semop **System Call Example** (continued)

```
78          for(i = 0; i < nsops; i++)
79          {
80              printf("\nsem_num = %d\n", sembuf[i].sem_num);
81              printf("sem_op = %d\n", sembuf[i].sem_op);
82              printf("sem_flg = 0%o\n", sembuf[i].sem_flg);
83              printf(" ");
84          }

85          sops = sembuf; /*Reset the pointer to
86                          sembuf[0].*/

87          /*Do the semop system call.*/
88          retrn = semop(semid, sops, nsops);
89          if(retrn == -1)  {
90              printf("\nSemop failed, error = %d\n", errno);
91          }
92          else {
93              printf ("\nSemop was successful\n");
94              printf("for semid = %d\n", semid);

95              printf("Value returned = %d\n", retrn);
96          }
97      }
```

Shared Memory

The shared memory type of IPC allows two or more processes (executing programs) to share memory and, consequently, the data contained there. This is done by allowing processes to set up access to a common virtual memory address space. This sharing occurs on a segment basis, which is memory management hardware-dependent.

This sharing of memory provides the fastest means of exchanging data between processes. However, processes that reference a shared memory segment must reside on one processor. Consequently, processes running on different processors (such as in a NFS network or a multiprocessing environment) may not be able to use shared memory segments.

A process initially creates a shared memory segment facility using the **shmget** system call. Upon creation, this process sets the overall operation permissions for the shared memory segment facility, sets its size in bytes, and can specify that the shared memory segment is for reference only (read-only) upon attachment.

If the memory segment is not specified to be for reference only, all other processes with appropriate operation permissions can read from or write to the memory segment.

shmat (shared memory attach) and **shmdt** (shared memory detach) can be performed on a shared memory segment.

shmat allows processes to associate themselves with the shared memory segment if they have permission. They can then read or write as allowed.

shmdt allows processes to disassociate themselves from a shared memory segment. Therefore, they lose the ability to read from or write to the shared memory segment.

The original owner/creator of a shared memory segment can relinquish ownership to another process using the **shmctl** system call. However, the creating process remains the creator until the facility is removed or the system is reinitialized. Other processes with permission can perform other functions on the shared memory segment using the **shmctl** system call.

System calls (documented in the *Operating System API Reference*) make these shared memory capabilities available to processes. The calling process passes arguments to a system call, and the system call either successfully or unsuccessfully performs its function. If the system call is successful, it performs its function and returns the appropriate information. Otherwise, a known error code (**-1**) is returned to the process, and the external variable **errno** is set accordingly.

Using Shared Memory

Sharing memory between processes occurs on a virtual segment basis. There is only one copy of each individual shared memory segment existing in the UNIX operating system at any time.

Before sharing of memory can be realized, a uniquely identified shared memory segment and data structure must be created. The unique identifier created is called the shared memory identifier (**shmid**); it is used to identify or refer to the associated data structure. This identifier is accessible by any process in the system, subject to normal access restrictions.

The data structure includes the following for each shared memory segment:

- operation permissions
- segment size
- segment descriptor (for internal system use only)
- PID performing last operation
- PID of creator
- current number of processes attached
- last attach time
- last detach time
- last change time

In UNIX System V Release 4, the definition for the associated shared-memory segment data structure **shmid_ds** is as follows:

```
/*
**      There is a shared mem id data structure for each segment in the system.
*/
struct shmid_ds {
    struct ipc_perm     shm_perm;       /* operation permission struct */
    int                 shm_segsz;      /* segment size */
    struct region       *shm_reg;       /* ptr to region structure */
    char                pad[4];         /* for swap compatibility */
    pid_t               shm_lpid;       /* pid of last shmop */
    pid_t               shm_cpid;       /* pid of creator */
    ushort              shm_nattch;     /* used only for shminfo */
    ushort              shm_cnattch;    /* used only for shminfo */
    time_t              shm_atime;      /* last shmat time */
    time_t              shm_dtime;      /* last shmdt time */
    time_t              shm_ctime;      /* last change time */
};
```

The C programming language data structure definition for the shared memory segment data structure **shmid_ds** is located in the **sys/shm.h** header file.

Note that the **shm_perm** member of this structure uses **ipc_perm** as a template. The **ipc_perm** data structure is the same for all IPC facilities; it is located in the **sys/ipc.h** header file and shown in the figure entitled "**ipc_perm** Data Structure".

The **shmget** system call performs two tasks:

- it gets a new shared memory identifier and creates an associated shared memory segment data structure

- it returns an existing shared memory identifier that already has an associated shared memory segment data structure

The task performed is determined by the value of the **key** argument passed to the **shmget** system call.

For the first task, if the **key** is not already in use for an existing shared memory identifier at the security level of the calling process and the **IPC_CREAT** flag is set in **shmflg**, a new identifier is returned with an associated shared memory segment data structure created for it provided no system-tunable parameters would be exceeded.

There is also a provision for specifying a **key** of value zero which is known as the private **key** (**IPC_PRIVATE**); when specified, a new **shmid** is always returned with an associated shared memory segment data structure created for it unless a system-tunable parameter would be exceeded. The **ipcs** command will show the **key** field for the **shmid** as all zeros.

For the second task, if a **shmid** exists for the **key** specified, the value of the existing **shmid** is returned. If it is not desired to have an existing **shmid** returned, a control command (**IPC_EXCL**) can be specified (set) in the **shmflg** argument passed to the system call. "Using shmget" discusses how to use this system call.

When performing the first task, the process that calls **shmget** becomes the owner/creator, and the associated data structure is initialized accordingly. Remember, ownership can be changed, but the creating process always remains the creator (see "Controlling Shared Memory"). The creator of the shared memory segment also determines the initial operation permissions for it.

Once a uniquely identified shared memory segment data structure is created, **shmop** (shared memory segment operations) and **shmctl** (shared memory control) can be used.

Shared memory segment operations consist of attaching and detaching shared memory segments. **shmat** and **shmdt** are provided for each of these operations (see "Operations for Shared Memory" for details of the **shmat** and **shmdt** system calls).

The **shmctl** system call permits you to control the shared memory facility in the following ways:

- by retrieving the data structure associated with a shared memory segment (**IPC_STAT**)

- by changing operation permissions for a shared memory segment (**IPC_SET**)

- by removing a particular shared memory segment from the UNIX operating system along with its associated shared memory segment data structure (**IPC_RMID**)

- by locking a shared memory segment in memory (**SHM_LOCK**)

- by unlocking a shared memory segment (**SHM_UNLOCK**)

See the section "Controlling Shared Memory" for details of the **shmctl** system call.

Getting Shared Memory Segments

This section describes how to use the **shmget** system call. The accompanying program illustrates its use.

Using shmget

The synopsis found in the **shmget**(2) entry in the *Operating System API Reference* is as follows:

```
#include   <sys/types.h>
#include   <sys/ipc.h>
#include   <sys/shm.h>

int   shmget (key, size, shmflg)
key_t  key;
int size, shmflg;
```

All of these include files are located in the **/usr/include/sys** directory of the UNIX operating system. The following line in the synopsis:

```
int shmget (key, size, shmflg)
```

informs you that **shmget** is a function with three formal arguments that returns an integer-type value. The next two lines:

```
key_t   key;
int size, shmflg;
```

declare the types of the formal arguments. **key_t** is defined by a **typedef** in the **sys/types.h** header file to be an integer.

The integer returned from this function (upon successful completion) is the shared memory identifier (**shmid**) that was discussed earlier.

As declared, the process calling the **shmget** system call must supply three arguments to be passed to the formal **key**, **size**, and **shmflg** arguments.

A new **shmid** with an associated shared memory data structure is provided if either

- **key** is equal to **IPC_PRIVATE**,

or

- **key** is a unique integer and **shmflg** ANDed with **IPC_CREAT** is "true" (not zero).

The value passed to the **shmflg** argument must be an integer-type value and will specify the following:

- operations permissions
- control fields (commands)

Access permissions determine the read/write attributes and modes determine the user/group/other attributes of the **shmflg** argument. They are collectively referred to as "operation permissions."

Table 10-3 reflects the numeric values (expressed in octal notation) for the valid operation permissions codes.

Table 10-3: Operation Permissions Codes

Operation Permissions	Octal Value
Read by User	00400
Write by User	00200
Read by Group	00040
Write by Group	00020
Read by Others	00004
Write by Others	00002

A specific octal value is derived by adding or bitwise ORing the octal values for the operation permissions desired. That is, if read by user and read/write by others is desired, the code value would be 00406 (00400 plus 00006). There are constants located in the **sys/shm.h** header file which can be used for the user (OWNER). They are:

```
SHM_R  0400
SHM_W  0200
```

Control flags are predefined constants (represented by all upper-case letters). The flags that apply to the **shmget** system call are **IPC_CREAT** and **IPC_EXCL** and are defined in the **sys/ipc.h** header file.

The value for **shmflg** is, therefore, a combination of operation permissions and control commands. After determining the value for the operation permissions as previously described, the desired flag(s) can be specified. This is accomplished by adding or bitwise ORing (|) them with the operation permissions; the bit positions and values for the control commands in relation to those of the operation permissions make this possible.

The **shmflg** value can easily be set by using the names of the flags in conjunction with the octal operation permissions value:

```
shmid = shmget (key, size, (IPC_CREAT | 0400));

shmid = shmget (key, size, (IPC_CREAT | IPC_EXCL | 0400));
```

As specified by the **shmget**(2) entry in the *Operating System API Reference*, success or failure of this system call depends upon the argument values for **key**, **size**, and **shmflg,** and system-tunable parameters. The system call will attempt to return a new **shmid** if one of the following conditions is true:

- **key** is equal to **IPC_PRIVATE** .
- **key** does not already have a **shmid** associated with it and (**shmflg** & **IPC_CREAT**) is "true" (not zero).

The **key** argument can be set to **IPC_PRIVATE** like this:

```
shmid = shmget(IPC_PRIVATE, size, shmflg);
```

The **SHMMNI** system-tunable parameter determines the maximum number of unique shared memory segments (**shmid**s) that may be in use at any given time. If the maximum number of shared memory segments is already in use, an attempt to create an additional segment will fail.

IPC_EXCL is another control command used in conjunction with **IPC_CREAT**. It will cause the system call to return an error if a shared memory identifier already exists for the specified **key** provided. This is necessary to prevent the process from thinking that it has received a new (unique) **shmid** when it has not. In other words, when both **PC_CREAT** and **IPC_EXCL** are specified, a unique shared memory identifier is returned if the system call is successful. Any value for **shmflg** returns a new identifier if the **key** equals zero (**IPC_PRIVATE**) and no system-tunable parameters are exceeded.

The system call will fail if the value for the **size** argument is less than **SHMMIN** or greater than **SHMMAX**. These tunable parameters specify the minimum and maximum shared memory segment sizes.

Refer to the **shmget**(2) manual page in the *Operating System API Reference* for specific associated data structure initialization for successful completion. The specific failure conditions and their error names are contained there also.

Example Program

Figure 10-8 is a menu-driven program. It allows all possible combinations of using the **shmget** system call to be exercised.

From studying this program, you can observe the method of passing arguments and receiving return values. The user-written program requirements are pointed out.

This program begins (lines 4-7) by including the required header files as specified by the **shmget**(2) entry in the *Operating System API Reference*. Note that the **sys/errno.h** header file is included as opposed to declaring **errno** as an external variable; either method will work.

Variable names have been chosen to be as close as possible to those in the synopsis for the system call. Their declarations are self explanatory. These names make the program more readable and are perfectly valid since they are local to the program.

The variables declared for this program and what they are used for are as follows:

key	used to pass the value for the desired **key**
opperm	used to store the desired operation permissions
flags	used to store the desired control commands (flags)
shmid	used for returning the message queue identification number for a successful system call or the error code (**-1**) for an unsuccessful one
size	used to specify the shared memory segment size
opperm_flags	used to store the combination from the logical ORing of the **opperm** and **flags** variables; it is then used in the system call to pass the **shmflg** argument

The program begins by prompting for a hexadecimal **key**, an octal operation permissions code, and finally for the control command combinations (flags) which are selected from a menu (lines 14-31). All possible combinations are allowed even though they might not be viable. This allows observing the errors for invalid combinations.

Interprocess Communication

Next, the menu selection for the flags is combined with the operation permissions; the result is stored in the **opperm_flags** variable (lines 35-50).

A display then prompts for the size of the shared memory segment; it is stored in the **size** variable (lines 51-54).

The system call is made next; the result is stored in the **shmid** variable (line 56).

Since the **shmid** variable now contains a valid message queue identifier or the error code (**-1**), it is tested to see if an error occurred (line 58). If **shmid** equals **-1**, a message indicates that an error resulted and the external **errno** variable is displayed (line 60).

If no error occurred, the returned shared memory segment identifier is displayed (line 64).

The example program for the **shmget** system call follows. We suggest that you name the source program file **shmget.c** and the executable file **shmget**.

Figure 10-8: shmget **System Call Example**

```
1     /*This is a program to illustrate
2     **the shared memory get, shmget(),
3     **system call capabilities.*/
4     #include    <sys/types.h>
5     #include    <sys/ipc.h>
6     #include    <sys/shm.h>
7     #include    <errno.h>
8     /*Start of main C language program*/
9     main()
10    {
11        key_t key;                  /*declare as long integer*/
12        int opperm, flags;
13        int shmid, size, opperm_flags;
14        /*Enter the desired key*/
15        printf("Enter the desired key in hex = ");
16        scanf("%x", &key);
17        /*Enter the desired octal operation
18          permissions.*/
19        printf("\nEnter the operation\n");
20        printf("permissions in octal = ");
21        scanf("%o", &opperm);
22        /*Set the desired flags.*/
23        printf("\nEnter corresponding number to\n");
24        printf("set the desired flags:\n");
25        printf("No flags              = 0\n");
26        printf("IPC_CREAT             = 1\n");
27        printf("IPC_EXCL              = 2\n");
```

(continued on next page)

Figure 10-8: shmget **System Call Example** (continued)

```
28        printf("IPC_CREAT and IPC_EXCL    = 3\n");
29        printf("            Flags          = ");
30        /*Get the flag(s) to be set.*/
31        scanf("%d", &flags);

32        /*Check the values.*/
33        printf ("\nkey =0x%x, opperm = 0%o, flags = %d\n",
34            key, opperm, flags);

35        /*Incorporate the control fields (flags) with
36          the operation permissions*/
37        switch (flags)
38        {
39        case 0:    /*No flags are to be set.*/
40            opperm_flags = (opperm | 0);
41            break;
42        case 1:    /*Set the IPC_CREAT flag.*/
43            opperm_flags = (opperm | IPC_CREAT);
44            break;
45        case 2:    /*Set the IPC_EXCL flag.*/
46            opperm_flags = (opperm | IPC_EXCL);
47            break;
48        case 3:    /*Set the IPC_CREAT and IPC_EXCL flags.*/
49            opperm_flags = (opperm | IPC_CREAT | IPC_EXCL);
50        }

51        /*Get the size of the segment in bytes.*/
52        printf ("\nEnter the segment");
53        printf ("\nsize in bytes = ");
54        scanf ("%d", &size);

55        /*Call the shmget system call.*/
56        shmid = shmget (key, size, opperm_flags);

57        /*Perform the following if the call is unsuccessful.*/
58        if(shmid == -1)
59        {
60            printf ("\nThe shmget call failed, error number = %d\n", errno);
61        }
62        /*Return the shmid upon successful completion.*/
63        else
64            printf ("\nThe shmid = %d\n", shmid);
65        exit(0);
66    }
```

Controlling Shared Memory

This section describes how to use the **shmctl** system call. The accompanying program illustrates its use.

Using shmctl

The synopsis found in the **shmctl**(2) entry in the *Operating System API Reference* is as follows:

```
#include <sys/types.h>
#include <sys/ipc.h>
#include <sys/shm.h>

int shmctl (shmid, cmd, buf)
int shmid, cmd;
struct shmid_ds *buf;
```

The **shmctl** system call requires three arguments to be passed to it. It returns an integer value which will be zero for successful completion or **-1** otherwise.

The **shmid** variable must be a valid, non-negative, integer value. In other words, it must have already been created by using the **shmget** system call.

The **cmd** argument can be replaced by one of following values:

IPC_STAT   return the status information contained in the associated data structure for the specified **shmid** and place it in the data structure pointed to by the **buf** pointer in the user memory area

IPC_SET   for the specified **shmid**, set the effective user and group identification, and operation permissions

IPC_RMID   remove the specified **shmid** with its associated shared memory segment data structure

SHM_LOCK   lock the specified shared memory segment in memory; must have appropriate privileges to perform this operation

SHM_LOCK   lock the shared memory segment from memory; must have appropriate privileges to perform this operation

To perform an **IPC_SET** or **IPC_RMID** control command, a process must have:

- an effective user id of OWNER/CREATOR, or

- an effective user id of **root** (if the system is running with the SUM privilege module), or

- the **P_OWNER** privilege.

Only **root** (if the SUM privilege module is installed) can perform a **SHM_LOCK** or **SHM_UNLOCK** control command.

A process must have read permission to perform the **IPC_STAT** control command.

The details of this system call are discussed in the example program. If you need more information on the logic manipulations in this program, read "Using shmget". It goes into more detail than would be practical for every system call.

Example Program

Figure 10-9 is a menu-driven program. It allows all possible combinations of using the **shmctl** system call to be exercised.

From studying this program, you can observe the method of passing arguments and receiving return values. The user-written program requirements are pointed out.

This program begins (lines 5-9) by including the required header files as specified by the **shmctl**(2) entry in the *Operating System API Reference*. Note that in this program **errno** is declared as an external variable, and therefore, the **sys/errno.h** header file does not have to be included.

Variable and structure names have been chosen to be as close as possible to those in the synopsis for the system call. Their declarations are self explanatory. These names make the program more readable and are perfectly valid since they are local to the program.

The variables declared for this program and what they are used for are as follows:

uid	used to store the **IPC_SET** value for the user identification
gid	used to store the **IPC_SET** value for the group identification
mode	used to store the **IPC_SET** value for the operation permissions
rtrn	used to store the return integer value from the system call
shmid	used to store and pass the shared memory segment identifier to the system call

command	used to store the code for the desired control command so that subsequent processing can be performed on it
choice	used to determine which member for the IPC_SET control command is to be changed
shmid_ds	used to receive the specified shared memory segment identifier's data structure when an IPC_STAT control command is performed
buf	a pointer passed to the system call which locates the data structure in the user memory area where the IPC_STAT control command is to place its return values or where the IPC_SET command gets the values to set.

Note that the shmid_ds data structure in this program (line 16) uses the data structure of the same name located in the sys/shm.h header file as a template for its declaration.

The next important thing to observe is that although the buf pointer is declared to be a pointer to a data structure of the shmid_ds type, it must also be initialized to contain the address of the user memory area data structure (line 17).

Now that all of the required declarations have been explained for this program, this is how it works.

First, the program prompts for a valid shared memory segment identifier which is stored in the shmid variable (lines 18-20). This is required for every shmctl system call.

Then, the code for the desired control command must be entered (lines 21-29); it is stored in the command variable. The code is tested to determine the control command for subsequent processing.

If the IPC_STAT control command is selected (code 1), the system call is performed (lines 39, 40) and the status information returned is printed out (lines 41-71). Note that if the system call is unsuccessful (line 139), the status information of the last successful call is printed out. In addition, an error message is displayed and the errno variable is printed out (lines 141). If the system call is successful, a message indicates this along with the shared memory segment identifier used (lines 143-147).

If the IPC_SET control command is selected (code 2), the first thing done is to get the current status information for the shared memory identifier specified (lines 88-90). This is necessary because this example program provides for changing only one member at a time, and the system call changes all of them. Also, if an invalid value happened to be stored in the user memory area for one of these members, it would cause repetitive failures for this control command until corrected. The next thing the program does is to prompt for a code corresponding to the member to be changed (lines 91-96). This code is stored in the choice variable (line 97). Now, depending upon the member picked, the program prompts for the new value (lines 98-120). The value is placed in the appropriate member in the user memory area data structure, and the system call is made (lines 121-128). Depending upon success or failure, the program returns the same messages as for **IPC_STAT** above.

If the **IPC_RMID** control command (code 3) is selected, the system call is performed (lines 125-128), and the **shmid** along with its associated message queue and data structure are removed from the UNIX operating system. Note that the **buf** pointer is ignored in performing this control command and its value can be zero or NULL. Depending upon the success or failure, the program returns the same messages as for the other control commands.

If the **SHM_LOCK** control command (code 4) is selected, the system call is performed (lines 130,131). Depending upon the success or failure, the program returns the same messages as for the other control commands.

If the **SHM_UNLOCK** control command (code 5) is selected, the system call is performed (lines 133-135). Depending upon the success or failure, the program returns the same messages as for the other control commands.

The example program for the **shmctl** system call follows. We suggest that you name the source program file **shmctl.c** and the executable file **shmctl**.

Figure 10-9: shmctl **System Call Example**

```
1    /*This is a program to illustrate
2    **the shared memory control, shmctl(),
3    **system call capabilities.
4    */
5    /*Include necessary header files.*/
6    #include    <stdio.h>
7    #include    <sys/types.h>
8    #include    <sys/ipc.h>
9    #include    <sys/shm.h>
10   /*Start of main C language program*/
11   main()
12   {
13       extern int errno;
14       int uid, gid, mode;
15       int rtrn, shmid, command, choice;
16       struct shmid_ds shmid_ds, *buf;
17       buf = &shmid_ds;
```

(continued on next page)

Interprocess Communication

Figure 10-9: shmctl **System Call Example** (continued)

```
18          /*Get the shmid, and command.*/
19          printf("Enter the shmid = ");
20          scanf("%d", &shmid);
21          printf("\nEnter the number for\n");
22          printf("the desired command:\n");

23          printf("IPC_STAT    =  1\n");
24          printf("IPC_SET     =  2\n");
25          printf("IPC_RMID    =  3\n");
26          printf("SHM_LOCK    =  4\n");
27          printf("SHM_UNLOCK  =  5\n");
28          printf("Entry       =  ");
29          scanf("%d", &command);

30          /*Check the values.*/
31          printf ("\nshmid =%d, command = %d\n",
32              shmid, command);

33          switch (command)
34          {
35          case 1:     /*Use shmctl() to get
36                      the data structure for
37                      shmid in the shmid_ds area pointed
38                      to by buf and then print it out.*/
39              rtrn = shmctl(shmid, IPC_STAT,
40                  buf);
41              printf ("\nThe USER ID = %d\n",
42                  buf->shm_perm.uid);
43              printf ("The GROUP ID = %d\n",
44                  buf->shm_perm.gid);
45              printf ("The creator's ID = %d\n",
46                  buf->shm_perm.cuid);
47              printf ("The creator's group ID = %d\n",
48                  buf->shm_perm.cgid);
49              printf ("The operation permissions = 0%o\n",
50                  buf->shm_perm.mode);
51              printf ("The slot usage sequence\n");
52              printf ("number = 0%x\n",
53                  buf->shm_perm.seq);
54              printf ("The key= 0%x\n",
55                  buf->shm_perm.key);
56              printf ("The segment size = %d\n",
57                  buf->shm_segsz);
58              printf ("The pid of last shmop = %d\n",
59                  buf->shm_lpid);
60              printf ("The pid of creator = %d\n",
61                  buf->shm_cpid);
62              printf ("The current # attached = %d\n",
63                  buf->shm_nattch);
64              printf("The last shmat time = %ld\n",
```

(continued on next page)

Figure 10-9: `shmctl` **System Call Example** (continued)

```
65                  buf->shm_atime);
66            printf("The last shmdt time = %ld\n",
67                  buf->shm_dtime);
68            printf("The last change time = %ld\n",
69                  buf->shm_ctime);
70            break;

              /* Lines 71 - 85 deleted */

86       case 2:    /*Select and change the desired
87                       member(s) of the data structure.*/

88            /*Get the original data for this shmid
89                  data structure first.*/
90            rtrn = shmctl(shmid, IPC_STAT, buf);

91            printf("\nEnter the number for the\n");
92            printf("member to be changed:\n");
93            printf("shm_perm.uid   = 1\n");
94            printf("shm_perm.gid   = 2\n");
95            printf("shm_perm.mode  = 3\n");
96            printf("Entry          = ");
97            scanf("%d", &choice);

98            switch(choice){
99            case 1:
100               printf("\nEnter USER ID = ");
101               scanf ("%d", &uid);
102               buf->shm_perm.uid = uid;
103               printf("\nUSER ID = %d\n",
104                    buf->shm_perm.uid);
105               break;

106           case 2:
107               printf("\nEnter GROUP ID = ");
108               scanf("%d", &gid);
109               buf->shm_perm.gid = gid;
110               printf("\nGROUP ID = %d\n",
111                    buf->shm_perm.gid);
112               break;

113           case 3:
114               printf("\nEnter MODE in octal = ");
115               scanf("%o", &mode);
116               buf->shm_perm.mode = mode;
117               printf("\nMODE = 0%o\n",
118                    buf->shm_perm.mode);
119               break;
120           }
121           /*Do the change.*/
122           rtrn = shmctl(shmid, IPC_SET,
123               buf);
124           break;
```

(continued on next page)

Figure 10-9: `shmctl` **System Call Example** (continued)

```
125         case 3:    /*Remove the shmid along with its
126                       associated
127                       data structure.*/
128            rtrn = shmctl(shmid, IPC_RMID, (struct shmid_ds *) NULL);
129            break;
130         case 4: /*Lock the shared memory segment*/
131            rtrn = shmctl(shmid, SHM_LOCK, (struct shmid_ds *) NULL);
132            break;
133         case 5: /*Unlock the shared memory
134                       segment.*/
135            rtrn = shmctl(shmid, SHM_UNLOCK, (struct shmid_ds *) NULL);
136            break;
137         }
138         /*Perform the following if the call is unsuccessful.*/
139         if(rtrn == -1)
140         {
41            printf ("\nThe shmctl call failed, error number = %d\n", errno);
142         }
143         /*Return the shmid upon successful completion.*/
144         else
145            printf ("\nShmctl was successful for shmid = %d\n",
146                 shmid);
147         exit (0);
148      }
```

Operations for Shared Memory

This section describes how to use the **shmat** and **shmdt** system calls. The accompanying program illustrates their use.

Using Shared Memory Operations: shmat and shmdt

The synopsis found in the **shmop**(2) entry in the *Operating System API Reference* is as follows:

```
#include <sys/types.h>
#include <sys/ipc.h>
#include <sys/shm.h>

void *shmat (shmid, shmaddr, shmflg)
int shmid;
void *shmaddr;
int shmflg;

int shmdt (shmaddr)
void *shmaddr;
```

Attaching a Shared Memory Segment

The **shmat** system call requires three arguments to be passed to it. It returns a character pointer value. Upon successful completion, this value will be the address in memory where the process is attached to the shared memory segment and when unsuccessful the value will be **-1**.

The **shmid** argument must be a valid, non-negative, integer value. In other words, it must have already been created by using the **shmget** system call.

The **shmaddr** argument can be zero or user supplied when passed to the **shmat** system call. If it is zero, the UNIX operating system picks the address where the shared memory segment will be attached. If it is user supplied, the address must be a valid address that the UNIX operating system would pick.

The following illustrates some typical address ranges.

> 0xc00c0000
> 0xc00e0000
> 0xc0100000
> 0xc0120000

Note that these addresses are in chunks of 20,000 hexadecimal. It would be wise to let the operating system pick addresses so as to improve portability.

The **shmflg** argument is used to pass the **SHM_RND** and **SHM_RDONLY** flags to the **shmat** system call.

Detaching Shared Memory Segments

The **shmdt** system call requires one argument to be passed to it. It returns an integer value which will be zero for successful completion or **-1** otherwise.

Interprocess Communication

Further details on **shmat** and **shmdt** are discussed in the example program. If you need more information on the logic manipulations in this program, read "Using shmget". It goes into more detail than would be practical for every system call.

Example Program

Figure 10-10 is a menu-driven program. It allows all possible combinations of using the **shmat** and **shmdt** system calls to be exercised.

From studying this program, you can observe the method of passing arguments and receiving return values. The user-written program requirements are pointed out.

This program begins (lines 5-9) by including the required header files as specified by the **shmop**(2) entry in the *Operating System API Reference*. Note that in this program **errno** is declared as an external variable; therefore, the **sys/errno.h** header file does not have to be included.

Variable and structure names have been chosen to be as close as possible to those in the synopsis. Their declarations are self explanatory. These names make the program more readable and are perfectly valid since they are local to the program.

The variables declared for this program and what they are used for are as follows:

addr	used to store the address of the shared memory segment for the **shmat** and **shmdt** system calls and to receive the return value from the **shmat** system call
laddr	used to store the desired attach/detach address entered by the user
flags	used to store the codes of the **SHM_RND** or **SHM_RDONLY** flags for the **shmat** system call
i	used as a loop counter for attaching and detaching
attach	used to store the desired number of attach operations
shmid	used to store and pass the desired shared memory segment identifier
shmflg	used to pass the value of flags to the **shmat** system call
retrn	used to store the return values from the **shmdt** system call
detach	used to store the desired number of detach operations

This example program combines both the **shmat** and **shmdt** system calls. The program prompts for the number of attachments and enters a loop until they are done for the specified shared memory identifiers. Then, the program prompts for the number of detachments to be performed and enters a loop until they are done for the specified shared memory segment addresses.

shmat

The program prompts for the number of attachments to be performed, and the value is stored at the address of the attach variable (lines 19-23).

A loop is entered using the attach variable and the **i** counter (lines 23-72) to perform the specified number of attachments.

In this loop, the program prompts for a shared memory segment identifier (lines 26-29); it is stored in the **shmid** variable (line 30). Next, the program prompts for the address where the segment is to be attached (lines 32-36); it is stored in the **laddr** variable (line 37) and converted to a pointer (line 39). Then, the program prompts for the desired flags to be used for the attachment (lines 40-47), and the code representing the flags is stored in the **flags** variable (line 48). The **flags** variable is tested to determine the code to be stored for the **shmflg** variable used to pass them to the **shmat** system call (lines 49-60). The system call is executed (line 63). If successful, a message stating so is displayed along with the attach address (lines 68-70). If unsuccessful, a message stating so is displayed and the error code is displayed (line 65). The loop then continues until it finishes.

shmdt

After the attach loop completes, the program prompts for the number of detach operations to be performed (lines 73-77) and the value is stored in the detach variable (line 76).

A loop is entered using the detach variable and the **i** counter (lines 80-98) to perform the specified number of detachments.

In this loop, the program prompts for the address of the shared memory segment to be detached (lines 81-85); it is stored in the **laddr** variable (line 86) and converted to a pointer (line 88). Then, the **shmdt** system call is performed (line 89). If successful, a message stating so is displayed along with the address that the segment was detached from (lines 95, 96). If unsuccessful, the error number is displayed (line 92). The loop continues until it finishes.

The example program for the **shmop** system calls follows. We suggest that you name the source program file **shmop.c** and the executable file **shmop**.

Figure 10-10: shmop **System Call Example**

```
1       /*This is a program to illustrate
2       **the shared memory operations, shmop(),
3       **system call capabilities.
4       */
5       /*Include necessary header files.*/
6       #include    <stdio.h>
7       #include    <sys/types.h>
8       #include    <sys/ipc.h>
9       #include    <sys/shm.h>
10      /*Start of main C language program*/
11      main()
12      {
13          extern int errno;
14          void *addr;
15          long laddr;
16          int flags, i, attach;
17          int shmid, shmflg, retrn, detach;

18          /*Loop for attachments by this process.*/
19          printf("Enter the number of\n");
20          printf("attachments for this\n");
21          printf("process (1-4).\n");
22          printf("        Attachments = ");

23          scanf("%d", &attach);
24          printf("Number of attaches = %d\n", attach);

25          for(i = 1; i <= attach; i++) {
26              /*Enter the shared memory ID.*/
27              printf("\nEnter the shmid of\n");
28              printf("the shared memory segment to\n");
29              printf("be operated on = ");
30              scanf("%d", &shmid);
31              printf("\nshmid = %d\n", shmid);

32              /*Enter the value for shmaddr.*/
33              printf("\nEnter the value for\n");
34              printf("the shared memory address\n");
35              printf("in hexadecimal:\n");
36              printf("            Shmaddr = ");
37              scanf("%lx", &laddr);
38              addr = (void*) laddr;
39              printf("The desired address = 0x%lx\n", (long)addr);

40              /*Specify the desired flags.*/
41              printf("\nEnter the corresponding\n");
42              printf("number for the desired\n");
43              printf("flags:\n");
44              printf("SHM_RND                = 1\n");
45              printf("SHM_RDONLY             = 2\n");
46              printf("SHM_RND and SHM_RDONLY = 3\n");
47              printf("            Flags      = ");
```

(continued on next page)

Figure 10-10: shmop **System Call Example** (continued)

```
48              scanf("%d", &flags);
49              switch(flags)
50              {
51              case 1:
52                  shmflg = SHM_RND;
53                  break;
54              case 2:
55                  shmflg = SHM_RDONLY;
56                  break;
57              case 3:
58                  shmflg = SHM_RND | SHM_RDONLY;
59                  break;
60              }
61              printf("\nFlags = 0%o\n", shmflg);

62              /*Do the shmat system call.*/
63              addr = shmat(shmid, addr, shmflg);
64              if(addr == (char*) -1) {
65                  printf("\nShmat failed, error = %d\n", errno);
66              }
67              else {
68                  printf ("\nShmat was successful\n");
69                  printf("for shmid = %d\n", shmid);
70                  printf("The address = 0x%lx\n", (long)addr);
71              }
72          }
73      /*Loop for detachments by this process.*/
74      printf("Enter the number of\n");
75      printf("detachments for this\n");
76      printf("process (1-4).\n");
77      printf("        Detachments = ");

78      scanf("%d", &detach);
79      printf("Number of attaches = %d\n", detach);
80      for(i = 1; i <= detach; i++) {
81          /*Enter the value for shmaddr.*/
82          printf("\nEnter the value for\n");
83          printf("the shared memory address\n");
84          printf("in hexadecimal:\n");
85          printf("            Shmaddr = ");
86          scanf("%lx", &laddr);
87          addr = (void*) laddr;
88          printf("The desired address = 0x%lx\n", (long)addr);

89          /*Do the shmdt system call.*/
90          retrn = shmdt(addr);
91          if(retrn == -1)  {
92              printf("Error = %d\n", errno);
93          }
94          else {
```

(continued on next page)

Figure 10-10: `shmop` **System Call Example** (continued)

```
95                    printf ("\nShmdt was successful\n");
96                    printf("for address  = 0x%lx\n", (long)addr);

97            }
98        }
99    }
```

IPC Programming Example for liber

To illustrate the use of UNIX system programming tools in the development of an application, we are going to pretend we are engaged in the development of a computer system for a library. The system is known as **liber**. The early stages of system development, we assume, have already been completed; feasibility studies have been done, the preliminary design is described in the coming paragraphs. We are going to stop short of producing a complete detailed design and module specifications for our system. You will have to accept that these exist. In using portions of the system for examples of the topics covered in this chapter, we will work from these virtual specifications.

We make no claim as to the efficacy of this design. It is the way it is only in order to provide some passably realistic examples of UNIX system programming tools in use. It is not an application, but rather is code fragments only.

liber is a system for keeping track of the books in a library. The hardware consists of a single computer with terminals throughout the library. One terminal is used for adding new books to the data base. Others are used for checking out books and as electronic card catalogs.

The design of the system calls for it to be brought up at the beginning of the day and remain running while the library is in operation. Associated with each terminal is a program specific to the function of that terminal, each running as a separate UNIX process. The system has one master index that contains the unique identifier of each title in the library. When the system is running the index is mapped into the address space of each process. Semaphores are used to synchronize access to the index. In the pages that follow fragments of some of the system's programs are shown to illustrate the way they work together. The startup program performs the system initialization; opening the semaphores and the index file; mapping the index file into memory; and kicking off the other programs. The id numbers for the semaphores (**wrtsem**, and **rdsem**) are written to a file during initialization, this file is then read by all the subsidiary programs so that all use the same semaphores.

All the programs share access to the index file. They gain access to it with the following code:

```
/*
 * Gain access to the index file, map it in.
 * After mapping, free the file descriptor so
 * that it will be available for other uses --
 * the mapping will remain until the program
 * exits, or until the mapping is removed either
 * by munmap() or by mapping over top of this one
 * with another call to mmap().  Note the use of
 * the read/write open mode -- all programs but
 * "add-books" should open just for read-only.
 */
if ((index_fd = open("index.file", O_RDWR)) == -1)
{
        (void) fprintf(stderr, "index open failed: %d\n", errno);
        exit(1);
}
/*
 * Establish the mapping.  As with the call to
 * open(), all programs but "add-books" should
 * map with PROT_READ for read-only access.
 */
if ((int)(index = (INDEX *)mmap(0, sizeof (INDEX), PROT_READ|PROT_WRITE,
    MAP_SHARED, index_fd, 0) == -1)
{
        (void) fprintf(stderr, "shmat failed: %d\n", errno);
        exit(1);
}
(void) close(index_fd);
```

The preceding code fragment establishes a mapping to the index file in the address space of the program. Access to the addresses at which the file is mapped affect the file directly, no further file operations are required. For instance, if the access deposits data at the accessed address, then the file will be modified by operation. If the access examines data, then the file will be accessed. In either case, the portion of the file containing the information will be obtained or restored to secondary storage automatically by the system and transparently to the application.

Of the programs shown, **add-books** is the only one that alters the index. The semaphores are used to ensure that no other programs will try to read the index while **add-books** is altering it. The checkout program locks the file record for the book, so that each copy being checked out is recorded separately and the book cannot be checked out at two different checkout stations at the same time.

The program fragments do not provide any details on the structure of the index or the book records in the data base.

```
                    /* liber.h - header file for the
                     *            library system.
                     */
typedef ... INDEX;      /* data structure for book file index */
typedef struct {        /* type of records in book file */
     char title[30];
     char author[30];
     .
     .
     .
} BOOK;
int index_fd;
int wrtsem;
int rdsem;
INDEX *index;

int book_file;
BOOK book_buf;

/*     startup program  */

/*
 * 1. Open index file and map it in.
 * 2. Open two semaphores for providing exclusive write access to index.
 * 3. Stash id's for shared memory segment and semaphores in a file
 *    where they can be accessed by the programs.
 * 4. Start programs:  add-books, card-catalog, and checkout running
 *    on the various terminals throughout the library.
 */

#include    <stdio.h>
#include    <sys/types.h>
#include    <sys/ipc.h>
#include    <sys/shm.h>
#include    <sys/sem.h>
#include    "liber.h"

void exit();
extern int errno;

key_t key;
int shmid;
int wrtsem;
int rdsem;
FILE *ipc_file;

main()
{
     .
     .
     .
```

(continued on next page)

Interprocess Communication

```
    /*
     * Open index file and map it.
     */

    /* See previous example */

    /*
     * Get the read/write semaphores.
     */
    if ((wrtsem = semget(key, 1, IPC_CREAT | 0666)) == -1)
    {
        (void) fprintf(stderr, "startup: semget failed: errno=%d\n", errno);
        exit(1);
    }

    if ((rdsem = semget(key, 1, IPC_CREAT | 0666)) == -1)
    {
        (void) fprintf(stderr, "startup: semget failed: errno=%d\n", errno);
        exit(1);
    }
    (void) fprintf(ipc_file, "%d\n%d\n", wrtsem, rdsem);

    /*
     * Start the add-books program running on the terminal in the
     * basement.  Start the checkout and card-catalog programs
     * running on the various other terminals throughout the library.
     */
    .
    .
    .
}

/*    card-catalog program*/

/*
 * 1. Read screen for author and title.
 * 2. Use semaphores to prevent reading index while it is being written.
 * 3. Use index to get position of book record in book file.
 * 4. Print book record on screen or indicate book was not found.
 * 5. Go to 1.
 */

#include        <stdio.h>
#include        <sys/types.h>
#include        <sys/ipc.h>
#include        <sys/sem.h>
#include     <fcntl.h>
#include     "liber.h"

void exit();
extern int errno;
```

(continued on next page)

```
struct sembuf sop[1];

main() {
     .
     .
     .

     while (1)
     {
          /*
           * Read author/title/subject information from screen.
           */

          /*
           * Wait for write semaphore to reach 0 (index not being written).
           */
          sop[0].sem_op = 1;
          if (semop(wrtsem, sop, 1) == -1)
          {
                    (void) fprintf(stderr, "semop failed: %d\n", errno);
                    exit(1);
          }
          /*
           * Increment read semaphore so potential writer will wait
           * for us to finish reading the index.
           */
          sop[0].sem_op = 0;
          if (semop(rdsem, sop, 1) == -1)
          {
                    (void) fprintf(stderr, "semop failed: %d\n", errno);
                    exit(1);
          }

          /* Use index to find file pointer(s) for book(s) */

          /* Decrement read semaphore */
          sop[0].sem_op = -1;
          if (semop(rdsem, sop, 1) == -1)
          {
                    (void) fprintf(stderr, "semop failed: %d\n", errno);
                    exit(1);
          }

          /*
           * Now we use the file pointers found in the index to
           * read the book file.  Then we print the information
           * on the book(s) to the screen.
           */

          /*
           * Note design alternatives for this portion of the
```

(continued on next page)

Interprocess Communication

```
                    * the code: the book file could be accessed by
                    * lseek()s to the portion of the file containing
                    * the record, and then read() could be used to
                    * obtain the file information.  Alternatively, the
                    * entire book file could be mapped into memory, and the
                    * the record accessed directly without further
                    * file operations, or the area of the file containing
                    * the book record could just be mapped and then unmapped
                    * when the access is complete.
                    */
                    .
                    .
                    .

        } /* while */
}
/*      checkout program */

/*
 * 1. Read screen for Dewey Decimal number of book to be checked out.
 * 2. Use semaphores to prevent reading index while it is being written.
 * 3. Use index to get position of book record in book file.
 * 4. If book not found print message on screen, otherwise lock
 *    book record and read.
 * 5. If book already checked out print message on screen, otherwise
 *    mark record "checked out" and write back to book file.
 * 6. Unlock book record.
 * 7. Go to 1.
 */

#include         <stdio.h>
#include         <sys/types.h>
#include         <sys/ipc.h>
#include         <sys/sem.h>
#include     <fcntl.h>
#include     "liber.h"

void exit();
long lseek();
extern int errno;
struct flock flk;
struct sembuf sop[1];
long bookpos;

main()
{
        .
        .
        .
        while (1)
        {
```

(continued on next page)

IPC Programming Example for liber   **10-85**

```
/*
 * Read Dewey Decimal number from screen.
 */

/*
 * Wait for write semaphore to reach 0 (index not being written).
 */
sop[0].sem_flg = 0;
sop[0].sem_op = 0;
if (semop(wrtsem, sop, 1) == -1)
{
        (void) fprintf(stderr, "semop failed: %d\n", errno);
        exit(1);
}
/*
 * Increment read semaphore so potential writer will wait
 * for us to finish reading the index.
 */
sop[0].sem_op = 1;
if (semop(rdsem, sop, 1) == -1)
{
        (void) fprintf(stderr, "semop failed: %d\n", errno);
        exit(1);
}

/*
 * Now we can use the index to find the book's record position.
 * Assign this value to "bookpos".
 */

/* Decrement read semaphore */
sop[0].sem_op = -1;
if (semop(rdsem, sop, 1) == -1)
{
        (void) fprintf(stderr, "semop failed: %d\n", errno);
        exit(1);
}

/*
 * Lock the book's record in book file, read the record.
 * Here again we have the design option of deciding to
 * access and update the database through the use of
 * seeks, read()s and write()s; or file mapping can
 * be used to access the file.  File mapping has the
 * disadvantage that it does not interact well with
 * enforcement-mode locking, although semaphores
 * could be used as an alternative synchronization
 * mechanism to file locking.  File mapping would have
 * potential efficiency advantages, eliminating the need
 * for repetitive file access operations and attendant
 * data copying.  For this example, however, we choose
```

(continued on next page)

Interprocess Communication

```
                    * not to use mapping to demonstrate the use of other
                    * system facilities.
                    */
                   flk.l_type = F_WRLCK;
                   flk.l_whence = 0;
                   flk.l_start = bookpos;
                   flk.l_len = sizeof(BOOK);
                   if (fcntl(book_file, F_SETLKW, &flk) == -1)

                   {
                            (void) fprintf(stderr, "trouble locking: %d\n", errno);
                            exit(1);
                   }
                   if (lseek(book_file, bookpos, 0) == -1)
                   {
                            (Error processing for lseek);
                   }
                   if (read(book_file, &book_buf, sizeof(BOOK)) == -1)
                   {
                            (Error processing for read);
                   }

                   /*
                    * If the book is checked out inform the client, otherwise
                    * mark the book's record as checked out and write it
                    * back into the book file.
                    */

                   /* Unlock the book's record in book file. */
                   flk.l_type = F_UNLCK;
                   if (fcntl(book_file, F_SETLK, &flk) == -1)
                   {
                            (void) fprintf(stderr, "trouble unlocking: %d\n", errno);
                            exit(1);
                   }
        } /* while */
}

/*    add-books program*/

/*
 * 1. Read a new book entry from screen.
 * 2. Insert book in book file.
 * 3. Use semaphore "wrtsem" to block new readers.
 * 4. Wait for semaphore "rdsem" to reach 0.
 * 5. Insert book into index.
 * 6. Decrement wrtsem.
 * 7. Go to 1.
 */

#include <stdio.h>
```

(continued on next page)

```
#include    <sys/types.h>
#include    <sys/ipc.h>
#include    <sys/sem.h>
#include    "liber.h"

void exit();
extern int errno;
struct sembuf sop[1];
BOOK bookbuf;

main()
{
    .
    .
    .
    for (;;)
    {
        /*
         * Read information on new book from screen.
         */

        addscr(&bookbuf);

        /* write new record at the end of the bookfile.
         * Code not shown, but
         * addscr() returns a 1 if title information has
         * been entered, 0 if not.
         */

        /*
         * Increment write semaphore, blocking new readers from
         * accessing the index.
         */
        sop[0].sem_flg = 0;
        sop[0].sem_op = 1;
        if (semop(wrtsem, sop, 1) == -1)
        {
                (void) fprintf(stderr, "semop failed: %d\n", errno);
                exit(1);
        }

        /*
         * Wait for read semaphore to reach 0 (all readers to finish
         * using the index).
         */
        sop[0].sem_op = 0;
        if (semop(rdsem, sop, 1) == -1)
        {
                (void) fprintf(stderr, "semop failed: %d\n", errno);
                exit(1);
```

(continued on next page)

Interprocess Communication

```
        }
        /*
         * Now that we have exclusive access to the index we
         * insert our new book with its file pointer.
         */

        /* Decrement write semaphore, permitting readers to read index. */
        sop[0].sem_op = -1;
        if (semop(wrtsem, sop, 1) == -1)
        {
                (void) fprintf(stderr, "semop failed: %d\n", errno);
                exit(1);
        }
    } /* for */
    .
    .
    .
}
```

The example following, **addscr**, illustrates two significant points about **curses** screens:

1. Information read in from a **curses** window can be stored in fields that are part of a structure defined in the header file for the application.

2. The address of the structure can be passed from another function where the record is processed.

```
                    /*  addscr is called from add-books.
                     *  The user is prompted for title
                     *  information.
                     */
#include <curses.h>

WINDOW *cmdwin;

addscr(bb)
struct BOOK *bb;
{
    int c;

    initscr();
    nonl();
    noecho();
    cbreak();

    cmdwin = newwin(6, 40, 3, 20);
    mvprintw(0, 0, "This screen is for adding titles to the data base");
    mvprintw(1, 0, "Enter  a  to add;  q  to quit: ");
    refresh();
    for (;;)
    {
        refresh();
        c = getch();
        switch (c) {
          case 'a':
                    werase(cmdwin);
                    box(cmdwin, '|', '-');
                    mvwprintw(cmdwin, 1, 1, "Enter title: ");
                    wmove(cmdwin, 2, 1);
                    echo();
                    wrefresh(cmdwin);
                    wgetstr(cmdwin, bb->title);
                    noecho();
                    werase(cmdwin);
                    box(cmdwin, '|', '-');
                    mvwprintw(cmdwin, 1, 1, "Enter author: ");
                    wmove(cmdwin, 2, 1);
                    echo();
                    wrefresh(cmdwin);
                    wgetstr(cmdwin, bb->author);
                    noecho();
                    werase(cmdwin);
                    wrefresh(cmdwin);
                    endwin();
                    return(1);
            case 'q':
                    erase();
                    endwin();
```

(continued on next page)

```
                    return(0);
            }
    }
}

#
# Makefile for liber library system
#

CC = cc
CFLAGS = -O
all: startup add-books checkout card-catalog

startup: liber.h startup.c
      $(CC) $(CFLAGS) -o startup startup.c

add-books: add-books.o addscr.o
      $(CC) $(CFLAGS) -o add-books add-books.o addscr.o

add-books.o: liber.h

checkout: liber.h checkout.c
      $(CC) $(CFLAGS) -o checkout checkout.c

card-catalog: liber.h card-catalog.c
      $(CC) $(CFLAGS) -o card-catalog card-catalog.c
```

11 STREAMS Polling and Multiplexing

Introduction

This chapter describes how STREAMS allows user processes to monitor, control, and poll Streams to allow an effective utilization of system resources. The synchronous polling mechanism and asynchronous event notification within STREAMS is discussed. STREAMS signal handling between modules and/or drivers and user processes is also discussed.

The remainder of this chapter is devoted to STREAMS input/output multiplexing. It defines a STREAMS multiplexor, and describes multiplexing drivers. A discussion of how STREAMS multiplexing configurations are created, is included. Code examples are included to illustrate using both the polling and multiplexing mechanisms.

STREAMS Input/Output Polling

This section describes the synchronous polling mechanism and asynchronous event notification within STREAMS.

User processes can efficiently monitor and control multiple Streams with two system calls: **poll** and the **I_SETSIG ioctl** command. These calls allow a user process to detect events that occur at the Stream head on one or more Streams, including receipt of data or messages on the read queue and cessation of flow control.

To monitor Streams with **poll**, a user process issues that system call and specifies the Streams to be monitored, the events to look for, and the amount of time to wait for an event. The **poll** system call blocks the process until the time expires or until an event occurs. If an event occurs, it returns the type of event and the Stream on which the event occurred.

Instead of waiting for an event to occur, a user process may want to monitor one or more Streams while processing other data. It can do so by issuing the **I_SETSIG ioctl** command, specifying one or more Streams and events [as with **poll**]. This **ioctl** does not block the process and force the user process to wait for the event but returns immediately and issues a signal when an event occurs. The process must specify a signal handler to catch the resultant **SIGPOLL** signal.

If any selected event occurs on any of the selected Streams, STREAMS causes the **SIGPOLL** catching function to be executed in all associated requesting processes. However, the process(es) will not know which event occurred, nor on what Stream the event occurred. A process that issues the **I_SETSIG** can get more detailed information by issuing a **poll** after it detects the event.

Synchronous Input/Output

The **poll** system call provides a mechanism to identify those Streams over which a user can send or receive data. For each Stream of interest, users can specify one or more events about which they should be notified. The types of events that can be polled are as follows:

POLLIN   A message other than an **M_PCPROTO** is at the front of the Stream head read queue. This event is maintained for compatibility with the previous releases of the UNIX System V.

POLLRDNORM	A normal (nonpriority) message is at the front of the Stream head read queue.
POLLRDBAND	A priority message (band > 0) is at the front of the Stream head queue.
POLLPRI	A high-priority message (M_PCPROTO) is at the front of the Stream head read queue.
POLLOUT	The normal priority band of the queue is writable (not flow controlled).
POLLWRNORM	The same as POLLOUT.
POLLWRBAND	A priority band greater than 0 of a queue downstream exists and is writable.
POLLMSG	An M_SIG or M_PCSIG message containing the SIG-POLL signal has reached the front of the Stream head read queue.

Some of the events may not be applicable to all file types. For example, it is not expected that the POLLPRI event will be generated when polling a regular file. POLLIN, POLLRDNORM, POLLRDBAND, and POLLPRI are set even if the message is of zero length.

The poll system call examines each file descriptor for the requested events and, on return, shows which events have occurred for each file descriptor. If no event has occurred on any polled file descriptor, poll blocks until a requested event or timeout occurs. poll takes the following arguments:

- An array of file descriptors and events to be polled.

- The number of file descriptors to be polled.

- The number of milliseconds poll should wait for an event if no events are pending (-1 specifies wait forever).

The following example shows the use of poll. Two separate minor devices of the communications driver are opened, thereby establishing two separate Streams to the driver. The pollfd entry is initialized for each device. Each Stream is polled for incoming data. If data arrives on either Stream, it is read and then written back to the other Stream.

```
#include <fcntl.h>
#include <poll.h>

#define NPOLL 2        /* number of file descriptors to poll */

main()
{
    struct pollfd pollfds[NPOLL];
    char buf[1024];
    int count, i;

    if ((pollfds[0].fd = open("/dev/comm/01", O_RDWR|O_NDELAY)) < 0) {
        perror("open failed for /dev/comm/01");
        exit(1);
    }

    if ((pollfds[1].fd = open("/dev/comm/02", O_RDWR|O_NDELAY)) < 0) {
        perror("open failed for /dev/comm/02");
        exit(2);
    }
```

The variable **pollfds** is declared as an array of the **pollfd** structure that is defined in **<poll.h>** and has the following format:

```
struct pollfd {
    int     fd;        /* file descriptor */
    short   events;    /* requested events */
    short   revents;   /* returned events */
}
```

For each entry in the array, **fd** specifies the file descriptor to be polled and **events** is a bitmask that contains the bitwise inclusive OR of events to be polled on that file descriptor. On return, the **revents** bitmask indicates which of the requested events has occurred.

The example continues to process incoming data as follows:

```
        pollfds[0].events = POLLIN;    /* set events to poll */
        pollfds[1].events = POLLIN;    /* for incoming data */
        pollfds[0].revents = 0;
        pollfds[1].revents = 0;


    while (1) {
        /* poll and use -1 timeout (infinite) */
        if (poll(pollfds, NPOLL, -1) < 0) {
            perror("poll failed");
            exit(3);
        }
        for (i = 0; i < NPOLL; i++) {
            switch (pollfds[i].revents) {

            case 0:                          /* no events */
                break;

            case POLLIN:
                /* echo incoming data on "other" Stream */
                while ((count = read(pollfds[i].fd, buf, 1024)) > 0)
                    /*
                     * the write loses data if flow control
                     * prevents the transmit at this time.
                     */
                    if (write(pollfds[(i+1)%2].fd, buf, count) != count)
                            fprintf(stderr,"writer lost data\n");
                pollfds[i].revents = 0;
                break;

            default:                         /* default error case */
                perror("error event");
                exit(4);
            }
        }
    }
}
```

The user specifies the polled events by setting the **events** field of the **pollfd**
structure to **POLLIN**. This requested event directs **poll** to notify the user of any
incoming data on each Stream. The bulk of the example is an infinite loop, where
each iteration polls both Streams for incoming data.

The second argument to the **poll** system call specifies the number of entries in the
pollfds array (2 in this example). The third argument is a timeout value indicating the number of milliseconds **poll** should wait for an event if none occurs. On a
system where millisecond accuracy is not available, *timeout* is rounded up to the
nearest value available on that system. If the value of *timeout* is **0**, **poll** returns
immediately. Here, the value of *timeout* is **-1**, specifying that **poll** should block
until a requested event occurs or until the call is interrupted.

If the **poll** call succeeds, the program looks at each entry in the **pollfds** array. If **revents** is set to **0**, no event has occurred on that file descriptor. If **revents** is set to **POLLIN**, incoming data is available. In this case, all data is read from the polled minor device and written to the other minor device.

If **revents** is set to a value other than **0** or **POLLIN**, an error event must have occurred on that Stream, because **POLLIN** was the only requested event. The following are **poll** error events:

POLLERR	A fatal error has occurred in some module or driver on the Stream associated with the specified file descriptor. Further system calls will fail.
POLLHUP	A hangup condition exists on the Stream associated with the specified file descriptor. This event and **POLLOUT** are mutually exclusive; a Stream cannot be writable if a hangup has occurred.
POLLNVAL	The specified file descriptor is not valid

These events may not be polled by the user, but will be reported in **revents** whenever they occur. As such, they are only valid in the **revents** bitmask.

The example attempts to process incoming data as quickly as possible. However, when writing data to a Stream, the **write** call may block if the Stream is exerting flow control. To prevent the process from blocking, the minor devices of the communications driver were opened with the **O_NDELAY** (or **O_NONBLOCK**, see note) flag set. The **write** will not be able to send all the data if flow control is exerted and **O_NDELAY** (**O_NONBLOCK**) is set. This can occur if the communications driver is unable to keep up with the user's rate of data transmission. If the Stream becomes full, the number of bytes the **write** sends will be less than the requested **count**. For simplicity, the example ignores the data if the Stream becomes full, and a warning is printed to **stderr**.

 NOTE For conformance with the IEEE operating system interface standard, POSIX, it is recommended that new applications use the **O_NONBLOCK** flag, which behaves the same as **O_NDELAY** unless otherwise noted.

This program continues until an error occurs on a Stream, or until the process is interrupted.

Asynchronous Input/Output

The **poll** system call enables a user to monitor multiple Streams in a synchronous fashion. The **poll** call normally blocks until an event occurs on any of the polled file descriptors. In some applications, however, it is desirable to process incoming data asynchronously. For example, an application may want to do some local processing and be interrupted when a pending event occurs. Some time-critical applications cannot afford to block, but must have immediate indication of success or failure.

The **I_SETSIG ioctl** call [see **streamio**(7)] is used to request that a **SIGPOLL** signal be sent to a user process when a specific event occurs. Listed below are events for the **ioctl I_SETSIG**. These are similar to those described for **poll**.

S_INPUT	A message other than an **M_PCPROTO** is at the front of the Stream head read queue. This event is maintained for compatibility with the previous releases of the UNIX System V.
S_RDNORM	A normal (nonpriority) message is at the front of the Stream head read queue.
S_RDBAND	A priority message (band > 0) is at the front of the Stream head read queue.
S_HIPRI	A high-priority message (**M_PCPROTO**) is present at the front of the Stream head read queue.
S_OUTPUT	A write queue for normal data (priority band = 0) is no longer full (not flow controlled). This notifies a user that there is room on the queue for sending or writing normal data downstream.
S_WRNORM	The same as **S_OUTPUT**.
S_WRBAND	A priority band greater than **0** of a queue downstream exists and is writable. This notifies a user that there is room on the queue for sending or writing priority data downstream.
S_MSG	An **M_SIG** or **M_PCSIG** message containing the **SIGPOLL** flag has reached the front of Stream head read queue.
S_ERROR	An **M_ERROR** message reaches the Stream head.
S_HANGUP	An **M_HANGUP** message reaches the Stream head.

| S_BANDURG | When used with **S_RDBAND**, **SIGURG** is generated instead **SIGPOLL** when a priority message reaches the front of the Stream head read queue. |

S_INPUT, **S_RDNORM**, **S_RDBAND**, and **S_HIPRI** are set even if the message is of zero length. A user process may choose to handle only high-priority messages by setting the *arg* to **S_HIPRI**.

Signals

STREAMS allows modules and drivers to cause a signal to be sent to user process(es) through an **M_SIG** or **M_PCSIG** message. The first byte of the message specifies the signal for the Stream head to generate. If the signal is not **SIGPOLL** [see **signal**(2)], the signal is sent to the process group associated with the Stream. If the signal is **SIGPOLL**, the signal is only sent to processes that have registered for the signal by using the **I_SETSIG ioctl**.

An **M_SIG** message can be used by modules or drivers that want to insert an explicit inband signal into a message Stream. For example, this message can be sent to the user process immediately before a particular service interface message to gain the immediate attention of the user process. When the **M_SIG** message reaches the head of the Stream head read queue, a signal is generated and the **M_SIG** message is removed. This leaves the service interface message as the next message to be processed by the user. Use of the **M_SIG** message is typically defined as part of the service interface of the driver or module.

Extended Signals

To enable a process to obtain the band and event associated with **SIGPOLL** more readily, STREAMS supports extended signals. For the given events, a special code is defined in **<siginfo.h>** that describes the reason **SIGPOLL** was generated. Table 11-1 describes the data available in the **siginfo_t** structure passed to the signal handler.

Table 11-1: `siginfo_t` **Data Available to the Signal Handler**

Event	si_signo	si_code	si_band	si_errno
S_INPUT	SIGPOLL	POLL_IN	band readable	unused
S_OUTPUT	SIGPOLL	POLL_OUT	band writable	unused
S_MSG	SIGPOLL	POLL_MSG	band signaled	unused
S_ERROR	SIGPOLL	POLL_ERR	unused	Stream error
S_HANGUP	SIGPOLL	POLL_HUP	unused	unused
S_HIPRI	SIGPOLL	POLL_PRI	unused	unused

STREAMS Input/Output Multiplexing

This section describes how STREAMS multiplexing configurations are created and also discusses multiplexing drivers.

Earlier, Streams were described as linear connections of modules, where each invocation of a module is connected to at most one upstream module and one downstream module. While this configuration is suitable for many applications, others require the ability to multiplex Streams in a variety of configurations. Typical examples are terminal window facilities, and internetworking protocols (which might route data over several subnetworks).

Figure 11-1 shows an example of a multiplexor that multiplexes data from several upper Streams over a single lower Stream. An upper Stream is one that is upstream from a multiplexor, and a lower Stream is one that is downstream from a multiplexor. A terminal windowing facility might be implemented in this fashion, where each upper Stream is associated with a separate window.

Figure 11-1: Many-to-One Multiplexor

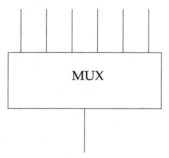

Figure 11-2 shows a second type of multiplexor that might route data from a single upper Stream to one of several lower Streams. An internetworking protocol could take this form, where each lower Stream links the protocol to a different physical network.

Figure 11-2: One-to-Many Multiplexor

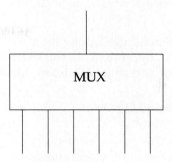

Figure 11-3 shows a third type of multiplexor that might route data from one of many upper Streams to one of many lower Streams.

Figure 11-3: Many-to-Many Multiplexor

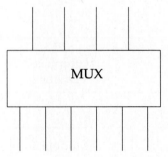

The STREAMS mechanism supports the multiplexing of Streams through special pseudo-device drivers. Using a linking facility, users can dynamically build, maintain, and dismantle multiplexed Stream configurations. Simple configurations like the ones shown in Figure 11-1 through Figure 11-3 can be further combined to form complex, multilevel, multiplexed Stream configurations.

STREAMS multiplexing configurations are created in the kernel by interconnecting multiple Streams. Conceptually, there are two kinds of multiplexors: upper and lower multiplexors. Lower multiplexors have multiple lower Streams between device drivers and the multiplexor, and upper multiplexors have multiple upper Streams between user processes and the multiplexor.

Figure 11-4 is an example of the multiplexor configuration that typically occurs where internetworking functions are included in the system. This configuration contains three hardware device drivers. The IP (Internet Protocol) is a multiplexor.

The IP multiplexor switches messages among the lower Streams or sends them upstream to user processes in the system. In this example, the multiplexor expects to see the same interface downstream to Module 1, Module 2, and Driver 3.

Figure 11-4: Internet Multiplexing Stream

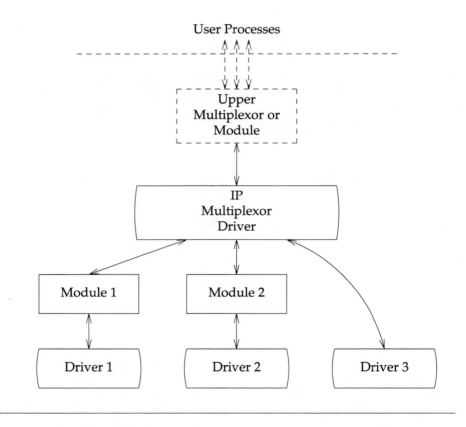

Figure 11-4 depicts the IP multiplexor as part of a larger configuration. The multiplexor configuration, shown in the dashed rectangle, generally has an upper multiplexor and additional modules. Multiplexors can also be cascaded below the IP multiplexor driver if the device drivers are replaced by multiplexor drivers.

Figure 11-5 shows a multiplexor configuration where the multiplexor (or multi-plexing driver) routes messages between the lower Stream and one upper Stream. This Stream performs X.25 multiplexing to multiple independent Switched Virtual Circuit (SVC) and Permanent Virtual Circuit (PVC) user processes. Upper multi-plexors are a specific application of standard STREAMS facilities that support multiple minor devices in a device driver. This figure also shows that more complex configurations can be built by having one or more multiplexed drivers below and multiple modules above an upper multiplexor.

Developers can choose either upper or lower multiplexing, or both, when designing their applications. For example, a window multiplexor would have a similar configuration to the X.25 configuration of Figure 11-5, with a window driver replacing the Packet Layer, a tty driver replacing the driver XYZ, and the child processes of the terminal process replacing the user processes. Although the X.25 and window multiplexing Streams have similar configurations, their multiplexor drivers would differ significantly. The IP multiplexor in Figure 11-4 has a different configuration than the X.25 multiplexor, and the driver would implement its own set of processing and routing requirements in each configuration.

Figure 11-5: X.25 Multiplexing Stream

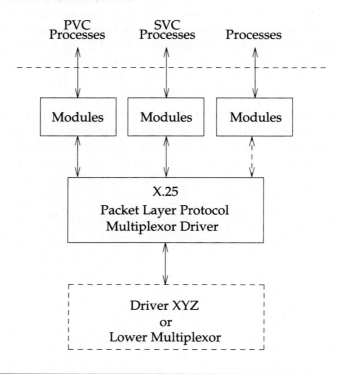

In addition to upper and lower multiplexors, you can create more complex configurations by connecting Streams containing multiplexors to other multiplexor drivers. With such a diversity of needs for multiplexors, it is not possible to provide general purpose multiplexor drivers. Rather, STREAMS provides a general purpose multiplexing facility, which allows users to set up the intermodule/driver plumbing to create multiplexor configurations of generally unlimited interconnection.

STREAMS Multiplexors

A STREAMS multiplexor is a driver with multiple Streams connected to it. The primary function of the multiplexing driver is to switch messages among the connected Streams. Multiplexor configurations are created at user level by system calls.

STREAMS-related system calls set up the "plumbing," or Stream interconnections, for multiplexing drivers. The subset of these calls that allows a user to connect (and disconnect) Streams below a driver is referred to as the multiplexing facility. This type of connection is referred to as a 1-to-M, or lower, multiplexor configuration. This configuration must always contain a multiplexing driver, which is recognized by STREAMS as having special characteristics.

Multiple Streams can be connected above a driver by **open** calls. There is no difference between the connections to these drivers, only the functions performed by the driver are different. In the multiplexing case, the driver routes data between multiple Streams. In the device driver case, the driver routes data between user processes and associated physical ports. Multiplexing with Streams connected above is referred to as an N-to-1, or upper, multiplexor. STREAMS does not provide any facilities beyond **open** and **close** to connect or disconnect upper Streams for multiplexing purposes.

From the driver's perspective, upper and lower configurations differ only in how they are initially connected to the driver. The implementation requirements are the same: route the data and handle flow control. All multiplexor drivers require special developer-provided software to perform the multiplexing data routing and to handle flow control. STREAMS does not directly support flow control among multiplexed Streams.

M-to-N multiplexing configurations are implemented by using both of the above mechanisms in a driver.

The multiple Streams that represent minor devices are actually distinct Streams in which the driver keeps track of each Stream attached to it. The STREAMS subsystem does not recognize any relationship between the Streams. The same is true for STREAMS multiplexors of any configuration. The multiplexed Streams are distinct and the driver must be implemented to do most of the work.

In addition to upper and lower multiplexors, more complex configurations can be created by connecting Streams containing multiplexors to other multiplexor drivers. With such a diversity of needs for multiplexors, it is not possible to provide general-purpose multiplexor drivers. Rather, STREAMS provides a general purpose multiplexing facility that allows users to set up the intermodule/driver plumbing to create multiplexor configurations of generally unlimited interconnection.

Building a Multiplexor

This section builds a protocol multiplexor with the multiplexing configuration shown in Figure 11-6. To free users from the need to know about the underlying protocol structure, a user-level daemon process is built to maintain the multiplexing configuration. Users can then access the transport protocol directly by opening the transport protocol (TP) driver device node.

An internetworking protocol driver (IP) routes data from a single upper Stream to one of two lower Streams. This driver supports two STREAMS connections beneath it. These connections are to two distinct networks; one for the IEEE 802.3 standard with the 802.3 driver, and the other to the IEEE 802.4 standard with the 802.4 driver. The TP driver multiplexes upper Streams over a single Stream to the IP driver.

Figure 11-6: Protocol Multiplexor

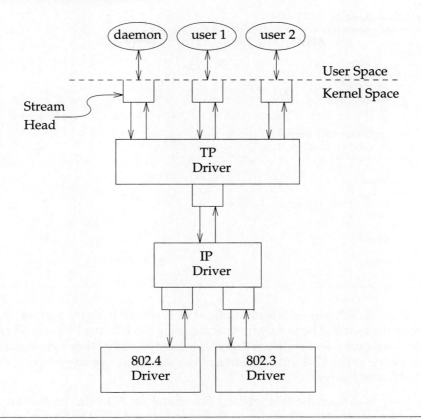

The following example shows how this daemon process sets up the protocol multiplexor. The necessary declarations and initialization for the daemon program are as follows:

```
#include <fcntl.h>
#include <stropts.h>

main()
{
    int fd_802_4,
        fd_802_3,
        fd_ip,
        fd_tp;

    /* daemon-ize this process */

    switch (fork()) {
    case 0:
        break;
    case -1:
        perror("fork failed");
        exit(2);
    default:
        exit(0);
    }
    setsid();
```

This multilevel multiplexed Stream configuration is built from the bottom up. Therefore, the example begins by first constructing the Internet Protocol (IP) multiplexor. This multiplexing device driver is treated like any other software driver. It owns a node in the UNIX file system and is opened just like any other STREAMS device driver.

The first step is to open the multiplexing driver and the 802.4 driver, thus creating separate Streams above each driver as shown in Figure 11-7. The Stream to the 802.4 driver may now be connected below the multiplexing IP driver using the **I_LINK ioctl** call.

Figure 11-7: Before Link

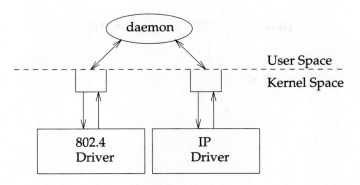

The sequence of instructions to this point is

```
if ((fd_802_4 = open("/dev/802_4", O_RDWR)) < 0) {
    perror("open of /dev/802_4 failed");
    exit(1);
}

if ((fd_ip = open("/dev/ip", O_RDWR)) < 0) {
    perror("open of /dev/ip failed");
    exit(2);
}

/* now link 802.4 to underside of IP */

if (ioctl(fd_ip, I_LINK, fd_802_4) < 0) {
    perror("I_LINK ioctl failed");
    exit(3);
}
```

I_LINK takes two file descriptors as arguments. The first file descriptor, fd_ip, must reference the Stream connected to the multiplexing driver, and the second file descriptor, fd_802_4, must reference the Stream to be connected below the multiplexor. Figure 11-8 shows the state of these Streams following the I_LINK call. The complete Stream to the 802.4 driver has been connected below the IP driver. The Stream head's queues of the 802.4 driver is used by the IP driver to manage the lower half of the multiplexor.

Figure 11-8: IP Multiplexor after First Link

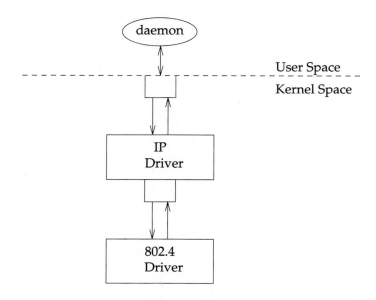

I_LINK returns an integer value, called **muxid**, which is used by the multiplexing driver to identify the Stream just connected below it. This **muxid** is ignored in the example, but is useful for dismantling a multiplexor or routing data through the multiplexor. Its significance is discussed later.

The following sequence of system calls is used to continue building the internet-working protocol multiplexor (IP):

```
if ((fd_802_3 = open("/dev/802_3", O_RDWR)) < 0) {
    perror("open of /dev/802_3 failed");
    exit(4);
}

if (ioctl(fd_ip, I_LINK, fd_802_3) < 0) {
    perror("I_LINK ioctl failed");
    exit(5);
}
```

All links below the IP driver have now been established, giving the configuration in Figure 11-9.

Figure 11-9: IP Multiplexor

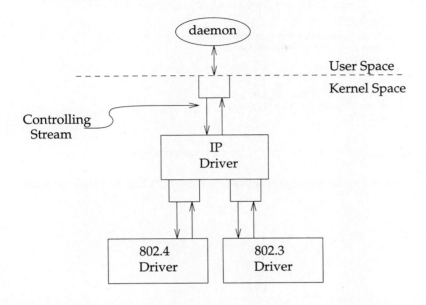

The Stream above the multiplexing driver used to establish the lower connections is the controlling Stream and has special significance when dismantling the multiplexing configuration. This will be illustrated later in this section. The Stream referenced by **fd_ip** is the controlling Stream for the IP multiplexor.

NOTE The order in which the Streams in the multiplexing configuration are opened is unimportant. If it is necessary to have intermediate modules in the Stream between the IP driver and media drivers, these modules must be added to the Streams associated with the media drivers (using I_PUSH) before the media drivers are attached below the multiplexor.

The number of Streams that can be linked to a multiplexor is restricted by the design of the particular multiplexor. The manual page describing each driver (typically found in Section 7) describes such restrictions. However, only one **I_LINK** operation is allowed for each lower Stream; a single Stream cannot be linked below two multiplexors simultaneously.

Continuing with the example, the IP driver is now linked below the transport protocol (TP) multiplexing driver. As seen earlier in Figure 11-6, only one link is supported below the transport driver. This link is formed by the following sequence of system calls:

```
if ((fd_tp = open("/dev/tp", O_RDWR)) < 0) {
    perror("open of /dev/tp failed");
    exit(6);
}

if (ioctl(fd_tp, I_LINK, fd_ip) < 0) {
    perror("I_LINK ioctl failed");
    exit(7);
}
```

The multilevel multiplexing configuration shown in Figure 11-10 has now been created.

Figure 11-10: TP Multiplexor

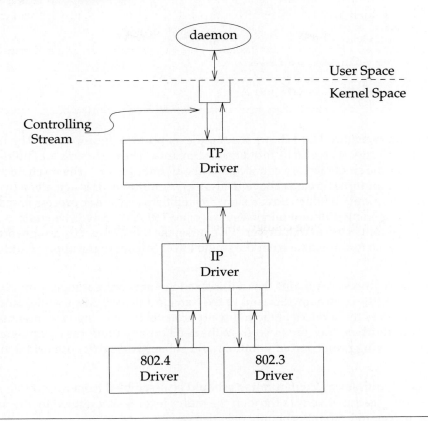

Because the controlling Stream of the IP multiplexor has been linked below the TP multiplexor, the controlling Stream for the new multilevel multiplexor configuration is the Stream above the TP multiplexor.

At this point, the file descriptors associated with the lower drivers can be closed without affecting the operation of the multiplexor. If these file descriptors are not closed, all later **read, write, ioctl, poll, getmsg**, and **putmsg** system calls issued to them will fail because **I_LINK** associates the Stream head of each linked Stream with the multiplexor, so the user may not access that Stream directly for the duration of the link.

The following sequence of system calls completes the daemon example:

```
        close(fd_802_4);
        close(fd_802_3);
        close(fd_ip);

        /* Hold multiplexor open forever */
        pause();
    }
```

To summarize, Figure 11-10 shows the multilevel protocol multiplexor. The transport driver supports several simultaneous Streams. These Streams are multiplexed over the single Stream connected to the IP multiplexor. The mechanism for establishing multiple Streams above the transport multiplexor is actually a by-product of the way in which Streams are created between a user process and a driver. By opening different minor devices of a STREAMS driver, separate Streams are connected to that driver. Of course, the driver must be designed with the intelligence to route data from the single lower Stream to the appropriate upper Stream.

The daemon process maintains the multiplexed Stream configuration through an open Stream (the controlling Stream) to the transport driver. Meanwhile, other users can access the services of the transport protocol by opening new Streams to the transport driver; they are freed from the need for any unnecessary knowledge of the underlying protocol configurations and subnetworks that support the transport service.

Multilevel multiplexing configurations should be assembled from the bottom up because the passing of **ioctl**s through the multiplexor is determined by the multiplexing driver and cannot generally be relied on.

Dismantling a Multiplexor

Streams connected to a multiplexing driver from above with **open**, can be dismantled by closing each Stream with **close**. The mechanism for dismantling Streams that have been linked below a multiplexing driver is less obvious, and is described below.

The **I_UNLINK ioctl** call disconnects each multiplexor link below a multiplexing driver individually. This command has the form:

> ioctl(*fd*, **I_UNLINK**, *muxid*);

where *fd* is a file descriptor associated with a Stream connected to the multiplexing driver from above, and *muxid* is the identifier that was returned by **I_LINK** when a driver was linked below the multiplexor. Each lower driver may be disconnected individually in this way, or a special *muxid* value of **-1** may disconnect all drivers from the multiplexor simultaneously.

In the multiplexing daemon program presented earlier, the multiplexor is never explicitly dismantled because all links associated with a multiplexing driver are automatically dismantled when the controlling Stream associated with that multiplexor is closed. Because the controlling Stream is open to a driver, only the final call of **close** for that Stream closes it. In this case, the daemon is the only process that opens the controlling Stream, so the multiplexing configuration is dismantled when the daemon exits.

For the automatic dismantling mechanism to work in the multilevel, multiplexed Stream configuration, the controlling Stream for each multiplexor at each level must be linked under the next higher level multiplexor. In the example, the controlling Stream for the IP driver was linked under the TP driver, which resulted in a single controlling Stream for the full, multilevel configuration. Because the multiplexing program relied on closing the controlling Stream to dismantle the multiplexed Stream configuration instead of using explicit **I_UNLINK** calls, the *muxid* values returned by **I_LINK** could be ignored.

An important side-effect of automatic dismantling on the close is that it is not possible for a process to build a multiplexing configuration with **I_LINK** and then exit. This is because **exit** closes all files associated with the process, including the controlling Stream. To keep the configuration intact, the process must exist for the life of that multiplexor. That is the motivation for implementing the example as a daemon process.

However, if the process uses persistent links with the **I_PLINK ioctl** call, the multiplexor configuration remains intact after the process exits. Persistent links are described later in this section.

Routing Data through a Multiplexor

As shown, STREAMS provides a mechanism for building multiplexed Stream configurations. However, the criteria on which a multiplexor routes data is driver-dependent. For example, the protocol multiplexor shown before might use address information found in a protocol header to determine over which subnetwork data should be routed. It is the multiplexing driver's responsibility to define its routing criteria.

One routing option available to the multiplexor is to use the *muxid* value to determine to which Stream data should be routed (remember that each multiplexor link is associated with a *muxid*). **I_LINK** passes the *muxid* value to the driver and returns this value to the user. The driver can therefore specify that the *muxid* value must accompany data routed through it. For example, if a multiplexor routed data from a single upper Stream to one of several lower Streams (as did the IP driver), the multiplexor could require the user to insert the *muxid* of the desired lower Stream into the first four bytes of each message passed to it. The driver could then match the *muxid* in each message with the *muxid* of each lower Stream, and route the data accordingly.

Persistent Links

With **I_LINK** and **I_UNLINK** **ioctl**s, the file descriptor associated with the Stream above the multiplexor used to set up the lower multiplexor connections must remain open for the duration of the configuration. Closing the file descriptor associated with the controlling Stream dismantles the whole multiplexing configuration. Some applications may not want to keep a process running merely to hold the multiplexor configuration together. Therefore, "free-standing" links below a multiplexor are needed. A persistent link is such a link. It is similar to a STREAMS multiplexor link, except that a process is not needed to hold the links together. After the multiplexor has been set up, the process may close all file descriptors and exit, and the multiplexor remains intact.

Two **ioctl**s, **I_PLINK** and **I_PUNLINK**, are used to create and remove persistent links that are associated with the Stream above the multiplexor. **close** and **I_UNLINK** are not able to disconnect the persistent links.

The format of **I_PLINK** is

> **ioctl**(*fd0*, **I_PLINK**, *fd1*)

The first file descriptor, *fd0*, must reference the Stream connected to the multiplexing driver and the second file descriptor, *fd1*, must reference the Stream to be connected below the multiplexor. The persistent link can be created in the following way:

```
upper_stream_fd = open("/dev/mux", O_RDWR);
lower_stream_fd = open("/dev/driver", O_RDWR);
muxid = ioctl(upper_stream_fd, I_PLINK, lower_stream_fd);
/*
 * save muxid in a file
 */
exit(0);
```

Figure 11-11 shows how **open** establishes a Stream between the device and the Stream head.

Figure 11-11: open of MUXdriver and Driver1

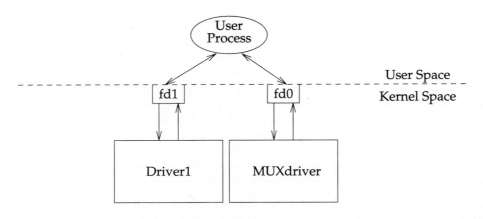

The persistent link can still exist even if the file descriptor associated with the upper Stream to the multiplexing driver is closed. The **I_PLINK ioctl** returns an integer value, **muxid**, that can be used for dismantling the multiplexing configuration. If the process that created the persistent link still exists, it may pass the **muxid** value to some other process to dismantle the link, if the dismantling is desired, or it can leave the **muxid** value in a file so that other processes may find it later. Figure 11-12 shows a multiplexor after **I_PLINK**.

Figure 11-12: Multiplexor after I_PLINK

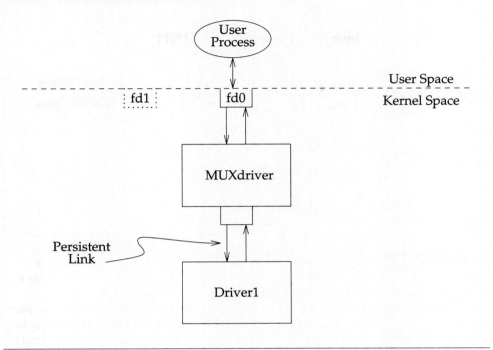

Several users can open the MUXdriver and send data to Driver1 since the persistent link to Driver1 remains intact. This is shown in Figure 11-13.

Figure 11-13: Other Users Opening a MUXdriver

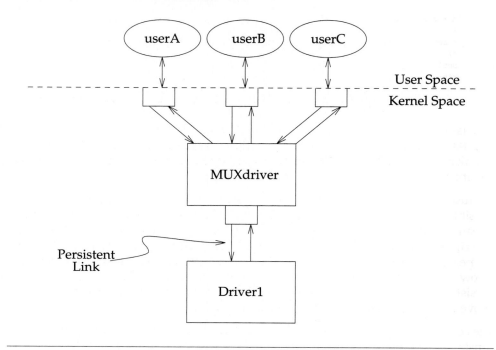

The **I_PUNLINK ioctl** is used for dismantling the persistent link. Its format is

   ioctl (*fd0*, **I_PUNLINK**, *muxid*)

where the *fd0* is the file descriptor associated with Stream connected to the multi-plexing driver from above. The *muxid* is returned by the **I_PLINK ioctl** for the Stream that was connected below the multiplexor. The **I_PUNLINK** removes the persistent link between the multiplexor referenced by the *fd0* and the Stream to the driver designated by the *muxid*. Each of the bottom persistent links can be disconnected individually. An **I_PUNLINK ioctl** with the *muxid* value of **MUXID_ALL** removes all persistent links below the multiplexing driver referenced by *fd0*.

The following dismantles the previously given configuration:

```
fd = open("/dev/mux", O_RDWR);
/*
 * retrieve muxid from the file
 */
ioctl(fd, I_PUNLINK, muxid);
exit(0);
```

The use of the ioctls I_PLINK and I_PUNLINK should not be intermixed with I_LINK and I_UNLINK. Any attempt to unlink a regular link with I_PUNLINK or to unlink a persistent link with I_UNLINK ioctl causes the errno value of EINVAL to be returned.

Because multilevel multiplexing configurations are allowed in STREAMS, it is possible to have a situation where persistent links exist below a multiplexor whose Stream is connected to the above multiplexor by regular links. Closing the file descriptor associated with the controlling Stream removes the regular link but not the persistent links below it. On the other hand, regular links are allowed to exist below a multiplexor whose Stream is connected to the above multiplexor with persistent links. In this case, the regular links are removed if the persistent link above is removed and no other references to the lower Streams exist.

The construction of cycles is not allowed when creating links. A cycle could be constructed by creating a persistent link of multiplexor 2 below multiplexor 1 and then closing the controlling file descriptor associated with the multiplexor 2 and reopening it again and then linking the multiplexor 1 below the multiplexor 2, but this is not allowed. The operating system prevents a multiplexor configuration from containing a cycle to ensure that messages cannot be routed infinitely, thus creating an infinite loop or overflowing the kernel stack.

12 Asynchronous I/O

Overview of Asynchronous I/O

The Asynchronous Input/Output (I/O) feature contains the following POSIX P1003.4 interface functions:

aio_cancel   cancel asynchronous read and/or write requests

aio_error   retrieve Asynchronous I/O error status

aio_fsync   asynchronously force I/O completion, and sets **errno** to ENOSYS

aio_read   begin asynchronous read

aio_return   retrieve return status of Asynchronous I/O operation

aio_suspend   suspend until Asynchronous I/O Completes

aio_write   begin asynchronous write

lio_listio   issue list of I/O requests

Together they provide a user application with the ability to overlap CPU processing with I/O operations. Additionally, Asynchronous I/O supports the **aio_memlock** function for high performance database applications.

> **NOTE** The **aio_cancel** and **aio_suspend** functions are supported only in the thread-based implementation of UNIX System V Release 4.2 Multiprocessor (SVR4.2 MP). The **lio_listio** function is supported only for raw slices of hard disks for both SVR4.2 MP and SVR4.2.

These routines are more fully described in their respective manual pages.

Chapter Organization

This chapter contains the following sections:

- Overview of Asynchronous I/O
- Advantages of Asynchronous I/O
- Using Asynchronous I/O
- Using the Interface Functions

- Using Other System Calls with Asynchronous I/O

- Tips on Using Asynchronous I/O

Notation Conventions

The Asynchronous I/O feature supports both UNIX System V Release 4.2
(SVR4.2) and UNIX System V Release 4.2 Multiprocessor (SVR4.2 MP). Functions
provided for SVR4.2 and SVR4.2 MP that can only be used on raw slices of hard
disks have been indicated in the following manner:

> `aio_memlock`$_{42}$

Functions provided for the SVR4.2 MP threads-based implementation only have
been indicated in the following manner:

> `aio_cancel`$_{MP}$
> `aio_suspend`$_{MP}$

Advantages of Asynchronous I/O

The Asynchronous Input/Output (I/O) mechanism provides a user process with the ability to overlap processing with I/O operations. In real time and transaction processing environments, applications may need to overlap their compute and I/O processing to improve the throughput and determinism on a per process or application basis. You can use Asynchronous I/O to enable read-ahead and write-behind to be performed in a controlled fashion. One process can have many I/O operations in progress while it is executing other code. Conversely, with synchronous I/O, the process would have been blocked waiting for each I/O operation.

Previously in UNIX System V, a call to the **read** system call was considered to be logically synchronous because the call could not return to the user until the requested data was read into the specified buffer in the calling process' address space. The user process was blocked until the data had been placed into the user's buffer and could not execute other instructions while the I/O was taking place. Non-blocking I/O could only be performed if the **O_NONBLOCK** flag was set on a call to **open** or **fcntl**. A non-blocking **read** call such as a call from a pipe, returns immediately with a failure indication if there is no data available. In contrast, a successful call to begin an asynchronous read returns to the calling process immediately after queuing a read request to the open file descriptor so that when data becomes available, the read request would be satisfied.

A call to the **write** system call is considered to be logically synchronous because the call does not return to the user until the requested data is written into the file system cache. After returning from the call, the user is free to reuse its buffers. However, the data is actually written to disk asynchronously at a later time. If the caller has set the **O_SYNC** flag on the call to **open** or **fcntl**, the call to **write** is truly synchronous and does not return to the user until the requested data is written out to disk. In contrast, a successful call to begin an asynchronous write queues a write request and returns immediately, without waiting for the I/O to be completed. When returning from the call, the data is not copied from the user buffers so the caller should not reuse the buffers until the I/O has completed.

An important part of the Asynchronous I/O application is the ability to request asynchronous notification of I/O completion. At the time the Asynchronous I/O request is made, the application may also request later notification on completion of the I/O.

An asynchronous read enables an application to control the amount of read-ahead that is performed so that the data can already be available when the database application needs it. With database and transaction processing software, often the writing out of data can be done asynchronously although you may need to know when the I/O has completed. The notification mechanism provided in UNIX System V fulfills this need.

NOTE The section titled "How to Use Asynchronous I/O with Your Application" describes how an application may use the interfaces specified in this document.

Performance

The Asynchronous I/O feature enhances performance by allowing applications to overlap processing with I/O operations. Using Asynchronous I/O enables an application to have more CPU time available to perform other processing while the I/O is taking place.

When **read** and **write** system calls return, the data is copied into or out of the user buffer, respectively. This usually requires copying data between user and kernel spaces, and may possibly also require real I/O. If only the copy operation is required, the user process must wait, and if I/O is necessary, the process will also be blocked. For applications such as real time and transaction processing, this waiting and blocking time may be so significant that there may be an application that supports concurrent execution of I/O and other work in the application.

With the Asynchronous I/O capability, an application can submit an I/O request without waiting for its completion, and perform other CPU work either until it is asynchronously notified of the completion of the I/O operation, or until it wishes to poll for the completion. For applications that involve large amounts of I/O data, this CPU and I/O overlapping can offer significant improvement on throughput.

Asynchronous I/O Control Block

The Asynchronous I/O interfaces use an Asynchronous I/O control block **aiocb** to provide information when making a request. The data structure of **aiocb_t** is shown below. See **aiocb**(7) for more details.

```
int               aio_fildes;      /* file descriptor            */
volatile void    *aio_buf;         /* buffer location            */
size_t            aio_nbytes;      /* length of transfer         */
off_t             aio_offset;      /* file offset                */
int               aio_reqprio;     /* request priority offset    */
struct sigevent   aio_sigevent;    /* signal number and offset   */
int               aio_lio_opcode;  /* listio operation           */
int               aio_flags;       /* flags                      */
```

Using Asynchronous I/O

The Asynchronous I/O feature comes in two versions; System V Release 4.2 and System V Release 4.2 MP, which is used for multiprocessing.

The POSIX P1003.4 technical committee specified a set of interfaces, a subset of which are supported by both SVR4.2 and SVR4.2 MP.

SVR4.2 MP supports all file types and is a threads-based, user-level implementation.

For database applications, there is a kernel-based implementation that offers higher performance and throughput. However, since database applications use only raw slices of hard disks, all file types are not supported. This implementation runs on SVR4.2 and SVR4.2 MP.

To summarize, SVR4.2 MP offers a thread-based implementation that supports all file types, as well as a high performance, kernel-based implementation that supports only raw slices of hard disks. SVR4.2 offers only the high performance, kernel-based implementation.

For both implementations, the POSIX interfaces are implemented and included in a single library, **libthread**, that provides the applications with access to this feature. This library is in both SVR4.2 and SVR4.2 MP, and is the only library needed to use Asynchronous I/O. **libthread** provides upward binary compatibility to SVR4.2 MP. The Asynchronous I/O routines are included in this library and therefore, you must link with **libthread** to use these routines.

Figure 12-1 shows the relationship between the Asynchronous I/O interface functions and the common threads library, the two versions of the UNIX Operating System, the interfaces for all the file types, and the Kernel Implementation used for raw slices of hard disks.

Figure 12-1: Asynchronous I/O Interface Functions

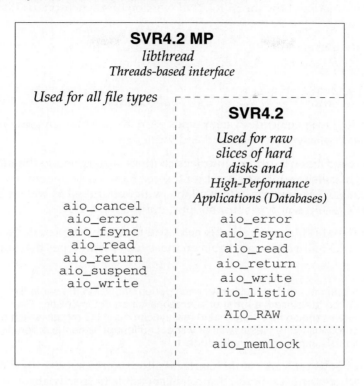

The following sections detail the various interfaces.

SVR4.2 MP Interface

The SVR4.2 MP version of Asynchronous I/O contains the following caveats:

- Uses all POSIX interfaces including **aio_suspend** and **aio_cancel**.

- Can implement Asynchronous I/O over all file types, not just raw disk slices and is implemented in the thread-based library **libthread**.

- Does not need to use **aio_memlock** to lock memory.

- Does not support **lio_listio**.

SVR4.2 MP Interface Operations

This section describes how the SVR4.2 MP version of Asynchronous I/O operates on the following:

- regular files
- device files
- STREAMS-based files.

It is not limited to specific file system types. Any device that supports **read** and **write** will accept asynchronous read and write requests.

There **aio_read** and **aio_write** interface routines correspond to the **read** and **write** system calls to support asynchronous read and write operations. These Asynchronous I/O operations are available with unbuffered as well as buffered I/O on those file system types that support unbuffered I/O.

Since unbuffered I/O is not available across all file system types, asynchronous unbuffered I/O will only be available on those file system types that support this capability.

 It is important that multiple threads performing I/O to the same file cooperate since the order of operations is non-deterministic. Even one thread should be careful not to mix synchronous I/O requests with asynchronous I/O requests (with or without buffering) since the order of operations is implementation dependent.

The asynchronous read and write interfaces allow you to specify the file offset indicating where the I/O should begin. It is possible to specify absolute file offsets for each I/O request and this type of access is defined to be random. It is also possible to indicate that the I/O should begin at the *current* file offset. Sequential access is defined to be multiple I/O requests from a single thread of control to the same file descriptor indicating that I/O should begin at the current file offset. See the section entitled *Asynchronous I/O Control Block* for more information.

Determining the value of the file pointer when Asynchronous I/O operations are in progress is difficult. Considering that there may be multiple outstanding asynchronous I/O operations, each of which may update the file pointer at any time, things may become complex for an application. An application should be careful not to mix calls to **read** and **write** or **lseek**, for example, with Asynchronous I/O operations. If sequential I/O is not requested, the order of I/O operations is implementation dependent. In general, until all asynchronous operations on a file are completed, the position of the file pointer is considered to be indeterminate.

An application can request cancellation of one or more Asynchronous I/O requests that the application had previously queued. The `aio_cancel` interface enables an application to cancel one or more outstanding Asynchronous I/O operations. Those that have not been started are canceled but those in progress may or may not be canceled.

An application can wait for Asynchronous I/O completion. If an application has completed all its *other work*, it may relinquish control of the CPU until some of its outstanding asynchronous I/O requests have completed.

An application can obtain completion status information by calling `aio_error` and `aio_return`.

 NOTE The completion of an asynchronous write on any device has the same semantics as a synchronous write to that device; for example, completion of a write to a STREAMS-based device means that the data has been copied into the stream's queue and does not imply that the data has been written to a device.

When an Asynchronous I/O request is made, the application can also request that it be notified when the I/O completes. This lets the application know immediately that the I/O has completed rather than having the application poll for completion status.

Single Threaded and Multithreaded Applications

Asynchronous I/O may be used by single threaded or multithreaded applications.

In multithreaded applications, multiple threads within a process share the same address space and therefore have access to the Asynchronous I/O control blocks of any other thread within that process. For example, one thread may begin an asynchronous read on an open file and another thread within that process may use the `aio_suspend` interface to determine if that read operation has completed. If this occurs, the application must make sure that the cooperating threads are properly synchronized.

Kernel Implementation

If you want higher performance for your applications, such as database applications, use the Kernel Implementation. The Kernel Implementation is available on both SVR4.2 and SVR4.2 MP. It contains the following caveats:

■ It supports Asynchronous I/O only on raw slices of hard disks.

- It supports the same interface but must be used with two additional interfaces, `aio_memlock` and the `AIO_RAW` flag.
  - The `aio_memlock` function must be called to lock the I/O buffer in memory before any other Asynchronous I/O operations can be performed.
  - The `AIO_RAW` flag has to be set in the `aiocb` control block so that the Asynchronous I/O operations will be performed by the kernel.

- It can be used on systems that only support raw disk slices such as SVR4.2.

- It supports `lio_listio`, but does not support `aio_suspend` and `aio_cancel`.

Accessing Raw Disk Slices

The aio_flags member of the `aiocb` control block must be set to `AIO_RAW` if you want to access raw disk slices. The following example shows you how to set this flag:

```
aiocb.aio_flags = AIO_RAW;
```

Using the Asynchronous I/O Memory Lock

The Asynchronous I/O interface uses `aio_memlock` to perform memory lock operations. See `aiomemlock`(7). Before starting an Asynchronous I/O request, the application must lock an area of memory to be used for the I/O buffer. The size of the locked area is determined by the number of requests that may be outstanding at any point in time. Only the I/O buffer area must be locked. Once this buffer has been locked with `aio_memlock`, it can not be resized or unlocked. When the application exits, the memory is unlocked automatically.

Error Handling

The Asynchronous I/O feature handles errors by returning a value of *-1* and placing an error number in the externally declared variable *errno*. It is included in `<errno.h>`. The value of `errno` or the `aio_error` function can be set to one of the following:

EAGAIN   The requested Asynchronous I/O operation was not queued because of system resource limitations. The first request to encounter a resource limitation and all later requests will be marked such that `aio_error` returns **EAGAIN**.

EFAULT	*aiocbp* or the *aio_buf* member points outside the allocated address space.
ECANCELED	The requested I/O was canceled before the I/O completed because of an explicit **aio_cancel** request.
EINVAL	All requests are **NULL** or have their **lio_listio** set to **LIO_NOP**. This is used for **lio_listio** only.
EINVAL	**nent** is zero. This is used for **lio_listio** only.
EINVAL	On SVR4.2, the request does not have the **AIO_RAW** flag bit set in **aio_flags**.
EFAULT	A memory fault occurred while accessing a **lio_listio** request. In this cause, **lio_listio** returns immediately without processing later requests in the list. On some implementations, memory faults might result in a **SIGSEGV** signal being delivered to the processes instead of returning the error code. This is used for **lio_listio** only.

Error Behavior

The following describes the detailed error behavior for the **lio_listio** and **aio_cancel** functions.

lio_listio   If the number of entries indicated by **nent** causes the system-wide limit **AIO_MAX** to be exceeded, **lio_listio** returns with **-1** and sets **errno** to **EAGAIN** after marking **EAGAIN** in all requests. If **nent** is greater than **AIO_LISTIO_MAX**, **lio_listio** returns immediately with **-1** and sets **errno** to **EINVAL**. No requests are processed or touched. Requests are processed as follows:

1. If there is a memory fault while accessing a request, **lio_listio** immediately returns **-1** or **EFAULT**, or causes a **SIGSEGV**.

2. If a resource problem occurs while queuing a request, **lio_listio** returns **-1** and sets **errno** to **EAGAIN** for all remaining requests.

3. If any other problem occurs with a request, **lio_listio** returns **-1** and sets **errno** to the appropriate error code. **lio_listio** continues processing requests and remembers what was wrong with the request in order for **lio_listio** to return this error code. The callback or signal will not be

executed for that request. Note that if different errors occur while processing requests, it is unspecified which error code gets returned. For example, it could be the first error encountered, or the last one.

4. If all requests from **1** through **nent** have **aio_lio_opcode** = **LIO_NOP** or **nent** is zero, **lio_listio** returns **-1** or **EINVAL**.

aio_cancel
                aio_cancel returns **AIO_CANCELED** if all requests were either canceled or completed and at least one request was canceled.

If an attempt was made to cancel a request that is in progress, but it is uncertain whether the request will be canceled, **aio_cancel** will return **AIO_NOTCANCELED**.

Using the Interface Functions

This section tells you how to use the four interface functions:

- aio_read
- aio_suspend_{MP}
- aio_write
- aio_cancel_{MP}

aio_read and aio_write

aio_read and **aio_write** allow an application to request an asynchronous read or asynchronous write operation. When initiating an asynchronous read or write, you can request asynchronous notification by supplying the address of a user-defined handler to be invoked when the I/O has completed. Since the address of the **aiocb** control block is passed as an argument to the handler, the I/O request that completed is easily identified and you need only implement one handler.

aio_suspend

An application may request asynchronous notification by supplying the address of a user-defined handler to be called on completion of the Asynchronous I/O request. This enables the application to perform other work while the I/O is in progress and guarantees that the application will be notified at the time the I/O completes so that any processing on that data may be performed immediately, if so desired.

For SVR4.2 MP, an application may also use the **aio_suspend** interface to block until at least one I/O operation completes or a timeout period expires. This interface is flexible because it enables any thread within a process to ask about one or more outstanding Asynchronous I/O operations and can specify how long to wait.

The **aio_suspend** routine returns 0 if at least one matching I/O request completed.

Beginning with SVR4.2 MP, a null pointer is returned on failure and *errno* is set to indicate that the *timeout* expired (**ETIME**) or an interrupt occurred (**EINTR**).

aio_cancel

Although rarely needed, **aio_cancel** is the only way to cancel an Asynchronous I/O request that has been blocked for input from a remote host that just crashed. Requests that have not been started are canceled, but those in progress may or may not be canceled.

Using Other System Calls with Asynchronous I/O

This section describes how an Asynchronous I/O application affects and is affected by the **fork, exec, exit** and **close** system calls.

fork and forkall

No Asynchronous I/O is inherited for **fork** and **forkall**. Asynchronous I/O operations that occur after the **fork** or **forkall** do not affect the copy of the **aiocb** control block in the child's address space and the child does not receive any notification from the completion of the parent's I/O. For example, if the parent process does a **forkall** while an I/O is in progress, the I/O completion will not be delivered to the child process.

exec and exit

Before calling **exec** and **exit**, you must attempt to cancel all outstanding Asynchronous I/O requests. Beginning with SVR4.2 MP, the **exit** function will wait for all outstanding Asynchronous I/O operations to complete before returning. It will unlock the area of memory locked by the **aiomemlock** call.

The **sbrk, brk** and **shmdt** functions will return **EBUSY** if the areas of locked memory are within the area affected by the call.

The **exec** function will fail if there are any outstanding Asynchronous I/O operations, so you must ensure that no requests are outstanding before calling **exec**.

close

When using the **AIO_RAW** flag on raw slices of hard disks, **close** will block until all outstanding asynchronous I/O operations are completed. When the call returns, the application is free to reuse the control block and buffers.

Beginning with SVR4.2 MP, if the **AIO_RAW** flag is not used, the **close**(*fd*) has to be trapped so that all outstanding requests to *fd* can be canceled. This is done by first calling **aio_cancel** until all have been canceled, and then **_close** to close the file.

How to Use Asynchronous I/O with Your Application

This section describes how the interfaces specified in this chapter may be used by applications. Points to remember include:

- The **aiocb** control block is the center of all asynchronous I/O requests. You must allocate a control block and assign values to its members before a call to **aio_read** or **aio_write** is made.

- Before an application exits or closes its file descriptors, it should ensure that all its Asynchronous I/O requests complete.

- If you want to lock an area of memory using **aio_memlock**, you must be sure that you are running the SVR4.2 version of the operating system.

A Guidelines for Writing Trusted Software

Writing Trusted Software

As a programmer on UNIX System V, you need to be aware of the special care you need to exercise when designing and writing software for any system. You want to ensure that the software you write and install for local applications is trusted.

The concept of trusting software is applicable to any system, regardless of the level of security implemented; the process of trusting software will lead to a more secure installation.

Trust is the belief that a system element upholds the security policy of an operating system. If this belief is founded on blind faith, disasters are likely to happen, so it makes sense to assign trust only when a system element has been shown to deserve that trust.

For user-level software, this means making sure that a command or library routine works as advertised, and prevents unauthorized users from circumventing access controls or mechanisms that protect sensitive system operations. In this section, trust refers not to blind faith, but to confirmed trustworthiness.

Scope of Trust

The first step in assigning trust to a command or library routine is to determine whether it has enough access to the system to require trust. Some commands do not require privilege or access to sensitive information. Such commands need not be trusted, since they pose no threat.

Other commands either occasionally or routinely obtain access to sensitive operations, or create that access for themselves through mechanisms like the **setuid-on-exec** feature. These commands must be trusted, since they operate in a sensitive environment.

The rules dictating which commands need trust and which commands do not are straightforward, but matching a command to a rule may not be. The following command classes must always be trusted:

- commands used by administrative personnel

- commands invoked by other trusted commands

- commands that use privilege (see the "Basic Security" "Security" chapter of the *Basic System Administration User and Group Management* guide for an explanation of privilege)

- commands that set their user or group identity to an administrative one on execution (`set-id`)

Deciding whether a command is "used by administrative personnel" or "uses privilege" can be difficult, since this distinction often varies from site to site and administrator to administrator.

Library routines have similar rules, but these routines are so pervasive the most reasonable rule is: each library routine must be trusted unless it can be shown not to be used by trusted code. This principle means that every element of a trusted command must itself be trusted. This principle includes the private routines within the command as well as all library routines used by the command.

How Trust Is Achieved

The rules for trust are different for commands and library routines. These rules are described in detail in the remaining sections of this chapter.

Trust is achieved by following all rules that pertain to writing a given piece of software and by documenting the methods used to follow those rules. This documentation must be supplied with every piece of trusted software. It describes the circumstances under which it is trusted, the methods used to make it trusted, and warnings about any practices that might jeopardize the trust placed in the software.

As with all code that is to be incorporated in a running system, trusted software needs to be reviewed and tested before it is installed. You can have reviewers and testers read this chapter so that they can familiarize themselves with the special requirements for trusted software.

How to Use This Chapter

This chapter is divided into sections describing the procedures needed to produce and install trusted software. You may want to read the "Creating and Managing User Accounts" and the "Basic Security" "Security" chapters of the *Basic System Administration User and Group Management* guide for background information.

It is a good idea to become familiar with the background material first, then proceed with reading the sections of this chapter that explain how to ensure trust in the kind of software you are writing. Reading the entire chapter is useful, but not essential. Many rules for ensuring trust are also good general programming practices, so they may also benefit any programming you do.

Finally, be aware that this chapter does not contain the definitive explanation of trust. Writing software is as much an art as it is a science, and the rules presented here are only guidelines to gain an understanding of the issues involved. It is by no means a guarantee that you will produce trusted software if you blindly obey the rules and dutifully mark the checklists. However, reading the advice here is a good beginning to learning how to write trusted software.

Trust and Security

Any discussion of software trust must be based on fundamental understanding of the security-related system elements. These elements are:

- Privileges
- Trusted Facility Management (TFM)
- Discretionary Access Controls (DAC)
- DAC Isolation Mechanism

The next subsections give a general explanation of these elements of security and trust. There are other descriptions in the *Basic System Administration User and Group Management* guide to which you may want to refer for other perspectives and information.

Privilege

Privilege means "the ability to override system restrictions." This ability is vested in three ways:

- in any user whose effective identity is **root**
- by way of the TFM feature
- through fixed privileges assigned to a command

There is a problem with the first approach to overriding system restrictions. A user (or command) allowed a reasonably mundane privileged action (for example, reading a protected file without explicit permission) also has permission to perform every other privileged action on the system, including the permission to overwrite all files on the system, add users, kill processes, start and stop network services, mount and unmount file systems, and many other sensitive operations. There is no restriction because there is no way to give a "little bit of **root**" to a user or command. Any process with an effective user-ID of "0" (**root**) is considered omnipotent.

The second and third approaches provide methods of giving a "little bit of **root**" to a user or command, and thus address the problem with the first approach. These approaches can be thought of as "Administrative Least Privilege" since they introduce the idea of discrete privileges that are associated with command files and processes.

The second and third approaches dissolve the bond between user identity and privilege, making privilege a process and command attribute instead of a user attribute. This approach makes sense because command behavior is much easier to describe and regulate than user behavior.

Process privileges are contained in two sets, "working" and "maximum." The working set contains the privileges in effect at any particular instant. This set controls the restrictions that the process can override at the moment. The procpriv(2) system call allows a command to set or clear privileges in the working set.

The maximum set represents the upper limit of privileges that a process can have in its working set. These privileges have no effect unless they are also in the working set, but they are held in reserve for the command to assert at any time. Using the procpriv system call, a command can clear a privilege in the maximum set but cannot set one.

The privilege set associated with a command's executable file determine what is put in the working and maximum privilege sets when a process executes the command. The file privilege set is called "fixed." Fixed privileges are useful for commands that do privileged things for ordinary users because they are granted unconditionally upon execution. The unconditional nature of fixed privileges, however, means that any program that uses them must strictly enforce all system policies it can override.

Trusted Facility Management

Historically, the only way a process could acquire privilege was if the value of the effective user-ID was "0", which is traditionally associated with the **root** login. This acquisition could be accomplished in one of two ways:

- logging in as a user whose real user-ID is "0" (i.e. **root**), or

- executing a command file that is **setuid-on-exec** and is owned by **root**. This results in a process effectively executing as **root**.

With this release, another method of acquiring privilege has been defined. This method is the Trusted Facility Management (TFM) mechanism. TFM provides an interface between users (not privileged) and commands (possibly privileged or requiring privilege). The primary elements of TFM are the **tfadmin**(1M) command, and the TFM database.

The `tfadmin` command is invoked with the desired command line as its arguments as in the following example:

```
tfadmin mount /dev/mydsk /my_mnt_point
```

The fixed privilege set of the `tfadmin` command file contains all privileges, so the `exec` system call turns on all privileges in the resulting process.

But the `tfadmin` command cannot be executed successfully by every user. To open it to such free access would be a violation of trust. When `tfadmin` is invoked, the first thing it does is to find out the real identity (real UID) of the invoking user. It then uses that identity to find the user's entry in the TFM Database.

A TFM database contains two pieces of information:

- the list of privileged commands that define specific roles
- the list of administrative roles and/or privileged commands to which the user is assigned

A trusted system may define administrative roles for selected system administrators. Each role is likely to be filled by a different administrator in order that all sensitive administrative functions not be handled by a single person. This division of administrative duties into separate roles reduces the chances for misuse of administrative power. All trusted administrators will be associated with at least one role and/or set of privileged commands; a very few administrators may be associated with more than one role, especially at small sites. But most users are not associated with any role.

When `tfadmin` finds the user's entry, it looks for the requested command in the list of specific commands, and if it does not find it, in the list of roles. Once the command is found and the user's entry verifies that the user is assigned to a role that has the authorization to use that command, `tfadmin` turns on the correct privileges (found in the database entry for the command) in its maximum set and executes the command. These privileges are propagated across the chain of execution of any child processes.

By providing a single point of privileged access to administrative commands and by basing that access on the real identity of the requesting user, `tfadmin` eliminates the need for privileged ID's and enhances administrative accountability.

Discretionary Access Control

Discretionary Access Control (DAC) on a file defines the permissible access to it by its owner, the owner's group, and all others. It is discretionary because the protection on this data object is set at the discretion of the owner of the object.

Discretionary Access Isolation

A DAC isolation mechanism is needed to protect files on base systems.

A review of the limitations and pitfalls of discretionary protection is in order. First, the discretion to change permissions on data resides with the owner. If ownership of a piece of data is obtained by a malicious or incompetent user, nothing can prevent that user from destroying all discretionary protections. Second, discretionary access controls cannot be used to prevent sensitive software or users from reading bad data, because the owner of a file can always make its data readable by the world, and the world includes sensitive people. Finally, discretionary access is based on effective user and group identity. Effective identities change whenever a set-id-on-exec command runs, and they remain changed until the command sets them back to the real identities or exits. Thus, sensitive discretionary access (and ownership) can be passed from a trusted command to an untrusted one by accident, exposing the system to attack.

UNIX System V protects sensitive data files by setting the ownership of all such files to **root** and supplying **setuid-on-exec** commands to give users controlled access to these files. This method provides protection because it makes protected files accessible only to the most restricted user.

This protection is adequate for most systems, but it is inadequate for protecting sensitive information on secure systems, because in practice, this has led to a proliferation of **setuid-on-exec** to **root** commands, some of which might be less careful than they should be about propagating the **root** user identity to other commands. As a result, not only did the file protection begin to fail, but what had been the most restricted user identity suddenly became much easier to obtain.

The next attempt was to set up "ghost" user identities other than **root** to own sensitive files. Ghost user identities are user ID's in the system that are inaccessible as a valid user account (i.e. no one can login with this ID. Programmers using this technique managed to protect **root** somewhat better, but still left open the risk of Trojan Horse attacks on the files they were trying to protect. Finally, it became clear that giving away ownership to files made attacks too easy. Giving away group access was preferable. True, it was still possible to gain unauthorized access through imperfect system commands, but at least that access was limited to reading and writing.

The currently recommended DAC isolation method calls for the existence of a "ghost" owner: **sys**. This owner has a locked password entry, to make logging in as that user impossible. In addition, no commands can set their user identity to **sys** upon execution. This makes it impossible for a non-privileged process to obtain this user identity. Groups are defined to provide protection isolated according to the kinds of commands and users needing access to protected files. Administrators are assigned multiple group lists that allow direct access to protected files while normal users may gain access only through set-gid commands. All files protected by this mechanism are owned by **sys** and have the appropriate system group identity.

Writing Trusted Commands

The following sections describe how to write trusted commands.

User Documentation

The first line of defense against system damage is accurate and complete documentation. Before a command can be trusted, its use, behavior, options, and influence over the system must be fully described. In addition to a full description of the command, any potentially harmful behavior should be noted, to allow users to avoid such hazards.

Parameter and Process Attribute Checking

The parameters given to a command at execution are the primary external influences over the behavior of the command. All parameters passed into a command at execution, therefore, must be checked and shown to be consistent by the command before processing starts. This means that a command that has, for example, two mutually exclusive modes of operation based on command line options must ensure that only one of these modes is requested at a time. This is particularly important when one operation might negate the other or cause an inconsistency in the system, or when the interfaces for two operations are similar enough to interact in a way that might be misinterpreted by the command.

Process attributes are also important, but, with rare exception, should not be checked explicitly by a command. The reason for this is that most process attributes are intended to be checked by the operating system itself and will cause identifiable errors if they are not right. It is unwise to make assumptions about the way a particular operating system decision will come out based on potentially flawed knowledge of how the decision is made. Some exceptions to this rule are the process `umask`, which should be set as needed by all trusted commands, and the process `ulimit`, which, if too small, may lead a trusted command to an error from which it cannot gracefully recover.

Privilege and Special Access

There are two forms of special access in UNIX System V. The first is the access granted by the set-id feature, and the second is privilege. In the past these have been bound together through the **root** effective user identity, and they continue to be bound in superuser-based versions of UNIX System V.

Set-id Commands

Commands that use the set-id feature to obtain access to files not otherwise available to an invoking user must carefully control not only their own use of these access permissions, but how these permissions are granted to other commands. There is always the possibility of a Trojan Horse when a command executes another command so care must be taken (see "Executing Other Commands") In this section, the issue is incorrect use of special access rights. In general, the best protection against either incorrect use or a Trojan Horse is to reset the effective user and group identity immediately on entry to a command and only use the special identities where they are explicitly needed. The code excerpt in Figure A-1 illustrates the procedure.

Figure A-1: Correct Regulation of Access in C Programs

```
static  uid_t      eff_uid, real_uid;
static  uid_t      eff_gid, real_gid;
        .
        .
        .
main(argc, argv)
int     argc;
char    *argv[];
{
        /*Variable declarations*/
        eff_uid = geteuid();
        eff_gid = getegid();
        real_uid = getuid();
        real_gid = getgid();
        if(seteuid(real_uid) < 0){  /*Set the effective UID to the real*/
                error("Cannot reset UID."); /*Report error and exit*/
        }
        if(setegid(real_gid) < 0){  /*Set the effective GID to the real*/
                error("Cannot reset GID."); /*Report error and exit*/
        }
              .
              .
              .
        if(setegid(eff_gid) < 0){                /*Assert the effective GID*/
                error("Cannot assert GID.");/*Report error and exit*/
        }
        fd = open("/etc/security_file", O_RDWR);
        if(setegid(real_gid) < 0){  /*Set the effective GID to the real*/
                cleanup();                   /*Restore consistency*/
                error("Cannot reset GID."); /*Report error and exit*/
        }
        if(fd < 0){
                error("Cannot open file."); /*Report error and exit*/
        }
        /*Process data*/
              .
              .
              .
        close(fd);
}
```

Privilege and Special Access in Shared Private Routines

A group of related commands occasionally share routines from a common object module. Such routines may provide database access, device setup and release, data conversion, etc. The desire to centralize these utility functions leads to creation of private "libraries." Although these are not usually libraries in the archive sense, they are collections of useful routines stored in a place that makes them accessible to a controlled group of commands. Since these routines are private, they are treated as subsections of the commands that use them. These routines are designed to cooperate closely with their calling programs, so they are expected to regulate privilege internally.

Exceptions to this rule occur when different commands have different views of the same routine or when the designer of a routine believes the routine may be added to a public library. A private database library may contain a routine to open and position the database. A command that only needs to query the database might want to assert only read access override privileges while a command that changes the database might want to assert both read and write access override privileges. Such a routine should make no assumptions about what privileges the calling routine wants to use, but should simply assume that the correct privileges are in place.

A library routine might also have broad enough usefulness to be a candidate for public use. The reasons why such a routine might not be placed in a public library range from a desire to keep the published interface as small as possible to name conflicts or even lack of staff to make the change. If a programmer believes that a routine is useful enough to merit consideration for a public library, the programmer should follow the rules for writing public library routines, even if the routine is initially private.

These guidelines apply equally well to special access permissions obtained through the set-id mechanism as they do to privilege. Wherever these access permissions are used instead of privilege, they should be turned on and off as though they were individual privileges, using the `seteuid` and `setegid` system calls as shown in Figure A-1

Error Checking

Almost every system call or library routine can, somehow, encounter an error during its operation. While many of these occur only because of programmer error, each such problem indicates a failure of either the system, the calling program or a transient parameter like access permission or available memory. If a programmer chooses to ignore a reported error, the result is a command that, should some basic assumption of the system fail, could corrupt its environment. For trusted commands, therefore, every possible error return must be checked and reported. This rule is not always followed to the letter, since in some cases it is more efficient to detect the error case downstream from the actual failure. Ignoring errors is risky and should not be done without strong justification.

Signal Handling

Signals pose a problem in trusted software because they are not predictable. There are two main areas of concern when it comes to handling signals:

1. maintaining system integrity when a trusted command receives a signal

2. use of privilege and special permission inside signal handling functions

If a signal is received by a trusted command, that command must not simply exit and leave the system in an inconsistent or insecure state. If a command contains critical sections that cannot be interrupted, every effort must be made to prevent signals from interrupting those sections.

On the other hand, a signal usually means either that a system problem has occurred (like memory exhaustion, an addressing error, or invalid operation) or that the user has decided to abort the operation. Regardless, it is not correct for a command to continue processing as though nothing had happened.

A system-generated signal usually signifies a flaw in the command and almost certainly means that further processing will be based on corrupt data. A user-generated signal signifies a change of heart by the requesting user and should be honored where possible by restoring the system to the state it was in before the command was invoked. If a command receives a signal after it is committed to a change, the command should finish any steps necessary to ensure consistency and exit.

Attempts to write signal-safe commands must take into account the possibility of unforeseen signals and signals that cannot be caught. On any given system, the set of possible signals is constant, but in general, systems are allowed to have their own implementation-specific signals.

It is better to keep the critical sections of a command as small as possible than to try to protect large critical sections against interruption. This principle means, for example, a command that changes a system database should make all changes on a copy of any sensitive part of the database (for example an index file) before replacing the original. This limits opportunity for an unknown signal to interrupt the sensitive part of the command.

When a trusted command is using privilege or some other extraordinary access and receives a signal, the command may enter a signal handler. Because signals are unpredictable, it is not a good idea for a command to change the privileges or other access attributes of its process inside a signal handler. When the handler returns to the main stream of processing, these attributes must be the same as they were before the signal occurred, or unpredictable processing will result.

Since signal handlers are not allowed to change process attributes, they should never do anything that might take advantage of privileges or special access. In general, a signal handler should set a flag and return or longjump away. Once the flag is set, the command can recognize the signal and respond to it in an orderly fashion.

Handling Sensitive Data

While it is important that trusted commands always protect the integrity of the data they manipulate, they must also prevent information disclosure that might damage system security. If commands are used exclusively by administrators or never gain access to sensitive information, then they are mostly exempt from this concern, but some commands are regularly used by non-administrators and use privilege or special access to read secret information.

An example is the **passwd** command. The **passwd** command retrieves information from the system password list (not normally readable by users) and reports (and sometimes changes) that information. In the process of obtaining the information, **passwd** must scan through records that are not intended for the eyes of the invoking user. If a signal were to cause **passwd** to write a core image with one or more records buffered, it would be possible for an enterprising programmer to extract secret information from the core image.

It is best to eliminate this possibility by designing databases and commands to handle only the sensitive information they are authorized to disclose. When it is impossible to eliminate the risk, programmers should limit the vulnerability of the command by clearing the contents of any sensitive buffers as soon as they cease to be needed.

Executing Other Commands

Whenever a command executes another command, it must first set its effective user and group identities to its real user and group identities unless the executed command needs the special access to do its job. If the executed command needs the special access, the executing command must take every possible step to ensure that it executes the correct command with proper parameters and cannot be misled into executing a Trojan Horse.

A Trojan Horse is a command that imposes itself on a process by looking like the needed command. It inherits permissions and other attributes (like file descriptors, environment, and so on), from the executing command, and can use these capabilities to disrupt the system. Measures to prevent Trojan Horse intrusion include the following:

- using full pathnames for execution

- avoiding the **system** and **popen** library routines, which use the shell to interpret command lines

- carefully making sure the **$PATH**, **$IFS**, and other environment variables are set to safe values whenever the shell must be used

- never allowing special-access rights or file descriptors to survive across an execution of a user-supplied command name

Using Library Routines

A trusted command must never use an untrusted library routine. This restriction means that a trusted command must never use a library routine that has an untrusted call anywhere in its calling sequence, nor a library routine that causes an untrusted command to be executed. The information derived from the untrusted command might influence the behavior of the trusted command, or the command might give away extraordinary access to the untrusted command; neither action is acceptable.

Trusting Shell Scripts

With the introduction of support for multiple file formats in UNIX System V, it is possible to have set-id and privileged shell scripts. In addition, there have always been shell scripts that are used by administrators. If a shell script can get administrative access to the system it must be trusted, so rules for trusting shell scripts are needed as well.

The primary rule of trusted shell scripts is: any shell script that uses privilege or special access rights is subject to spoofing and must not be available to non-administrators.

User Documentation

The documentation needed for a trusted shell script is the same as that for any other trusted command. See the "User Documentation" part of the "Trusting Commands" section.

Privilege and Special Access

The shell offers no way to control special access rights granted by the set-id feature. Without this control, such a shell script must be extremely simple before it can be trusted. In general, it is not a good idea to use the set-id mechanisms for shell scripts. Only trusted commands should be used in shell scripts.

The shell has the ability to regulate privilege through the new built-in **privs** command.

Guidelines for Writing Trusted Software

Figure A-2: Correct Use of Privilege in a Shell Script

```
#! /sbin/sh -p
privs -allprivs max          #Turn off all working privileges
if [ $? -ne 0 ]
then                         #The priv command will report the error
        exit $?
fi

        .
        .
        .
privs +mount max
if [ $? -ne 0 ]
then                         #The mount command will report the error
        exit $?
fi
/sbin/mount /dev/mydsk /mnt
privs -allprivs max
if [ $? -ne 0 ]
then                         #The priv command will report the error
        exit $?
fi

        .
        .
        .
```

Executing Commands

Shell scripts consist mainly of commands, which makes them especially vulnerable to spoofing attacks. Only trusted commands should be used in shell scripts. Also, all commands that are not known to be built into the shell itself must be executed either by their full pathname or through the **/sbin/tfadmin** command provided by the TFM feature.

Sometimes, a script will need to use a command with privilege regardless of TFM data. When this situation occurs, privileges are assigned to the script by way of TFM. Fixed privileges are assigned by way of the **filepriv** command. In this case, the script should turn on only the needed privileges and execute the command using a full pathname (see Figure A-2).

Another way of executing a privileged command is through the **/sbin/tfadmin** command, since this allows the TFM mechanisms to decide whether the user of the script should have the privilege. In this instance, all commands to be executed in the script must exist in the TFM database, and all users who execute the script must have access to them. This case is illustrated in Figure A-3.

In order for a script to propagate privileges whether they are acquired by way of **tfadmin** or **filepriv**, the **#!** line must be the first line of the script.

Figure A-3: Shell Script Using Commands From TFM Database

```
#! /sbin/sh -p
if [ $? -ne 0 ]
then                        #The priv command will report the error
        exit $?
fi
        .
        .
        .
if [ $? -ne 0 ]
then                        #The mount command will report the error
        exit $?
fi
tfadmin mount /dev/mydsk /mnt
if [ $? -ne 0 ]
then                        #The priv command will report the error
        exit $?
fi
        .
        .
        .
```

Error Checking

Most commands report the errors they encounter and exit with a non-zero return code on failure. Shell scripts, therefore, usually do not need to bother reporting errors. Nonetheless, shell scripts should check for errors. A command that fails and reports an error indicates a problem in the shell script. If that error might cause the system to be left in an inconsistent state by the script, the error must be caught and handled. Whether the error is specially reported depends on the particular circumstances.

For example, if the failing command redirects its standard error output to a file or to **/dev/null**, the shell script must report an error to avoid failing silently.

If, on the other hand, the command does nothing to redirect messages, then the command's error message should be enough to tell the user what happened.

Guidelines for Writing Trusted Software

Trusting Public Library Routines

While commands obtain their privilege and special access through kernel mechanisms, library routines obtain their access rights and privileges from the commands that call them. Additionally, library routines usually serve a single purpose instead of offering a spectrum of options. These differences dictate the rules for library routines described below.

Documentation

The most important aspect of trusting a library routine is the documentation used by a programmer to decide how and when that routine should be used. This description should include basic elements such as the interface to the routine, what the routine does, and what error conditions might be encountered by the routine. Additionally, any privileged routine should have a description of the privileges it can use and the reason it might use each privilege. Also, any interesting side effects of the routine should be detailed. These include opening, closing, deleting or creating files, executing commands, setting global variables, allocating heap storage, changing process attributes, sending signals, or any other behavior that is not immediately obvious to the reader.

Finally, the description should include a section describing any non-trusted uses of the routine. If, for example, a user can cause the routine to fill past the end of a buffer by feeding it too much data, this possibility should be stated in the description. By supplying as much information as possible to the programmer who will use the routine, the documenter allows the programmer to choose routines wisely and use them correctly.

Privilege and Special Access

Public libraries provide many useful functions, such as file IO buffering, memory allocation, and mathematical processing. These routines are intended for use by a wide variety of applications, with a wide variety of needs and goals.

A library routine, therefore, should not try to guess the intent of the calling program. It should simply do its job and return. The rule for public library routines and privilege or special access is: no public routine should change the privilege or access environment of a process unless that is its primary purpose. There should be no exceptions to this rule, since a trusted command must always be in full control of its privileges and special access rights.

Reporting Errors

The only way a command can detect and recover from an error is to use the information reported by the system calls and library routines that encountered the error. A library routine, therefore, must report every possible error case as informatively as possible to the calling program. Where several different failure modes are possible, each should be reported uniquely so that the calling program can take any necessary corrective action or can restore system integrity before exiting. It is not correct for a library routine to cause a process to exit as the result of an error, since the calling program may need to clean up before exiting. The rule is: library routines must report all errors as accurately as possible.

Handling Sensitive Data

Library routines sometimes need to retrieve sensitive data for a trusted command. The designer of such routines must be aware of the risk that this data might be accidentally disclosed in a core file or some other unprotected data object. For a more detailed discussion of this problem and its solutions, see the "Handling Sensitive Data" section of "Trusting Commands".

Executing Commands

Whenever a library routine executes a shell level command it must take great care to ensure that the command is executed correctly and with the right parameters. For library routines that handle requests to execute a command this requirement is limited to making sure the request is followed exactly as issued. Library routines (like **system** or **popen**) that execute commands independently of the specific request must use full pathnames, and be certain that the commands they execute are themselves trusted.

Installing Trusted Commands and Data

The access isolation and privilege mechanisms described in the "Creating and Managing User Accounts" chapter of the *Basic System Administration User and Group Management* guide depend on the software installation procedures. Defining special levels and group identities serves no purpose if those levels and groups are not used correctly. Defining a set of privileges and kernel level mechanisms to enforce and control them serves no purpose if every command gets all fixed privileges. As much care must be put into defining the installation parameters of a command and its data objects as goes into writing the command and designing its data. This section establishes principles upon which installation decisions can be made.

Assigning Access Controls

All trusted data must be protected from unauthorized changes. This decision is based on the question "does any non-administrator need to use this information?" not "is this information too sensitive for non-administrators to see?"

Discretionary access controls provide a finer access granularity. These permissions should be assigned based on logical groupings of data according to the needs of a set of commands and administrators. Since the discretionary controls are the only protections available to the base system, they should be assigned as though they were protecting a system on which all files are public and writable unless restricted by DAC.

The actual permissions placed on a given file depend entirely on the needs of the commands that use the file. The group bits, however, should be used instead of the owner bits to grant controlled access to files. This methodology allows the designer to use set-uid root for non-access related privilege and still take advantage of DAC controls on a least privilege system.

Assigning Privileges and Special Permissions

Privileges are assigned to executable files (commands) based on the needs of the command and the knowledge that the command will not misuse the privileges. These two factors are equally important: Even though a programmer knows that a command will not abuse a particular privilege, the command must need that privilege or it does not get it. Furthermore, even though a command needs a privilege, it must be shown to use the privilege properly or it does not get it.

After determining what privileges a command can have, the next step is to determine whether the command needs privileges that are propagated through **tfadmin**, or fixed privileges.

Using fixed privilege calls for extremely careful programming. A command with fixed privilege must never use untrusted data for security-relevant decision making. This means that a shell script can never have fixed privilege, since the environment a shell script inherits is untrusted and influences the shell's behavior (a command that uses the **system** or **popen** library routines can never have fixed privilege for the same reason). Other possible disqualifications are the following:

- commands that are controlled by user-supplied script files
- commands that are controlled by data from standard input

Privileges acquired through **tfadmin** are more carefully controlled, so they do not require the extensive limitations placed on fixed privilege. Any privileged command, however, must uphold system policies when it uses privilege and must obey both the spirit and the letter of the rules of trust described in these guidelines.

Special access rights should be used in favor of privileges wherever possible. A program that needs discretionary access to a well-defined set of files should be **setgid** to the group to which those files belong. The files should be as accessible as necessary to their group. If, for example, a command needs to read a file **foo** and read and write a file **bar** and the group of the files **foo** and **bar** is **sys**, the command should be **setgid** to **sys**. The file **foo** should be readable by group while the file **bar** should be both readable and writable by group. The P_DACREAD and P_DACWRITE privileges should not be used for this purpose, since they give too much access to the command.

Summary

Trusting a command or library routine requires a solid understanding of the risks encountered by the command or library, the policies of the system, and the principles of trust. These guidelines offer a brief look at the policies available with UNIX System V, and a discussion of the principles of trust. The risks encountered by a particular command or library must be determined by the programmer attempting to make it trusted.

While some of the rules presented here may seem overly exacting, or even clumsy, the strenuousness of the rules is the price paid for a secure system. Every rule and principle described in these guidelines originates from some aspect of an observed attack on a computer system. The programmer who ignores these rules does so, not at his or her own risk, since the programmer is unlikely to be affected by the attack, but at the risk of everyone who uses that programmer's software. The responsibility of writing trusted software, therefore, must not be taken lightly.

GL^{Glossary}

Glossary

The following terms are used throughout the UNIX System V Programming Series. This glossary includes terms found in:

- *Programming with UNIX System Calls*
- *UNIX Software Development Tools*
- *Character User Interface Programming*
- *Graphical User Interface Programming*
- *Network Programming Interfaces*
- *Programming in Standard C*

a.out	`a.out`, historically for "assembler output," is the default file name for an executable program produced by the C compilation system.
abortive release	An abrupt termination of a transport connection, which may result in the loss of data.
access permissions	Access checking is performed whenever a subject (a process) tries to access an object (such as a file or directory). Permission to access an object is granted or denied on the basis of mode bits.
ADJUST	The mouse button or keyboard equivalent used to adjust a selection (cf. SELECT); usually the middle button on a right hand mouse.
alias file	A script which contains alias definitions, each on a separate line. An alias file is optional, but if one is written, it must be named as an argument when `fmli` is invoked.
alias	A short name that can be used in FMLI scripts in place of a long pathname or a list of paths to search. An FMLI developer defines aliases in an alias file. Alias definitions have the format *alias=pathname*.
alternate keystrokes	A sequence of keystrokes, usually beginning with a CTRL key and consisting entirely of keys that are standard on all keyboards, which cause the same action to occur that occurs when a named key is

pressed. Alternate keystrokes are necessary because many keyboards do not have a complete set of the named keys used by FMLI applications. For example, when the named key ⟨↑⟩ is not available on a keyboard, users can type the alternate keystrokes ⟨ **CTRL-u** ⟩.

anchor

Either end of a **Scrollbar** widget or a **Slider** widget. The part of the widget that remains fixed while the *elevator* or *drag box* moves along.

ANSI

ANSI is an acronym for the American National Standards Institute. ANSI establishes standards in the computing industry from the definition of ASCII (see below) to the measurement of overall datacom system performance. ANSI standards have been established for the Ada, FORTRAN, and C programming languages.

API

Application programmer interface.

application

An executable program, usually unique to one type of users' work, such as an accounting application. Applications are frequently interactive environments in which the user can perform various related tasks. See "FMLI application."

archive

An archive, or statically linked library, is a collection of object files each of which contains the code for a function or a group of related functions in the library. When you call a library function in your program, and specify a static linking option on the **cc** command line, a copy of the object file that contains the function is incorporated in your executable at link time. For further information, see "C Compilation System" in *Programming in Standard C*.

argument

A character string or number that follows a command and controls its execution in some way. There are two types of arguments: options and operands. Options change the execution or output of the command. Operands provide data that will be operated on by the command. Arguments to the **open** command are saved in built-in variables readable (only) by the frame opened. Options are also called flags. Operands specify files or directories to be operated on by the program. For example, in the command line:

```
$ cc -o hello hello.c
```

all the elements after the **cc** command are arguments. For further information of how command line arguments are passed to C programs, see "C Compilation System" in *Programming in Standard C*.

In the C language, function arguments are enclosed in a pair of parentheses immediately following the function name. You can find formal definitions of the functions supplied with the C compilation system in **cc**(1).

ASCII
An acronym for American Standard Code for Information Interchange. ASCII code uses one byte of computer memory to represent each character. Each alphanumeric and special character has an ASCII equivalent. When files and directories are printed according to the ASCII code equivalent of the first letter of their names, the order is called ASCII collating sequence. The order is special characters first, numbers second, then upper case and lower case letters.

assembler
Assembly language is a programming language that uses symbolic names to represent the machine instructions of a given computer. An assembler is a program that accepts instructions written in the assembly language of the computer and translates them into a binary representation of the corresponding machine instructions. Because each assembly language instruction usually has a one-to-one correspondence with a machine instruction, programs written in assembly language are not portable to different machines.

asynchronous execution
The mode of execution in which Transport Interface routines will never block while waiting for specific asynchronous events to occur, but instead will return immediately if the event is not pending.

automatic data
Data that is persistent only during the invocation of a procedure. It describes data belonging to a process. Automatic data occupies the stack segment. See *static data*.

background process group

> Any process group that is not the foreground process group of a session that has established a connection with a controlling terminal.

backquoted expression

> A command line enclosed in backquotes, whose output is returned as a value. The output of the command replaces the backquotes and the command line within the backquotes. In FMLI, this output can be used as an argument for another command, assigned to a variable, or assigned to a descriptor.

banner line

> The top line of the screen in FMLI applications, used to display the application's title and a **Working** message that indicates when the application is busy.

bottom level

> Lowest of the four lower RPC levels; programs written to this level can control many transport-specific details.

buffer

> A buffer is a space in computer memory where data is stored temporarily in convenient units for system operations. Buffers are often used by programs such as editors that access and alter text or data frequently. When you edit a file, for instance, a copy of its contents are read into a buffer; the copy is what you change. For your changes to become part of the permanent file, you must write the buffer's contents back into the permanent file. This replaces the contents of the file with the contents of the buffer. When you quit the editor, the contents of the buffer are flushed.

button

> Generic term for any of several widgets, specifically **RectButton** widgets and **OblongButton** widgets. The RectButtons are implicitly defined in *flattened widgets*, as well. A button, when pressed usually initiates certain actions, like popping up a menu or executing an application routine.

cable

> In a **Scrollbar** widget, the cable is the "line" on which the *elevator* moves. One end of the cable is connected to the *anchor* and the other is connected to the *elevator*.

callback	A callback routine is a routine written by an application programmer and associated with a specific widget *resource*. The callback routine is invoked as a result of a specific activity associated with that widget (that is, the widget calls back the program via that routine). For example, the **XtNselect** *resource* contains the name of the callback routine that is entered when a *button* is pushed or when a **CheckBox** is selected; the **XtNverification** resource contains the name of the callback routine to invoke when a **Text-Field** widget is exited. The act of associating the name of a callback routine with a widget resource is called *registration*.
cast	An expression which describes the nature or use of that which follows it to the interpreter. In FMLI, casts are used: (1) to describe whether a file is a menu definition file, a form definition file, or a text frame definition file; (2) to indicate how often to evaluate a descriptor.
character class table	A character class table is used for character classification and conversion. The table is built by the commands **chrtbl**(1M) and **wchrtbl**(1M), and located in the file **usr/lib/***locale***/LC_CTYPE**.
child process	See "**fork**."
choices menu	A menu that can be provided to show a list of possible entries to a form field. An FMLI application developer defines choices where appropriate through the use of the **rmenu** descriptor.
click	The act of pressing and releasing a mouse button without moving the mouse *pointer* more than a few pixels.
click-move-click	A method of user interaction with a set of objects where the user clicks MENU to display the objects, moves the pointer over the one of interest, then clicks MENU or SELECT to select or activate the object.
client	The transport user in connection-mode that requests a transport connection.

CLTS	Connectionless Transport Service
command line	The next-to-the-last line on the screen in FMLI applications, where users can enter an application's commands without using the menus provided in the application.
command menu	A menu provided automatically in FMLI applications that lists a sub-set of the FMLI built-in commands and any application-specific commands that have been defined in a commands file. Users can execute a command in the Command Menu by selecting it, as in any menu. The Command Menu can be made current by pressing the $\boxed{\text{CMD-MENU}}$ function key.
command	one of a set of executables built into FMLI, such as **open** and **close**, to which descriptors of type command must evaluate. A command line consists of the command followed by its arguments. For example:

$$\text{\$ cc file1.c file2.c}$$

instructs the operating system to execute the C compiler program, which is stored in the file **cc**, and to use the source files **file1.c** and **file2.c** as input. A command line can extend over multiple terminal lines.

commands file	A script in which an FMLI developer can redefine or disable FMLI built-in commands, and define new, application-specific commands. The contents of a commands file are reflected in the Command Menu. Users can execute a command by selecting it from the Command Menu, or by typing it on the FMLI command line. A commands file is optional, but if one is written, it must be named as an argument when **fmli** is invoked.
compiler	A compiler is a program that translates a source program written in a higher-level language into the assembly language of the computer the program is to run on. An assembler translates the assembly language code into the machine instructions of the computer. In the C compilation system, these instructions are stored in object files that correspond to each of your source files. Each object file contains a binary **representation** of the C language code in the

corresponding source file. The link editor links these object files with each other, and with any library functions you have used in your source code, to produce an executable program called **a.out** by default. For further information, see "C Compilation System" in *Programming in Standard C*.

composite widget
See *widget*. A widget that is a parent of other widgets, that physically contains other widgets.

connection establishment
The phase in connection-mode that enables two transport users to create a transport connection between them.

connection-mode
A circuit-oriented mode of transfer in which data is passed from one user to another over an established connection in a reliable, sequenced manner.

connection-oriented transport
Connection-oriented transports are reliable and support byte-stream deliveries of unlimited data size.

connectionless transport
Connectionless transports have less overhead than connection-oriented transports but are less reliable and maximum data transmissions are limited by buffer sizes.

container
A widget that defines a region that holds zero or more sub-objects of a given type.

control area
The area located directly under the header of a *window*. It is used to display "command buttons," if the application in the window provides them.

controlling process
A session leader that established a connection to a controlling terminal.

controlling terminal
A terminal that is associated with a session. Each session may have, at most, one controlling terminal associated with it and a controlling terminal may be associated with only one session. Certain input sequences from the controlling terminal cause signals to be sent to process groups in the session associated with the controlling terminal; see **termio**(7).

conversation
The negotiation and the data transfer between *Source* and *Destination*. Both tasks are accomplished through *selection mechanism*.

core image	A core image is a copy of the memory image of a process. A file named **core** is created in your current directory when the UNIX operating system aborts an executing program. The file contains the core image of the process at the time of the failure. For further information, see "Using debug from the Command Line" in *Programming in Standard C*.
current context	When using the GUI debugger, the current context for a Window Set determines what is displayed in each of the windows. The current context is determined by the current frame of the current process. For further information, see "Using debug with the Graphical User Interface" in *Programming in Standard C*.
current frame	When using the GUI debugger, the current frame, along with the current process, determines the current context. The current frame is shown with a pointing hand to its left in the Process Pane of the Context Window. For further information, see "Using debug with the Graphical User Interface" in *Programming in Standard C*.
current process	When using the GUI debugger, the current process, along with the current frame, determines the current context. The current process is shown with a pointing hand to its left in the Process Pane of the Context Window. For further information, see "Using debug with the Graphical User Interface" in *Programming in Standard C*.
current program	When using the GUI debugger, the current program is the program containing the current process. The current program may also contain other processes derived from the same executable file. For further information, see "Using debug with the Graphical User Interface" in *Programming in Standard C*.
current	The frame, menu item, form field, or activity in which the cursor is positioned. An element of the FMLI screen which is current is usually distinguished in some way from other screen elements being displayed—the current frame, for example, may be shown in bright video, while non-current frames may be shown in half-bright video. User input is

processed by, or applies to, the current frame, item, and so on.

daemon

A background process that performs a system-wide public function. The UNIX System process `init` may spawn daemon processes that exist throughout the lifetime of the system. Daemons (often) continue to run after their parents terminate. An example of a daemon process is `calendar`(1).

data symbol

A data symbol names a variable that may or may not be initialized. Normally, these variables reside in read/write memory during execution. Compare "text symbol."

data transfer

The phase in connection-mode or connectionless-mode that supports the transfer of data between two transport users.

datagram transport

See *connectionless transport*.

datagram

A unit of data transferred between two users of the connectionless-mode service.

debugging

Debugging is the process of locating and correcting errors in executable programs. For further information, see "Using debug from the Command Line", "Using debug with the Graphical User Interface", and "Appendix C - sdb" in *Programming in Standard C.*

default

A default is the way a program will perform a task in the absence of other instructions, that is, in default of your specifying something else.

descriptor

An element of the Form and Menu Language that defines some aspect of the look (appearance or location of an element of your application), or feel (an action to take in response to user input). A descriptor is coded in the format *dname=value*, where *dname* is one of the set of Form and Menu Language descriptors and *value* is, or generates, an expression of a type appropriate for the particular descriptor. Each Form and Menu Language descriptor is only meaningful in a particular context (that is, a menu frame, a form frame, and so on).

deserializing	Converting data from XDR format to a machine-specific representation.
Desktop	Synonymous with the workspace. It is a metaphor of the screen to something that many users are familiar with (for example, screen representation of a user's office desk with a calculator, clock, file folders, and so on).
destination	The ending point of the drag-and-drop operation. It is also referred as the requester.
dimmed	A visual effect on an object. A control, such as a *button*, is dimmed if its visible manifestation represents the state of just one of several objects that are in inconsistent states. When such a control is manipulated (for example, by clicking SELECT over the button), it is no longer dimmed because the manipulation sets the state for all the objects.
directory	A directory is a type of file used to group and organize other files or directories. A subdirectory is a directory that is pointed to by a directory one level above it in the file system. A directory name is a string of characters that identifies the directory. It can be a simple directory name, a relative path name, or a full path name. For further information, see "Using the File System" in the *User's Guide.*
display width	Display width is the width in screen columns required to display the characters of a particular code set. Display width is defined in the character class table.
double click	To press and release a mouse button twice in succession.
downstream	In a stream, the direction from stream head to driver.
drag area	In a **Scrollbar** widget, the drag area is the center portion of the *elevator* that is moved by the mouse.
drag box	In a **Slider** widget, the drag box is the portion of the slider that is moved by the mouse.
drag-and-drop	A single atomic action to achieve a *Conversation* between *Source* and *Destination*.

dragging   The act of moving the *pointer* while a mouse button or
                            keyboard equivalent is pressed.

driver   In a stream, the driver provides the interface between
                            peripheral hardware and the stream. A driver can
                            also be a pseudo-driver, such as a multiplexor or log
                            driver [see **log**(7)], which is not associated with a
                            hardware device.

DTM   Desktop manager.

dynamic frame   A frame whose contents are determined at run-time.

dynamic linking   Dynamic linking refers to the process in which exter-
                            nal references in a program are linked with their
                            definitions when the program is executed. For
                            further information, see "C Compilation System" in
                            Programming in Standard C.

effective group ID
effective user ID   An active process has an effective user ID and an
                            effective group ID that are used to determine file
                            access permissions. The effective user ID and effec-
                            tive group ID are equal to the process's real user ID
                            and real group ID respectively, unless the process or
                            one of its ancestors evolved from a file that had the
                            set-user-ID bit or set-group ID bit set [see **exec**(2)].

elevator   The center portion of a **Scrollbar** widget; that part
                            which moves along the *cable*.

ELF   ELF is an acronym for the executable and linking for-
                            mat of the object files produced by the C compilation
                            system. For further information, see "Object Files" in
                            Programming in Standard C.

environment   A set of UNIX system shell variables created and
                            assigned values by the system when a user logs in.
                            The system executes programs that set these variables
                            based on information it gets from **/etc/profile**, the
                            shell, **login**(1), and the user's **.profile** file. In
                            FMLI, variables can be added to the environment
                            with the **set**(1F) built-in utility, and removed from
                            the environment with the **unset**(1F) utility. FMLI
                            also defines a local environment that contains vari-
                            ables known only to the FMLI application.

ETSDU	Expedited Transport Service Data Unit
EUC	Extended UNIX system code. See *Programming with UNIX System Calls*
executable program	On the UNIX operating system, an executable program is a compiled and linked program or a shell program. The command to execute either is the name of the file containing the program. A compiled and linked program is called an executable object file. Compare "object file."
executable	A program that can be processed or executed by the computer without any further translation; a file that has execute permission, such as an **a.out** file, or a shell script.
exit	The **exit** function causes a process to terminate. **exit** closes any open files and cleans up most other information and memory used by the process. An exit status, or return code, is an integer value that your program returns to the operating system to say whether it completed successfully or not. For further information, see "Introduction" in *Programming in Standard C.*
expedited data	Data that is considered urgent. The specific semantics of expedited data is defined by the transport protocol that provides the transport service.
expedited transport service data	The amount of expedited user data the identity of which is preserved from one end of a transport connection to the other.
expert level	Second-lowest of the four lower RPC levels. Programs written to this level can control client and server characteristics, interface with **rpcbind** and manipulate service dispatch.
expression	An expression is a mathematical or logical symbol or meaningful combination of symbols.
FALSE	A value to which a Boolean descriptor can evaluate. FALSE must be the word "false," irrespective of case, or a non-zero return code.

File Class Database	Contains file class definitions where each definition consists of a file class name and a list of properties. The properties define the visual and metaphor behavior of files belonging to the file class.
file descriptor	A file descriptor is an integer value assigned by the operating system to a file when the file is opened by a process.
file system type	Each different file system implementation that is incorporated into the VFS architecture is referred to as a file system type. A file system type may support different file types. The traditional System V file system type, a secure file system type, a high performance file system type, and an MS-DOS file system type are examples of potential file system types.
file system	A UNIX file system is a hierarchical collection of directories and other files that are organized in a tree structure. The base of the structure is the root (/) directory; other directories, all subordinate to root, are branches. The collection of files can be mounted on a block special file. Each file of a file system appears exactly once in the inode list of the file system and is accessible via a single, unique path from the root directory of the file system. For further information, see "Using the File System" in the *User's Guide*.
file type	The general expected characteristics of a file are determined by its file type. File types include regular file, character special file, block special file, FIFO, directory, and symbolic link. Each file type is supported within some file system type
file	A file is a potential source of input or a potential destination for output; at some point, then, an identifiable collection of information. A file is known to the UNIX operating system as an inode plus the information the inode contains that tells whether the file is a plain file, a special file, or a directory. A plain file contains text, data, programs, or other information that forms a coherent unit. A special file is a hardware device or portion thereof, such as a disk partition. A directory is a type of file that contains the names and inode addresses of other plain, special, or

directory files. For further information, see "Using the File System" in the *User's Guide*.

filter	A filter is a program that reads information from the standard input, acts on it in some way, and sends its result to the standard output. It is called a filter because it can be used in a pipeline (see "pipe") to transform the output of another program. Filters are different from editors in that they do not change the contents of a file. Examples of UNIX operating system filters are **sort**, which sorts the input, and **wc**, which counts the number of words, characters, and lines in the input. See **sort**(1) and **wc**(1) for more information.
flag	See "argument."
flat widget	See *widget*. A single widget that maintains a collection of similar user-interface components that together give the appearance and behavior of many widgets.
flattened widget	Same as *flat widget*.
FMLI application	An application developed using the Form and Menu Language Interpreter (FMLI) to provide and maintain a user interface relying only on standard characters. An FMLI application can provide access to other applications.
focus	To specify a particular area of the screen. (See *input focus* and *keyboard focus*).
folder	A folder represents a directory in a file system. A folder can contain other folders and files.
foreground process group	Each session that has established a connection with a controlling terminal will distinguish one process group of the session as the foreground process group of the controlling terminal. This group has certain privileges when accessing its controlling terminal that are denied to background process groups.
fork	**fork** is a system call that splits one process into two, the parent process and the child process, with separate, but initially identical, text, data, and stack segments. See **fork(2)** for more information.

form field	An area of a form consisting of a field label and a field input area into which a user can enter input.
form	A visual element of an FMLI application displayed in a frame. A form is made up of fields that allow a user to provide input to the application.
frame definition file	A file in which the contents, appearance, functionality, and placement of a menu, form, or text frame are defined using the Form and Menu Language.
frame ID number	A number assigned by FMLI to a frame when it is opened. A frame ID number appears at the left in the title bar of a frame. The frame ID number allows users to navigate among frames by number.
frame	An independently-scrollable, bordered region of the screen, used to display FMLI forms, menus, and text. A frame includes a title bar, frame border, contents, and—for frames containing more than three lines—a scroll box.
fundamental block size	The minimal file allocation unit. In the case of disk-based file systems this is a disk sector or a multiple of disk sectors, smaller than or equal to the preferred block size (see below).
gadget	A windowless object; an object that could be defined as a widget but, instead, is defined as having its parent's window resources.
grab	To position the mouse pointer on a *resize corner* and take hold of it for the purpose of resizing the window.
hard key	A physical key on a computer's keyboard. For example, the "Return" or "Enter" key is illustrated as [Return].
header file	A header file is a file that usually contains shared data declarations that are to be copied into source files by the compiler. Header file names conventionally end with the characters **.h**. Header files are also called include files, for the C language **#include** directive by which they are made available to source files. For further information, see "C Compilation System" in *Programming in Standard C*.

Help Desk	A central place on the desktop where users can get help on the desktop metaphor or any applications that have registered help information with the desktop manager.
HELP	The mouse button or keyboard equivalent used to bring up a GUI Help window.
highlighted	A visual indication that an object is in a special state. For two-color ("monochrome") objects, the colors are exchanged. Multi-color objects cannot be highlighted.
Home Window	The folder window that shows the desktop directory, which is the root of the user's folder hierarchy.
I/O	I/O stands for input/output, the process by which information enters (input) and leaves (output) a computer system. For further information, see "C Compilation System" in *Programming in Standard C*.
Icon Menu	The pop-up menu associated with an icon. When the mouse MENU button is pressed on an icon, the icon menu pops up. By default, this menu has a minimum of three buttons: Open, Delete, and File Properties. More buttons are possible, depending on the file class of the icon.
icon	A graphical representation of an object. The visual consists of a glyph and a label centered below the glyph. In FMLI, it is a symbol used to indicate an available function. For example, the caret (^) is an icon displayed in a frame's border to indicate the contents can be scrolled upwards.
ideogram	An ideogram is a language symbol usually based on a pictorial representation of an object or concept. An ideogram may or may not have a phonetic value.
include file	See "header file."
initial frame	The frame, or frames, named as arguments when the **fmli** command is invoked. Initial frames are displayed automatically when an FMLI application is started, and remain on display in the work area until the FMLI session is terminated.

initialization file	A script in which an FMLI developer can define global attributes of an application using the Form and Menu Language. Such things as a transient introductory frame, a customized banner line, colors for various display elements, and restrictions on user access to the UNIX system can be defined. An initialization file is optional, but if one is written it must be named as an argument when **fmli** is invoked.
input focus	To have the cursor on a particular field, designating that field as "next."
instance	A specific *realization* of a widget; one particular widget as opposed to a class of widgets.
intermediate level	Second-highest of the four lower RPC levels; programs written to this level specify the transport they require.
interpreter	A program that allows you to communicate with the operating system. It reads the commands you enter and interprets them as requests to execute other programs, access files, or provide output.
interrupt	A signal to stop the execution of a process. From the keyboard, interrupts are usually initiated by pressing the [**DELETE**] or [**BREAK**] key. **stty**(1) will report the interrupt key for your session as **intr**. In FMLI, the ability of users to interrupt a process defined in an **action** or **done** descriptor can be enabled or disabled through the use of the **interrupt** descriptor.
interrupt	A signal to stop the execution of a process. From the keyboard, interrupts are usually initiated by pressing the [**DELETE**] or [**BREAK**] key. **stty**(1) will report the interrupt key for your session as **intr**. In FMLI, the ability of users to interrupt a process defined in an **action** or **done** descriptor can be enabled or disabled through the use of the **interrupt** descriptor.
ISO	ISO is an acronym for the International Standards Organization. ISO establishes standards in the computing industry for international markets.
kernel	The kernel is the basic resident software of the UNIX operating system. The kernel is responsible for most system operations: scheduling and managing the work done by the computer, maintaining the file

system, and so forth. The kernel has its own text, data, and stack areas.

keyboard focus

The area of the *screen* that will accept the next input from the keyboard.

lexical analysis

Lexical analysis is the process by which a stream of characters (often comprising a source program) is broken up into its elementary words and symbols, called tokens. The tokens can include the reserved words of a programming language, its identifiers and constants, and special symbols such as =, :=, and ; . Lexical analysis enables you to recognize, for instance, that the stream of characters `printf("hello, world\n");` is a series of tokens beginning with `printf` and not with, say, `printf("h`. In compilers, a lexical analyzer is often called by a syntactic analyzer, or parser, that analyzes the grammatical form of tokens passed to it by the lexical analyzer. For further information, see *UNIX Software Development Tools*

library

A library is a file that contains object code for a group of commonly used functions. Rather than write the functions yourself, you arrange for the functions to be linked with your program when an executable is created (see "archive"), or when it is run (see "shared object").

line discipline

The line discipline is a STREAMS module that processes line data in the I/O stream to control the format and flow of data into and out of the system — erase and kill character handling, for example. See also "stream."

link editing

Link editing refers to the process in which a symbol referenced in one module of a program is connected with its definition in another. With the C compilation system, programs are linked statically, when an executable is created, or dynamically, when it is run. For further information, see "C Compilation System" in *Programming in Standard C*.

local management

The phase in either connection-mode or connectionless-mode in which a transport user establishes a transport endpoint and binds a transport address to the endpoint. Functions in this phase

	perform local operations, and require no transport layer traffic over the network.
makefile	A **makefile** is a file that is used with the program **make** to keep track of the dependencies between modules of a program, so that when one module is changed, dependent ones are brought up to date. For further information, see *UNIX Software Development Tools*.
menu frame	A screen display showing a number or choices from which a user can make a selection(s), and which invokes some action when a selection is made.
MENU	The mouse button or keyboard equivalent used to display (*pop up*) a menu.
menu	When unqualified, any of the three states of a GUI menu: *popup menu*, *stay-up menu*, or *pinned menu*.
message line	The third line from the bottom of the screen in FMLI applications, used to display one-line messages and instructions to the user.
message queue identifier	A message queue identifier (**msqid**) is a unique positive integer created by a **msgget** system call. Each **msqid** has a message queue and a data structure associated with it.
message queue	In a stream, a linked list of messages awaiting processing by a module or driver.
message	In a stream, one or more blocks of data or information, with associated STREAMS control structures. Messages can be of several defined types, which identify the message contents. Messages are the only means of transferring data and communicating within a stream.
metacharacters	Metacharacters are ASCII characters with special meanings during pattern processing.
module	A module is a program component that typically contains a function or a group of related functions. Source files and libraries are modules.

multi-select menu	A menu which allows the user to mark one or more items and then select all marked items.
multiplexor	A multiplexor is a driver that allows streams associated with several user processes to be connected to a single driver, or several drivers to be connected to a single user process. STREAMS provides facilities for constructing multiplexors and for connecting multiplexed configurations of streams.
named key	A keyboard key which has a name indicating the function it performs. For example, `TAB`, `DELETE`, or `ENTER`.
network client	A process that makes remote procedure calls to services.
network service	A collection of one or more remote programs.
non-current	A frame, or other element on display which is not the element in which the cursor is currently positioned.
null pointer	In the C language, a null pointer is a C pointer with a value of 0.
object file	An object file contains a binary representation of programming language code. A relocatable object file contains references to symbols that have not yet been linked with their definitions. An executable object file is a linked program. Compare "source file."
OLWM	OPEN LOOK Window Manager.
onstop event	When using the GUI debugger, an onstop event specifies an action for the debugger to perform whenever a process stops for any reason. The action may be one or more of the commands available through the debugger's command line interface. For further information, see "Using debug with the Graphical User Interface" in *Programming in Standard C*.
optimizer	An optimizer improves the efficiency of the assembly language code generated by a compiler. That, in turn, will speed the execution time of your object code. For further information, see "Commonly Used cc Command Line Options" in "C Compilation System" in *Programming in Standard C*.

option	See "argument."
orderly release	A procedure for gracefully terminating a transport connection with no loss of data.
orphaned process group	A process group in which the parent of every member in the group is either itself a member of the group, or is not a member of the process group's session.
pane	The rectangular area within a window where an application displays text or graphics.
parent process ID	A new process is created by a currently active process [see **fork**(2)]. The parent process ID of a process is the process ID of its creator.
parent process	See "**fork**."
parser	A parser, or syntactic analyzer, analyzes the grammatical form of tokens passed to it by a lexical analyzer (see "lexical analysis"). For further information, see *UNIX Software Development Tools*
path name	A path name designates the location of a file in the file system. It is made up of a series of directory names that proceed down the hierarchical path of the file system. The directory names are separated by a slash character (/). The last name in the path is the file. If the path name begins with a slash, it is called an absolute, or full, path name; the initial slash means that the path begins at the root directory. A path name that does not begin with a slash is known as a relative path name, meaning relative to your current directory. For further information, see "Using the File System" in the *User's Guide*.
peer user	The user with whom a given user is communicating above the Transport Interface.
permissions	Permissions define a right to access a file in the file system. Permissions are granted separately to you, your group, and all others. There are three basic permissions: read, write, and execute. For further information, see "Using the File System" in the *User's Guide*.

ping	A call to procedure **0** of an RPC program. Pinging is used to verify the existence and accessibility of a remote program. Pinging can also be used to time network communications.
pinned menu	A MoOLIT menu that has a *pushpin* that is "in." This menu behaves much like a control area in a pinned command window.
pipe	A pipe causes the output of one program to be used as the input to another program, so that the programs run in sequence. You create a pipeline by preceding each command after the first command with the pipe symbol (|), which indicates that the output from the process on the left should be routed to the process on the right.

$$\texttt{\$ who | wc -l}$$

causes the output of the **who** command, which lists the users who are logged in to the system, to be used as the input of the **wc**, or word count, command with the **-l** option. The result is the number of users logged in to the system. See **who**(1) and **wc**(1) for more information.

pixel	An addressable point on the *screen*.
pixmap	A bitmap of an area of the screen stored within the program. A "pixmap" is also a defined data type in the Xt Intrinsics.
pointer	The *screen* representation of the location of the mouse or equivalent.
pop up	As a noun, *pop up* is a generic term referring to a MoOLIT window other than the base window. As a verb, this phrase is the act of making a menu or MoOLIT popup window visible. As an adjective, it is used to refer to a window that can be popped up and is spelled with or without a dash, as in "popup menu" or "pop-up menu."
popup menu	A MoOLIT menu that was brought up by pressing MENU. While MENU remains pressed, the menu remains a popup menu and operates in a *press-drag-release* mode.

portability	Portability refers to the degree of ease with which a program can be moved, or ported, to a different operating system or machine.
post	The FMLI activity of reading and interpreting a frame definition file, displaying the frame described therein, and making that frame current.
preference	Synonymous with property settings or options. This document uses the term preference to avoid confusion with properties that mean name-value pairs.
preferred block size	The unit of transfer for block devices in read/write operations (also known as "logical block size").
preprocessor	A preprocessor is a program that prepares an input file for another program. The preprocessor component of the C compiler performs macro expansion, conditional compilation, and file inclusion.
press	The act of pressing a mouse button or keyboard key. This is distinct from the act of releasing the button or key, so that both can be discussed separately. Thus **press SELECT** means to press, but not release, the SELECT mouse button or keyboard equivalent key.
press-drag-release	A method of user interaction with a set of objects where the user presses MENU to display the objects, *drags* the pointer over the objects until it is over the one of interest, then releases MENU to select or activate the object.
primary source window	When using the GUI debugger, the primary source window is displayed when you select the Source Window button in the Windows menu. The primary window is always updated to show the current source line whenever the current process stops. For further information, see "Using debug with the Graphical User Interface" in *Programming in Standard C.*
primitive widget	See *widget*. A widget that does not have any child widgets; one that either performs a specific action, allows input or allows output.
privilege	Having appropriate privilege means having the capability to perform sensitive system operations [see **procpriv**(2)].

process group ID	Each active process is a member of a process group and is identified by a positive integer called the process group ID. This ID is the process ID of the group leader. This grouping permits the signaling of related processes [see **kill**(2)].
process group leader	A process group leader is a process whose process ID is the same as its process group ID.
process group lifetime	A process group lifetime begins when the process group is created by its process group leader, and ends when the lifetime of the last process in the group ends or when the last process in the group leaves the group.
process group	Each process in the system is a member of a process group that is identified by a process group ID. Any process that is not a process group leader may create a new process group and become its leader. Any process that is not a process group leader may join an existing process group that shares the same session as the process. A newly created process joins the process group of its parent.
process lifetime	A process lifetime begins when the process is forked and ends after it exits, when its termination has been acknowledged by its parent process. See **wait**(2).
process	An instance of a program being executed. A number that identifies an active process. In the UNIX System, it incorporates the concept of an execution environment, including contents of memory, register values, name of the current directory, status of files, and various other information. See **ps**(1) for more information on how to determine the process ID of any process currently active on your system.
program	A set of instructions and data kept in an ordinary file.
property	A name-value pair. Both the name and the value are strings. A number of attributes may also be attached to each property. Properties are used throughout the desktop manager. DTM uses desktop properties. Each file class described in the file database consists of a list of properties. These properties are called class properties. Each file in a file system may have instance properties associated with it. See *Graphical*

	User Interface Programming for a detailed explanation of properties.
push a button	The act of moving the *pointer* to a *button widget* and then *selecting* the button.
pushpin	A *screen* object that is part of a *popup menu*. It can be pointed to and selected. When it is first selected, it is "pushed in" and causes the menu to stay up after the user moves out of it. When it is again selected, it is pulled out and the menu pops down.
quota	A mechanism for restricting the amount of file system resources that a user can obtain. The quota mechanism sets limits on both the number of files and the number of disk blocks that a user may allocate. Implemented by UFS.
read queue	In a stream, the message queue in a module or driver containing messages moving upstream.
real group ID real user ID	Each user allowed on the system is identified by a positive integer (0 to **UID_MAX**) called a real user ID. Each user is also a member of a group. The group is identified by a positive integer called the real group ID. An active process has a real user ID and real group ID that are set to the real user ID and real group ID, respectively, of the user responsible for the creation of the process.
realized	In the context of the X Toolkit Intrinsics, the point at which all the data structures of a widget have been allocated. Windows and other information are not created when the widget is created with the **XtCreateWidget** routine, but are created in a later call to **XtRealizeWidget** on the widget itself or on an ancestor widget.
register, registration	To make a routine name known to the API. When the application programmer develops a *callback* routine, that routine needs to be registered when the widget is created so that it can be properly invoked.
regular expression	A regular expression is a string of alphanumeric characters and special characters that describes, in a short-hand way, a pattern to be searched for in a file.

For further information, see *UNIX Software Development Tools*.

release
: The act of releasing a pressed button or keyboard key, as in "release MENU."

remote program
: Software that implements one or more remote procedures.

resize corners
: Hollow, L-shaped symbols located on all four corners of a *window* which, when *grabbed*, are used to change the size of the *window*.

resource translation
: The mechanism by which resource values are made accessible to widgets. The list of resources is contained in the **app-defaults** files. Each entry in these files consists of a resource name/value pair of the form: *app_name.resource_name*: *value*. Using an asterisk in place of the *app_name* makes the entry available to any application that recognizes the *resource_name*. Any hardcoded value takes precedence over what is set in the resource file.

resource
: An attribute of a widget or a widget class. A resource is a named data value in the defining structure of a widget.

root directory/current directory
: Each process has associated with it a concept of a root directory and a current directory for the purpose of resolving pathname searches. The root directory of a process need not be the root directory of the root file system.

routine
: A routine is another name for a function.

RPC language
: A C-like programming language recognized by the **rpcgen** compiler.

RPC Package
: The collection of software and documentation used to implement and support remote procedure calls in System V. The RPC Package implements and is a superset of the functionality of the RPC Protocol.

RPC Protocol
: The message-passing protocol that is the basis of the RPC package.

RPC/XDR	See *RPC language*.
saved group ID saved user ID	The saved user ID and saved group ID are the values of the effective user ID and effective group ID prior to an **exec** of a file [see **exec**(2)].
screen	The surface on your computer monitor where information is displayed.
screen-labeled keys	The eight function keys, F1 through F8, found on many keyboards, to which the labels displayed on the last line of the screen in FMLI applications correspond. The screen-labels indicate the operations assigned to the function keys.
script	A file which contains the definition of a frame (a frame definition file), the definition of global attributes of an FMLI application (an initialization file), the definitions of application specific commands (a commands file), a list of aliases for pathnames (an alias file), or UNIX system shell commands.
scroll indicators	Symbols contained in the scroll box of FMLI frames, to indicate that additional material is available above or below the current frame borders. The up symbol is a caret (^) or up-arrow character, and the down indicator is a **v** or down-arrow character.
scrolling	An attribute of FMLI frames which allows a fixed-size frame to accommodate a larger amount of information than can be displayed in it at one time. The first frameful of information is displayed when the frame is opened, and users can press named keys or their alternate keystrokes to move forward to a new frameful of information, or to move back to a previous frameful.
secondary	When using the GUI debugger, the secondary source window is indicated by an asterisk ('*') in the window header, and is not updated when the current process stops. Secondary source windows are created with the New Source option. For further information, see "Using debug with the Graphical User Interface" in *Programming in Standard C*.

SELECT	The mouse button or keyboard equivalent used to select and move an object, manipulate a control, or set the input focus.
select	To move the *pointer* to an object and press the *SELECT* mouse button. The result is to initiate either an application action or a change in the window content or structure.
Selection Mechanism	The primary mechanism that X11 defines for clients that want to exchange information. Refer to both Xlib and Inter-Client Communication Manual (ICCCM, [5]) documents for more details.
semaphore identifier	A semaphore identifier (**semid**) is a unique positive integer created by a **semget** system call. Each semid has a set of semaphores and a data structure associated with it.
serializing	Converting data from a machine-specific representation to XDR format.
server	The transport user in connection-mode that offers services to other users (clients) and enables these clients to establish a transport connection to it.
service indication	The notification of a pending event generated by the provider to a user of a particular service.
service primitive	The unit of information passed across a service interface that contains either a service request or service indication.
service request	A request for some action generated by a user to the provider of a particular service.
session ID	Each session in the system is uniquely identified during its lifetime by a positive integer called a session ID, the process ID of its session leader.
session Leader	A session leader is a process whose session ID is the same as its process and process group ID.
session lifetime	A session lifetime begins when the session is created by its session leader, and ends when the lifetime of the last process that is a member of the session ends, or when the last process that is a member in the session leaves the session.

session	A session is a group of processes identified by a common ID called a session ID, capable of establishing a connection with a controlling terminal. Any process that is not a process group leader may create a new session and process group, becoming the session leader of the session and process group leader of the process group. A newly created process joins the session of its creator.
shared memory identifier	A shared memory identifier (**shmid**) is a unique positive integer created by a **shmget** system call. Each **shmid** has a segment of memory (referred to as a shared memory segment) and a data structure associated with it. (Note that these shared memory segments must be explicitly removed by the user after the last reference to them is removed.)
shared object	A shared object, or dynamically linked library, is a single object file that contains the code for every function in the library. When you call a library function in your program, and specify a dynamic linking option on the **cc** command line, the entire contents of the shared object are mapped into the virtual address space of your process at run time. As its name implies, a shared object contains code that can be used simultaneously by different programs at run time. For further information, see "C Compilation System" in *Programming in Standard C*.
shell	The shell is the UNIX system program that handles communication between you and the system. The shell is known as a command interpreter because it translates your commands into a language understandable by the system. A shell normally is started for you when you log in to the system. A shell program calls the shell to read and execute commands contained in an executable file. For further information, see "Shell Tutorial" in the *User's Guide*, and the **sh**(1) page.
signal event	When using the GUI debugger, the signal event suspends the process and performs the associated commands whenever the process receives the specified signal. Multiple events may be created for the same signal. For further information, see

"Using debug with the Graphical User Interface" in *Programming in Standard C*.

signal
: A signal is a message you send to a process or that processes send to one another. You might use a signal, for example, to initiate an interrupt (see above). A signal sent by a running process is usually a sign of an exceptional occurrence that has caused the process to terminate or divert from the normal flow of control.

simplified interface
: The simplest level of the RPC package.

single-select menu
: A menu from which a user can select only one item at a time.

SLK
: See screen-labeled keys.

source file
: Source files contain the programming language version of a program. Before a computer can execute the program, the source code must be translated by a compiler and assembler into the machine language of the computer. Compare "object file."

source
: The starting point of the drag-and-drop operation. It is also referred as the holder.

special processes
: The process with ID 0 and the process with ID 1 are special processes referred to as proc0 and proc1; see **kill**(2). proc0 is the process scheduler. proc1 is the initialization process (**init**); proc1 is the ancestor of every other process in the system and is used to control the process structure.

standard error
: Standard error is an output stream from a program that normally is used to convey error messages. On the UNIX operating system, the default case is to associate standard error with the user's terminal.

standard input
: Standard input is an input stream to a program. On the UNIX operating system, the default case is to associate standard input with the user's terminal.

standard output
: Standard output is an output stream from a program. On the UNIX operating system, the default case is to associate standard output with the user's terminal.

static data	Static represents a condition persistent throughout a process. Static data occupies the data segment and the bss segment.
static linking	Static linking refers to the process in which external references in a program are linked with their definitions when an executable is created. For further information, see "C Compilation System" in *Programming in Standard C*.
stay-up menu	A MoOLIT menu that was brought up and made to stay on the screen for one round of use. The controls in this menu behave like controls in an unpinned command window, except that the menu is removed from the screen even if nothing is selected from the menu.
stop event	When using the GUI debugger, a stop event suspends the process and performs the associated commands, if any, whenever the specified condition in the program's address space becomes true. For further information, see "Using debug with the Graphical User Interface" in *Programming in Standard C*.
stop expression	When using the GUI debugger, stop expressions are special expressions accepted by the stop command. The expression may include one or more of location, (expression), or *lvalue, joined by the special && (and) or || (or) operators. For further information, see "Using debug with the Graphical User Interface" in *Programming in Standard C*.
stream head	In a stream, the stream head is the end of the stream that provides the interface between the stream and a user process. The principal functions of the stream head are processing STREAMS-related system calls, and passing data and information between a user process and the stream.
stream	A stream is a full-duplex data path within the kernel between a user process and driver routines. The primary components are a stream head, a driver and zero or more modules between the stream head and driver. A stream is analogous to a shell pipeline except that data flow and processing are bidirectional. For further information, see "Standard I/O" in "C Compilation System" in *Programming in Standard C*.

STREAMS	A set of kernel mechanisms that support the development of network services and data communication drivers. It defines interface standards for character input/output within the kernel and between the kernel and user level processes. The STREAMS mechanism is composed of utility routines, kernel facilities and a set of data structures.
string	A string is a contiguous sequence of characters treated as a unit. In the C language, a character string is an array of characters terminated by the null character, \0.
sub-object	A sub-object is the equivalent of a *primitive widget* contained in a *flattened widget*. In a Flat Exclusives or F NonExclusives widget, the sub-objects are the equivalents of **RectButtons**. In a Flat CheckBox, the sub-objects are the equivalents of **CheckBox** widgets.
SVID	System V Interface Definition, which defines the standard interface for SVR4 and is the basis of other UNIX operating system standards.
syntax	Command syntax is the order in which commands and their arguments must be put together. The command always comes first. The order of arguments varies from command to command. Language syntax is the set of rules that describes how the elements of a programming language may legally be used.
syscall event	When using the GUI debugger, a syscall event suspends the process and performs the associated commands whenever the process enters or exits the specified system calls. Multiple events may be created for the same system call. For further information, see "Using debug with the Graphical User Interface" in *Programming in Standard C*.
system call	A system call is a request from a program for an action to be performed by the UNIX operating system kernel. For further information, see "C Compilation System" in *Programming in Standard C*.
templates	Files that are used to be the initial structure and/or content of newly created files. Template files are specified for each file class by the **TEMPLATES** class property. (OEMs and ISVs can add new templates).

terminal attributes	Characteristics of the video screen which can be manipulated by an FMLI application developer to provide visual cues to the application's functionality. They include underlining, half-bright, bright, and blinking display of characters, an alternate character set for line drawing, and others.
text frame	a visual element of an FMLI application displayed in a frame. A text frame displays lines of text; for example, help on how to fill in a form field.
text symbol	A text symbol names a program instruction. Instructions reside in read-only memory during execution. Compare "data symbol."
toggle	This is an action performed on an object with two states; it is the switching from one state to the other.
top level	Highest of the four lower RPC levels; programs written to this level specify the type of transport they require.
transaction	A transaction refers to the specific transaction type involving icons dragged from one area on the desktop and dropped onto another area. A drag-and-drop transaction is said to be started when a trigger message is sent to the destination client. During the life of a transaction, information is exchanged between the source client and the destination client via the selection mechanism. The transaction is closed when a done message is sent by the destination client to the source client. Note that a transaction starts after a client has determined the drop location and wants to convey the drag-and-drop information to the client that had registered drag-and-drop interest on the drop location. See *Graphical User Interface Programming* for more details on the drag-and-drop mechanism.
translation	See *resource translation*.
transport address	The identifier used to differentiate and locate specific transport endpoints in a network.
transport connection	The communication circuit that is established between two transport users in connection-mode.

transport endpoint	The local communication channel between a transport user and a transport provider.
transport interface	The library routines and state transition rules that support the services of a transport protocol.
transport provider	The transport protocol that provides the services of the Transport Interface.
transport service data unit	The amount of user data whose identity is preserved from one end of a transport connection to the other.
transport user	The user-level application or protocol that accesses the services of the Transport Interface.
TRUE	A value to which a Boolean descriptor can evaluate. Any value other than those defined for FALSE is interpreted as TRUE.
TSDU	Transport Service Data Unit
UFS	The Unified File System, a derivative of the 4.2BSD file system. It offers file hardening, supports large and fragmented block allocations for files, and distributed inode and free block management. Additionally, it supports quotas (see above).
universal address	A machine-independent representation of a network address.
upstream	In a stream, the direction from driver to stream head.
user ID	A user ID is an integer value, usually associated with a login name, that the system uses to identify owners of files and directories. The user ID of a process becomes the owner of files created by the process and by descendent processes (see "fork").
utility	A software tool of general programming usefulness built-in to FMLI, such as fmlgrep or message, which can be used inside backquoted expressions, and which is executed when the backquoted expression is evaluated. A built-in utility has a performance advantage over a UNIX shell utility in that it does not fork a new process.

variable	In a program, a variable is an object whose value may change during the execution of the program or from one execution to the next. A variable in the shell is a name representing a string of characters.
virtual circuit transport	See *connection-oriented transport*.
virtual circuit	A transport connection established in connection-mode.
Vnode	The operating system's internal representation of a file (previously known as a file-system-independent inode).
white space	One or more space, tab, and/or newline characters. White space is normally used to separate strings of characters, and is required to separate a command from its arguments when it is invoked. For this toolkit, these characters are space, tab, newline, and [Return.]
widget class	A collection of code and data structures that provides a generic implementation of a part of a look-and-feel.
widget	A specific example or realization of a *widget class*.
window set	When using the GUI debugger, a Window Set consists of a Context window, Command window, Event window, Disassembly window, and one or more Source windows. The windows in a set all operate on the same current process. For further information, see "Using debug with the Graphical User Interface" in *Programming in Standard C*.
window	A work area on the screen that you use to run and display an application.
word wrapping	An attribute of text frames which prevents words from being split across two lines when the text frame is displayed. Word wrapping can be turned on or off by the developer in the text frame definition file.
work area	In FMLI applications, the area of the screen running from the second line from the top to the fourth line from the bottom. The work area is used to display menus, forms, and text frames.

wrapping	An attribute of frames which allows a user to navigate through a list of menu items or form fields as if it were a circular list. Forward or backward navigation keys always cause movement to the next logical item or field. The next logical item or field may differ according to the navigation key being used (see the table in Appendix B for complete details).
write queue	In a stream, the message queue in a module or driver containing messages moving downstream.
X/Open	X/Open is short for the X/Open Company Limited, a consortium of computer firms dedicated to achieving open UNIX systems.
XDR language	A protocol specification language for data representation. RPC language builds on and is a superset of XDR.
XDR	eXternal Data Representation. Provides an architecture independent representation of data.
zombie	A process that has executed the **exit** system call and no longer exists, but which leaves a record containing an exit code and some timing statistics for its parent to collect. The zombie state is the final state of a process.

IN Index

Index

Y

Z